STATE OF THE WORLD 1985

Other Norton/Worldwatch Books

Lester R. Brown / *The Twenty-Ninth Day:
Accommodating Human Needs and Numbers to the
Earth's Resources*

Lester R. Brown / *Building a Sustainable Society*

Lester R. Brown et al. / *State of the World-1984*

Lester R. Brown, Christopher Flavin, and Colin
Norman / *Running on Empty: The Future of the
Automobile in an Oil-Short World*

Daniel Deudney and Christopher Flavin / *Renewable
Energy: The Power to Choose*

Erik P. Eckholm / *Losing Ground: Environmental
Stress and World Food Prospects*

Erik P. Eckholm / *The Picture of Health:
Environmental Sources of Disease*

Denis Hayes / *Rays of Hope: The Transition to a
Post-Petroleum World*

Kathleen Newland / *The Sisterhood of Man*

Colin Norman / *The God That Limps: Science and
Technology in the Eighties*

Bruce Stokes / *Helping Ourselves: Local Solutions to
Global Problems*

STATE OF THE WORLD
1985

*A Worldwatch Institute Report on
Progress Toward a Sustainable Society*

PROJECT DIRECTOR
Lester R. Brown

PROJECT ASSOCIATE
Edward C. Wolf

EDITOR
Linda Starke

SENIOR RESEARCHERS
Lester R. Brown
William U. Chandler
Christopher Flavin
Sandra Postel
Edward C. Wolf

RESEARCHER
Cynthia Pollock

W·W·NORTON & COMPANY
NEW YORK   LONDON

Published simultaneously in Canada by Penguin Books Canada Ltd, 2801 John Street, Markham,
Ontario L3R 1B4
Printed in the United States of America

The text of this book is composed in Baskerville, with display type set in Caslon. Composition and
manufacturing by The Haddon Craftsmen, Inc.
First Edition

ISBN 0-393-01930-6

ISBN 0-393-30218-0 PBK.

W. W. Norton & Company, Inc., 500 Fifth Avenue, New York, N.Y. 10110
W. W. Norton & Company Ltd., 37 Great Russell Street, London WC1B 3NU

1 2 3 4 5 6 7 8 9 0

Acknowledgments

Producing a *State of the World* report each year depends on the support and aid of countless individuals and institutions. Among the principal groups making the report possible are the funders. This annual series was initiated with the active support of William Dietel, President of the Rockefeller Brothers Fund, which helped launch the Institute a decade ago. In addition to RBF, both the Winthrop Rockefeller Trust and David Rockefeller are helping fund the report.

Beyond this, the report draws on the Institute's ongoing research, which is supported by several foundations—the Geraldine R. Dodge, William and Flora Hewlett, W. Alton Jones, Edna McConnell Clark, Andrew W. Mellon, and Edward John Noble Foundations. All these provide general support that gives us a flexibility and an efficiency in operation that few other research institutes can claim. In addition, Worldwatch has enjoyed from its inception financial support from the United Nations Fund for Population Activities, headed by Rafael Salas.

This year, as in 1983, Linda Starke edited the manuscript, coaxing prose out of numerous recalcitrant drafts. By sharpening authors' thinking and polishing their writing, Linda has smoothed the reader's journey immeasurably. Her skills as an editor and her sure sense of graphic design enabled us to produce *State of the World* on an accelerated schedule without compromising quality.

One of the great privileges of writing at Worldwatch Institute is the opportunity to test one's ideas against an exceptionally talented and knowledgeable set of reviewers both within and outside the Institute. This year outside reviewers included Gerald O. Barney, Gail Finsterbush, Robert Goodland, Scott McVay, and Andrew Rice, who reviewed the entire manuscript at short notice; the final version is stronger due to their eleventh-hour efforts. The following people reviewed individual chapters and generously shared their expertise: Peter Blair, Deborah Bleviss, Leon Bouvier, John Bredehoeft, Winston Brill, Tom Bull, Clark Bullard, Ben Burr, T.T. Chang, Donald Duvick, Jae Edmonds, Malin Falkenmark, Andrea Fella, David L. Fluharty, Kenneth Frederick, Howard Geller, Major M. Goodman, Holly L. Gwin, John Harte, Carl Haub, Maureen Hinkle, Judith Jacobsen, Mary Kent, Carlo LaPorta, Jay Lear, Thomas E. Lovejoy, Amory Lovins, Thomas Merrick, Douglas Merry, Alan Miller, David Moulton, Elliott A. Norse, Helen Peters, Donald Plucknett, Fred Potter, John Reilly, Peter Rogers, Marc Ross, Nigel J.H. Smith, Joseph Speidel, Maryla Webb, and J.T. Williams.

Special thanks go to Nancy Birdsall of the World Bank for sharing background papers prepared for the *World Development Report;* William Kellogg and Walter Orr Roberts of the National Center for Atmospheric Research for reviewing sections of *State of the World* that deal with climate; Stephen Schneider, also of the Center, for sharing his latest thinking on the effects of population growth on climate; Milena P. Roos for her experienced assistance in unearthing and obtaining documents within the United Nations system; and Boyd Chugg of the U.S. Department of Agriculture, whose historical data on world agriculture and food production have provided a foundation for our analysis.

We were fortunate to have such a diverse, thorough, and qualified group of reviewers; the authors alone bear the responsibility for any errors that remain.

Any success that *State of the World* achieves rests squarely on the shoulders of the Worldwatch Institute staff, who have done much more than the term "support staff" implies. Blondeen Gravely, Jodi Johnson, and Susan Norris managed the tide of drafts and revisions, coped with crises on the word processing system, and mastered a complex coding system so the book could be typeset directly from disks. Cynthia Pollock assisted with the research for Chapter 3 as well as writing part of Chapter 8; Brian Brown and Marion Guyer contributed to the research and analysis in several other chapters. Colleen Bickman's efficient management of publication sales and devious sense of humor both proved indispensable. David Macgregor designed an ambitious and effective outreach system for *State of the World* without missing a stride in his duties as editor of the Worldwatch Papers. The report's value as a reference was greatly enhanced by Alice Fins, who joined us coming down the home stretch to produce a detailed index.

Blondeen Gravely, Felix Gorrell, and Marge Hubbard share the administrative and financial responsibilities that make our research possible. Along with the guidance of our Board of Directors, their cumulative expertise and unfailing good judgment provide the even keel the Institute requires to chart new waters in each year's *State of the World*.

Lester R. Brown

Contents

Tables and Figures

LIST OF TABLES

LIST OF FIGURES

Chapter 2. Reducing Hunger

Chapter 3. Managing Freshwater Supplies

Chapter 4. Maintaining World Fisheries

Chapter 7. Increasing Energy Efficiency

Chapter 8. Harnessing Renewable Energy

Foreword

At this time last year we had just completed *State of the World-1984*, our first global assessment of progress toward a sustainable society. We believed there would be a strong interest in such an assessment but we did not anticipate that the U.S. edition would go into three printings during the first year. Nor did we foresee that the book would be excerpted in more than 50 periodicals—ranging from *Natural History* to the *International Herald Tribune* to *The Statesman* of Pakistan.

The strong response to *State of the World-1984* (SOTW-84) demonstrates the depth of interest in interdisciplinary studies and suggests their usefulness in policymaking. Over a third of the world's people live in countries that have undertaken Year 2000 studies, patterned on the *Global 2000 Report to the President* done in the United States five years ago. Leaders and citizens everywhere express concern at these perplexing resource and environmental problems, and some have started to seek solutions that reinforce rather than undermine each other.

The events of 1984 revealed a world conscious of its problems but at a loss as to how to confront them. In Mexico City, the U.N. International Conference on Population refocused the world's attention on its growing numbers but saw basic commitments to population assistance challenged. A prolonged African drought turned into famine, though relief efforts and media attention did spark an interest in causal factors. Civil wars, insurgencies, terrorist attacks, and tensions between various religious and ethnic groups continued to distract leaders' attention from the forces shaping the "current" of events.

Against this backdrop, the interest of world political and corporate leaders in *State of the World* has been particularly heartening. In Latin America, former Colombian president Carlos Lleras Restrepo wrote a lengthy summary of *SOTW-84* for publication in *El Tiempo*, that country's leading newspaper. A personal letter from President Julius Nyerere of Tanzania indicates that *State of the World* was for him a "useful survey" that had become part of his personal library. Closer to home, Ted Turner, head of the Turner Broadcasting System, purchased 1,400 copies for distribution to key decision makers in the United States—including Chief Executive Officers of the Fortune 500, members of Congress, and the Cabinet. Turner called it "the most important book I have read in several years."

A good beginning was made in distributing *SOTW-84* internationally. Our North American publisher, W.W. Norton, holds English rights worldwide. In Beijing, the Institute of Scientific and Technical Information of China had a team of six translators at work on the book within weeks of its U.S. publication. Their efforts are being paralleled in Japan by the Defense of the Green Earth Foundation, which has also purchased in advance the rights to *SOTW-85*. Discussions are being held with the American

Center Library on an English edition for India. In Indonesia, we expect the Obor Institute, long our publisher there, to do a local edition. Rights for Spanish have been purchased by Fondo de Cultura Economica, a major publishing house in Mexico City. If negotiations for Portuguese rights in Brazil are completed successfully, coverage of the western hemisphere will be complete. In Europe, Panstwowe Wydawnictwo Ekonomiczne is planning a Polish edition and negotiations are under way on a German one.

At a time when some global problems seem insurmountable, it is reassuring to know that information illuminating them can be disseminated worldwide so quickly. The chapter on the economics of nuclear power from *SOTW-84* was published in an expanded version as a Worldwatch Paper, for example. As soon as the study received news coverage, telephone orders were received within a matter of hours—from Japanese utilities, members of the German Bundestag, and Wall Street investment firms. The sales patterns of *SOTW-84* and associated Worldwatch Papers sometimes say a lot about the nature of the issues. When the chapter on acid rain from this year's edition first appeared as Worldwatch Paper 58, the Canadian embassy purchased 2,000 copies for distribution in the United States.

In addition to the interest shown by political leaders and corporate planners, the academic world has also responded well to *SOTW-84*. Its principal selling point on campuses appears to be its integrative character and the linkages it establishes among major fields of study. In addition to serving as a reference for researchers, it is being adopted as a text for courses in agriculture, demography, ecology, geography, international affairs, and that relatively new genre of courses typically labeled Environment, Technology, and Society that is now found on almost all campuses.

Each year's *State of the World* will be a fresh assessment. Although each annual edition will cover the same basic issues—energy, environment, food, population, and economic trends—we will be looking at them from a different perspective, for no single volume could cover all these issues and their interrelationships. This year, for example, we have devoted a section of the first chapter to population-induced climate change, a subject that we think deserves far more attention. With more time to gather data, we hope to expand this analysis into a full chapter in *SOTW-86*. Similarly, this year we note the famine unfolding in Africa; next year we hope to analyze the social consequences of failed agricultural and population policies.

State of the World is intended to be an integrative document, cutting across disciplines and fields of interest. It could not of course displace the specialized reports of various agencies, such as *State of Food and Agriculture* by the U.N. Food and Agriculture Organization, *State of the World's Population* by the U.N. Fund for Population Activities, or *World Economic Outlook* by the International Monetary Fund. Rather, it attempts to draw upon their findings, relating them to each other. *State of the World* also relies on national assessments such as those prepared by the Conservation Foundation for the United States and by the Centre for Science and Environment for India. Another report in this vein is scheduled to be published jointly by the World Resources Institute and the International Institute for Environment and Development in early 1986. Tentatively entitled *The World Resources Report*, it will have an extensive statistical appendix that should provide sorely needed data on resource and environmental trends, much as the World Bank's *World Development Report* details economic indicators for the developing countries.

We appreciate the many articles and reports received from researchers the world over. As with *SOTW-84,* we welcome comments and suggestions. Queries may be directed to me or to the authors of individual chapters.

Lester R. Brown
Worldwatch Institute
1776 Massachusetts Avenue, N.W.
Washington, D.C. 20036

December 1984

STATE OF THE
WORLD
1985

1

A False Sense of Security

Lester R. Brown

Although human activities have always altered the natural environment, the scale of disruptions in the late twentieth century is unprecedented. The collective actions of a world population approaching five billion now appear capable of causing continental and even global changes in natural systems. As human pressures build, the relationship between people and their natural support systems can cross key thresholds, leading to a breakdown.

Nowhere is that breakdown more tragically evident than in Africa, where famine is spreading across the continent. As recently as 1970, Africa was essentially self-sufficient in food. In 1984, however, some 140 million Africans—out of a total of 531 million—were fed with grain from abroad. In the years ahead, the continent's dependence on imported grain will almost certainly be even greater.[1]

The spotlight of public attention focused in late 1984 on emergency food relief; the media regularly attributed the famine to drought. But the drought, though a triggering event, is not the basic cause. Per capita grain production

peaked in Africa in 1967 and has been declining nearly 1 percent per year ever since. The drought merely brought this long-term deterioration into focus. The decline is largely attributable to three well-established trends: the fastest population growth of any continent in history, widespread soil erosion and desertification, and the failure by African governments to give agriculture the support that it needs.[2]

Population growth both expands food needs and contributes to endemic soil erosion, which is dimming the food prospect of virtually every African country from the Mediterranean to the Cape of Good Hope. A 1978 report from the U.S. Agency for International Development office in Addis Ababa indicated that Ethiopia was losing a billion tons of topsoil annually—foreshadowing the famine now gripping that ancient country. In graphic language it described "an environmental nightmare unfolding before our eyes . . . a result of the acts of millions of Ethiopians struggling for survival: scratching the surface of eroded land and eroding it further, cutting down the trees for warmth and fuel and leaving the country denuded. . . . Over one billion—one billion—tons of topsoil

Units of measurements are usually metric unless common usage dictates otherwise.

flow from Ethiopia's highlands each year."[3] Similar language could be used to describe the population-induced deterioration of forests and soils in much of Africa.

Amid all the media coverage of the African food crisis a fundamental point is being overlooked. There are no developments in prospect on either the agriculture or the family planning side of the food/population equation that will arrest the slide in per capita food production.

The sheer number of people seeking to survive on arid, marginal land in Africa may be driving a self-reinforcing process of dessication.

In addition, there is now evidence that population growth may be driving climate change in Africa. The sheer number of people seeking to survive on arid, marginal land may be driving a self-reinforcing process of desiccation, literally drying out the continent. Coming at a time of declining food output, this suggests a breakdown in the relationship between people and environmental support systems that could lead Africa into a crisis of historic dimensions—one that goes far beyond short-term emergency food relief. This continent-wide disintegration could gradually shift attention from the East-West confrontation, which has dominated world affairs for a generation, to the deteriorating relationship between people and life-support systems that now threatens the security and survival of so many.

The deterioration of our environmental support systems is not restricted to Africa, however. It takes many forms and can be seen in industrial and developing countries alike. Acid rain and air pollu-

tants from the combustion of fossil fuels in automobiles and power plants are laying waste to the forests of central Europe. Indeed, acid rain may be destroying the forests of Czechoslovakia, Poland, and West Germany even faster than the axe and plow destroyed those of India and El Salvador. More serious than the immediate loss of forests in Europe is the failure of reforestation efforts in the devastated areas where newly planted seedlings have withered and died.

The loss of forests is not the only cost of growing dependence on fossil fuels. Their combustion is also releasing carbon dioxide to the atmosphere on a scale that is likely to cause climatic shifts that could disrupt food production, reduce dependable water supplies, and eventually jeopardize coastal cities and towns.

When natural systems are severely stressed by human activity, their vulnerability increases. One graphic illustration of this: In 1983 a forest fire spread through Indonesian Kalimantan (Borneo) destroying some 3.5 million hectares of forests and defying the conventional wisdom that moisture-laden tropical rain forests will not burn naturally. Drought combined with forest degradation from logging, agricultural settlement, and the spread of shifting cultivation to dry out the forest and provide a layer of kindling. Fires ignited by lightning and slash-and-burn cultivators began to burn uncontrollably. As fires blazed and smoldered for some three months, valuable timber tracts were destroyed and countless plant and animal species disappeared in an evolutionary instant. This conflagration, little noticed outside the scientific community although it consumed an area larger than Taiwan, may be a harbinger of disruptions to come in other tropical rain forests.[4]

As our numbers move steadily toward

five billion, new manifestations of population pressures are surfacing. In China, authorities are now trying to conserve land by encouraging cremation instead of interment in the traditional burial mounds seen throughout the countryside. Where mounds occupy too much cropland, Beijing recommends that ancestral remains be consolidated in a single community plot. Veneration of ancestors continues, but in this crowded country the living compete with the dead for land.[5]

Difficult choices are not confined to China. West Germans may now have to choose between reducing automobile use and sacrificing their forests. For many Third World countries the choice is between an abrupt lowering of birth rates and a certain decline in living standards.

Trade-offs between food and energy are particularly difficult. In Brazil some 1.3 million hectares of cropland were planted to sugarcane in 1984 as part of a massive government program to become self-sufficient in liquid fuels. This reduced the outlay of scarce foreign exchange, but it also increased the pressures on soil and the competition with the food sector for resources.

Although these new signs of environmental stress appear each year, many people find them easy to ignore. The world has been lulled into a false sense of security by recent progress in slowing population growth, reducing dependence on oil, and replenishing granaries. Only when environmental deterioration begins to affect the economic statistics does the world seem to take notice.

Economic trends and ecological systems interact continuously in ways that we sometimes fail to understand and with consequences that we frequently do not anticipate. Policies that are economically successful in the short run can be ecologically and economically disastrous

in the long run. The U.S. crop surpluses of the early eighties, for example—sometimes cited as a sign of a healthy agriculture—are partly the product of careless overplowing. The very practices that lead to excessive erosion often yield short-term production gains or even surpluses, creating an illusion of progress.

Only when environmental deterioration begins to affect the economic statistics does the world seem to take notice.

Our understanding of these new stresses is far from complete. Unfortunately, the consequences of our action or inaction are of an entirely new magnitude. National energy policies could determine the extent and pace of a worldwide change in climate. Population policies may help determine whether Africa becomes a virtual wasteland. The scale of environmental disruptions we face lends urgency to our efforts to return to a sustainable path—to bring population growth and our economic and social systems into a long-term balance with the resource base that supports us.

This chapter outlines some of the key links between the global economy and the natural systems and resources that underpin it, focusing on how resource depletion and human alterations of natural systems are adversely affecting the economy. It also briefly considers some facets of this complex relationship, such as population-induced climate change, that we plan to examine in more detail in *State of the World-1986*. Subsequent chapters analyze resource pressures in greater detail and consider the policy initiatives needed to alleviate these pressures and put the world economy on a sustainable path.

THE ECONOMY/ECOSYSTEM INTERACTION

Despite the central importance of the economy/ecosystem relationship, relatively little attention has been devoted to analyzing it. There are several understandable reasons for this neglect: Rapid, sustained growth of the world economy is historically rather recent; an analysis of the interaction is a difficult interdisciplinary undertaking; and ecosystems are not well understood. Since mid-century the world output of goods and services has nearly quadrupled, an unprecedented achievement and a testimony to human energy and ingenuity. Unfortunately, this explosive growth has left little time to assess the effects on the earth's natural systems and resources.

In a world where the broad-based advance of knowledge has led to a high degree of specialization, the need for interdisciplinary research has increased even as its pursuit has become intellectually more demanding. This challenge was boldly recognized in September 1984 at a meeting of the International Council of Scientific Unions in Ottawa. Members from some 20 scientific unions and 71 national academies of science passed a unanimous resolution urging a worldwide project to study the interaction of the earth's physical, chemical, and biological processes. For those assembled, it had become clear that our lack of understanding of these processes and how they are being affected by human activity poses a risk to society that should be reduced.[7]

The interactions between the global economy and the earth's natural systems, cycles, and resources are legion. Acid rain affects forest productivity, which in turn raises costs in the forest products industry. Population growth hastens deforestation, which may reduce rainfall. Fossil fuel combustion raises atmospheric levels of carbon dioxide, which in turn alters climate and eventually world agriculture. The growing demand for protein triggers overfishing, which in turn leads to the collapse of fisheries. These are but a few of the important links between the economy and the ecosystem.

Of these linkages, one that seems destined to attract attention soon is that between soil erosion and Third World debt. Soil erosion can undermine not only a country's food production capacity but its debt servicing capacity as well, for it leads to widening food deficits, mounting debt, and eventually to food shortages. A nation whose people face starvation can hardly be blamed for failing to make debt payments. Indeed, at a meeting of the Organization of African Unity in November 1984, Conference Chair Julius Nyerere urged African governments to withold payment on their $152-billion foreign debt, owed mostly to European and U.S. banks.[8]

The changing relationship between the global economy, now producing some $12-trillion worth of goods and services per year, and the natural systems and resources that underpin it raises difficult questions in analysis and in the conduct of international affairs. Unfortunately, there is no overarching body of theory that integrates economic trends and ecological forces. Economic analysts turn to highly developed theory in their field and ecologists rely on well-established ecological principles. But there is no easy way to integrate the two approaches.

Despite this lack of integration, experience tells us that the ecological indicators of today foreshadow the economic trends of tomorrow. If we are interested in food prices at the end of the century, we should be looking at soil erosion rates today. The less soil we have, the more food will cost. For some idea of the cost of lumber and the price of housing a generation hence, we should be following deforestation rates today. If we want to know what types of seafood we will be eating a decade from now, we should be analyzing the areas of overfishing today.

Add to this need for interdisciplinary research the interaction of these forces across international boundaries, and the complex analytical task ahead becomes evident. In effect, the emergence of a highly developed international economy provides a way of transmitting scarcities from one country to another, a sort of domino theory of ecological stress and collapse. Soil erosion, for example, has historically been a local problem: Civilizations whose food systems were undermined by erosion in times past declined in isolation. But in the integrated world economy of the late twentieth century, food—like oil—is a global commodity. A country that loses an excessive amount of topsoil needs to import more food and thereby raises the pressure on soils elsewhere.

A highly developed international economy provides a way of transmitting scarcities from one country to another, a sort of domino theory of ecological stress and collapse.

These forces interact not only among countries but also between generations. Fossil fuel combustion today promises to alter the climate of tomorrow. Our inadvertent destruction of plant and animal species impoverishes the world of our children and grandchildren. At issue is whether we can act on behalf of future generations by moderating our reproductive behavior and by shifting to technologies and consumption patterns that are sustainable.

THE LOSS OF ECONOMIC MOMENTUM

In last year's *State of the World,* we noted the loss of momentum in world economic growth since 1979, a trend that 1984 data appear to confirm. The present recovery, led by the resurgent U.S. economy, has only marginally boosted the average economic growth for the past five years. With a slowdown in prospect for 1985, it appears more and more likely that world economic growth during this decade may not average much more than 2 percent annually.

Most immediately, the global economic slowdown reflects the depletion of oil reserves and the associated price hikes. These increases, initially engineered by the Organization of Petroleum Exporting Countries, are not the result of the absolute exhaustion of reserves, for vast reserves still remain. Rather, they are supported by a subtle shift from a buyer's to a seller's market, a shift that in turn stems from several factors. New oil resources are generally more costly to develop, particularly those involving offshore drilling in new fields and the use of secondary and tertiary recovery methods in older ones. Perhaps even more important, this market shift reflects the realization that there is no alternative to cheap oil. All other options are more costly, some much more so than others.

An analysis of world economic growth over the past 34 years shows it has slowed markedly following each of the two major oil price increases: During the 23 years from 1950 through 1973, when oil was priced at roughly $2 a barrel, the world economy expanded at a robust 5.0 percent per year. (See Table 1-1.) After the 1973 oil price hike, the rate of growth averaged just 3.5 percent per year through 1979. Following the second oil price hike it slowed further.

Global economic growth during the eighties is scarcely keeping pace with that of population, a sharp contrast with the situation from 1950 to 1973. When the world economy was increasing at some 5 percent per year, it far exceeded even the most rapidly expanding national populations. Now that it is only 2 percent, however, this is no longer the case. Countries with rapidly increasing populations that are merely keeping pace with the global rate of economic growth are experiencing declines in per capita income.

The abundance of cheap petroleum associated with the exceptionally rapid 7.6 percent annual growth in oil production from 1950 to 1973 made it relatively easy to expand both industrial and agricultural output at a healthy pace. In effect, cheap oil sharply boosted the earth's carrying capacity. Since the oil price hikes and the associated rise in energy costs across the board, rapid expansion has been far more difficult. In the agricultural sector, for example, before the first oil price hike world grain output was expanding at over 3 percent a year. Since 1973 it has grown at just under 2 percent annually, barely keeping pace with population growth. The shift from a buyer's to a seller's market in world oil

has affected grain production in two ways. First, it has increased the cost of production inputs, thus reducing the amount farmers can produce with a given investment. Second, it has slowed the growth in demand for grain by virtually eliminating gains in per capita income.

Oil is the first major resource whose supply has been restricted enough to measurably constrain economic expansion, but over the long term the loss of topsoil through erosion is likely to be more important. In *State of the World-1984* we estimated the worldwide loss of topsoil from cropland in excess of new soil formation at 22.7 billion tons annually. This year, based on fresh data for the United States and China, we have raised our estimate to 25.4 billion tons.[9] Afflicting industrial and developing countries alike, soil erosion is draining land of productivity on every continent. For subsistence farmers in Africa or Andean peasants in Latin America, where use of oil-based inputs is negligible or nonexistent, the loss of topsoil is a more serious threat to food production than oil price rises are.

Supplies of fresh water are also constraining both agricultural and industrial expansion. Food is being produced in

Table 1-1. Annual Growth in World Economic and Grain Output at Three Oil Price Levels, 1950–84

Period	Oil Price Per Barrel	World Economic Output[1]		World Grain Output	
		Total	Per Capita	Total	Per Capita
	(current dollars)		(percent)		
1950–73	2	5.0	3.1	3.1	1.2
1973–79	12	3.5	1.7	1.9	0.1
1979–84	28	2.0	0.3	2.0	0.3

[1]Constant dollars.

SOURCES: Oil price data from International Monetary Fund (IMF); economic data from U.S. Department of State and IMF; population data from United Nations; grain production data from the U.S. Department of Agriculture.

key agricultural regions of the world by the overdrafting of water supplies. Groundwater overdrafts are rampant in many of China's northern provinces, for example. In the Beijing-Tianjin region of northeast China, a combination of agricultural and industrial uses is lowering the water table by 1 to 4 meters per year. And in the south Indian state of Tamil Nadu, irrigation expansion has lowered the underground water table some 25–30 meters over the past decade. Overdrafting in the water-short Soviet central Asian republics commonly takes the form of excessive river withdrawals. These have reduced the amount of water reaching the Caspian and Aral seas, shrinking both. In the United States, the depletion of the Ogallala aquifer in the southern Great Plains and the diversion of irrigation water to Sunbelt cities in Arizona, California, and Florida have led to an unanticipated decline in national irrigated area of 3 percent since 1978. Aquifer depletion is now taking its place beside oil depletion and soil erosion as a constraint on growth in world food production.[10]

Other constraints on global economic expansion include those imposed by the sustainable yield of fisheries and grasslands, two of nature's major protein-producing biological systems. After more than tripling between 1950 and 1970, growth in the world fish catch slowed abruptly. Averaging nearly 6 percent annually before 1970, it has dropped to a mere 1 percent in the years since. (See Table 1-2.) In per capita terms, the world catch has fallen some 10 percent from its peak in 1970. Within the total harvest, the fish farming segment accounts for about one eighth and is expanding steadily, indeed rapidly in some local situations. As with agriculture, however, aquacultural growth is constrained by the availability of land and water.

Table 1-2. Annual Growth in World Fish Catch, Total and Per Capita, 1950–83

Period	Annual Growth in Catch	
	Total	Per Capita
	(percent)	
1950–70	5.9	3.8
1970–83	1.0	−0.8

SOURCE: United Nations Food and Agriculture Organization, *Yearbook of Fishery Statistics* (Rome: various years).

Although less carefully monitored, growth in the world production of beef —the principal product of the world's grasslands and second only to fish as a source of animal protein—came to a halt in 1976. Except in a few locations, grasslands cannot support more beef cattle. World beef output has not expanded significantly over the last eight years, despite the continuing conversion of tropical rain forests into grasslands. As a result, per capita beef production worldwide has fallen one tenth since 1976. The decline has been disproportionately great where grassland deterioration is more extensive (as in the Sahel), where red meat consumption is being reduced for health reasons, or where income drops have been precipitous (in Brazil, for example.)[11]

Fish production can be expanded through fish farming and beef production can be raised by improving grasslands and by putting more cattle in feedlots, but these are both much more energy-intensive and capital-consuming than were the inputs that led to impressive worldwide gains during the fifties and sixties, when these two biological systems had not yet been fully exploited.

Contributing to the overall economic slowdown of the last five years is the reduced growth of world food output, a matter that should be of concern to policymakers everywhere. Average life expectancy in the Third World jumped from 43 years in 1950 to 53 years in the early seventies. But progress since then has been less impressive. Indeed, in those parts of the world where the food situation is deteriorating, life expectancy may actually be declining.[12]

These trends raise two key questions: Why, in an age of advancing technology, is the world no longer able to sustain the economic and social gains of the century's third quarter? And, closely related, what needs to be done to get the world back on track? How can we restore the broad-based improvement in living conditions that existed throughout most of the third quarter of this century?

In those parts of the world where the food situation is deteriorating, life expectancy may actually be declining.

The trends described above indicate that existing policies are not working well. Policy adjustments are needed, particularly with regard to population growth. Underlining the urgency of reformulating these policies is the realization that rapid population growth often has two negative effects. On the demand side, it requires a rapid expansion in the output of food and other basic goods merely to maintain the status quo. But more worrisome is the realization that population growth may now be indirectly undermining efforts to increase output of essential items such as food. Such a scenario is unfolding in Africa, where population growth may be driving climate change, leading to a reduction in rainfall and, ultimately, food production.

POPULATION-INDUCED CLIMATE CHANGE

Meteorologists have long recognized that human activity could alter climate in urban communities. It is commonly known, for example, that cities create heat islands, areas where temperatures are consistently higher than in the surrounding countryside. Daily weather forecasts for large cities in the north temperate zone usually differentiate between temperatures in the downtown area and the suburbs—with the former always being higher, sometimes by as much as several degrees Fahrenheit.

Recently another question has emerged: Could changes in land cover, such as deforestation in the Third World, alter climate? The contribution of population growth to deforestation, overgrazing, soil erosion, and desertification in the Third World is highly visible and widely recognized. What is new is the realization that these processes—and, therefore, population growth indirectly—may be driving climate changes in regions as diverse as the semiarid Sudano-Sahelian zone of Africa and the rain forests of the Amazon.

In a sense, the question of whether human activities in the Third World are inducing climate change centers on the stability and resilience of biological systems. Long-standing ecosystems consist of a complex of plant and animal species that interact to their mutual advantage. The principal stabilizing elements are perennial vegetation, a stable water table, adequate underground water and stream flows, and an intact, productive soil profile. These elements permit ecosystems to withstand external buffeting such as short-term climatic fluctuations. A drought, for instance, will visibly alter a semiarid system in the short run, perhaps even leading to a widespread loss of plants and animals, but when it rains the area quickly returns to normal, reestablishing its equilibrium. But a system under exceptional stress may not recover in the expected manner.

These natural climatic fluctuations make it difficult to separate out the possible human effects on climate. A reconstructed climatic history of the Sahel over the last 10,000 years, for example, shows extreme fluctuations, from periods of wetness to dryness. A rather detailed history over just the last few centuries shows that the Sahel periodically experienced severe, prolonged drought. And early in this century, a decade-long drought that was particularly severe during 1911 and 1914 reduced the annual discharge of the Nile by 35 percent and the depth of Lake Chad by about 50 percent; river flows and lake levels fell throughout West Africa.[13]

Meteorologists have traditionally dismissed the notion of large-scale human-induced climate change, arguing that the forces driving global atmospheric circulation would override any local, human-induced alterations. One prominent meteorologist, F. Kenneth Hare of the University of Toronto, points out: "One school of thought—certainly dominant among professionals—says that the high incidence and prolonged duration of recent droughts are simply aspects of a natural fluctuation, due to some deep-seated oscillation of the general circulation of the atmosphere (and maybe the ocean)." Although this is the conventional view, Hare notes that some meteorologists are beginning to wonder whether human activity may now be affecting regional climates.[14]

Previous assessments have often been handicapped by exclusive reliance on conventional meteorological models and tools. But it is now possible to draw on relevant information from several fields, including agriculture, ecology, and hydrology as well as meteorology, and to piece together a plausible hypothesis that population-induced local climate change is indeed under way in Africa, and perhaps in northeastern Brazil and the Amazon Basin as well.

Any assessment of this hypothesis must begin with the understanding that the continents are watered by the oceans and that change induced by population growth must involve interfering with the mechanics of this process. Africa, for example, is watered by moisture-laden air masses from the Indian and Atlantic oceans. The Indian subcontinent receives rain from clouds moving inland from the Indian Ocean and the Bay of Bengal. The Brazilian Amazon derives almost all its water initially from the Atlantic Ocean.

Rainfall normally follows three principal paths: rapid runoff, groundwater recharge, and evaporation. Rapid runoff is water that steadily makes its way back to the ocean via streams and rivers. Aquifers are recharged by water that permeates the soil, percolating below the root zone where it cannot be used by plants. And finally, some rainfall evaporates from soil or from plants, either directly as water intercepted by the plants or indirectly through transpiration.

At a typical site in the central Amazon, such as one that was carefully studied near Manaus, Brazil, roughly one fourth of rainfall evaporates directly and nearly one half reenters the atmosphere in the form of transpiration from plants. Together, direct evaporation and transpiration return three fourths of the rainfall to the atmosphere, leaving one fourth as runoff that makes its way back to the Atlantic. (See Table 1–3.) Such high levels of cloud recharge have led ecologists to refer to tropical rain forests as "rain machines."

When land is deforested, however, this ratio is roughly reversed, with a quarter of the rainfall being returned to the atmosphere and three quarters running off quickly. Rainfall in the region is accordingly reduced, as the atmosphere holds less returned moisture that can become rain later in the cycle. This pattern increases with distance from the coast, for the recharge of rain clouds by evaporation, both direct and indirect, becomes the dominant source of rainfall in the interior. Even in semiarid regions, evaporation supplies much of the moisture in rainfall. A National Academy of Sciences study estimates, for example, that one third to two thirds of all rainfall in the Sahel comes from soil moisture evaporation.[15]

As indicated, water initially enters the Amazon area in moisture-laden air masses from the Atlantic Ocean. As these progress westward, they are continually discharging moisture in the form of rain and being recharged by evaporation and transpiration. On the average, water in the Amazon that does not return to the ocean completes the cycle every 5.5 days. During this process some of the water works its way out of the evaporative cycle as runoff and be-

Table 1-3. Water Balance in Amazonian Watershed Near Manaus, Brazil

Path of Rainfall	Proportion of Rainfall
	(percent)
Evaporation of rainfall intercepted by vegetation and from forested soil	26
Transpiration from vegetation	48
Total evapotranspiration	74
Stream runoff	26
Total rainfall	100

SOURCE: Eneas Salati and Peter B. Vose, "Amazon Basin: A System in Equilibrium," *Science*, July 13, 1984.

gins the long trip back to the Atlantic. Moisture left in the air when it reaches the Andes moves southward into central Brazil and the Chaco/Paraguay river regions, where it becomes part of the rainfall cycle in major farming areas.[16]

As the Amazon rain forest is converted to cropland or grassland or is cleared by logging, the share of rainfall that runs off increases. This swells the stream flow while decreasing evaporation and hence the amount of water in the area's hydrological cycle. The net effect is lower average rainfall, particularly in the western reaches. Such changes, particularly those that reduce the amount of water in the Amazon's hydrological regime, would almost certainly reduce the amount that reaches the Paraguayan Chaco and the central Brazilian plateau. In a landmark article in *Science*, Eneas Salati and Peter B. Vose observe that this "might affect climatic patterns and agriculture in south central Brazil."[17] Brazil's efforts to resettle the excess population from its northeast and south and to expand beef production by converting the Amazon rain forest to grassland may indirectly threaten food production in the country's agricultural heartland.[18]

Several attempts have been made to assess the overall effect of deforestation on the Amazon Basin's climate. Perhaps the most comprehensive and authoritative analysis is one by Ann Henderson-Sellers, using a three-dimensional general-circulation computer model created at the Goddard Institute for Space Studies in the United States. Incorporating several variables, this model suggests a gradual decline in average rainfall in the Amazon Basin as deforestation progresses.[19]

The actual reduction of rainfall in the Amazon is not known, but Philip Fearnside, a resident researcher at the Brazilian Institute for Amazonian Research, reports that in 1979 Manaus went 73 consecutive days without rain. Salati and Vose observe that "if such long dry periods were to become commonplace or extended there would inevitably be a marked change in the natural vegetation." Others have concluded that even a reduction in precipitation of 10–20 percent would alter the Amazon ecosystem. The key question, of course, is at what point these human interventions overcome the traditional stabilizing forces and set in motion changes in vegetation and climate that will lead to a Brazilian Amazon very different from the one we now know.[20]

Changes in land use also affect local rainfall by altering the albedo, the amount of sunlight reflected back into space. The conversion of forests to cropland or grassland and sometimes to desert, for example, increases the albedo. Where this happens, as on the fringes of the Sahara, the affected areas reflect more heat into space. Frequently associated with this is an increase in what meteorologists call subsidence—a large-scale sinking air motion as air descends from higher altitudes to maintain the ground-level heat balances. This high-altitude air is dry and thus reduces rainfall. One consequence of this process, first observed in the mid-seventies, is that once desertification is under way it can become self-reinforcing, gaining momentum over time.[21]

Given these effects of land-use changes on the hydrological cycle and on albedo, it should come as no surprise that deserts are expanding in areas where rapidly growing populations are generating wholesale shifts in land use, such as Africa, northeastern Brazil, northwestern India, and northwestern China. Recently the United Nations Environment Programme undertook a survey to assess desertification in countries in the Sudano-Sahelian region of Africa. (See Table 1-4.) The 14 most populous countries in this group have a combined population of 230 million people, 43 percent of the African total. The survey focused on five manifestations of desertification—sand dune encroachment, the deterioration in rangelands, forest depletion, the deterioration of irrigation systems, and problems in rainfed agriculture.

Not one of the 70 indicators—5 for each of the 14 countries—showed any improvement. According to 13 of the 70 indicators, there was no significant change over the seven years under review. Some 35, or half the total measurements, showed a moderate deterioration. The remaining 21 showed a serious deterioration. The 3 indicators showing the most consistent deterioration were rangelands, forests, and rainfed agriculture. Field observers confirm the survey findings, describing them as somber but realistic.

Perhaps because of the Sahelian drought of the early seventies and the continent-wide drought experienced in Africa in 1983 and 1984, more attention has been focused on changing land-use patterns caused by population pressure and the possible effects on local climate. In addition to the evidence from agriculture and meteorology, and the desertification trends, hydrological data also suggest that Africa is "drying out." In a hydrological analysis measuring changes in river flows, J. Sircoulon observes that "the Senegal, Niger, and Chari rivers, coming from wetter regions to the south . . . have undergone a severe decrease of runoff during the last 15 years. . . . Lake Chad has shown a systematic decrease of level since 1963. At that time the lake's surface covered 23,500 sq. kilometers, and the volume of stored water was 105 billion cubic meters. In 1973, ten years later, the surface had been divided by 3

Table 1-4. Rate of Desertification in the Sudano-Sahelian Region, 1977–84

Country	Sand Dune Encroachment	Deterioration in Rangelands	Forest Depletion	Deterioration of Irrigation Systems	Rainfed Agriculture Problems
Burkina Faso[1]	o	+	+	+	+ +
Cameroon	o	+	+	o	+
Chad	+ +	+ +	+	+ +	+ +
Ethiopia	+	+ +	+ +	+	+
Guinea	o	o	+	+	+ +
Kenya	o	+ +	+	o	+
Mali	+	+ +	+ +	+	+
Mauritania	+	+ +	+ +	+	+
Niger	+	+ +	+	+ +	+
Nigeria	o	+	+ +	o	+
Senegal	+	+ +	+	+	+ +
Somalia	+	+	+	+ +	+
Sudan	+ +	+	+	+	o
Uganda	o	+ +	o	o	+

[1]Formerly Upper Volta.
Key: o = stable, + = some increase, + + = significant increase
SOURCE: Adapted from Leonard Berry, "Desertification in the Sudano-Sahelian Region 1977–84," *Desertification Control* (Nairobi), May 1984.

and the volume by four. Since this date, the lake has been cut into two parts. The northern part dries up every year, with only a small inflow through the 'Grande Barriere'."[22]

Most meteorologists have been reluctant to attribute significant climate shifts to human changes in land use. Although the evidence that can now be assembled from several fields of study is not yet conclusive, it is rather persuasive. In reflecting on this, Canadian meteorologist Kenneth Hare has concluded in an analysis of desertification in Africa that "we seem to have arrived at a critical moment in the history of mankind's relation to climate. For the first time we may be on the threshold of man-induced climatic change."[23] Knowing what we do about the extent of deforestation over the past generation and about the way the hydrological cycle works, it would be

surprising if climate were not changing.

The time may have come for national political leaders and international development agencies to seriously consider the possibility that human population growth may now be driving climate change. More significantly, it is driving that change in directions that will not benefit the people affected. It is reducing rainfall in areas where rain is needed for crop production and livestock grazing. And it is expanding deserts, which in turn is shrinking the land area available for producing food, grazing livestock, and producing firewood. Those responsible for family planning programs will be amazed to learn that their effectiveness—or lack of it—may be altering the climate of their country, perhaps irreversibly.

FOSSIL FUELS AND CLIMATE CHANGE

Prior to the modern age, atmospheric carbon dioxide (CO_2) levels were rather stable, changing only very slowly over long periods of geological time. Carbon dioxide is used by plants in photosynthesis and is then returned to the atmosphere when the plants decompose. In the absence of any major change in the amount of vegetation on earth, atmospheric CO_2 levels remained constant. With the advent of the fossil fuel age, however, this began to change. Hydrocarbons that had accumulated underground over long spans of geologic time were brought to the surface and burned for fuel. As fossil fuel burning increased, so did the carbon dioxide released into the atmosphere.

At the end of the nineteenth century, two scientists—Svante Arrhenius, a prominent Swedish chemist, and T.C. Chamberlain, a geologist at the University of Wisconsin—independently concluded that atmospheric carbon dioxide played a central role in maintaining the earth's heat balance. They observed that carbon dioxide was transparent to incoming sunlight but that it intercepted some of the heat radiating outward from the earth's surface, reflecting it back to earth. Thus a buildup in atmospheric carbon dioxide would warm the earth, a process dubbed the "greenhouse effect."[24]

Although the increase in atmospheric CO_2 probably began a century or more ago, it was relatively insignificant up through the mid-twentieth century. Since then, however, it has accelerated. In 1958, scientists at the U.S. Observatory on Mauna Loa, Hawaii, began collecting regular samples of air and analyzing them for CO_2 content. Their records show a steady rise in atmospheric carbon dioxide from an annual average of 316 parts per million in 1958 to 343 parts per million in 1983, an increase of 9 percent in scarcely a quarter-century. (See Figure 1-1.) Fossil fuel combustion dominates the carbon dioxide buildup, although the steady shrinkage in the earth's forest cover also adds CO_2 to the atmosphere. George Woodwell and his colleagues at the Marine Biological Laboratory in Woods Hole estimate that deforestation may now be adding between 1.8 billion and 4.7 billion tons of carbon to the atmosphere per year. Although less than the contribution from fossil fuels, this is still a large additional source of atmospheric carbon dioxide.[25]

In 1950, worldwide fossil fuel combustion emitted 1.6 billion metric tons of carbon. By 1979 carbon emissions had climbed to a record 5.14 billion tons, more than triple the earlier level. (See Figure 1-2.) During the three years following the oil price hike in 1979—which reversed, at least temporarily, the long-term trend in world oil consumption—carbon emissions fell by more than 5 percent. More impressive, however, is the 10 percent fall in carbon emissions per $1,000 of gross world product since 1979.[26] (See Table 1-5.) In effect, the sharp gains in oil-use efficiency and associated reduction in petroleum use

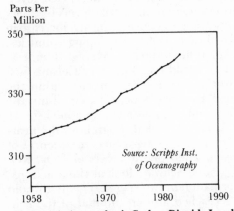

Figure 1-1. Atmospheric Carbon Dioxide Levels at Mauna Loa, Hawaii, 1958-83

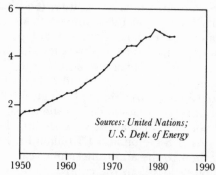

Figure 1-2. World Carbon Emissions From Fossil Fuel Combustion, 1950-83

Table 1-5. Carbon-Emissions Intensity of World Economic Output, 1950–82

Year	Gross World Product[1] (trillion dollars)	Total Carbon Emissions (million metric tons)	Carbon Per $1,000 of GWP (kilograms)
1950	2.94	1,583	538
1955	3.78	1,975	522
1960	4.68	2,495	533
1965	5.99	3,037	507
1970	7.67	3,934	513
1971	8.02	4,080	509
1972	8.41	4,236	504
1973	8.99	4,454	495
1974	9.30	4,463	480
1975	9.42	4,453	473
1976	9.87	4,696	476
1977	10.29	4,825	469
1978	10.71	4,861	454
1979	11.05	5,144	466
1980	11.27	5,058	449
1981	11.43	4,931	431
1982	11.59	4,875	421

[1]1980 dollars.
SOURCES: Worldwatch Institute estimates based on data from United Nations, U.S. Department of Energy, U.S. Department of State, and International Monetary Fund.

more than offset the growth in coal and gas use. Greater reliance on renewable energy sources has also helped reduce the carbon-emissions intensity of world economic output.

Advances in meteorological modeling, combined with the data from Mauna Loa, provide a basis for estimating the climatic impact of large-scale fossil fuel burning. By the early eighties there was a near consensus about the general effects of the CO_2 rise on the earth's climatic system. William W. Kellogg and Robert Schware point out that if industrial countries expand fossil fuel use 4 percent per year (the rate prevailing from 1900–80), atmospheric CO_2 levels will double preindustrial levels by 2030, without even considering any increase in fossil fuel use for developing countries. Under this scenario, average temperatures would rise 3 degrees Celsius (just over 5 degrees Fahrenheit) within the next 45 years, a period well within the life span of today's young adults.[27]

To help think through both the near-term and the long-term consequences of rising atmospheric levels of CO_2, Kellogg and Schware look at climatic transformation in two stages. The first would be reached around the end of the century, when the world would be on average a half-degree Celsius warmer than in

1980. This would correspond to an atmospheric CO_2 rise from the 343 parts per million at present to 360–370 parts per million. Although such a modest average increase does not appear particularly striking or ominous, temperatures in some regions would rise much more. The warming effect is amplified, for example, toward the poles. Thus in the northern tier of industrial countries, such as in North America or Europe, temperatures would increase 2–3 degrees Celsius (3–5 degrees Fahrenheit). Boston's climate would be similar to that of Washington, D.C., today. In Europe, a comparable shift would give Copenhagen a temperature regime resembling that of Paris.

In the second stage, when the doubling of CO_2 levels would raise global average temperature by 3 degrees Celsius, the temperate-zone northern hemisphere would experience a rise of 4–6 degrees Celsius, some 9 degrees Fahrenheit. Under this climatic regime Boston would have an average temperature close to that of Miami today: It would be a virtually frost-free city with swimming possible throughout most of the year. It is also likely to be more humid.

There would also be shifts in rainfall patterns associated with a CO_2 rise, but meteorologists are much less certain of these changes than they are about those in temperature. On average there would be more rainfall, though in substantial areas there would be less, as the global climatic patterns shifted with the alteration in atmospheric dynamics associated with the increase in temperature. Both North America and the Soviet Union would be likely losers in terms of average rainfall. The U.S. cornbelt, the U.S.-Canadian Great Plains wheat-growing area, and the principal grain-growing regions of the Soviet Union would all have less soil moisture even if rainfall remained the same, since higher temperatures would increase evaporation. China would stand to lose rainfall in the northern part of the country (the region already suffering from water scarcity) and to gain in the south, thus worsening the existing water imbalance between the two regions. Regions that stand to gain include Western Europe, most of Saharan Africa, the Indian subcontinent, and Australia.[28]

As atmospheric CO_2 levels go up the sea level will also rise. Thermal expansion alone from the temperature increase would raise average sea levels by some five feet as the oceans slowly warm by absorbing heat from the atmosphere. In addition, melting ice in both Greenland and Antarctica would contribute to the rise in sea level. There also would be a substantial melting of floating ice in the Arctic Ocean, although this would not appreciably affect sea levels.[29]

The rise in sea level anticipated with a doubling of atmospheric CO_2 could range up to five to seven meters, but because the transfer of heat from the warmer atmosphere to the oceans, particularly the lower levels, is a slow process, the full effect of doubled atmospheric CO_2 on ocean levels could take two centuries or longer. Even a short-term rise of one meter, however, would adversely affect many coastal cities and low-lying agricultural lands. The inundation of agricultural lowlands would reduce world rice output, much of which is produced on the river floodplains of Asia.

With seas that are five to seven meters higher, vast areas of rice land in the floodplains of the Ganges, the Yellow, and the Mekong rivers would become uncultivatable in the absence of dikes to hold back the sea. Such structures would be among the largest public works projects ever undertaken, requiring vast amounts of capital. For a low-lying country such as Bangladesh, where 13 million people live less than three meters above sea level, the significance of such a rise is obvious.[30]

The rise in temperature will bring with it another set of problems. Where temperature stress is already troublesome for both plants and animals, a rise in the average temperature of 9 degrees Fahrenheit, such as that projected for the north temperate zone, would entail unbearable heat stress. And over time it would lead to changes in vegetation, with species now prevalent being replaced by more heat-tolerant ones.

With a global warming there would be winners as well as losers. Canada, the Soviet Union, and other countries with hefty winter heat bills would find relief. Longer growing seasons in the extreme latitudes would also benefit these same countries.

Much of the literature emphasizes the need to adjust to such changes, but the costs of doing so could be high. For example, the evolution of agriculture over the last several centuries in both the Old World and the New has been keyed to a particular climatic regime. Cropping patterns, agricultural practices, and irrigation and drainage systems are shaped by local temperature and rainfall conditions. If these begin to change, with some areas becoming wetter and others drier, then the drainage systems now adequate will become redundant where rainfall is declining, whereas new systems will have to be constructed where it is increasing. Similarly, some regions that now have irrigation will no longer require it, while others will need it even more.

A major shift away from the climatic regime that has governed the evolution of agriculture will bring with it heavy capital investment needs.

The bottom line of climate change's impact on agriculture is an increase in capital requirements. The value of some drainage and irrigation systems will depreciate; some will be rendered worthless by the climate change. In other cases capital investments will be required for new drainage or irrigation systems to maintain land productivity. In any event, a major shift away from the climatic regime that has governed the evolution of agriculture over the centuries will bring

with it heavy capital investment needs. In a world that is finding it difficult to mobilize enough agricultural investment capital to eliminate hunger even with a stable climatic regime, the prospect of having to raise vast amounts of additional capital merely to maintain the productivity of existing systems is daunting indeed.

In addition to analyzing the effect of rising atmospheric CO_2 on climate, meteorologists are now examining the effect of trace gases. Fossil fuel combustion, the manufacture of synthetic chemicals, deforestation, and biomass combustion produce some 40 trace gases, including chlorofluorocarbons, methane, and nitrous oxide. Growth in the release of these gases has closely paralleled that of CO_2—and for the same reasons. The most recent assessment of the effect of trace gases on climate, conducted by a team of U.S. meteorologists, concluded that "the magnitude of this warming in the future can potentially be as large as the warming due to projected increases in CO_2."[31]

As awareness of the threat posed by the global CO_2 buildup now under way has begun to permeate the scientific community, various options have been considered for preventing or at least minimizing the problem. It is technically possible to remove carbon dioxide from the smokestacks of coal-fired thermal power plants, for example, but doing so requires a great deal of energy, enough to reduce a plant's effective generating capacity by 30–80 percent. Such a process would thus be prohibitively costly.[32]

Another, far more attractive option is to engage in serious efforts to conserve energy, thus reducing fossil fuel combustion. U.S. Department of Energy projections show world CO_2 emissions doubling from 5 billion tons of carbon in 1984 to 10.3 billion tons in 2025. Our own projections—based on average economic and population growth rates of

3.2 and 1.2 respectively during the period but assuming a concerted effort to use existing technologies to boost energy efficiency wherever it is profitable to do so—show that carbon emissions could be held to 7.9 billion tons. If allowance is made for a likely slower rate of economic growth (a 2 percent rate, say, comparable to the last five years), the future development of more-energy-efficient technologies, and an emergency effort to save forests from acid rain by accelerating the transition to renewable energy, then it is possible to envisage a world where carbon emissions never rise much above current levels, and eventually begin to decline as fossil fuels are depleted or phased out.[33]

If such a "CO_2-benign" strategy were to materialize, holding carbon emission levels at 5 billion tons per year, it would limit the rise in atmospheric CO_2 from the current 343 parts per million to 420 parts per million in 2050. This would be an increase of less than one fourth, far below the doubling that the Department of Energy projects. It would markedly slow the change in climate, buying time with which to develop alternative energy sources and to make any adjustments called for by the climatic change.[34]

Yet another key component of such a strategy would be to develop energy sources that did not generate carbon dioxide, such as nuclear power and the many sources of renewable energy that are now available. It seems unlikely that nuclear power will be an economically viable energy option, particularly when the costs of decommissioning worn-out power plants are added to construction and operating costs that are already prohibitive in many countries. (For a detailed discussion of the nuclear power option, see *State of the World-1984*.) But the possibilities of developing renewable energy resources that do not produce net carbon dioxide—such as hydropower, photovoltaics, wind power, solar panels, energy crops, and fuelwood plantations—are seemingly endless. Energy efficiency and the development of renewable energy resources are discussed at length in Chapters 7 and 8.

Over the long term, the contribution of conventional oil resources and natural gas to rising CO_2 levels will be fairly modest since the reserves of these two fossil fuels are being rapidly depleted. The only fossil fuel that remains in large enough quantities to markedly raise global atmospheric CO_2 levels is coal. In some ways this is fortuitous: Some 60 percent of the world's coal reserves lie under just three countries—China, the Soviet Union, and the United States—with most of the remainder in Australia, India, Poland, South Africa, the United Kingdom, and West Germany.[35]

In contrast to many issues arising in the management of the global commons, which rest on the cooperation of scores of countries, agreement among only these three countries to restrict coal burning would go a long way toward heading off a CO_2-induced global warming. Whether all would see it in their interest to do so is another matter. The Soviet Union, for example, might conclude that a warming and the associated lengthening of growing season would on balance be of benefit, particularly if its efforts to divert the flow of its major rivers southward should succeed. Such a view could make Moscow less eager to cooperate in a global effort to check the buildup of carbon dioxide.

BREAKING OUT OR BREAKING DOWN

The demographic transition, a conceptual device used by demographers to explain the relationship between population growth and levels of development, has three stages. In the first, which characterizes traditional societies, both birth and death rates are high. Societies have existed under these circumstances for long stretches, for thousands or even hundreds of thousands of years, without any appreciable change in population size. Births and deaths are largely in balance.

In the second portion of the demographic transition, living conditions get better as public health improves, vaccines become available, and food production expands. In this stage births remain high but deaths fall. The result is rapid population growth. A society at this point would typically have a crude birth rate of 45 and a crude death rate of 15, yielding an annual population growth of 3 percent.

The third stage sees living conditions improve further, birth control become widely available and used, and births declining to again roughly offset deaths. A balance between births and deaths in a modern society usually occurs with crude birth and death rates of around 13. The United Kingdom, West Germany, and Hungary are among the dozen or so countries that have completed the demographic transition, reestablishing an equilibrium between births and deaths.

Societies can remain in either the first or the final stage of the demographic transition indefinitely. This is not true, however, of the middle phase. Populations growing at 3 percent per year multiply twentyfold in a century. Many developing countries have been in the middle stage since roughly mid-century. Those now in the fourth decade of 3 percent annual population growth are en route to the twentyfold increase in a century that this arithmetic dictates. Unfortunately, it is difficult to imagine any country, even one that was sparsely populated at mid-century, surviving

such an increase with its biological support systems and social institutions intact.

The evidence of recent years suggests that countries stuck in the second stage for more than a few decades experience mounting population pressures, pressures that eventually destroy forests, grasslands, and croplands. As these resources deteriorate, mortality rates begin to rise to reestablish the balance between births and deaths that nature demands. Countries that do not make it to the demographic equilibrium of the third stage will eventually return to the demographic equilibrium of the first. Nature provides no long-term alternative.

The mechanics of this "demographic regression," rooted in the changing balance between population size and basic resources, are becoming clear. For countries that remain in the second stage for an extended period, population growth eventually shrinks the cropland per person. Such areas are also likely to be losing topsoil due to erosion. In these situations, the technological advances in agriculture—plus any increases in fertilizer use that can be afforded—may not be sufficient to maintain per capita food production. The government must either use foreign exchange to import food or obtain food assistance from abroad. Because societies in the middle stage of the demographic transition are largely agrarian, a decline in per capita food production invariably translates into a decline in per capita income.

Many of the countries that have broken out of the second stage of the demographic transition have done so with the aid of cheap energy and relatively favorable population/land ratios. Others are finding it increasingly difficult to reach the point where gains in per capita income and the use of birth control begin to reinforce each other with substantial gains in living standards.

Kilograms

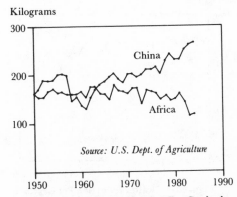

Figure 1-3. Grain Production Per Capita in China and Africa, 1950-84

through the end of the century.[36]

Africa, in contrast, shows no movement toward the third stage of the demographic transition. And time is running out. Population growth for the continent as a whole is close to 3 percent. The share of the population using birth control is minuscule. Grain production per capita in Africa was quite steady throughout the fifties and sixties, but it turned downward after reaching a post-war high of 180 kilograms per year in 1967. During the mid-eighties, grain production per person is nearly one fifth below the level of the late sixties. As noted in the opening of this chapter, several countries are reporting starvation deaths.[37]

In a recent report, the World Bank expressed concern about rising death rates in several African countries. Bank officials feel that in the absence of a major initiative, a number of countries will experience a disintegration of social institutions and will revert to "bush" economies. The seriousness of this situation led several West European members of the Bank in mid-1984 to call for the establishment of an emergency rescue fund for Africa. Without a sharply expanded effort in both family planning and farming, the prospect is that much of the continent will drop back into the first stage of the demographic transition.[38]

Without a sharply expanded effort in both family planning and farming, much of Africa will drop back into the first stage of the demographic transition.

The prospect of moving from the middle to the final stage of the demographic transition is perhaps best assessed by trends in per capita food production. China and Africa, with populations of just over 1 billion and 531 million respectively, illustrate contrasting prospects. China appears to be breaking out and Africa, having failed to do so, appears to be breaking down. (See Figure 1-3.)

As recently as the early seventies, per capita food production in China was little improved from the mid-fifties, the years immediately preceding the agriculturally disastrous Great Leap Forward. During the past decade, however, per capita food production in China has climbed at an encouraging rate. The rate of population growth has been halved since the early seventies, dropping to just over 1 percent per year. Grain production per capita in the mid-eighties averages over 250 kilograms per year, up by one fourth from the 200 kilograms per year of the early seventies. Even though China has serious environmental problems in agriculture, including soil erosion, and although its cropland base is likely to continue shrinking during the century's closing two decades, there is a good prospect that living standards in the nation will continue to improve

Other major areas of the world have also remained in the second stage for a dangerously long period. The southernmost Andean countries in Latin America

—Bolivia, Chile, Ecuador, and Peru— have experienced a decline in per capita food production for more than a decade. Indeed, the trend in per capita grain production in these four countries is remarkably similar to that of Africa. (See Figure 1-4.) Grain output kept pace with population growth during the fifties and sixties but then was eventually overwhelmed by the increase in human numbers. As a result, per capita grain production has fallen by roughly one fourth over the past 15 years. The forces leading to a decline in per capita grain production in the South Andes are precisely the same as those in Africa—rapid population growth, widespread soil erosion and desertification, and lack of attention to agricultural development.[39]

If data were available for northeastern Brazil, a region containing some 43 million people, it would undoubtedly show a similar trend and for the same reasons. In addition to high birth rates and widespread soil erosion, this region may be suffering from climate change as well. Another major area of the world at risk is the Indian subcontinent. Population growth ranges from 2.4 percent in India to roughly 3 percent per year in Bangladesh, Nepal, and Pakistan. Under these conditions, grain output per person in the early eighties is little changed from the early fifties.[40]

With a population of 960 million and a growth rate in excess of 2.2 percent per year, the subcontinent has remained in

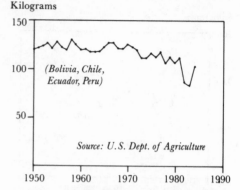

Kilograms

(Bolivia, Chile, Ecuador, Peru)

Source: U.S. Dept. of Agriculture

Figure 1-4. Grain Production Per Capita in South Andean Countries, 1950-84

the middle stage of the demographic transition for a dangerously long period of time. Cropland per person is shrinking, soil erosion continues, and population growth remains rapid, making it increasingly difficult for these countries to set in motion the self-reinforcing trends of rising food production per person and falling birth rates.

Under the circumstances now unfolding there is growing uncertainty about how many countries in the middle of the demographic transition will be able to break out. By the end of the century the world may be divided into two groups: countries that have progressed into the final stage and those that have fallen back to the first stage. There are unlikely to be many countries left in the middle. The demographic transition in each nation will have been largely completed or aborted.

2

Reducing Hunger

Lester R. Brown

During the third quarter of this century world food production surged ahead, outstripping population growth and holding out the hope that hunger could be banished. Over the last decade, however, growth in production has slowed, raising doubts about the long-term food prospect. Despite advances in technology, the effort to reduce hunger is at a standstill. The failure to adequately feed all of humanity hangs heavily on the collective conscience, dimming the many remarkable achievements of the late twentieth century.

The shifting contours of the world food economy are dominated by two major developments. One is the leveling off of per capita food production since 1973 following a quarter-century of steady gains. The other is the divergence among continents and major countries that this global trend obscures. In some regions per capita food production is surging ahead; in others it is falling steadily.

China and Africa illustrate these contrasts, as discussed in Chapter 1. The

impressive gains in per capita grain production in China have provided that country with a substantial safety margin, one that would permit it to weather two successive poor harvests without any serious malnutrition. In Africa, on the other hand, the food situation is deteriorating. The 1 percent annual decline in per capita grain output since 1967 has been aggravated by the drought of 1983 and 1984. Even before the drought, nearly a fifth of Africa's people were being sustained by imported grain.[1]

There is a similarly sharp contrast in the agricultural performances of the United States and the Soviet Union. Over the past generation the United States has become the world's breadbasket, supplying a larger share of world grain imports than Saudi Arabia does of oil imports. Meanwhile, the Soviet Union, which has both the world's largest cropland area and a farm sector plagued by mismanagement and undermined by soil erosion, is now projected to import a record 50 million tons of grain this year, more than any country in history. Ironically, its principal supplier is the United States. Each day two U.S. freighters loaded with grain head for the Soviet Union, indicating that economic interests can override ideological differences. Indeed, the long line of ships that links American farms with Soviet dining tables may carry within it the seeds of a lasting detente.

THE CROPLAND TREND

From the beginning of agriculture until roughly mid-century, growth in the world's cropland area more or less kept pace with that of world population. The great bulk of the year-to-year growth in food supply came from expanding cultivated area. Improvements in land productivity came slowly or not at all. At mid-century, this began to change. A 1984 study by the U.S. Department of Agriculture (USDA) showed that growth in the world's cropland slowed markedly during the fifties, averaging less than 1 percent per year—roughly half that of population. Thereafter the rate of growth in cropland area continued to slow, falling below 0.3 percent per year in the seventies. USDA projects that this slowing will continue, falling to 0.2 percent in the eighties and 0.15 percent in the nineties. (See Table 2-1.) If these trends do materialize, the world cropland base will expand about 4 percent between 1980 and 2000, while population growth is projected to expand by some 40 percent.[2]

Net growth in the world cropland area in any given year reflects the difference between the majority of countries, which are still adding some new cropland, and a much smaller, though growing, number where the cropland area is shrinking. In some of the latter group the shrinkage results from the abandonment of mar-

Table 2-1. Estimated Growth in World Cropland Area, 1950–80, With Projections to 2000

Period	Growth Per Year
	(percent)
Late fifties	1.0
Seventies	0.3
Eighties	0.2
Nineties	0.15

SOURCE: Francis Urban and Thomas Vollrath, *Patterns and Trends in World Agricultural Land Use* (Washington, D.C.: U.S. Government Printing Office, 1984).

ginal land in favor of more-intensive use of the most productive land. Such decline has been under way now for close to two decades in Western Europe, Eastern Europe, and Eastern Asia, including both China and Japan. In West Germany and Poland, for example, the postwar peak in arable land area occurred in 1955. In France, Japan, and Yugoslavia, it was 1960; in China, the peak was in 1963.[3]

Roughly a third of the world's people now live in countries where cropland area is shrinking.

Roughly 1.5 billion of the world's people, about a third of the total, now live in countries where cropland area is shrinking. China and Italy, for example, have lost 5.1 and 4.8 percent of their cropland since the decline began. (See Table 2-2.) Changes such as these reflect the relationship between the numerous plus and minus forces affecting the cropland area. Expansion commonly results from pushing back the frontiers of settlement, irrigation projects, drainage projects, the clearing of forests, or the plowing of grassland. The addition by new settlement projects is perhaps best illustrated by Brazil, which is encouraging new farms and ranches in the Cerrado and the Amazon Basin, and by Indonesia, which is attempting to resettle people from densely populated Java to the outer islands of Sumatra, Kalimantan, and Sulawesi.

New irrigation projects have played a central role in adding to the cultivated area of semiarid countries such as Pakistan and Mexico. Indeed, throughout history irrigation has played a major role in boosting cropland productivity and expanding the earth's food-producing capacities. The growing pressures on this key input to agricultural production are discussed at length in Chapter 3.

Land reclamation by drainage figures prominently in the Soviet Union, where some 700,000 hectares per year is to be

Table 2-2. Selected Countries With Declining Cropland Area, 1980

Country	Postwar Peak in Arable Land Area	Decline From Peak Year to 1980
	(year)	(percent)
China	1963	−5.1
France	1960	−13.3
Hungary	1955	−6.6
Ireland	1960	−29.4
Italy	1955	−4.8
Japan	1960	−19.6
Netherlands	1955	−18.0
Poland	1955	−9.7
Portugal	1963	−18.1
South Korea	1968	−5.3
Sweden	1955	−21.0
West Germany	1955	−13.9
Yugoslavia	1960	−5.6

SOURCE: Francis Urban and Thomas Vollrath, *Patterns and Trends in World Agricultural Land Use* (Washington, D.C.: U.S. Government Printing Office, 1984).

reclaimed during the early eighties. For the Soviet Union, at least, this rivals the annual additions from irrigation. In Central America, cropland area expansion comes at the expense of forests, while in East Africa and Argentina recent growth has come mostly from grassland conversion. The same has been true for some of the Great Plains states in the United States; Colorado's Weld County and Montana's Petroleum County have taken steps to prohibit the plowing of grasslands, which are vulnerable to wind erosion once the grass cover is removed.[4]

On the other side of the ledger, cropland can be lost to such nonfarm uses as industrialization and to urbanization, one of the most globally pervasive demographic trends of this century. According to U.N. projections, the urban share of world population is projected to increase from 29 percent in 1950 to 50 percent by 2000, boosting the number of city-dwellers from 725 million to a projected 3.1 billion.[5]

The amount of cropland disappearing under cities is not known, but individual country data and various surveys do provide some indication. For example, two USDA surveys—one in 1967 and the other in 1975—indicated that some 2.5 million hectares of prime U.S. cropland were converted to urban and built-up uses during the eight-year period. A study of urban encroachment on agricultural land in Europe (grasslands as well as croplands) from 1960 to 1970 found that West Germany was losing 0.25 percent of its agricultural land yearly, or 1 percent every four years. For France and the United Kingdom, the comparable figure was 0.18 percent per year, nearly 2 percent for the decade.[6]

While attention has focused on urban encroachment, cropland is also being lost to village expansion. Unfortunately, little research has been conducted on this loss. In one analysis using data over several decades for his native Bangladesh, Akef Quazi concludes that growth in the number of families and that of the area occupied by the village are closely related. One reason for this correlation is that homes are "made up of locally available materials, such as bamboo, thatch, and corrugated iron sheets and, as such, are never strong enough to hold an upper story." Quazi reports that "every new village homestead is being built on cropland." Although undoubtedly there are occasional exceptions, Quazi's general point is a sound one, for Bengali villages are usually surrounded by the rice fields on which they depend.[7]

Further east, in Beijing, Chinese planners are becoming alarmed over the loss of cropland to village home construction. One consequence of the shift to a family-based, market-oriented farm system is that the millions of peasants who are becoming wealthy invariably make building a new home their top priority. Planners in Beijing have concluded that one way to minimize cropland conversion is to encourage peasants to construct two-story homes. Even so, the new affluence in the countryside is exacting a heavy toll on scarce cropland.[8]

Apart from the expansion of human settlements per se, industrialization also consumes large areas of land. Indeed, one of the principal causes of cropland shrinkage in Western Europe and Japan since the mid-fifties has been factory construction, which was particularly rapid from the mid-fifties through the mid-seventies. More recently, industrial development has begun to claim land in developing countries as well. Land-hungry China has been especially affected: Factories must be built in the east and south, where most Chinese live, which is also where most farmland is located. Dwight Perkins, a Harvard scholar on China, notes that the 10 percent annual industrial growth steadily consumes cropland. He believes planners are

aware of this but that "there is no way around the fact that good farmland (flat, located near transport, etc.) often makes an excellent factory site."[9]

The automobilization of societies also claims cropland for highways, parking lots, garages, and filling stations. Growth in the world automobile fleet from 48 million in 1950 to 331 million in 1982 has claimed millions of hectares of farmland for these purposes.[10] As with factory sites, the flat, well-drained land that is ideal for farming is also well-suited for highways and parking lots.

In addition to the conversion of cropland to nonfarm uses, excessive economic demands and mismanagement are claiming cropland through desertification, severe erosion, waterlogging and salinization of irrigated land, and the diversion of irrigation water to nonfarm uses. Soil erosion claims cropland either through sheet erosion or as a result of gully formation. Although severe gullying, leading to land abandonment, is now commonplace, it has received the least official attention where it is most advanced. A U.N. report on cropland in Latin America notes its severe dimensions in the Andean countries, where gullys are advancing through the steeply sloping countryside like the tentacles of a giant malignancy. As these gullys eat their way across fields, farmers who are already hungry for land continue to till what is left, right up to the gully's edge —thus accelerating its progress across the land.[11]

A report for Europe describes the extensive abandonment of farmland in Italy: "It is generally agreed that in Italy 2 million hectares have been abandoned in the last ten years. . . . The farming measures used on this marginal land have led to deterioration of the soil so that the land was consumed in the literal sense of the term."[12] Similarly, some of the decline in the harvested area of cereals in Yugoslavia and Bulgaria over the past two decades reflects the movement from eroded, worn-out soils in farm areas with rugged terrain.[13]

Other sources of cropland loss have received little attention. For example, land for burial has claimed millions of hectares over the past generation. In most countries this loss is minimized by using cemeteries. But in China, as mentioned in Chapter 1, the dead are buried under mounds that are often located on good farmland. A study of this practice in the immediate vicinity of Beijing reported that from 1949 until 1964 burial mounds claimed 213 hectares (526 acres) of fertile cropland. Multiplied thousands of times over for the country as a whole, it is clear why this loss concerns Chinese political leaders. Accordingly, the government has launched a campaign to encourage cremation. Zhang Yizhi, an official in the ministry of civil affairs, observes that "we have to practice cremation in cities and in densely-populated rural areas. Otherwise the living and the dead will have to scramble for land." Although it is difficult to persuade people to change centuries-old traditions, Zhang believes that the shift to the family responsibility system will facilitate this transition: "If the peasants want to become more prosperous, they will not be able to let the dead occupy the limited land that is available for farming."[14]

Another factor in the world cropland equation is the low productivity of the new fields. In Nigeria and Brazil, where expansion of cultivated area has been greatest, cereal yields have increased little or none since 1950. The increasing use of fertilizer and other inputs is being offset by the declining quality of cropland.[15]

In some countries, the land lost to nonfarm uses is being replaced by land of lower productivity. The Science Council of Canada reports that "half of the farmland lost to urban expansion is coming from the best one twentieth of our farmland."[16] It takes an estimated 240 acres of new land in Canada's western provinces to replace 100 acres of land lost to urban expansion in the higher-rainfall eastern provinces. And in some countries there has been a "retreat from the margin" because of overexpansion. This occurred in the Soviet Union during the early eighties, for example, as a result of overexpansion into marginal lands.

By the year 2000 the area of new land to be plowed will obviously be limited. Indeed, new land being added will barely offset the losses projected. For planning purposes it is best to assume that virtually all growth in world food output by century's end will have to come from raising land productivity.

WATER AND BREAD

The lack of unexploited water resources may constrain growth in world food output even more than the scarcity of unexploited fertile land. In countries as widely separated as Mexico and Pakistan, freshwater scarcity prevents the spread of high-yielding wheats. In the Soviet Union, water shortages are frustrating efforts to expand feedgrain production for that country's swelling livestock herds. As new irrigation options are exhausted, the link between water and bread becomes increasingly obvious.

Although irrigated agriculture started several thousand years ago, only in the twentieth century has it covered much of the earth's surface. (For a fuller discussion of the reliance on irrigation throughout the world, see Chapter 3.) In 1800 an estimated 8 million hectares of the world's cropland were irrigated. Although irrigation increased substantially from 1900 to 1950, the bulk of the expansion has occurred since then, with the total irrigated area reaching 261 million hectares by 1982. (See Table 2-3.)

Some 15 percent of the world's cropland is irrigated, up from 11 percent in the early sixties. Although irrigation was once concentrated in the Middle East, where it first developed, the center of gravity has now shifted to Asia. As of 1980, 120 million hectares of the world's 261 million irrigated hectares—some 46 percent—were located in Asia. Today the Middle East and North Africa account for only 8 percent of the world total, as does the Soviet Union, and less than 10 percent is in the United States. Latin America accounts for under 10 percent of the world's irrigated land and subsaharan Africa has only 2 percent.[17]

Irrigation can use either underground water or surface water from rivers, streams, or lakes. Early irrigation systems relied on surface water, usually that which was backed up behind an embankment of some sort so that it would flow by gravity onto the fields. Using underground water requires more energy since the water must be lifted. Irrigation-water distribution techniques also vary. For crops such as rice, flooding is commonly used. Water is fed or pumped onto a field enclosed by a small embank-

Table 2-3. Estimated World Irrigated Area, 1900–82

Year	Irrigated Area
	(million hectares)
1900	40
1950	94
1982	261

SOURCE: W. R. Rangeley, "Irrigation—Current Trends and a Future Perspective," World Bank Seminar, Washington, D.C., February 1983.

ment until the entire surface is covered. This system requires that land be flat, either naturally or as a result of artificial leveling. Another traditional practice, furrow irrigation, is commonly used for row crops such as corn, potatoes, and vegetables. With the advent of cheap energy, many farmers pumping water from underground began distributing the water through sprinkler systems, an energy-intensive method.

At the country level, irrigation plays an important role in each of the big four food producers—the United States, the Soviet Union, China, and India. Growth in irrigated area in China since mid-century has been impressive, increasing from scarcely 20 million hectares in 1950 to some 48 million by 1980. Much of the increase was achieved by labor-intensive construction practices, and it is largely responsible for the increase in multiple cropping from an average of 1.3 crops per hectare in 1950 to 1.6 in 1980.[18]

India's net irrigated area in 1950 was 21 million hectares, almost exactly the same as China's. But as of 1980 it totaled only some 39 million hectares. The most rapid growth has occurred since the mid-sixties, following the introduction of high-yielding wheat and rice varieties that were both more responsive to the use of water and more exacting in their demands. This enhanced profitability stimulated widespread investments by small farmers in wells of their own so they could more fully exploit the yield potential of the new varieties.[19]

U.S. irrigated area has expanded throughout the period from 1950 to 1978 but at a decelerating rate. Growth in the irrigated area from the mid-fifties through the mid-seventies was concentrated in the southern Great Plains, largely based on water from the Ogallala aquifer. Since 1978 U.S. irrigated area has actually declined as a result of that aquifer's depletion and the diversion of water to nonfarm uses in the sunbelt states.[20]

Soviet irrigated area has grown steadily in recent decades. With some 18 million hectares under irrigation, Soviet plans call for an addition of roughly 700,000 hectares a year during the mid-eighties. An annual growth rate of nearly 4 percent makes this sector one of the fastest-growing in the Soviet economy. Such increase reflects the urgency that the Soviets attach to expanding the irrigated area, because for them it both boosts food production and minimizes the wide swings in crop output that result from highly variable rainfall.[21]

Irrigation often holds the key to cropping intensity, especially in monsoonal climates where the wet season is followed by dry months with little or no rain. Where temperatures permit year-round cropping, as they often do where the monsoon dominates rainfall, irrigation permits the production of two, three, or even more crops per year.

A billion and a half people are now fed with the additional food produced with chemical fertilizer.

Given the projected growth in world food demand, the irrigated area is certain to expand. The question is how rapidly. Projections by the U.N. Food and Agriculture Organization (FAO) show a possible 53 million hectares being added between 1980 and 1990, an increase of one fourth within a decade.[22] Whether or not these figures do materialize will be influenced by capital availability. Not only does it take a great deal of capital to irrigate this much land, but the cost per hectare of future expansion is rising since the least costly sites have largely been developed.

As the cost of bringing new land under irrigation rises at the margin, and as the cost of energy to pump underground water also rises, attention will focus more on improving the efficiency of both existing irrigation systems and water use. Unfortunately, the world in the mid-eighties is not paying any more attention to water-use efficiency than it was to oil-use efficiency in 1970. Increasingly, modification of irrigation practices to use water more economically will be the key to expanding irrigated food production.

THE FERTILIZER LINK

The mid-nineteenth-century discovery by German agricultural chemist Justus von Liebig that it was possible to replace all the nutrients removed from the soil by crops led to the modern chemical fertilizer industry. More than any other technological advance, it has spurred some remarkable food production gains.

In the years following von Liebig's discovery, an embryonic chemical fertilizer industry developed, but a century was to pass before the industry came into its own, emerging as an important industrial sector of the world economy. As the frontiers of agricultural settlement disappeared after World War II and as population growth accelerated, demand for fertilizer began to climb. In 1950 the world used less than 14 million tons of chemical fertilizer. Within a decade that figure had doubled. And in the next decade it doubled again. By 1984 world fertilizer consumption totaled 121 million tons, nearly a ninefold increase in 34 years. (See Table 2-4.) Eliminating its use today would probably cut world food production by at least a third. At a minimum, a billion and a half people are now fed with the additional food produced with chemical fertilizer.

Table 2-4. World Fertilizer Use, 1950–84

Year	Fertilizer Use
	(million metric tons)
1950	13.5
1955	18.3
1960	27.0
1965	23.1
1970	63.0
1971	68.3
1972	72.0
1973	77.2
1974	83.6
1975	82.4
1976	90.0
1977	95.6
1978	99.4
1979	106.9
1980	113.1
1981	116.1
1982	114.3
1983	116.1
1984	121.0

SOURCE: U.N. Food and Agriculture Organization, *FAO 1977 Annual Fertilizer Review* (Rome: 1978), Paul Andrilenas, U.S. Department of Agriculture, private communication, September 1983, and Worldwatch Institute estimates for 1984.

The increase in world fertilizer use since mid-century has been driven by population growth and by the expanding appetite for animal protein. As the stork outruns the plow, the role of fertilizer increases. The reduction in world cropland area per person since 1950 has been offset by raising per capita fertilizer use from 5 kilograms in 1950 to over 25 kilograms by 1980. In simple terms, more people now means less cropland per person, requiring more fertilizer to satisfy a

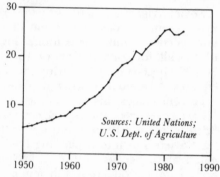

Kilograms

Sources: United Nations; U.S. Dept. of Agriculture

Figure 2-1. World Fertilizer Use Per Capita, 1950-84

given dietary level. (See Figure 2-1.)

The soil nutrients most needed by plants are nitrogen, phosphorus, and potassium. Many other elements also feed plants: Magnesium, calcium, and sulfur, for example, are considered minor nutrients. And there are trace nutrients such as zinc, boron, and copper. In both quantitative and economic terms, however, the chemical fertilizer industry is based almost entirely on nitrogenous, phosphatic, and potassic fertilizers. Among these three, nitrogen dominates, accounting for just over half of world fertilizer output; phosphate and potash account for roughly one quarter each.[23]

Historically, Western Europe, the United States, and Japan dominated world output but since nitrogen fertilizer is synthesized from atmospheric nitrogen, it can be produced wherever energy is available. Following the 1973 oil price increase, most new nitrogen plants have been built in oil-exporting countries, particularly those that flare natural gas. Since so many of these are developing countries—China, India, Indonesia, Mexico, and several Middle Eastern oil exporters—this shift has markedly boosted the Third World share of nitrogen fertilizer production.[24]

Phosphate and potash, on the other

hand, are mined only by the handful of countries that have indigenous reserves. Most of the world's phosphate is mined in Morocco and the United States, principally in Florida. In 1980 these two countries together exported 31 million tons of phosphate rock, nearly three fifths of the world total. Most of the remainder was exported by Jordan and Israel in the Middle East; by Togo, Tunisia, and Senegal in Africa; and by the Soviet Union.[25]

Production of potash, the third major nutrient, is dominated by the Soviet Union and Canada, which together account for 55 percent of world production capacity. East and West Germany divide rather equally an additional 21 percent, and most of the remainder is produced in the United States and France. Given the international interdependence of the world fertilizer economy, anything that affects international trade—such as export embargoes, the formation of export cartels, or external debt—can affect farmers' use of phosphate or potash.[26]

World fertilizer consumption, like the production of nitrogen fertilizer, is shifting toward the Third World. As of 1981 the industrial countries were consuming 72 million tons of chemical fertilizer, 63 percent of the world total. Developing countries were using 43 million tons, just over a third of the total, but their consumption has been growing far more rapidly, suggesting that by the year 2000 usage may be rather evenly divided between the North and the South, though per capita use will be far higher in the former.[27]

All the big four food producers are heavy users of fertilizer. The Soviet Union, which has invested heavily in manufacturing facilities, now uses more fertilizer than any other country except the United States. Despite this edge, Soviet grain output is scarcely half that of the United States, confirming the widespread inefficiency in fertilizer use that is regularly reported in Soviet journals.[28]

Fertilizer application rates vary widely not only among countries but also among different crops. Countries with the most fertilizer-intensive agriculture include Japan and several in Western Europe. U.S. farmers in the corn belt also apply fertilizer quite generously, whereas those in the semiarid western plains use it sparingly. Cereals, grown on some 70 percent of the world's cropland, account for the largest share of fertilizer use. Other heavily fertilized crops include cash crops, particularly those grown for export such as cotton and tobacco.

In recent years the growth in world fertilizer use has slowed markedly. After growing 7.5 percent annually from 1950 through 1973, it dropped to 5.6 percent per year during 1973–79 and to 2.5 percent per year since the 1979 oil price increase. (See Table 2-5.) This slowdown is not due to any single influence but rather to several, many of them associated directly or indirectly with rising oil prices.

Table 2-5. World Grain Production and Fertilizer Use at Three Oil Price Levels, 1950–84

Period	Oil Price Per Barrel	Annual Growth	
		Grain Production	Fertilizer Use
	(current dollars)	(percent)	
1950–73	2	3.1	7.5
1973–79	12	1.9	5.6
1979–84[1]	28	2.0	2.5

[1]1984 grain production and fertilizer use estimated by Worldwatch Institute.
SOURCES: Based on data from International Monetary Fund and U.S. Department of Agriculture.

Where fertilizer use is high, diminishing returns are setting in. As applications increase, so do crop yields, but only up to a point. At the lower levels of use the crop yield response to each additional kilogram of fertilizer is strong, but as application rates rise the increase diminishes, until eventually there is no response. A broad-brush comparison of changes in the ratio of world grain production to fertilizer use over time confirms this diminishing response. In 1950 world fertilizer use was just under 14 million tons and grain production was 623 million tons, yielding 46 tons of grain produced for every ton of fertilizer used. Fifteen years later this response ratio had been cut in half, with each ton of fertilizer yielding some 23 tons of grain. By 1979 the ratio had fallen to just over 13, where it has remained for the last four years. This leveling off suggests that farmers are not finding it profitable to increase greatly their use of chemical fertilizer.[29]

In many Third World countries, mounting foreign debt has constrained fertilizer use. The more foreign exchange required to service debt, the less is available for importing fertilizer. Brazil, for example—the western hemisphere's second ranking food producer—has severely restricted its fertilizer imports. Several other heavily indebted Third World countries have done the same.[30]

Closely associated with both external debt and internal deficits is the pressure to reduce or eliminate subsidies for fertilizer use and for food consumption, both of which reduce the profitability of fertilizer use. In some instances national governments have decided on their own to reduce these subsidies in an effort to lower deficits. In other cases the pressure has come from the International Monetary Fund as a condition for continued funding or for the renegotiation of debt repayment.[31]

Fertilizer consumption has also lagged because of depressed economic conditions in rural areas. Weak farm prices and mounting farm debt have even arrested the growth in fertilizer consumption in the United States. After an extraordinary growth, stretching from 1940 through 1980, fertilizer use in the world's leading food producer dropped sharply during the early eighties. (See Figure 2-2.)

Where intensive agriculture is practiced, as in the U.S. corn belt, the energy embodied in the fertilizer—including that used in manufacturing, transporting and applying it—often exceeds that used as tractor fuel. Of the total energy invested in fertilizer, roughly four fifths is used to produce it and one fifth to distribute and apply it. Some 70 percent of nitrogenous fertilizer is produced with natural gas, and the remainder is produced with naphtha, fuel oil, and coal. But regardless of the energy source, rising energy costs are reducing the profitability of fertilizer use.[32]

The ratio between the price of grain and that of fertilizer has changed over the past few decades, and the real cost of fertilizer now constrains use to some ex-

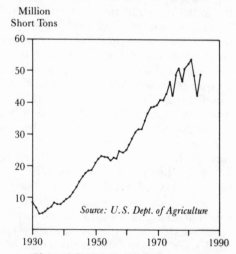

Figure 2-2. U.S. Fertilizer Consumption (Material Weight), 1930-84

tent. For example, in the United States 3.4 tons of wheat were required to purchase a ton of nitrogen fertilizer in 1960. A breakthrough in nitrogen synthesis in 1963 increased the energy efficiency of synthetic nitrogen fixation by some 40 percent and reduced nitrogen fertilizer costs beginning in the late sixties. As use of this new technology spread, fertilizer prices declined. By the early seventies only 1.6 tons of wheat were needed to buy a ton of nitrogen fertilizer. After the oil price hikes of 1973 this trend was reversed, however, and the amount of grain required to purchase a given amount of fertilizer increased somewhat. In 1984, some 2.1 tons of wheat bought one ton of nitrogen fertilizer.[33]

In contrast to the 1950–80 period, when world fertilizer use increased rather predictably, it has become quite erratic since 1980—sometimes increasing, sometimes decreasing, but certainly not maintaining the uninterrupted growth of the preceding three decades. As a general matter the fertilizer use projections of recent years have been lowered with each successive assessment. When the FAO did its *Agriculture: Toward 2000* study in 1979, it projected that fertilizer consumption in the 90 developing countries (excluding China) would increase from 19 million tons in 1980 to 93 million tons by the end of the century.[34] This increase of 8.3 percent per year was consistent with the historical trend, but it now appears that growth will be far slower, that the future will not be a simple extrapolation of the past.

Projections of global use are also being downgraded. An assessment undertaken in 1981 by an FAO/U.N. Industrial Development Organization/World Bank group projected that by 1985–86 world fertilizer use would reach 147 million tons. By early 1984 USDA was projecting 1988 world usage at 142 million tons of fertilizer.[35]

Future fertilizer use will be influenced heavily by the continuing spread of irrigation and by the energy/food-price relationship. However, in at least one major food-producing region—the southern Great Plains of the United States—the irrigated area has begun to decline, making substantial further growth in fertilizer use there unlikely. Energy prices over the long term seem certain to rise. Offsetting this at least partially is the temporary shift toward the use of flared natural gas as a nitrogen fertilizer feedstock. As long as gas supplies hold up, this will tend to check the rise in nitrogen fertilizer manufacturing costs, though not those of phosphate and potash.

ADVANCES IN TECHNOLOGY

Any assessment of the world food prospect must consider advances in agricultural technology. The doubling of world food output over the past generation is largely the product of the expanded use of irrigation, chemical fertilizer, and improved varieties. With cereals, which dominate food output, the development of hybrid corn and the dwarf rices and wheats have been centrally important.

Interestingly, the basic discoveries that led to these advances are by no means recent. Early agriculturalists in the Middle East discovered that diverting river water onto their fields increased their yields. The principles of chemical fertilization were discovered more than a century ago. Likewise, the laws of heredity were first formulated by Mendel in the mid-nineteenth century. It was the massive application of these interacting technologies and insights after World War II, however, that set the stage for the unprecedented growth in world food supplies.

The mid-eighties are a particularly rich time in agricultural research, with advances in biotechnology—including recombinant DNA, tissue culture, and cloning—opening new frontiers in farm technology. Exciting though these technologies are, they have nonetheless been greatly overplayed by the popular press. The goals of agricultural research remain the same—how to get more grain per hectare of land or more milk per cow.

The goals of agricultural research remain the same—how to get more grain per hectare of land or more milk per cow.

Biotechnology can help accelerate the research effort. It is not a new tool kit but an additional tool to put in the existing kit, one that will further progress toward existing goals. Its role is put into perspective by Thomas N. Urban, president of Pioneer Hi-Bred International, the world's largest producer of hybrid seed corn. He observes that "the new techniques will be helpful in speeding up our work but they will not change conventional breeding methods."[36] The same point was made by the U.S. Office of Technology Assessment in its 1981 report on applied genetics: "The new tools will be used to complement, but not replace, the well-established practices of plant and animal breeding."[37]

An examination of the historical yield trend of the three principal cereals grown in the United States—corn, wheat, and sorghum—provides both some sense of the potential for raising yields in countries where agricultural modernization is only beginning and an indication of the longer-term constraints in agriculturally advanced societies.[38]

The yield trend for grain sorghum in the United States since mid-century illustrates clearly the S-shaped curve that

biologists expect all biological growth functions to follow. (See Figure 2-3.) From the mid-fifties until the late sixties, yields of this crop nearly tripled, climbing from 1,200 kilograms to 3,300 kilograms per hectare. This remarkable growth was made possible by the rapid spread of hybrid sorghum and irrigation, particularly in the U.S. southern plains, and by heavy increases in chemical fertilizer applications. The principal benefits from these three technologies came between 1955 and 1966, the steeply rising part of the S-shaped curve.

Although there has been some fluctuation since then, there is little indication of any further increase in average yield. Lacking another major breakthrough of some sort, future increases in U.S. sorghum yields are likely to be modest. Indeed, as the Ogallala aquifer under the southern plains is depleted, many farmers will revert to dryland farming, in which case sorghum yields in 2000 could well be markedly lower than today.

Corn yields have also increased dramatically, nearly tripling between 1950 and the early eighties. (See Figure 2-4.) This impressive gain is primarily the result of continuously improving hy-

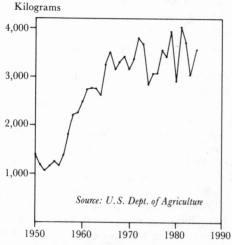

Figure 2-3. U.S. Grain Sorghum Yield Per Hectare, 1950-84

Kilograms

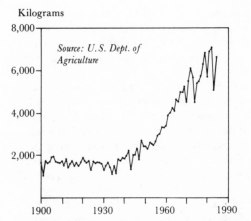

Figure 2-4. U.S. Corn Yield Per Hectare, 1900-84

brids interacting with the increasing application of chemical fertilizer. Although the rise in corn yields has slowed since the early seventies, it still shows a modest upward trend. As with sorghum, U.S. corn yields have also shown greater variability as they increased.

Year-to-year fluctuations from 1950 through 1969 were quite modest. In 1970, however, when the corn blight struck, yields dropped sharply because the predominant corn varieties contained little resistant stock. Yields declined even further in 1974 because of bad weather—a combination of heavy spring rains that postponed planting and an early frost that damaged much of the crop before it was ripe. And in 1980 and 1983, drought played a major role. It will be some years before it can be determined whether U.S. corn yields are leveling off as those for sorghum have.

With wheat, yield increases in the United States have been less dramatic than for corn or sorghum. But after several years of static or declining levels during the seventies, they have resumed their upward trend. In contrast to corn, which is grown under high rainfall conditions, and sorghum, which is planted largely on irrigated land, most U.S. wheat is grown under dryland condi-

tions, thus limiting the potential response to fertilizer use.

Although rice yields in Japan started increasing well before those of cereals in the United States, the steady rise that spanned several decades has been interrupted in recent years. (See Figure 2-5.) Over the last decade there has been little increase in Japanese rice yields, which average roughly 4.5 tons per hectare of milled rice. As with sorghum and corn in the United States, using more fertilizer has little effect on yields.

To assess fully the potential for boosting world food output, current yields in developing countries need to be compared with those of the more agriculturally advanced countries. In the mid-eighties Argentine corn yields, for example, were scarcely half those of the United States, suggesting that over time corn yields in Argentina, a country with similar soils and climate, could be doubled as agriculture modernizes.

Two of the most widely discussed potential breakthroughs in agricultural research are the development of nitrogen-fixing cereals and of more photosynthetically efficient crops. Although the former is technically possible, evidence is mounting that if cereals are engineered to behave like legumes, they will pay a yield penalty. In simplest

Kilograms

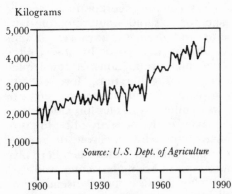

Figure 2-5. Rice Yield Per Hectare in Japan, 1900-84

terms, if the nitrogen-fixing bacteria that attach themselves to the roots of the cereals are supported with photosynthate from the plant, the drain on the plant's metabolic energy will reduce the energy available to form grain.

Evidence is mounting that if cereals are engineered to behave like legumes, they will pay a yield penalty.

Sharply increasing the photosynthetic efficiency will not be easy either. Some gains have been made by plant breeders who have improved leaf arrangements in order to collect more sunlight. Dwarf wheats and rices have upright leaves, for example, that enable them to absorb more sunlight than traditional varieties can. Of these two possible advances, only increased photosynthetic efficiency could actually raise yields. Nitrogen fixation by cereals would simply reduce chemical fertilizer use and hence the energy intensity of cereal production. Both breakthroughs are long shots, however, representing basic feats of biological engineering.

In livestock research, there are also signs of diminishing returns. The commercialization of artificial insemination of dairy cows a generation ago set the stage for a rapid upgrading of dairy herds and dramatic advances in milk production per cow. In the United States, milk production per cow tripled over the past generation. More recently, transplanting embryos from superior cows to inferior ones has provided a way to maximize the progeny of highly productive cows. But the role of embryo transplantation in raising dairy herd productivity will be modest compared with that played by artificial insemination: Whereas artificial insemination permits

a proven sire to father thousands of offspring per year, an outstanding cow can produce only 50–60 viable embryos per year for transplant into less productive cows.[39]

In applied agricultural research, as in any other area of endeavor governed by economics, the easy things are usually undertaken first. After several decades of sustained progress in raising crop and livestock productivity, it is becoming more difficult to maintain the rate of gain. Returns may be diminishing on investment in agricultural research. Doubling or tripling U.S. research expenditures on sorghum, for example, is not likely to have much effect on yields. Likewise, the ability of researchers in Japan to raise rice yields appears limited, regardless of the level of research expenditures.

The bottom line in assessing the potential of advancing technology to increase world food output rests with photosynthesis, nature's process for converting solar energy into biochemical energy, a form that can be used by animals. This process, which is unlikely to be bypassed, is governed by the basic laws of physics and chemistry—something worth keeping in mind lest pie-in-the-sky assessments of technology achieve more currency than they deserve.

FOOD SECURITY TRENDS

Since 1973, as noted, world grain production has barely kept pace with population growth. (See Table 2-6.) The difference between a 3 percent growth rate of grain production and one of 2 percent is the difference between a world where a rising tide of food output is improving diets across the board and one where food production is barely keeping pace with population. As indicated earlier, the rising price of oil affects the demand for food as well as the supply. The lack of growth in per capita income for the world since 1979 has virtually eliminated the income component of food demand growth. Eliminating hunger and malnutrition thus requires not only producing more food but also raising purchasing power among the poor.

Discussions of food security at the global level commonly focus on food reserves, typically measured in terms of carry-over stocks—those stores of grain on hand when harvest of the new crop begins. (See Table 2-7.) These reserves clearly do provide some security, but the cropland idled under U.S. farm programs is also a reserve, though one year removed. Except during the 1972–75 period, these two reserves together have maintained a remarkable stability in the world grain market.

A poor harvest in the Soviet Union in the summer of 1972, followed by a decision in Moscow to offset crop shortfalls by imports rather than by belt-tightening and also by a U.S. election-year decision to idle a rather large amount of cropland, set the stage for severe world wheat shortages beginning in the late summer of 1972. When poor harvests followed during the next two years in major food-producing regions such as China, the Indian subcontinent, the Soviet Union, and the United States, the rebuilding of world grain stocks was unfortunately delayed.

The combination of carry-over stocks and idled U.S. cropland amounted to the equivalent of 243 million tons of grain in 1984, a decrease from 277 million tons the previous year. Nonetheless, even this reduced level of grain and cropland reserves equaled 56 days of world food consumption, more than enough to maintain relatively stable prices in world grain markets.

With over 90 percent of the world grain harvest consumed in the country in which it is produced, food security, particularly in the poor countries, is influenced by the relationship between growth in food output and that of population.[40] Since 1973, as indicated, the race between food production and population growth has been a standoff. Although per capita grain production for the world as a whole has been static during this period, it has increased steadily

Table 2-6. World Grain Production, Total and Per Capita, at Three Oil Price Levels, 1950–84

Period	Oil Price Per Barrel	Annual Growth		Grain Production Per Person
		Grain Production	Population	
	(current dollars)		(percent)	
1950–73	2	3.1	1.9	1.2
1973–79	12	1.9	1.8	0.1
1979–84	28	2.0	1.7	0.3

SOURCES: International Monetary Fund, *International Financial Statistics,* various issues; U.S. Department of Agriculture, Economic Research Service, *World Indices of Agricultural and Food Production, 1950–83* (unpublished printout) (Washington, D.C.: 1984); United Nations, *Monthly Bulletin of Statistics,* New York, various issues.

Table 2-7. Index of World Food Security, 1960–84

Year	Reserves		Total	World Consumption
	World Carry-Over Stocks of Grain	Grain Equiv. of Idled U.S. Cropland		
	(million metric tons)			(days)
1960	200	36	236	104
1965	142	70	212	81
1970	164	71	235	75
1971	183	46	229	71
1972	143	78	221	67
1973	148	25	173	50
1974	133	4	137	41
1975	141	3	144	43
1976	196	3	199	56
1977	194	1	195	53
1978	221	22	243	62
1979	197	16	213	54
1980	187	0	187	47
1981	220	0	220	55
1982	254	13	267	64
1983[1]	185	92	277	65
1984[2]	205	38	243	56

[1]Preliminary.   [2]Projection based on May 15 estimate of U.S. cropland idled.
SOURCES: Reserve stocks from U.S. Department of Agriculture (USDA), *Foreign Agriculture Circulars*, October 1983 and May 1984; cropland idled in the United States from Randy Weber, USDA, private communications, August 1983 and June 1984.

in some regions of the world while decreasing in others and showing no perceptible movement up or down in still others.

Among the trouble spots are Africa and the south Andean countries of Latin America, as described in Chapter 1. These regions with declining food production per person typically have fragile ecosystems, most often semiarid or mountainous, and rapid population growth. Africa's postwar peak in per capita grain production came in 1967 at 180 kilograms. By 1982 it had fallen 20

percent. In 1983 it fell an additional 14 percent because of the continent-wide drought. Although in 1970 Africa was nearly self-sufficient in food, by 1984 imports had reached 24 million tons. (See Table 2-8.)

Africa is losing the battle to feed itself. Malnutrition and hunger are on the increase. That so many Africans are starving today is a tragedy. But the even greater tragedy is that African governments and the international community are doing so little about the causal factors. More often than not food-price

Table 2-8. The Changing Pattern of World Grain Trade, 1950–84[1]

Region	1950	1960	1970	1980	1984[2]
		(million metric tons)			
North America	+23	+39	+56	+131	+126
Latin America	+1	0	+4	−10	−4
Western Europe	−22	−25	−30	−16	+13
E. Eur. and Soviet Union	0	0	0	−46	−51
Africa	0	−2	−5	−15	−24
Asia	−6	−17	−37	−63	−80
Australia and New Zeal.	+3	+6	+12	+19	+20

[1]Plus sign indicates net exports; minus sign, net imports.   [2]Preliminary.
SOURCES: United Nations Food and Agriculture Organization, *Production Yearbook* (Rome: various years);
U.S. Department of Agriculture, *Foreign Agriculture Circulars*, August 1983 and November 1984; adjustments
by Worldwatch Institute.

policies are designed to pacify urban consumers rather than to stimulate development in the countryside. Except for a few countries such as Kenya, soil conservation programs are largely nonexistent. African leaders are only beginning to sense the urgency of braking population growth. Family planning programs, where they exist, are still in an embryonic stage.

After Africa, food security is deteriorating most rapidly in mountainous Third World countries, largely because their ecosystems are fragile and highly vulnerable to mismanagement. Land hunger in the Andean countries—Bolivia, Chile, Ecuador, and Peru—is evident in the push of unterraced farming up the mountainsides. Even to the casual observer it is evident that much of the soil on the steeply sloping, freshly plowed mountainsides will soon be washed to the stream beds below, leaving only bare rock and hungry people. One of the most fragile mountain ecosystems is that of Nepal, nestled in the high Himalayas. Grain production per person there peaked in 1961 and has declined some 27 percent or roughly 1 percent per year since then.[41] As with Africa and the Andean countries, there is nothing in prospect in this mountainous

kingdom in either farming or family planning that promises to arrest this deterioration in the foreseeable future. For these areas, as for Africa, the prospects for food security are not at all promising.

FOOD PRICES: THE BOTTOM LINE

Assessing the food prospect is not simply a matter of determining in a technical sense how much food the world's farmers can produce. They can produce far more than they now are. The real issue is at what cost and, most importantly, how this cost will relate to the purchasing power of the billion and a half poorest people in the world, who already spend most of their income on food.

The cost of food production is determined by the resources available, such as land, water, fertilizer, and pesticides, and the skill with which they are combined. Historically, advancing technology has more than offset any restrictions imposed by resource availability, but over the past decade or so this has become more difficult. As a result, growth in food production has slowed.

As noted earlier in this chapter, growth in the world's cropland area is now scarcely perceptible. USDA now projects that between 1985 and the end of the century the world cropland area will increase roughly 3 percent, just about enough to provide for one year's increase in demand.[42]

The most important force driving the cost of food production upward is the shrinkage of cropland per person.

Although irrigation has recently played a major role in boosting land productivity, for much of humanity water is becoming scarce. In some situations farmers are overdrawing supplies merely to produce food at current levels. In the United States, for example, the irrigated area actually declined some 3 percent between 1978 and 1982. This new trend is indicative of the growing difficulties in many other parts of the world in expanding the irrigated area. While the irrigated area worldwide will continue to expand, it will not do so nearly as rapidly as in the past.

Perhaps the most important force driving the cost of food production upward is the shrinkage of cropland per person. To maintain per capita food production as cropland shrinks, more purchased inputs must be used, including fertilizer, water, and pesticides. The trends can be measured most precisely for fertilizer. In 1950, when a quarter of a hectare was harvested per person, per capita fertilizer use was 5 kilograms. (See Table 2-9.) In 1984, when this area had shrunk to 0.15 hectares, fertilizer use had increased to 25 kilograms per person. Given the difficulties in expanding the cropland area and the momentum of

world population growth, this pattern is certain to continue. As the harvested grain area moves toward one tenth of a hectare at the turn of the century, ever larger amounts of fertilizer will have to be applied to maintain per capita food output, contributing to higher production costs.

Although all projections of world food supply and demand incorporate projections for the cropland area, none take into account the record amount of topsoil being lost from the world's cropland base through erosion. The loss of some 25.4 billion tons of topsoil from the world's cropland in excess of new soil being formed is reducing the inherent productivity of land. The linkage between soil erosion and production costs has been analyzed in detail by an interdisciplinary team of scientists who studied land in southern Iowa. They concluded that a shift of cropland from a slightly eroded to a severely eroded condition would boost annual fertilizer application requirements per acre by 40 pounds of nitrogen, 3 pounds of phosphate, and 13 pounds of potash. This increase in fertilizer would be required

Table 2-9. World Grain Area and Fertilizer Use Per Capita, 1950–84

Year	Grain Area Per Capita	Fertilizer Use Per Capita
	(hectares)	(kilograms)
1950	0.24	5.4
1955	0.23	6.7
1960	0.21	8.9
1965	0.20	11.9
1970	0.18	17.1
1975	0.18	20.4
1980	0.16	25.6
1984	0.15	25.4

SOURCE: Worldwatch Institute estimates, based on data from U.S. Department of Agriculture and United Nations Food and Agriculture Organization.

merely to maintain the output. They also looked at changes in the fuel requirements for tillage as the topsoil washed away, forcing farmers to include more subsoil in the plow layer. Increasing the degree of erosion from slight to severe would raise tillage fuel requirements by 38 percent.[43]

As the fertilizer required to satisfy food needs continues to increase, the world is faced with two rising cost curves. The first is associated with additional expenditures on fertilizer due to the shrinkage of cropland per person. And second, rising energy costs over the long term will increase the cost per unit of chemical fertilizer—the nitrogen, phosphate, and potash—required to boost land productivity.

For the world as a whole to reestablish the upward trend in per capita food production, either the growth of food production must accelerate or that of population must slow. Given the resource constraints described in this chapter—

land, water, and energy—it will be difficult to reestablish a 3 percent rate of growth in food production. The hope of reducing hunger thus rests more heavily than ever on population policies and family planning programs.

Consumers everywhere face higher food prices over the long term. This politically sensitive economic indicator perhaps more than any other leads to consumer dissatisfaction and political unrest. Headlines describing food price protests and food riots are becoming commonplace: Witness recent demonstrations in Brazil, the Dominican Republic, Morocco, Poland, and Tunisia.[44] Reductions in food subsidies imposed on deficit-ridden Third World borrowers by the International Monetary Fund as a condition for new loans have led to the coining of a term—IMF riots. Rising demands on the earth's food-producing resources as some 81 million people are added each year are beginning to translate into political unrest and instability.

3

Managing Freshwater Supplies

Sandra Postel

Like energy, water is an essential ingredient in virtually every human endeavor. Its availability is vital to feeding the world's growing population, producing the material goods that raise living standards, and preserving the integrity of natural systems upon which life itself depends. Yet in most nations remarkably little is known with certainty about how much water is used where, when, and by whom. Although virtually every political leader could quote the current price of a barrel of oil, few would know the cost of securing an additional 1,000 cubic meters of water.

Long taken for granted, fresh water may in many areas become a constraint on economic growth and food production over the coming decades. In the past, rivers and streams have been dammed and diverted to provide dependable water supplies to areas in need. Engineering feats, such as the Aswan Dam in Egypt and the California

This chapter appeared as Worldwatch Paper 62, *Water: Rethinking Management in an Age of Scarcity.*

Aqueduct in the United States, have literally made deserts bloom. Yet increasing competition for a limited supply and the rising economic and environmental costs of traditional water strategies demand a new approach to the management of fresh water. Few governments have even recognized the need for such a reevaluation, much less begun to design the necessary policies for the future. Unfortunately, an abundance of time, as with an abundance of water, may very well prove illusory.

THE WATER CYCLE AND RENEWABLE SUPPLIES

Numbers alone fail to tell water's true story. Enough rain and snow falls over the continents each year to fill Lake Huron 30 times, to magnify the flow of the Amazon River sixteenfold, or to cover the earth's total land area to a depth of 83 centimeters. Yet lack of water to grow crops periodically threatens millions with famine. Water tables in southern India, northern China, the Valley of Mexico, and the U.S. Southwest are falling precipitously, causing wells to go dry. Rivers that once ran year-round now fade with the end of the rainy season. Inland lakes and seas are shrinking.

Unlike coal, oil, wood, and most other vital resources, water is usually needed in vast quantities that are too unwieldy to be traded internationally. Rarely is it transported more than several hundred kilometers from its source. Thus while fresh water everywhere is linked to a vast global cycle, its viability and adequacy as a resource is determined by the amount available locally or regionally and by the way it is used and managed.

Each year, the sun's energy lifts some 500,000 cubic kilometers of water from the earth's surface—86 percent from the oceans and 14 percent from land. (One cubic kilometer equals one billion cubic meters or one trillion liters; in standard U.S. usage, the equivalent is about 264 billion gallons.) An equal amount falls back to earth as rain, sleet, or snow, but fortunately not in the same proportions. Some 110,300 cubic kilometers falls over land (excluding Greenland and Antarctica), whereas only 71,500 is evaporated from it. Thus, this solar-powered cycle annually distills and transfers 38,800 cubic kilometers of water from the oceans to the continents. To complete the natural cycle, the water then makes its way back to the sea as "runoff."[1]

By virtue of this cyclic flow between the sea, air, and land, fresh water is a renewable resource. Under the planet's existing climatic conditions, approximately the same volume is made available each year. Today's supply is the same as when civilizations first dawned in the fertile river valleys of the Ganges, the Tigris-Euphrates, and the Nile. Viewed globally, fresh water is still un-deniably abundant: For each human inhabitant there is now an annual renewable supply of 8,300 cubic meters, which is enough to fill a six-meter-square room 38 times, and several times the amount needed to sustain a moderate standard of living.[2]

Natural variations in climate and the vagaries of weather easily cast shadows over this picture of plenty, however, for water is not always available when and where it is most needed. Nearly two thirds of each year's runoff flows rapidly away in floods, often bringing more destruction than benefit. The other third is stable, and is thus a reliable source of water for drinking or irrigating crops year-round. Water that infiltrates and flows underground provides the base flow of rivers and streams and accounts for most of the stable supply. The controlled release of water from lakes and reservoirs adds a bit more, bringing the total stable supply to about 14,000 cubic kilometers, or 3,000 cubic meters per person—the present practical limit of the renewable freshwater supply.

Asia and Africa are the continents facing the greatest water stress. Supplies for each Asian today are less than half the global average, and the continent's runoff is the least stable of all the major land masses. (See Table 3-1.) Lofty mountain ranges and a monsoon climate make rainfall and runoff highly variable. China's Huang He, or Yellow River, has had at least one major change of course every century of the 2,500 years of recorded Chinese history. In India, 90 percent of the precipitation falls between the months of June and September, and most of the runoff flows in the Ganges and Brahmaputra basins in the North. Failure of the 1979 monsoon led to one of the worst droughts of recent record and reduced India's production of foodgrains by 16 percent. In Africa, the Zaire River (formerly the Congo)—second in volume only to the Amazon—accounts

Table 3-1. Distribution of Renewable Freshwater Supplies, By Continent

Region	Average Annual Runoff	Share of Global Runoff	Share of Global Population	Share of Runoff That Is Stable
	(cubic kilometers)[1]	(percent)		
Africa	4,225	11	11	45
Asia	9,865	26	58	30
Europe	2,129	5	10	43
North America[1]	5,960	15	8	40
South America	10,380	27	6	38
Oceania	1,965	5	1	25
Soviet Union	4,350	11	6	30
World	38,874	100	100	36[2]

[1]Includes Central America, with runoff of 545 cubic kilometers. [2]Average.
SOURCES: Adapted from M.I. L'vovich, *World Water Resources and Their Future,* translation ed. Raymond L. Nace (Washington, D.C.: American Geophysical Union, 1979); population figures are mid-1983 estimates from Population Reference Bureau, *1983 World Population Data Sheet* (Washington, D.C.: 1983).

for about 30 percent of the continent's renewable supplies but flows largely through sparsely populated rain forest. Two thirds of the African nations have at least a third less annual runoff than the global average. Drought conditions that persistently plague the continent's dry regions have in recent years threatened over 20 nations with famine.[3]

North and South America and the Soviet Union all appear to have abundant water resources for their populations, though again great geographic disparities exist. South America appears the most richly endowed continent, yet 60 percent of its runoff flows in the channel of the Amazon, remote from most people and a hard source to tap. North and Central America together have a per capita water supply twice the global average, but natural supplies are limited in broad areas of the west, particularly in the southwestern United States and northern Mexico. The Soviet Union's three largest rivers—the Yenisei, the Lena, and the Ob'—all flow north through Siberia to the Arctic Seas, far

from the major population centers. Finally, Europe joins Asia as a continent with a substantially greater share of the world's people than of its fresh water. The continent's per capita runoff is only half the global average, and supplies are especially short in southern and eastern Europe. Fortunately, for much of the continent a generally temperate climate and a large number of smaller rivers with fairly steady flows allow a comparatively large share of the runoff to be tapped.

A detailed breakdown of supplies by country confirms water's unequal distribution. (See Table 3-2.) Per capita runoff ranges from over 100,000 cubic meters in Canada to less than 1,000 in Egypt. Yet even these national figures hide important disparities. On a per capita basis, Canada is the most water-wealthy nation in the world, but two thirds of its river flow is northward, while 80 percent of its people live within 200 kilometers of the Canadian-U.S. border. Similarly, Indonesia appears to be a relatively water-rich nation, yet over 60 percent of the population live on the

Table 3-2. Average Annual Per Capita Runoff in Selected Countries, 1983, With Projections for 2000[1]

Country	1983	2000	Change
	(thousand cubic meters)		(percent)
Canada	110.0	95.1	−14
Norway	91.7	91.7	0
Brazil	43.2	30.2	−30
Venezuela	42.3	26.8	−37
Sweden	23.4	24.3	+4
Australia	21.8	18.5	−15
Soviet Union	16.0	14.1	−12
United States	10.0	8.8	−12
Indonesia	9.7	7.6	−22
Mexico	4.4	2.9	−34
France	4.3	4.1	−5
Japan	3.3	3.1	−6
Nigeria	3.1	1.8	−42
China	2.8	2.3	−18
India	2.1	1.6	−24
Kenya	2.0	1.0	−50
South Africa and Swaziland	1.9	1.2	−37
Poland	1.5	1.4	−7
West Germany	1.4	1.4	0
Bangladesh	1.3	0.9	−31
Egypt	0.09	0.06	−33
World	8.3	6.3	−24

[1]Estimates are for runoff originating within each specific country and do not include inflow from other countries.
SOURCES: M.I. L'vovich, *World Water Resources and Their Future,* translation ed. Raymond L. Nace (Washington D.C.: American Geophysical Union, 1979); population figures are mid-1983 estimates from Population Reference Bureau, *1983 World Population Data Sheet* (Washington D.C.: 1983).

island of Java, which has less than 10 percent of the country's runoff. Especially for the water-poor nations of Europe, Africa, and Asia, water flowing in from neighboring countries can be a vital addition to the runoff originating within their own borders. (The runoff estimates in Table 3-2 are consistent with a global water balance and thus include only runoff originating within each particular country.) Inflow accounts for roughly 70 percent of Czechoslovakia's water supplies, for example, roughly half of East and West Germany's, and 90 percent of Bulgaria's. Egypt, one of the most water-short nations in the world, is almost entirely dependent on the water of the Nile that enters the country from Sudan.[4]

Given existing climatic conditions and current population projections, the per capita global water supply at the end of the century will have declined by 24 percent, while the stable, reliable component of that water will have dropped from 3,000 to 2,280 cubic meters per person. Population continues to grow fastest in some of the most water-short regions. Per capita supplies in Kenya and Nigeria, for example, will diminish by 50 and 42 percent, respectively. Supplies per person in Bangladesh and Egypt will diminish by a third, and in India by a fourth. Moreover, if projected climatic shifts from the rising concentration of atmospheric carbon dioxide materialize, water supplies may diminish in some areas already chronically water-short, including major grain-producing regions of north China and the United States.[5]

COMPETING USES

When analysts speak of the "demand" for water, they typically refer to water's use as a commodity—as a factor of production in agriculture, industry, or household activities. Yet water in rivers, lakes, streams, and estuaries also is home to countless fish and plants, acts as a diluting and purifying solvent, and offers a source of aesthetic enjoyment and richness that adds immeasurably to the quality of life. No society can draw on all its available supplies and hope to maintain the benefits water freely offers when left undisturbed. The need to protect these natural functions is thus a critical backdrop to considering society's pattern of water use.

Although the practice of irrigation dates back several thousand years to early Egyptian and Babylonian societies, and although water has been tapped to supply homes and small industries for centuries, for most of humanity's history water use expanded at a moderate pace. (Throughout this chapter, the terms water use, withdrawal, and demand are used interchangeably; water consumption will be distinguished.) Over this century, however, demands have soared with rapid industrialization and the need to feed an expanding world population. According to estimates prepared by Soviet scientists in the early seventies for the U.N. International Hydrological Decade (1965–74), which are among the most comprehensive historical data available, world water use in 1900 was 400 billion cubic meters, or 242 cubic meters per person. By 1940 global usage had doubled, while population had increased about 40 percent. (See Figure 3-1.) A rapid rise in water demand then began at mid-century: By 1970 annual per capita withdrawals had climbed to over 700 cubic meters, 60 percent higher than in 1950. Both agricultural and industrial water use increased twice as much during these 20 years as they had over the entire first half of the century.[6]

Today, humanity's annual water withdrawals equal about a tenth of the total renewable supply and about a quarter of the stable supply—that which is typically

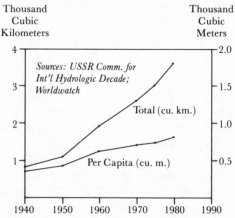

Figure 3-1. World Water Use, Total and Per Capita, 1940-80

available throughout a year. Agriculture claims the lion's share of world water use, accounting for about 70 percent of total withdrawals. As fertile land became more scarce, irrigation enabled farmers to get higher yields from existing fields, essentially substituting water for new cropland. With a controllable, year-round source of water, farmers also found it profitable to invest in fertilizer and to plant higher-yielding crop varieties. Yields of rain-fed rice, for example, typically increase by 50 percent if the effects of flood and drought can be eliminated, by 130 percent if controlled irrigation and drainage and some fertilizer are introduced, and by 280 percent or more if advanced irrigation techniques, generous amounts of fertilizer, pest control, and high-yielding seeds are used.[7]

Roughly a third of today's harvest comes from the 17 percent of the world's cropland that is irrigated. Irrigation thus greatly helps meet the challenge of feeding an ever-growing population. Since 1950, the irrigated area worldwide has increased from 94 million to 261 million hectares. During the sixties, irrigation water was brought to an additional 6 mil-

lion hectares each year; since 1970, an additional 5.2 million hectares have been added annually. (See Table 3-3.) At today's average rates of water use (some 11,000–12,000 cubic meters per irrigated hectare per year), and assuming irrigation continues to expand at a slightly diminishing rate, an additional 820 cubic kilometers of water will be needed for irrigation each year by the turn of the century—a 25–30 percent increase over existing levels.[8]

Besides demanding a large share of any region's available supplies, irrigation results in a large volume being "consumed"—removed from the local water supply through evaporation and transpiration. Crops must consume some water in order to grow, but typically much more water is transported and applied to fields than the crops require. Often less than half the water withdrawn for irrigation returns to a nearby stream or aquifer, where it can be used again. In the United States, for example, 55 percent of agricultural withdrawals are consumed, which in turn accounts for 81 percent of all the water consumed annually nationwide.[9]

Industry is the second major water-

Table 3-3. Growth in Irrigated Area, By Continent, 1950–82

Region	Total Irrigated Area, 1982	Growth in Irrigated Area		
		1950–60	1960–70	1970–80[1]
	(million hectares)		(percent)	
Africa	12	25	80	33
Asia[2]	177	52	32	34
Europe[3]	28	50	67	40
North America	34	42	71	17
South America	8	67	20	33
Oceania	2	0	100	0
World	261	49	41	32

[1]Percentage increase between 1970 and 1982 prorated to 1970–80 to maintain comparison by decade.
[2]Includes the Asian portion of the Soviet Union. [3]Includes the European portion of the Soviet Union.
SOURCE: W.R. Rangeley, "Irrigation—Current Trends and a Future Perspective," World Bank Seminar, Washington, D.C., February 1983.

using sector of society, accounting for about a quarter of water use worldwide. Producing energy from nuclear and fossil-fueled power plants is by far the largest single industrial water use. Water is the source of steam that drives the turbogenerators, and vast quantities are used to cool power plant condensers. Unlike in agriculture, however, only a small fraction of this water is consumed. Most existing power plants have "once-through" cooling systems that return water to its source immediately after it passes through the plant. U.S. power plants, for example, consume only 2 percent of their withdrawals. Thus, especially when plants are situated next to large lakes or rivers, the volume of cooling water withdrawn is usually of less concern than the discharge of heated water back to the source. If lake or stream temperatures get too high, oxygen levels may drop, threatening fish and other aquatic life.[10]

Producing energy from nuclear and fossil-fueled power plants is by far the largest single industrial water use.

Excluding energy production, two thirds of the remaining industrial withdrawals go to just five industries: primary metals, chemical products, petroleum refining, pulp and paper manufacturing, and food processing. In countries with an established industrial base and water pollution laws in effect, withdrawals for these industries are not likely to increase. Most pollution control techniques involve recycling and reusing water, thus reducing an industry's demand for new supplies. Industrial use has declined, or is expected to decline soon, in countries such as Finland, Sweden, and the United States. In contrast,

Portugal, the Soviet Union, Turkey, and several of the Eastern bloc nations are projecting a doubling of their industrial withdrawals over the century's last quarter. Increases of no more than 50 percent are expected in Czechoslovakia, France, and East and West Germany.[11]

Industry typically accounts for less than 10 percent of total withdrawals in most Third World countries, compared with 60–80 percent in most industrial nations. (See Table 3-4.) Much of the developing world is just embarking on the industrialization path taken by other countries four decades ago. Water demands for power production, manufacturing, mining, and materials processing are thus poised for a rapid increase if industries adopt the water-intensive technologies that those of the industrial world did. Industrial water use in Latin America, for example, is projected to jump 350 percent during the century's last quarter, compared with nearly 180 percent for municipal uses and 70 percent for irrigation. (See Figure 3-2.) Among the targets set for the United Na-

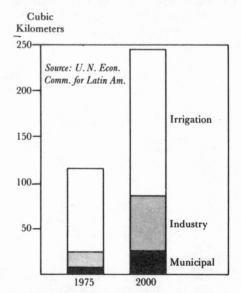

Figure 3-2. Water Demands in Latin America, 1975, With Projections for 2000

Table 3-4. Estimated Water Use in Selected Countries, Total, Per Capita, and by Sector, 1980

Country	Daily Water Withdrawals		Share Withdrawn by Major Sectors		
	Total	Per Capita	Agriculture	Industrial	Municipal[1]
	(billion liters)	(thousand liters)	(percent)		
United States	1,683	7.2	34	57	9
Canada	120	4.8	7	84	9
Soviet Union	967	3.6	64	30	6
Japan[2]	306	2.6	29	61	10
Mexico[2]	149	2.0	88	7	5
India[2]	1,058	1.5	92	2	6
United Kingdom	78	1.4	1	85	14
Poland	46	1.3	21	62	17
China	1,260	1.2	87	7	6
Indonesia[2]	115	0.7	86	3	11

[1]Along with residential use, figures may include commercial and public uses, such as watering parks and golf courses. [2]1975 figures for Mexico; 1977 for India, Indonesia, and Japan.
SOURCES: U.S. data, U.S. Geological Survey; Canadian data, Harold D. Foster and W.R. Derick Sewell, *Water: The Emerging Crisis in Canada* (Toronto: James Lorimer & Company, 1981); Soviet, U.K., Polish data, U.N. Economic Commission for Europe; Japanese, Indian, Indonesian data, *Global 2000 Report;* Mexican data, U.N. Economic Commission on Latin America; Chinese data, Vaclav Smil, *The Bad Earth.*

tions Second Development Decade is an 8 percent average annual rate of industrial growth for the Third World. Though this may prove too ambitious a goal, given the debt burden many of these countries face, the developing world's industrial water use could easily double by the end of the century.[12]

Water used by households—for drinking and cooking, bathing, washing clothes, and other activities—varies greatly with both income levels and the way in which water is supplied. In urban households with piped water available at the touch of a tap, daily use typically ranges between 100 and 350 liters per person. Households with water-intensive appliances, such as dishwashers and washing machines, and those where water is used to irrigate large lawns and gardens can use over 1,000 liters per person daily. In many developing coun-

tries, where water is supplied through a public hydrant, daily usage ranges between 20 and 70 liters per person. Areas such as Kenya, where women may walk several kilometers to draw water for their families, can record usages close to the biological minimum—2–5 liters per person daily.[13]

Residential and other municipal uses of water account for less than a tenth of water withdrawals in many nations, and only about 7 percent of total withdrawals worldwide. In industrial countries where population growth is slow and most households are already adequately supplied with water, growth in domestic demand is slowing and probably will continue to do so. In parts of Europe that are still converting from community wells to individual piped-water systems —including Czechoslovakia, Poland, Portugal, Romania, and Turkey—demand for drinking water is expected to double over the next two decades. The largest increase will probably occur in the Third World, where freshwater supplies are not yet universally available. The World Health Organization estimates that as of 1980 only 75 percent of the developing world's urban dwellers and 29 percent of its rural population were served with drinking water. The United Nations has set a goal of providing safe water to all by 1990, which, although unlikely to be met, will contribute to a probable doubling of Third World domestic water demands by the end of the century.[14]

Even given these large increases in water withdrawals for irrigation, industrial, and domestic needs, total use worldwide by the year 2000 is still likely to be less than half the stable renewable supply. Yet projections by leading hydrologists show that meeting demands in North Africa and the Middle East will require virtually all the usable freshwater supplies in these regions. Usage in southern and eastern Europe, as well as central and southern Asia, will also be uncomfortably close to the volume of supplies these regions can safely and reliably tap.[15] Moreover, even if supplies appear more than adequate, no region is immune from the consequences of mismanagement and abuse that are already arising and that are bound to worsen as competing demands escalate.

THE CONSEQUENCES OF MISMANAGEMENT

When a resource begins to show physical signs of abuse, economic and ecological consequences are usually not far behind. Water's seeming ubiquity has blinded society to the need to manage it sustain-

ably and to adapt to the limits of a fixed supply. Mounting pressures are currently manifest in pervasive pollution, depletion of groundwater supplies, falling water tables, and damage to ecological systems. Failure to heed these signs of stress, and to place water use on a sustainable footing, threatens the viability of both the resource base itself and the economic systems that depend on it.

Each liter of polluted water discharged untreated contaminates many additional liters of fresh water in the receiving stream. The disposal of synthetic chemicals and heavy metals, which pose dangers in extremely low concentrations, is an especially grave threat to the quality of water supplies. Without adequate treatment, the growing volume and toxicity of wastes could render as much as a fourth of the world's reliable supply unsafe for use by the year 2000.[16]

Many industrial countries now require that wastewaters meet specified standards of quality before they are discharged. Yet in most Third World countries, pollution controls are either nonexistent or unable to keep pace with urbanization and industrialization. In China, for example, only about 2 percent of the 28 billion cubic meters of wastewater discharged each year is treated. Already, a third of the water in its major rivers is polluted beyond safe health levels, and fish and shrimp have disappeared from 5 percent. China's first large wastewater treatment plant began operating in Beijing in the fall of 1980, but the volume of sewage far outpaces the facility's capacity to treat it. Wastewater flows in Beijing have increased twenty-sevenfold over the last three decades, and volumes for the country as a whole are projected to triple or quadruple by the end of the century. Vaclav Smil, a specialist on China's environment, writes that the country's water pollution problem "will require very heavy and sustained investment—not to achieve zero discharges but merely to bring the appalling situation within reasonable limits after decades of no control."[17]

In virtually all of Latin America, municipal sewage and industrial effluents are discharged into the nearest rivers and streams without treatment. The pulp and paper and the iron and steel industries—two of the region's biggest polluters—have been growing twice as fast as the economy as a whole. Yet cleanup efforts have typically been postponed because of their high cost. Purifying Colombia's Bogota River, for example—one of the continent's most contaminated waterways—would cost an estimated $1.4 billion, a high price for a debt-ridden country to pay. Unless governments begin attacking urban and industrial pollution soon, however, they will inevitably face the prospect of a water supply too polluted for their people to drink.[18]

A similar situation exists in the Soviet Union. Industrial wastewaters comprise 10 percent of the Volga River's average flow at Volgograd, and three fourths of the wastes are untreated. A major effort was begun in the mid-seventies to cleanse the river, but apparently enforcement has been too slack to encourage industries to install the costly technologies. Under these conditions, the Volga simply cannot sustain the existing high level of withdrawals and also remain of acceptable quality. According to Thane Gustafson, a U.S. specialist on Soviet affairs: "Footdragging by industry on pollution control will make it necessary to use more water for dilution. All these effects add up to a greater demand for water by the end of the century than the available supplies can satisfy."[19]

Vast quantities of the earth's water move slowly underground through the pores and fractures of geologic formations called aquifers. Some hold water thousands of years old and receive little annual replenishment from rainfall. Like oil reserves, water in these "fossil aquifers" is essentially nonrenewable; if tapped, it will in time be depleted. Even where recharge does occur, groundwater is often pumped at rates that exceed the replenishment, causing water tables to fall and depleting future water reserves. Such overpumping—which geologists call water "mining"—supports only a fragile and short-term prosperity at best, for eventually the water becomes too salty to use, too expensive to pump to the surface, or runs out altogether.

After several decades of steady growth, the total irrigated area in the High Plains is now declining.

One fifth of the irrigated cropland in the United States is supported by water mined from a vast underground reserve called the Ogallala aquifer. Stretching from southern South Dakota to northwest Texas, the aquifer underlies portions of eight states and spans an area roughly three times as big as the state of New York. Natural recharge is minimal in this semiarid region, and farmers have profitably irrigated corn, sorghum, and cotton only by drawing on water stored for thousands of years. Irrigation with Ogallala water began to expand rapidly in Texas in the forties, and when powerful pumping and irrigation systems were introduced it spread northward into Oklahoma, Kansas, and Nebraska during subsequent decades. By 1978, over eight million hectares were under irrigation in the states most heavily dependent on the Ogallala, compared with just 2.1 million in 1944. (See Figure 3-3.) Over the last four decades, 500 cubic kilometers of groundwater have been withdrawn. Hydrologists estimate that the aquifer is now half depleted under 900,000 hectares of Kansas, New Mexico, and Texas.[20]

Faced with rising pumping costs, diminishing well yields, and low commodity prices, farmers are taking land out of irrigation. After several decades of steady growth, the total irrigated area in the High Plains is now declining. In just four years, 1978 to 1982, irrigated land in Texas dropped by 20 percent, in Oklahoma by 18 percent, and in New Mexico by 9 percent. Collectively, in these and the other three states that draw most heavily on the Ogallala (Colorado, Kansas, and Nebraska), the total area under irrigation declined by 592,000 hectares, or 7 percent. In Nebraska, where a smaller portion of the Ogallala has been depleted, irrigation is still expanding. Yet in 1982, net returns from Northern Plains production of corn—the dominant irrigated crop in Nebraska—were less than half the national average, and it appears that eventually farmers there will begin switching crops, converting to dryland farming, or leaving agriculture altogether.[21]

Economists and government leaders are concerned about the potential collapse of a lucrative regional farming economy. The U.S. Army Corps of Engineers has even looked at the feasibility of massive river diversions to supply water to farmers now dependent on the diminishing Ogallala. But few have asked the more fundamental question of whether it makes sense to deplete this resource at a time when the nation can afford to preserve it. The U.S. Government is paying farmers to idle rain-fed cropland in order to lessen a price-depressing surplus of crops; at the same time, it is allowing the wholesale exhaustion of a unique water reserve to grow those same crops. Moreover, among the consequences predicted for much of the central and western United States from the rising level of atmospheric carbon dioxide is a reduction in the renewable water supply and an increase in the frequency and severity of droughts.[22] By exploiting the Ogallala today, farmers are foreclosing options to draw on it in the future when it may really be needed to meet vital food needs domestically and abroad. Failure to preserve this resource is shortsighted, and an error future generations will rightfully find hard to forgive.

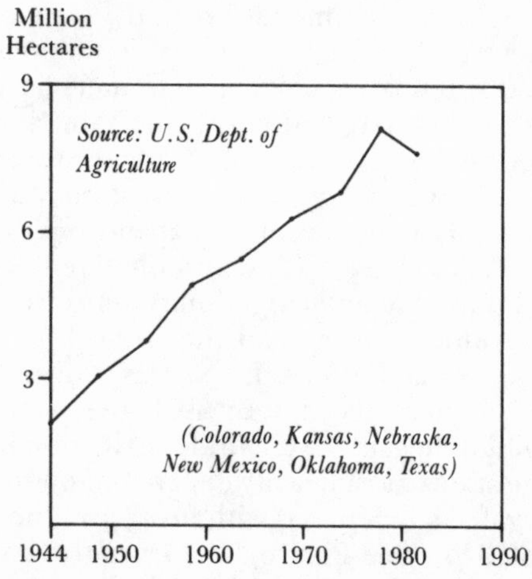

Many other U.S. aquifers are suffering from overuse. Among the severest cases is one underlying Tucson, Arizona—the largest American city completely dependent on groundwater. Only about 35 percent of the water withdrawn to supply Tucson's residents, farms, and copper mines is replaced each year by recharge, and water tables in some areas have fallen over 50 meters. The Santa Cruz River is no longer sufficiently fed by underground water to keep it flowing during dry spells. Water levels have also dropped precipitously around El Paso in Texas and Ciudad Juarez in Mexico from the mining of the aquifer they share. In portions of the Dallas-Fort Worth metropolitan area, water tables have fallen

Figure 3-3. Irrigated Area in Six States That Rely Heavily on the Ogallala Aquifer, 1944-82

more than 120 meters over the last 25 years.[23]

Though rarely as well-documented as cases in the United States, excessive groundwater pumping and subsequent lowering of the water table appears to be increasingly common worldwide. (See Table 3-5.) Over the seventies, water levels dropped 25–30 meters in areas of Tamil Nadu in southern India, a conse-

Table 3-5. Selected Cases of Excessive Water Withdrawals

Region	Status
Colorado River Basin, United States	Yearly consumption exceeds renewable supply by 5 percent, creating a water deficit; Colorado River is increasingly salty; water tables have fallen precipitously in areas of Phoenix and Tucson.
High Plains, United States	The Ogallala, a fossil aquifer that supplies most of the region's irrigation water, is diminishing; over a large area of the southern plains, the aquifer is already half depleted.
Northern China	Groundwater overdrafts are epidemic in northern provinces; annual pumping in Beijing exceeds the sustainable supply by 25 percent; water tables in some areas are dropping up to 1–4 meters per year.
Tamil Nadu, India	Heavy pumping for irrigation has caused drops in water level of 25–30 meters in a decade.
Israel, Arabian Gulf, and coastal United States	Intrusion of sea water from heavy pumping of coastal aquifers threatens to contaminate drinking water supplies with salt.
Mexico City; Beijing, China; Central Valley, California; Houston-Galveston, Texas	Groundwater pumping has caused compaction of aquifers and subsidence of land surface, damaging buildings, streets, pipes, and wells; hundreds of homes in a waterfront Texas community have been flooded.
California, United States	Water from Owens Valley and Mono Basin have been diverted to supply southern water users; Owens Lake has dried up, and Mono Lake's surface area has shrunk by a third.
Southwestern Soviet Union	Large river withdrawals have reduced inflow to the Caspian and Aral seas; the Caspian sturgeon fishery is threatened; the Aral's fisheries are virtually gone and the sea's volume may be halved by the turn of the century.

SOURCE: Worldwatch Institute, based on various sources.

quence of uncontrolled pumping for irrigation. Overpumping is epidemic in China's northern provinces, where some 10 major cities rely heavily on groundwater for their basic supply. In Beijing, annual groundwater withdrawals exceed the sustainable supply by 25 percent, and water tables in some parts of the city have been dropping over 1 meter each year. In one district of Tianjin, a major manufacturing and commercial city, water tables are falling an astonishing 4.4 meters annually.[24]

Large withdrawals of groundwater may have other costly effects besides the depletion of future supplies. If water pumped from an aquifer susceptible to compaction is not replaced by recharge, the aquifer may compress, resulting in subsidence of the overlying land. Subsidence in Mexico City has damaged buildings and streets and disrupted the sewage system. In China, portions of Beijing have been sinking 20–30 centimeters annually since 1950, and rates of 10 centimeters per year have been measured in Tianjin. In the Houston-Galveston area of Texas, where water levels have declined 60 meters during the last half-century, portions of the land surface have sunk over 2 meters. High tides in the Gulf have flooded residential developments that, because of subsidence, are now closer to sea level.[25]

In coastal areas, heavy pumping may alter the volume and flow of groundwater discharging to the ocean and thereby allow sea water to invade the aquifer. Salt-water intrusion threatens to contaminate the drinking water supplies of many cities and towns along the U.S. Atlantic and Gulf coasts; it is especially severe in several Florida cities where pumping has pulled the water table below sea level. Israel, Syria, and the Arabian Gulf states are also battling threats of salt-water intrusion. Once it occurs, such contamination is difficult, if not impossible, to reverse.[26]

Excessive demands also take a toll on lakes, estuaries, and inland seas that are sustained by freshwater inflow from nearby rivers and streams. The Aral Sea in the southern Soviet Union is shrinking because of large withdrawals from its two major tributaries, the Amu Darya and Syr Darya. These two rivers help support Soviet central Asia's lucrative agricultural economy, which includes roughly half the nation's irrigated cropland. The population of several central Asian republics has grown by 30 percent over the last decade, adding to pressures on the available water supply and to the importance of maintaining a thriving economy to secure more jobs in the region. The Aral's level had remained fairly stable between 1900 and 1960, but has since dropped 9 meters. Fisheries that once figured prominently in the regional economy have virtually disappeared. Although officials are taking some measures to save portions of the Aral, they appear resigned to it shrinking further. Some scientists have projected that before the end of the century the sea may drop another 8–10 meters and its volume may be reduced by half.[27]

A similar scenario threatens to unfold further west, in the Caspian Sea. The Volga River is the Caspian's main source of inflow, helping to replenish the large quantities of water evaporated from the sea each year. Construction of huge dams on the river during the fifties and subsequent large irrigation withdrawals dramatically reduced the river's discharge into the Caspian. The sea reached its lowest level in centuries in 1977, having dropped more than 3 meters over the preceding half-century. The level has risen somewhat in recent years because of unusually heavy rains that increased the Volga's flow. But Soviet scientists do not expect this fortuitous occurrence to continue. According to U.S. geographer Philip Micklin, who discussed the situation with scientists during a five-month stay in the Soviet Union in 1984, additional diversions for irrigation are planned for the Volga, and the Caspian's level is expected to drop further over the next decade. The sea supports bountiful fisheries, including 90 percent of the world's catch of sturgeon. Salmon and migratory herring spawn in the Volga and feed in the North Caspian. Substantial damage to these fisheries is likely to occur if the sea's level declines much further.[28]

Shrinking inland seas are a dramatic consequence of heavy water withdrawals to meet irrigation and other water demands. But an equally grave threat is the quiet loss of fish and other aquatic life from rivers and streams whose altered flow patterns can no longer sustain them. As long as water withdrawals remain well below a region's average sustainable supply, streamflows will be sufficient to safeguard most ecological values. Yet where a large share of surface water is diverted from its natural channels, these benefits may be lost.

Over the last decade, many nations have begun to realize this danger, but they are not prepared to avert it. Setting minimum flow levels to protect wildlife requires large quantities of data and the expertise of hydrologists, fishery biologists, and aquatic ecologists. The quick and inexpensive methodologies are simply not accurate enough to be reliable. A common one, for example, sets minimum flow requirements as a fixed percentage (such as 10 percent) of the average annual flow. But this makes no allowance for the large flow variability that typifies many river basins, nor for the long-term, cumulative effects on fish of low flows for extended periods of time. More sophisticated methods usually involve a computer model that quantifies, for each particular species, the amount of habitat available in a given stretch of the stream at each stage of its life cycle and under varying streamflow

conditions. Though more accurate, such methods are time-consuming and costly, requiring much field data and scientific expertise to interpret them.[29] A paper issued in 1984 by the Canadian Inquiry on Federal Water Policy acknowledges that "in Canada, we are only beginning to appreciate the magnitude of water needs for the support of the ecosystem. We do not have very reliable estimates of instream requirements."[30]

Farmers in the Indian state of Madhya Pradesh now refer to their once fertile fields as "wet deserts."

Among the least affordable consequences of irrational water use is the degradation of valuable cropland from poor irrigation practices. Irrigation water is typically brought to crops through unlined canals and ditches that allow vast quantities of water to seep down to the water table. Where drainage is inadequate, the water level gradually rises, eventually entering the crops' root zone and waterlogging the soil. In the Indian state of Madhya Pradesh, for example, a large irrigation project that originally was expected to increase crop production tenfold led to extensive waterlogging and, consequently, a reduction in corn and wheat yields. Farmers there now refer to their once fertile fields as "wet deserts."[31]

In dry climates, waterlogging may be accompanied by salinization as water near the surface evaporates and leaves behind a damaging residue of salt. According to some estimates, waterlogging and salinization are sterilizing some 1 million to 1.5 million hectares of fertile soil annually. The problem is especially severe in India and Pakistan (where an estimated 12 million hectares have been degraded), the Valley of Mexico, the

Helmud Valley in Afghanistan, the Ti-
gris and Euphrates basins in Syria and
Iraq, the San Joaquin Valley in California, the North Plain of China, and Soviet
central Asia.[32] In these areas, waterlogging and/or salinization threaten to diminish the very gains in food production
that costly new irrigation projects are intended to yield.

AUGMENTING DEPENDABLE
SUPPLIES

When natural water supplies become
inadequate to meet a region's demands,
water planners and engineers historically have responded by building dams
to capture and store runoff that would
otherwise flow through the water cycle
"unused" and by diverting rivers to
redistribute water from areas of lesser to
greater need. As the demand for water
has increased, so have the number and
scale of these engineering endeavors to
augment available supplies. Tens of
thousands of dams now span the world's
rivers. Collectively, their reservoirs store
roughly 2,000 cubic kilometers of runoff, increasing by 17 percent the 12,000
cubic kilometers of naturally stable
runoff derived from groundwater and
lakes. Most of this capacity has been
added since mid-century, when the pace
of large dam construction abruptly
quickened. All but 7 of the 100 largest
dams in the world were completed after
World War II.[33]

Many industrial countries are now
finding, however, that the list of possible
dam sites is growing shorter and that the
cost of adding new storage facilities is
rising rapidly. In the United States, for
example, reservoir capacity grew on average 80 percent per decade between
the twenties and the sixties. As the nar-

row valley sites were gradually exploited, any new capacity required
broader, earth-filled dams. By the sixties, 36 times more dam material was
needed to create a given reservoir capacity than in the twenties. With a corre-
sponding escalation in construction
costs, reservoir development markedly
declined.[34]

In most of Europe, a favorable climate
and geography for securing water supplies has lessened the need to build large
storage reservoirs, compared with, for
example, the western United States. Yet
to meet rising demands, many European
nations plan large increases in reservoir
capacity over the next decade. (See
Table 3-6.) A 1981 report prepared by
the U.N. Economic Commission for
Europe (ECE) raises doubts, however,
about the ambitious plans of several
countries materializing. Both high costs
and growing opposition to the flooding
of farmlands and valleys are becoming
major barriers to dam construction. Notwithstanding government forecasts that
"optimistically predict" a doubling or
tripling in reservoir capacity, the ECE
assessment concludes that some countries have already reached the practical
limits of their reservoir development.[35]

Lagging the industrial world's big
dam era by two decades, dam construction in the developing world is now in its
heyday. Two thirds of the dams over 150
meters high slated for completion this
decade are in the Third World.[36] Designed mainly for generating hydroelectric power and supplying water for irrigation, large dams and reservoirs offer
promises of greater energy independence and food self-sufficiency. Their
lure is understandable as large-scale solutions to a set of large development
dilemmas. Unfortunately, high costs,
poor planning, and environmental disruption are leaving a legacy of failed expectations that suggest they are not the
panacea once envisioned.

Table 3-6. Reservoir Capacity in Selected Countries, 1970, With Projections for 1990

Country	Total Capacity	Projected Increase in Capacity, 1970–90
	(cubic kilometers)	(percent)
Belgium	0.1	79
Bulgaria	2.7	296
Canada	518.0	—
Czechoslovakia	3.3	76
East Germany	0.9	156
France	2.0	—
Greece	8.7	78
Poland	26.0	127
Portugal	5.3	119
Romania	2.6	746
Sweden	27.1	0
Soviet Union	830.0	60
United Kingdom	1.5	47
United States	670.0	15
West Germany	2.3	—

SOURCE: United Nations Economic Commission for Europe, *Long-Term Perspectives for Water Use and Supply in the ECE Region* (New York: United Nations, 1981).

Sri Lanka's Mahaweli Development Programme encompasses construction of four large dams across the Mahaweli River to help achieve goals of tripling the nation's electric generating capacity and irrigating an additional 130,000 hectares of cropland. Yet with only two dams completed, the project has already been plagued with problems. Capital costs nearly doubled in just four years, severely straining the government's finances. Inspections by agencies donating to the project—including the Agency for International Development and the World Bank—uncovered serious design and construction problems that in 1982 led to the conclusion that without major corrective efforts the irrigation canals would not function as planned. Studies had warned that unless deforested hillsides were replanted, runoff would wash large amounts of soil downstream, threatening a buildup of silt in reservoirs and irrigation canals and a lowering of soil fertility. Yet reforestation did not begin until more than a decade after initiation of the project, and by the end of 1982 replanting had taken place on less than 1 percent of the area targeted for it. Writer John Madeley notes, "The homes of 45,000 people are being flooded by the Victoria Dam, and, when they move into the new resettlement zone, their hopes of making a new living will not have been helped by the lack of attention to replanting."[37]

The experience Sri Lanka has had with the Mahaweli project is by no means unique. Though undertaken with good intentions of raising food production and living standards, large dam schemes are often so costly and complex that other critical tasks—often essential to the project's success—are neglected. As described earlier, vast areas of valuable cropland are becoming waterlogged and salt-laden because of excessive seepage from reservoirs and canals and poor drainage from fields. Deforestation and overgrazing are disrupting water's flow through the landscape. Natural forests and grasslands absorb runoff and allow it to move slowly through the subsurface. As hillsides are denuded, rainfall and soil run rapidly off in floods, filling expensive reservoirs with silt and causing dry-weather streamflows to disappear.

Especially in the Third World, managing watersheds to stabilize runoff is critical to reversing a vicious cycle of flooding, soil loss, declining crop production, and perennial drought. In Malaysia, conversion of natural forest to rubber and palm oil plantations has doubled peak runoff and cut dry-season flows in half.

Deforestation on the small island of Dominica has contributed to a 50 percent reduction in dry-weather flows there.[38] Though virtually impossible to quantify, it may well be that deforestation—now estimated at 11.3 million hectares per year—is diminishing the Third World's stable runoff by as much as expensive new dams and reservoirs are augmenting it. Unless the threats posed by deforestation, waterlogging, and soil salinization are countered, large dam schemes may end up wasting capital and degrading land while bringing few last-

ing benefits to those they are intended to serve.[39]

As with dams and reservoirs, projects to divert water from one river basin to another have grown in number and scale in response to rising demand. Proposals to import water from some distant source have been made for virtually every major region facing a shortage. Most were developed during an era of cheap energy, relatively cheap capital, and when environmental values rarely entered the debate over project costs and benefits. The collective history of

Table 3-7. Current Status of Selected Major River Diversion Projects

Project	Distance	Planned Annual Volume	Estimated Capital Cost	Current Status
	(kilometers)	(cubic kilometers)	(billion dollars)	
Chan Jiang River–North China Plain, China	1,150	15.0	5.2[1]	Decision in 1983 to begin construction
Northern European Rivers–Caspian Sea Basin, Soviet Union	3,500	20.0	3.1	Construction to begin 1986
Siberian Rivers–Central Asia, Soviet Union	2,500	25.0	41.0	Preparing engineering designs; decision pending
Central Arizona Project, United States	536	1.5	3.5	Deliveries to Phoenix to begin Dec. 1985; to Tucson, 1991.
California State Water Project, United States	715	5.2	3.8[2]	Operating at 60 percent of planned capacity
Midwest Rivers–High Plains, United States[3]	600–1,600	2.0–7.4	5.5–35.0	No action

[1]A published estimate considered low by project analysts; cost could easily double.   [2]Includes only costs incurred and projected through 1995; State has yet to develop new proposals (and cost estimates) to significantly increase the project's capacity over existing levels.   [3]Five different diversions were studied. Lower figure of each range is for diversion of Missouri River into western Kansas, the least costly alternative; higher figure is for diversion of several south-central rivers into Oklahoma and Texas panhandles, the most costly alternative.
SOURCE: Worldwatch Institute, based on various sources.

these large diversion schemes is marked by long study times, periodic abandonment, multibillion-dollar cost estimates, and growing concern over their ecological effects. (See Table 3-7.) Some of these projects will probably never leave the drawing boards. Those that do, and that are actually completed, may be more a product of political expediency than an objective analysis of alternative ways to achieve a given end.

Managing watersheds to stabilize runoff is critical to reversing a vicious cycle of flooding, soil loss, declining crop production, and perennial drought.

In China, officials and scientists began in the early fifties to study the possibility of diverting water from the Chang Jiang (Yangtze) River Basin in central China to the water-poor regions of the north. After years of lying dormant, the project was given a boost in February 1983 when the government approved the first stage of work on what is known as the East Route. This mainly involves reconstructing the old Grand Canal, which will offer navigation benefits regardless of whether other phases of the project are completed. The long-term plans call for pumping water 660 kilometers north to the Huang He, the Yellow River, from which it would flow an additional 490 kilometers by gravity into the vicinity of Tianjin. Chinese water planners estimate that the diversion will require several dozen pumping stations with a total installed capacity of about 1,000 megawatts—equal to one very large nuclear or coal plant. The system would transfer about 15 cubic kilometers of water in an average year, and up to double that volume in a dry year. Most of the water would be used to expand or improve irri-

gation on 4.3 million hectares; the remainder would enhance Tianjin's municipal and industrial water supply.[40]

With an estimated price tag of $5.2 billion, which analysts say could easily double, Chinese officials are understandably proceeding cautiously. Bruce Stone, one of a team of experts studying the Chinese diversion proposals, makes a convincing case that the water transfer may be an unnecessarily costly and risky way to raise grain production from the North China Plain. He notes that most of the irrigated cropland near Tianjin now yields only 1.8 tons per hectare, while a smaller portion yields 2.3 tons. The production increase gained by expanding irrigation to 1 average-yielding hectare could therefore be obtained equally by upgrading 3 or 4 hectares already under irrigation to produce the higher yields. Moreover, without better management and drainage of irrigated lands, the diverted water may worsen the salinization of North Plains' farmland. Salinization is already reducing yields on 2.7 million hectares, and another 4.7 million are threatened.[41]

Officials in the Soviet Union have in recent years revived century-old ideas of diverting north-flowing rivers to the more populous southern European and central Asian regions. One project aims to transfer water from northern European lakes and rivers to the Volga drainage basin, the primary purpose being to stabilize the level of the Caspian Sea. Even more ambitious is the proposed diversion of Siberian rivers south to the central Asian republics, where water deficits of 100 cubic kilometers are projected by the turn of the century. The region's burgeoning population and intensifying political clout have increased pressure to find some solution to its pending water shortage and unemployment problems. Thane Gustafson observed in 1980 that apparently "the latitude enjoyed by technical specialists to criticize or oppose the diversion projects has become hostage to the projects' political priority." The greatest single obstacle to proceeding with the diversions, he noted, was "the tightness of investment capital, which makes a full-scale commitment by the leadership unlikely in the near term."[42]

In January 1984, nevertheless, the USSR Council of Ministers called for a detailed engineering design for the entire 2,500–kilometer route from the Ob' River to the Amu Darya. Construction could begin by 1988 if the designs are accepted, and water that now drains into the Arctic may be heading to the cotton lands and industries of central Asia by the end of the century. Cost estimates for the initial transfer capacity of 25 cubic kilometers are $18 billion for the main diversion canal and $23 billion for the facilities to distribute the water once it reaches its destination. Meanwhile, some Soviet scientists still maintain there is considerable potential to increase the efficiency of water use in the destination region. According to one estimate, conservation in agriculture and industry could save up to half the initial volume of the proposed transfer. Moreover, as with China's project, the diverted water could spread the already severe salinization of irrigated land.[43]

In the United States, no new federal water projects have been authorized since 1976, though since the turn of the century authorization bills have been introduced into the U.S. Congress about every two years. More importantly, actual funding for water project construction (excluding wastewater treatment) has declined steadily over the past eight years; appropriations in 1984 were about 70 percent less in real terms than in 1976.[44] Tight capital and $200–billion federal deficits are forcing to an end a long era of massive water subsidies. Historically, few of these projects have returned sufficient benefits to justify their

high costs. Long before the first drops of Central Arizona Project water were destined for Phoenix and Tucson, for example, economist Thomas Power of the University of Montana stated that not only was the project's benefit-cost ratio less than one, "it may well only return a few cents of each dollar invested in it."[45]

Public opposition is adding another large hurdle to water project construction in the United States—in some cases, perhaps an insurmountable one. The California State Water Project (SWP) is a case in point. One of the most complex water schemes ever designed, SWP is now operating at 60 percent of its planned annual capacity. Capital costs to date total about $3.4 billion, and the need to lift much of the water 590 meters over the Tehachapi Mountains guarantees high energy bills: Pumping costs in 1983 totaled over $100 million.[46]

Two successive state administrations in California have failed to win sufficient support for additional SWP facilities that would allow more northern water to be transferred to Los Angeles and the agricultural valleys in the south. The voters rejected one proposal, called the Peripheral Canal, in a 1982 referendum. This defeat reflected concern about the canal's ecological effects around the Sacramento–San Joaquin Delta and, more fundamentally, about the merits of costly water exports versus stronger conservation efforts by southern water users. Another proposal, known as the "through-delta" plan, died in the California assembly in August 1984 when it appeared to proponents that another public referendum could not be avoided. Approval of any plan within the next few years that would substantially increase the volume of water shipped south appears increasingly doubtful.[47]

As the prospects for dams and diversions to augment dependable water supplies become less promising, the potential to store surplus runoff underground is receiving more attention. Artificially recharging underground aquifers—either by spreading water over land that allows it to percolate downward or by injecting it through a well—is one way to both stabilize water tables and increase the amount of runoff stored for later use. Underground storage also avoids damming a free-flowing river, minimizes competition for valuable land, and prevents large losses of water through evaporation, which are among the principal objections to surface reservoirs.

More than 20 countries now have active projects to artificially recharge groundwater. Yet in just a few cases has the practice been adopted on a large scale. Israel transports 300 million cubic meters of water from north to south every year through its National Water Carrier System and stores two thirds of it underground. The water is used to meet high summer demands and offers a reliable source of supply during dry years. In the United States, local water agencies in California, which have been recharging groundwater since the twenties, now place nearly 2.5 billion cubic meters in underground basins each year. The state's Department of Water Resources also began to seriously investigate groundwater storage as the options for damming more surface streams became increasingly limited. By 1980, the department had 34.5 million cubic meters stored in two separate State Water Project demonstration areas. Preliminary estimates for seven groundwater basins indicate a potential for augmenting the SWP's annual yield by about 500 million cubic meters, at unit costs at least 35–40 percent lower than the median cost of water from new surface reservoirs. Also, the U.S. Congress enacted legislation in the fall of 1984 authorizing demonstration projects in 17 western states to recharge aquifers, including the diminishing Ogallala.[48]

Underground storage may hold special potential for Third World countries subjected to the destructive flooding and perennial dry spells of a monsoon climate. Capturing excessive runoff and storing it underground can convert damaging flood waters into a stable source of supply, while avoiding the large evaporation losses that occur with surface reservoirs. In India, subsurface storage has sparked interest as a way of providing a reliable source of irrigation water for the productive soils of the Gangetic Plain. According to some estimates, a fully irrigated Plain could grow crops sufficient for three fourths of India's population. On the North Plain of China, also prone to chronic drought, water from nearby surface streams is diverted into an underground storage area with a capacity of 480 million cubic meters. When fully recharged, the aquifer will supply irrigation water for 30,000 hectares of farmland. Several counties in Hebei Province are also artificially recharging aquifers to combat sinking water tables.[49]

Many aquifers are also recharged unintentionally by seepage from irrigation canals. In such cases, managing groundwater in conjunction with the surface irrigation water can help prevent waterlogging and salinization and may allow for an expansion of irrigated area without developing additional surface water sources. Such a strategy has been tried in the Indus Valley of Pakistan where a 60,000–kilometer network of canals sits atop a vast groundwater reservoir. By the mid-sixties, leakage from the canals had tripled the volume of recharge to the aquifer, and the resulting rise in the water table caused extensive waterlogging. Following a World Bank-sponsored study of the area, the Pakistan Government began to subsidize the installation of tubewells to tap the vast amount of water that had collected underground over the decades. About 11,000 public wells have been installed under the government program, and individual farmers have constructed over 100,000 private wells, which, though built to supply them with irrigation water, also help control waterlogging. Unfortunately, much of the water pumped is too saline for use unless mixed with purer surface water, and poor operation and maintenance have apparently made the public wells a burden to the government. Yet the strategy of jointly managing groundwater and surface water may offer substantial benefits where the physical setting is right and the needed technical and institutional coordination can be developed.[50]

Artificial recharge on a small scale has helped augment local water supplies for decades. The North Dakota town of Minot, for example, opted for this approach when faced with chronic water shortages and rapidly declining groundwater levels. Its complete recharge system cost only 1 percent as much as building a pipeline to the Missouri River, another of the town's supply alternatives. After six months of operation, water levels in portions of the aquifer had risen more than six meters.[51] Despite a host of similar local-level success stories, however, the practice is far from realizing its potential. According to Jay H. Lehr, Executive Director of the National Water Well Association in the United States, the efficiency of storing surplus runoff underground "has been proven the world over. The costs, while by no means negligible, are reasonable in the face of other sound alternatives and a steal when compared to the grandiose water schemes of the mega minds of the Army Corps of Engineers and the Bureau of Reclamation."[52] Soviet scientist M.I. L'vovich has predicted that "the 21st century will undoubtedly be the century of underground reservoirs."[53]

Of the less conventional ways to augment a region's freshwater supplies— such as seeding clouds to induce precipitation, towing icebergs, and desalting sea water—desalination appears to hold the greatest near-term potential. Indeed, with the oceans holding 97 percent of all the water on earth, desalted sea water seems to offer the ultimate solution to a limited renewable freshwater supply. Several technologies have proved effective, but their large energy requirements make them too expensive for widespread use. Desalting sea water is typically 10 times more costly than supplying water from conventional sources, and applying the process to brackish (slightly salty) water is 2.5 times more costly. Total desalination capacity worldwide is now 2.7 cubic kilometers per year, less than one tenth of 1 percent of global water use. Sixty percent of the world's capacity is in the Arabian Peninsula and Iran, where surface water is virtually nonexistent and even groundwater is often too salty to drink. Yet even in these energy-rich countries, producing and transporting the desalted water inland is in some cases prohibitively expensive. Though perhaps the ultimate source, desalination is unlikely to deliver its promise of a limitless supply of fresh water any time soon.[54]

CONSERVING WATER

As affordable options to augment dependable water supplies diminish, the key to feeding the world's growing population, sustaining economic progress, and improving living standards will be learning to use existing supplies more efficiently. Using less water to grow grain, make steel, and flush toilets increases the water available for other uses as surely as building a dam or diverting a river does. The outlines of a strategy to curb water demand are clear, though no single blueprint can apply to every region. The challenge is to combine the technologies, economic policies, laws, and institutions that work best in each water setting.

Since agriculture claims the bulk of most nations' water budgets and is by far the largest consumer, saving even a small fraction of this water frees a large amount to meet other needs. Raising irrigation efficiencies worldwide by just 10 percent, for example, would save enough water to supply all global residential water uses. As discussed previously, vast quantities of water seep through unlined canals while in transit to the field, and much more water is applied to crops than is necessary for them to grow. The rising cost of new irrigation projects, the limited supplies available to expand watering in many areas, and the high cost of pumping are forcing governments, international lending agencies, and farmers alike to find ways of making agricultural water use more efficient.

Most farmers in developing as well as industrial countries use gravity-flow systems to irrigate their fields. The oldest method, and generally the least expensive to install, these systems distribute water from a groundwater well or surface canal through unlined field ditches or siphons. Typically, only a small portion reaches the crop's root zone; a large share runs off the field. Sprinkler systems, which come in many varieties, apply water to the field in a spray. They use more energy than gravity systems and require a larger capital investment to install, but they have brought irrigation to rolling and steep lands otherwise suited only for dryland farming. One design—the center pivot system—was largely responsible for the rapid expansion of irrigation on the U.S. High Plains in recent decades.[55]

Drip or trickle irrigation systems, developed in Israel in the sixties, supply water and fertilizer directly onto or below the soil. An extensive network of perforated piping releases water close to the plants' roots, minimizing evaporation and seepage losses. These costly systems thus far have been used mainly for high-value orchard crops in water-short areas. Today drip irrigation is used on about 10 percent of Israel's irrigated land, where experiments in the Negev Desert have shown per-hectare yield increases of 80 percent over sprinkler systems. Introduced into the United States in the early seventies, these systems now water nearly 200,000 hectares and are slowly being used on row crops too. In Brazil's drought-plagued northeast, a project sponsored by the Inter-American Development Bank is experimenting with one design to irrigate crops where farm incomes are low and water supplies are scarce.[56]

Raising irrigation efficiencies worldwide by just 10 percent would save enough water to supply all global residential water uses.

Most irrigation experts agree that the actual efficiency of water use obtained in the field depends as much on the way the irrigation system is managed as on the type used. Although drip irrigation may be inherently more efficient by design, the wide average range of efficiency for each system—40–80 percent for gravity flow, 75–85 percent for a center pivot sprinkler, and 60–92 percent for a drip system—shows that management is a key determinant. Farmers using conventional gravity-flow systems, for example, can cut their water demands by 30 percent by capturing and recycling the water that would otherwise run off the field. Some U.S. jurisdictions now require these tailwater reuse systems. Farmers are also finding, however, that they often make good economic sense because pumping tailwaters back to the main irrigation ditch generally requires less energy than pumping new water from the source, especially from a deep well.[57]

Farmers can also reduce water withdrawals by scheduling their irrigation according to actual weather conditions, evapotranspiration rates, soil moisture, and their crops' water requirements. Although this may seem like fine tuning, careful scheduling can cut water needs by 20–30 percent. At the University of Nebraska's Institute of Agriculture and Natural Resources, a computer program called "IRRIGATE" uses data gathered from small weather stations across the state to calculate evapotranspiration from the different crops grown in each area. Farmers can call a telephone hotline to find out the amount of water used by their crops the preceding week, and then adjust their scheduled irrigation date accordingly. The California Department of Water Resources is launching a similar management system with a goal of saving 740 million cubic meters of water annually by the year 2010. The Department is also demonstrating irrigation management techniques through mobile laboratories equipped to evaluate the efficiencies of all types of irrigation systems—gravity, sprinkler, and drip—and to recommend ways that farmers can use their water more efficiently.[58]

Israel has pioneered the development of automated irrigation, in which the timing and amount of water applied is controlled by computers. The computer not only sets the water flow, it also detects leaks, adjusts water application for wind speed and soil moisture, and optimizes fertilizer use. The systems typically pay for themselves within three to five years through water and energy savings and higher crop yields. Motorola Israel Ltd., the main local marketer of automated systems, has begun exporting its product to other countries; by 1982 over 100 units had been sold in the United States. Israel's overall gains in agricultural water use efficiency, through widespread adoption of sprinkler and drip systems and optimum management practices, have been impressive: The average volume of water applied per hectare declined by nearly 20 percent between 1967 and 1981, allowing the nation's irrigated area to expand by 39 percent while irrigation water withdrawals rose by only 13 percent.[59]

In the Third World, where capital for construction of new projects is increasingly scarce, better management of existing irrigation systems may be the best near-term prospect for increasing crop production and conserving water supplies. Lining irrigation canals, for example, can help reduce water waste, prevent waterlogging, and eliminate the erosion and weed growth that makes irrigation ditches deteriorate.[60] Yet canal lining is expensive, and other options may prove more cost-effective. Seepage from canals is not necessarily water wasted since it increases the potential groundwater supply. By coordinating the use and management of groundwater and surface water, as in the case of the Indus Valley described earlier, the total efficiency of water use in an agricultural region can be increased.

Farmers also need control of their irrigation water in order to make good use of fertilizer and other inputs that increase crop yields. Concrete turnouts that allow farmers to better dictate the timing and flow of water to their fields, for example, are being built in India, Pakistan, and elsewhere. At a pilot project in Egypt, funded by the U.S. Agency for International Development, improved management of irrigation systems is largely credited with boosting rice yields 35 percent. Water savings alone will often justify such investments: By some estimates, better irrigation management in Pakistan could annually save over 50 cubic kilometers—four times the storage capacity of the nation's Tarbela Dam—at one fourth the cost of developing new water supplies.[61]

Curbing industrial demand for water, the second major draw on world supplies, tackles problems in two ways: It frees a large volume of fresh water to meet other competing demands, and it can greatly reduce the volume of polluted water discharged to local rivers and streams. In most developing countries, industry's demand for water is growing faster than that of either agriculture or municipalities. A slowdown is thus essential for sustained economic growth in water-short regions and for battling pollution problems that are fast making available supplies unfit for use.

In many industries, much of the water used is for cooling and other processes that do not require that it be of drinking-water quality. A large share of the water initially withdrawn can thus be recycled several times before disposing of it. Thermal power plants can cut their requirements by 98 percent or more by using recycled water in cooling towers rather than the typical once-through cooling methods. Palo Verde, a nuclear power plant built in the desert outside Phoenix, Arizona, for example, is near no body of water; it will draw on nearby communities' treated wastewater, which the plant will reuse 15 times. The water needs of other industries also vary greatly, depending on the degree of recycling: Manufacturing a ton of steel may take as much as 200,000 liters or as little as 5,000, and a ton of paper may take 350,000 liters or only 60,000. Moreover, recycling the materials themselves can also greatly cut industrial water use and wastewater discharges. Manufacturing a ton of aluminum from scrap rather than virgin ore, for instance, can reduce the volume of water discharged by 97 percent.[62]

For the manufacturing industries that use a great deal of water—primary metals, chemicals, food products, pulp and paper, and petroleum—the cost of water is rarely more than 3 percent of total manufacturing expenses. Incentives to use water more efficiently have come either from strict water allocations or stringent pollution control requirements. In Israel, where virtually all available freshwater supplies are being tapped, the government has set quotas on the amount any industrial plant may receive. A water-use standard per unit of production is established for each industry, and a particular plant's allocation is then calculated by multiplying the standard by the anticipated level of production. As new technologies are developed, the standards are made more stringent. Consequently, average water use per unit value of industrial production has declined in Israel by 70 percent over the last two decades.[63]

Manufacturing a ton of aluminum from scrap rather than virgin ore can reduce the volume of water discharged by 97 percent.

In Sweden, industrial water use quintupled between 1930 and the mid-sixties but has since shown a marked decline. Strict environmental protection requirements for the pulp and paper industry, which accounts for about 80 percent of the country's industrial withdrawals, fostered widespread adoption of recycling technologies. Despite more than a doubling of production between the early sixties and late seventies, the industry cut its total water use by half—a fourfold increase in water efficiency. Indeed, largely because of these savings, Sweden's total water withdrawals in the mid-seventies were only half the level projected a decade earlier.[64]

Pollution controls spawned by federal and state laws are also helping to curb manufacturing water use in many areas of the United States. Surveys of Californian industries show, for example, that total water use in manufacturing declined during the seventies despite a 14 percent increase in the number of plants. Echoing Sweden's experience, the pulp and paper industry led in water reductions, with a 45 percent decline in withdrawals between 1970 and 1979. Nationwide, industrial withdrawals have not yet turned the corner, probably because of long delays in passing the pollution control requirements authorized by the Clean Water Act. Yet declines should occur when and where strict standards are enforced.[65]

Developing countries are in a prime position to take advantage of these new recycling technologies. Building water efficiency and pollution control into new plants is vastly cheaper than retrofitting old ones. Experience in the West shows that industries will have little incentive to adopt these measures without either sufficiently high water and wastewater fees or stringent pollution control requirements. Many of the technologies available are able to reduce water use and wastewater flows at least 90 percent and thus can contribute greatly to alleviating water supply and pollution problems in growing industrial areas. A recent study of an integrated iron and steel plant near Sao Paulo in Brazil, for example, showed that the plant was withdrawing 12,000 cubic meters of water per hour—highly polluted with the city's sewage—and that it was discharging 22,000 tons of iron oxide and 2,600 tons of grease annually into the nearby Santos estuary. For an estimated $15 million, or less than $1 per ton of annual production, the plant could install a recirculating water system that would cut water use by 94 percent and pollutant discharges by 99 percent.[66]

Household and other municipal water demands rarely account for more than 15 percent of a nation's water budget, and worldwide they claim only about 7 percent of total withdrawals. Yet storing, treating, and distributing this water, as well as collecting and treating the resulting wastewater, is increasingly costly. Large capital investments are required, making water and wastewater utilities especially sensitive to scarce capital and high interest rates. In the United States, for example, water and wastewater utilities require an average of $8.5 billion in new investment each year. Capital needs for 1982–90 are expected to total about $100 billion, and some estimates go much higher.[67] Reducing municipal water use can ease these financial burdens by allowing water and wastewater utilities to scale down the capacity of new plants, water mains, and sewer pipes and to cut the energy and chemical costs associated with pumping and treating the water.

Many household fixtures and appliances use much more water than necessary to perform their varied functions. Most toilets in the United States, for example, use 18–22 liters per flush, while water-conserving varieties recommended by the Plumbing Manufacturers Institute average about 13. A typical West German toilet requires only 9 liters per flush, and a new model that meets government standards uses about 7.5 liters, just a third as much as conventional U.S. models. Showerheads often spray forth 20 or more liters per minute; water-conserving designs can cut this at least in half. Water-efficient dishwashers and washing machines can reduce water use 25–30 percent over conventional models. With simple conservation measures such as these, indoor water use can easily be reduced by a third.[68] (See Table 3-8.)

Table 3-8. United States: Annual Household Water Use and Potential Savings With Simple Conservation Measures[1]

Activity	Share of Total Indoor Water Use	Without Conservation	With Conservation	Savings
	(percent)	(thousand liters per capita)		(percent)
Toilet flushing	38	34.5	16.4	52
Bathing	31	27.6	21.8	21
Laundry and dishes	20	18.0	13.1	27
Drinking and cooking	6	5.5	5.5	0
Brushing teeth, misc.	5	4.1	3.7	10
Total	100	89.7	60.5	33

[1]Estimates based on water use patterns for a typical U.S. household. European toilets, for example, often use less water than the figures given here would imply.
SOURCE: Adapted from U.S. Environmental Protection Agency, Office of Water Program Operations, *Flow Reduction: Methods, Analysis Procedures, Examples* (Washington, D.C.: 1981).

Consumers installing these devices and appliances will almost always save money, since they will reduce not only water use but the energy used in heating water. A typical household in the United States, for example, could expect investments in common water-saving fixtures and appliances to pay for themselves through lower water, sewer, and energy costs in just a few months, or within four years at most. Israel, Italy, and the states of California, Florida, Michigan, and New York now have laws requiring the installation of various water-efficient appliances in new homes, apartments, and offices.[69]

Despite its potential financial benefits to consumers and utilities, municipal conservation is still typically viewed only as a means of combating drought, rarely as a long-range water strategy. Programs developed by water-short communities to foster lasting reductions in water use, however, have yielded fruitful results. In Tucson, Arizona, a combination of price increases and public education efforts to · encourage installation of household water-saving devices and replacement of watered lawns with desert landscaping led to a 24 percent drop in per capita water use. As a result, the Tucson utility's pumping costs were reduced and the drilling of new water-supply wells was deferred. Planners thus expected customer water bills to be lower over the long term than they would have been without the conservation efforts.[70]

In El Paso, Texas, one of the most water-short cities in the United States, pricing and education efforts are also credited with a substantial reduction in water use. Long-term water supply projections show conservation meeting about 15–17 percent of the city's future water needs. Besides slowing the rate of depletion of El Paso's underground water supplies, the conservation measures are saving water for an average cost of about $135 per 1,000 cubic meters—8 percent less than the average cost of existing water supplies.[71]

Many other options are available to reduce the demand for fresh water. Some areas are finding, for example, that brackish water and treated wastewater can meet many of their water needs.

In Saudi Arabia, brackish water irrigates salt-tolerant crops such as sugar beets, barley, cotton, spinach, and date palms, thereby saving the best-quality water for drinking and other household uses. Treated municipal wastewater is also reused there to irrigate crops and gardens, to recharge aquifers, and as a supply for certain industries. Power plants in Finland, Sweden, the United Kingdom, and the United States are beginning to use brackish water or saltwater for cooling.[72]

In perennially dry South Africa, water policy specifically calls upon users to "make use of the minimum quantity of water of the lowest acceptable quality for any process." Over the next several decades, cities and industries are projected to recycle between 60 and 70 percent of the water they withdraw. Engineers estimate that the cost of treating raw sewage to a quality suitable for drinking is very likely competitive with that of developing the next surface water source. In Israel, 30 percent of municipal wastewater was already being reused in 1981, most of it for irrigation. With completion of the Dan Region Wastewater Reuse Project serving the Tel Aviv metropolitan area, projections are that the proportion of municipal wastewater reused will climb to 80 percent by the turn of the century.[73]

PRIORITIES FOR A NEW WATER ECONOMY

Much of the profligate waste and inefficiency in today's use of water results from policies that promote an antiquated illusion of abundance. People rarely pay the true cost of the water they use. Economists often suggest pricing water at its marginal cost—the cost of supplying the next increment from the best available source. Consumers would thus pay more as supplies become scarcer. Market forces would foster conservation and a reallocation of water supplies to their highest valued uses. In California, for example, the value added per cubic kilometer of water is 65 times greater in industry than in agriculture.[74] Increasing competition for water and rising prices thus dictate a shift in water use from farming to manufacturing. The extent to which a market-driven reallocation should take place is partially a political decision, since it would alter a region's basic character and social fabric; but by economic criteria, it is efficient.

In reality, water is rarely priced at marginal cost; charges often bear little relation to the real cost and quantity of water supplied. Many homeowners in Great Britain, for instance, are charged for water according to the value of their property, a practice that dates to Victorian times. In Indonesia, Malaysia, Saudi Arabia, South Africa, Tanzania, most East European countries, and many others, the government pays all or most of the capital costs for major irrigation projects. Farmers in the United States supplied with irrigation water from federal projects pay, on average, less than a fifth of the real cost of supplying it.[75] Taxpayers are burdened with the remainder, and farmers use more water than they would if asked to pay its full cost.

When water users supply themselves rather than relying on a public project, they typically pay only the cost of getting the water to their farm, factory, or home. But if their withdrawals are diminishing a water source or harming an ecosystem, they should bear the costs that their private actions impose on society. American farmers pumping water from the Ogallala aquifer, for example, pay nothing extra for the right to earn their profits by depleting an irreplaceable resource. On the contrary, many get a tax break by claiming a depletion allowance based on the drop in water level beneath their land that year. The greater the depletion, the greater the allowance—hardly an incentive to conserve.[76] A more appropriate policy would be to tax groundwater pumping in all areas where aquifers are being depleted. That way the public gets some compensation for the loss of its resource, and farmers are encouraged to curb their withdrawals.

In much of the Third World, where the cost per hectare of building new irrigation systems often exceeds per capita gross national product, pricing water at its full cost may not always be feasible. Water is often supplied for free or is heavily subsidized because it is so vital to food production. Yet most experts agree that the inefficient operation and poor maintenance of irrigation systems is largely due to farmers' perceptions that they have no responsibility for them. International lending agencies are now investing handsome sums to rehabilitate irrigation systems that sound operation and maintenance could have kept in good working order. Having farmers pay some share of water costs gives them a stake in the system, besides generating revenue to improve operations.[77]

A combined strategy of charging Third World farmers for some share of system costs and organizing them into "water user associations" to coordinate management tasks and the collection of fees appears a promising way of improving irrigation management. Arguing for more attention to pricing and water user organizations in Thailand, economist Ruangdej Srivardhana of Kasetsart University in Bangkok says that in order for Thai farmers to improve their practices "the feeling that the irrigation facilities belong to and are useful to them is crucial."[78] Charging a modest price for an initial allotment and higher fees for water used above this amount would encourage farmers to conserve without overburdening them. Moreover, where groundwater supplies are available, farmers may be able to profitably construct irrigation wells with minimal public support. In India, over 1.7 million private tubewells had been installed by the late seventies, aided by the availability of credit with very reasonable interest and repayment terms. For many farmers on the Indo-Gangetic Plain, installation of these wells has yielded rates of return greater than 50 percent.[79]

Water users must also begin to pay for treating the water they pollute. Especially in many areas of the Third World, water bodies cannot long be expected to provide a source of high-quality drinking and irrigation water *and* to dilute the increasing tonnage of waste dumped into them each year. Dilution alone simply cannot maintain adequate water quality in a society undergoing rapid industrialization and urbanization. Industries should pay the full cost of using water in their production, which includes the cost of discharging most of it in a form suitable for reuse. Controlling pollution is costly: Funds for protecting quality now account for over half the U.S. budget for water resource development and amount to $25 billion annually.[80] Developing countries may not have the financial resources to subsidize costly pollution controls while at the same time continuing to improve irrigation systems and install drinking water services. Industrialization should proceed in tandem with industries' ability to pay for controlling the pollution they generate. Sacrificing water quality for industrial growth cannot be a winning proposition in the long run.

Existing laws and methods for allocating water supplies are often heavily biased toward those wanting to withdraw water and against those desiring that it remain in place. The old English common law, which required that a riparian landowner not diminish the quantity or quality of water remaining for downstream users, inherently protected stream ecology and habitats. Yet this rule was changed early in the American experience to give riparians the right to "reasonable use" of the water, thus allowing for alterations in streamflows. In the drier states of the American West, an appropriative system was adopted that is even more biased toward withdrawals: Water rights are allocated successively to those who put water to "beneficial use." Establishing such a use, and thus a water right, often required an actual diversion from the stream. As legal expert James Huffman notes, this was not a problem "until the combination of changing values and diminishing water supplies brought the issue of instream flow maintenance to the public attention."[81]

A number of options exist for governments seeking to preserve an ecological balance in their rivers and streams. In the United States, for example, Montana passed a law in 1973 that allows government agencies to acquire prospective water rights. Much of the state's water has not yet been appropriated, so under this legislation a large share of it can be reserved to protect stream ecology. Because of these reserved rights, much of the Yellowstone River will never be withdrawn for use. Many rivers and streams in the United States, however, are already fully appropriated during the dry season of the year. Preserving water quality and fish and wildlife habitats thus requires some form of regulation that limits withdrawals during periods of diminished flow. One of the most powerful tools available, though as yet little used, is what legal experts call the "public trust" doctrine. Dating back to Roman times, it asserts that governments hold certain rights in trust for the public and can take action to protect them from private interests. Its application has potentially sweeping effects since even exist-

ing water permits or rights could be revoked in order to prevent violation of the public trust.[82]

In a landmark decision handed down in February 1983, the California Supreme Court declared that the water rights of the City of Los Angeles, which allow diversions from the Mono Lake Basin, are subject to the public trust doctrine. Mono Lake, a hauntingly beautiful water body on the eastern side of the Sierra, has diminished in surface area by a third, largely because Los Angeles is diverting water from its major tributaries. The lake is also becoming more saline, threatening its brine shrimp population, which in turn feeds millions of local and migratory birds. By invoking the public trust doctrine, the California Court paved the way for a state agency or the courts to decide that Los Angeles must reduce its diversions from the Mono Lake Basin. California law professor Harrison C. Dunning writes: "Although ramifications of the ruling may not be apparent for years, there can be no doubt that it will raise new obstacles for those who would divert California's natural stream flows to farm and city use. . . . From now on, the state must protect what the court calls 'the people's common heritage of streams, lakes, marshlands and tidelands'."[83]

Where demands are already at the limits of the available supply, regulations may be necessary to put water use on a sustainable footing. Strategies geared toward balancing the water budget are lacking in most areas of falling water tables or shrinking surface supplies. Despite pleas by hydrologists, for example, no Indian states have passed laws to regulate the installation of tubewells or to limit groundwater withdrawals. In the southern state of Tamil Nadu, authorities are doing little to curb overpumping that in some areas has caused groundwater levels to drop 30 meters in just a decade. Hydrologists note that the "long-term effects are probably understood, but until the water disappears, it is hardly likely that anyone is going to do anything about the situation."[84]

At least one example worth emulating has emerged in the United States: the 1980 Arizona Groundwater Management Act. Facing a rapidly dwindling water supply, the state is requiring its most overpumped areas to achieve "safe yield" by the year 2025. At this level no more groundwater is withdrawn than is recharged; the resource is thus in balance. Achieving this goal will by no means be painless. Conservation measures will be required of all water users and all groundwater withdrawals will be taxed. No subdivided land can be developed without proof of an assured water supply. If by the year 2006 it appears that conservation alone will not achieve the state's goal, the government can begin buying and retiring farmland. Shifts in Arizona's economy have already begun: Between 1978 and 1982, the state's irrigated area declined 8 percent. Other water-short regions should recognize that such shifts are bound to occur, and that they will be less traumatic if, as Arizona is doing, they are eased by thoughtful planning. Many governments will be watching as the real test of Arizona's law begins in the nineties.[85]

Finally, planners and educators must dispel the myth that conservation is exclusively a short-term strategy to alleviate droughts and other immediate crises. Only in such dry nations as South Africa and Israel is conservation made an integral part of planning future water supplies. In these countries, which are already tapping most of their available sources, continually striving to increase the efficiency of water use is imperative if growth is to continue. But even in nations with untapped rivers and aquifers, measures to conserve, recycle, and reuse fresh water may in many cases make the

resource available at a lower cost and with less environmental disruption than developing these new supplies. Conservation's potential will never be realized until it is analyzed as a viable long-term option comparable to drilling a new well or building a new reservoir.

The Soviet Union's planned diversion of Siberian rivers may meet only one fourth of the deficit expected in central Asia.

Steps toward this end were taken in the United States during the late seventies. In a June 1978 water policy message to the nation, President Carter resolved to make conservation a national priority. Government agencies began to make federal grants and loans for water projects conditional upon inclusion of cost-effective conservation measures. Numerous analyses suggested that substantial savings would accrue both to the government and to communities and their residents from measures to curb water demand. Unfortunately, the Reagan administration took several steps backward when it demoted these conservation requirements to voluntary guidelines and disbanded the Water Resources Council, which had been pushing for a more economically efficient and environmentally sound water policy. California has taken the lead where the federal government has faltered: A 1983 law requires every major urban water supplier in the state to submit by the end of 1985 a management plan that explicitly evaluates efficiency measures as an alternative to developing new supplies.[86]

Most governments continue to expect traditional dam and diversion projects to relieve regional water stresses. Yet the engineering complexities of these projects, along with their threats of ecological disruption, multibillion–dollar price tags, and 20–year lead times leave little hope that they will deliver water in time to avert projected shortages—if, indeed, they are completed at all. In the Third World, unless deforestation and erosion are curbed and irrigation systems are better managed and maintained, large projects may waste scarce capital and diminish the productivity of cropland. Moreover, even the most grandiose schemes will not be ultimate solutions to regional water problems. The Soviet Union's planned diversion of the Siberian rivers, for example, may meet only one fourth of the deficit expected in central Asia. Water delivered to Arizona through the Central Arizona Project will make up for only half of the state's annual groundwater depletions and thus will not alone balance the water budget. Against an insatiable demand, the best any dam or diversion can do is to slow the depletion of supplies or delay the day when they fall short.

In an era of growing competition for limited water sources, heightened environmental awareness, and scarce and costly capital, new water strategies are needed. Continuing to bank on new large water projects, and failing to take steps toward a water-efficient economy, is risky: Vital increases in food production may never materialize, industrial activity may stagnate, and the rationing of drinking-water supplies may become more commonplace.

Alternatives to large dam and diversion projects exist. Water crises need not occur. Securing more-dependable supplies in the Third World can and should continue, but it may better be done with smaller projects more amenable to coordinated land and water management, with incremental development of groundwater, and especially with joint management of surface and underground supplies. In water-short areas of industrial countries, people and economic activity must begin adapting to water's limited availability. Supplies in Soviet central Asia, for example, simply cannot support a booming population and an expanding farming economy for long. Oasis cities such as Phoenix and Los Angeles can no longer expect to grow and thrive by draining the water supplies of other regions. Conservation and better management can free a large volume of water—and capital—for competing uses. Thus far, we have seen only hints of their potential.

4

Maintaining World Fisheries

Lester R. Brown

The world's fisheries occupy an important niche in the global ecosystem, the world economy, and the human diet. Their annual harvest—74 million tons in 1983—exceeds world beef production by a substantial margin. Yielding an average of 16 kilograms per capita live weight for a world population of 4.76 billion, fisheries supply 23 percent of all animal protein consumed. More importantly, in many low-income countries, as well as in a few industrial ones, fish are the principal source of animal protein.[1]

Millions of people make their living from supplying fish: Two million Latin Americans, for example, earn a living this way. And on the densely populated island of Java, which is heavily dependent on the catch from the surrounding waters, 1.8 million Javanese fish fulltime. The World Bank estimates that 12 million workers worldwide support themselves by fishing or fish farming; millions more are involved in the transportation, processing, and marketing of their catches.[2]

It is no surprise, then, that the collapse of the Southeast Pacific anchovy fishery in the early seventies, due to overfishing and ocean variability, caught the attention of many who had assumed that humanity would ultimately turn to the oceans for food. This widely publicized case now appears to have been just the most extreme example of a worldwide pattern: As recently as a generation ago overfishing was the exception. Now in some regions it seems to be the rule.

GLOBAL SUPPLY AND DEMAND

Between 1950 and 1970, the world fish catch increased from 21 million to 66 million metric tons, more than tripling within two decades. (See Table 4-1.) An unprecedented expansion in world population combined with an equally unprecedented rise in per capita incomes boosted demand for animal protein. On the supply side, advances in fishing technology and the availability of cheap oil led to the development of distant-water fishing fleets that literally scoured the oceans in search of edible sea life.

During the fifties and sixties this extraordinary growth in the catch led to a feeling that the oceans contained infinite supplies of fish. Projections made at this time commonly indicated the catch would eventually reach 200–400 million tons annually. In quantity terms, the per capita harvest went from just over 8 kilograms in 1950 to nearly 18 kilograms in 1970, a doubling that contributed to improvements in human nutrition in many countries.

By the seventies, however, there were signs of overfishing: After increasing at nearly 6 percent per year from 1950 to

Table 4-1. World Fish Production, Total and Per Capita, 1950–83

Year	Population	Fish Production[1]	Production Per Capita
	(billion)	(metric tons)	(kilograms)
1950	2.513	21.1	8.4
1955	2.745	28.9	10.5
1960	3.026	40.2	13.3
1965	3.344	53.2	15.9
1970	3.678	65.6	17.8
1971	3.746	66.1	17.6
1972	3.815	62.0	16.3
1973	3.885	62.7	16.1
1974	3.957	66.5	16.8
1975	4.033	66.4	16.5
1976	4.107	69.4	16.9
1977	4.182	68.5	16.4
1978	4.258	70.2	16.5
1979	4.336	71.2	16.4
1980	4.415	72.3	16.4
1981	4.495	75.1	16.7
1982	4.577	76.8	16.8
1983	4.660	74.0	15.9

[1]Includes oceanic catch, freshwater catch, and fish farming.
SOURCE: United Nations Food and Agriculture Organization, *Yearbook of Fishery Statistics* (Rome: various years).

1970, growth in the annual world fish catch slowed to less than 1 percent. And in per capita terms, the growth of nearly 4 percent per year during the fifties and sixties became a decline of almost 1 percent yearly after 1970.

Most of the fish caught are used directly for human consumption. But part of the catch—largely the inferior species or waste from the processing of table-grade fish—is fed to hogs and chickens. Despite the leveling off in the world fish catch, the amount used for fish meal, for fertilizer, and as a source of fish oil has changed little over the last decade, remaining fairly steady at 20 million tons, close to 30 percent of the world catch.[3]

In some countries, such as Japan and Thailand, non-table fish are commonly fed to higher-value fish produced by fish farmers. The relative contribution of oceanic fishing versus fish farming is slowly changing, as growth in the oceanic catch slows and that of aquaculture steadily expands. As of the mid-eighties, fish farming accounts for roughly 9 million of the 75-million-ton global harvest —nearly one eighth of the total. A growing emphasis on this approach is evident in the lending of international aid agencies such as the World Bank and the U.N. Food and Agriculture Organization (FAO). Assistance that previously concentrated on investments in better boats and improved ports and processing facilities shifted toward fish farming during the seventies, as it became clear that there were a limited number of fisheries in which investment in additional capacity would be profitable.[4]

The oceanic fish catch is composed of an indescribable diversity of aquatic organisms: The FAO reports that more than 100 species of finfish, crustaceans, and shellfish are harvested on a commercial scale. Of this long list, some 22 species commonly yield 100,000 tons or more per year, and just 5—herrings, cods, jacks, redfishes, and mackerels, plus the associated relatives of these species—account for more than 40 million tons, well over half the annual catch. (See Table 4-2.)

The most prolific of these are the herrings (in the North Atlantic), sardines,

Table 4-2. World Fish Catch By Species, 1980

Species	Quantity
	(thousand metric tons)
Herrings, sardines, anchovies, etc.	16,225
Cods, hakes, haddocks, etc.	10,720
Jacks, mullets, sauries, etc.	7,338
Redfishes, basses, congers, etc.	5,247
Mackerels, snoeks, cutlassfishes, etc.	4,226
Tunas, bonitos, billfishes, etc.	2,490
Shrimps, prawns, etc.	1,681
Squids, cuttlefishes, octopuses, etc.	1,572
Clams, cockles, arkshells, etc.	1,177
Flounders, halibuts, soles, etc.	1,084
Oysters	973
Sea-spiders, crabs, etc.	848
Shads, milkfishes, etc.	818
Salmons, trouts, smelts, etc.	770
Carps, barbels, and other cyrinids	616
Mussels	614
Sharks, rays, chimaeras, etc.	583
Krill, planktonic crustaceans, etc.	425
Tilapias and other cichlids	367
Scallops, pectens, etc.	364
Freshwater mollusks	267
Lobsters, spiny-rock lobsters, etc.	108
All other	13,676
Total	72,191

SOURCE: United Nations Food and Agriculture Organization, *Yearbook of Fishery Statistics* (Rome: 1981).

anchovies, and pilchards, which yielded a harvest of over 16 million tons in 1980, much of which is consumed indirectly in the form of pork and poultry produced with fish meal. Herrings are not a high-value table fish, although they are consumed directly in both industrial and developing countries. Second on the list is the cod family, with a catch of nearly 11 million tons in 1980. Included in this group are the heavily fished Atlantic cod, the haddock, and the Alaska pollack, a fish that has soared in importance over the past decade.

The place of fish in the human diet varies widely around the world. Per capita fish consumption in the Soviet Union, for example, is roughly twice as high as in the United States. Faced with difficulty in expanding livestock output during the fifties and sixties, the Soviets decided it would be easier to satisfy their animal protein needs by investing heavily in distant-water fisheries. As a result they were at the forefront of launching fish processing factory ships, which permitted their fleet to range to the world's far corners in search of protein, profits, and foreign exchange.[5]

In some industrial countries, such as Japan and Norway, fish figure prominently in the diet. The Japanese, with a per capita seafood consumption of 200 pounds per year, consume far more fish than they do red meat or poultry. Given the nation's low ratio of land to people, the government decided long ago that it would use its scarce land resources to produce its starchy staple—rice—and would obtain as much of its animal protein from the ocean as possible. This, combined with a strong cultural preference for seafood over red meat, led to the evolution of the Japanese "fish and rice" diet.[6]

Although per capita fish consumption in Third World countries is lower on average than in the industrial world, it is nonetheless a key protein source in the diet of coastal peoples. A scrap of dried fish in a rice dish can often mean the difference between a nutritionally adequate diet and one seriously deficient in protein. Thus the worldwide decline in the per capita fish harvest does not augur well for future nutritional improvements in developing countries.

A scrap of dried fish in a rice dish can often mean the difference between a nutritionally adequate diet and one seriously deficient in protein.

The composition of national seafood consumption patterns also varies widely. For example, in the United States tuna occupies a prominent position in overall seafood consumption: With tuna sandwiches and salads a common fare, U.S consumption accounts for more than one third of the world tuna catch. To the extent that tuna stocks are stressed, this is largely the responsibility of American consumers; conversely, the fortunes of the world's tuna fishing fleets rest on the American appetite for this fish. European appetites are in some ways similar to those in North America but there are also some notable differences. Herring, for example, is a favored seafood item, particularly in the Scandinavian countries and in West Germany. Japan and the countries along the Mediterranean's northern shore—Spain, Portugal, and Italy—consume most of the million and a half tons of squid caught yearly. In fact, just as Americans consume over one third of the world tuna catch, the Japanese consume nearly half that of squid.[7]

Geographic patterns of marine protein consumption have shifted over the last three decades as transportation systems have expanded and processing techniques have advanced. A generation ago inland regions of Third World countries consumed little fish, but with improvements in preserving and transporting, this is slowly changing. At that time, very little of the catch was frozen; today close to one fifth is marketed in this form. Meanwhile the drying of fish, the traditional method of preservation in Third World countries, has declined as transportation advances have effectively shortened the distance from catcher to consumer.[8]

Biological constraints on supplies, mismanagement of fisheries, investments in fish farming, and changing tastes all interact to reshape seafood consumption patterns over time. The relative importance these influences are likely to have in the years ahead is discussed in the remainder of this chapter.

THE EXTENT OF OVERFISHING

An FAO assessment of the status of the 19 principal fisheries that account for most of the catch in the Northwest Atlantic gives an idea of the contemporary pressures on this resource base. The stocks of 4 have been depleted, and 9 others are described as "fully exploited." In FAO terminology, this often means that they are heavily overfished—that their yield has been reduced well below their biological maximum, but that the stocks have not yet been fully depleted.[9]

The silver hake, for example, has a potential yield of 250,000 tons but the catch in 1965 totaled 383,000 tons, more than half again its estimated sustainable yield. By the early seventies it dropped to 270,000 tons and in 1981 just 62,000 tons were caught, scarcely a quarter its estimated potential. Assuming this decline is due to stock depletion, it is easy to calculate overfishing's reduction of the catch. Of the 6 other principal Northwest Atlantic fisheries, 3—including squid—are believed to be only moderately exploited and the status of 3 others is listed as unknown because their biological potential has not been determined. There has not been enough information gathered on the crab and clam population of the Northwest Atlantic, for instance, to establish biological potential and hence to determine whether overharvesting has occurred.[10]

There are a few species that are overexploited in some regions while scarcely touched in others. For instance, the cephalopod fisheries (octopus, squid, and cuttlefish) in the east central Atlantic have been heavily harvested. All three are overexploited. After several annual harvests of well over 100,000 tons of octopus, the catch in 1980 fell to 48,000 tons. Similarly, over 30,000 tons of squid were caught each year during the seventies; the harvest in 1980 was only 11,000 tons, well below the estimated potential of 40,000 tons.[11]

By the early eighties 11 major oceanic fisheries—6 in the Atlantic and 5 in the Pacific—had been depleted to the point of collapse. They range from the Peruvian anchovy, which had an estimated potential of 9 million tons, to the Alaska king crab, with a possible yield of nearly 100,000 tons. This mismanagement is an expensive error. For example, the North Atlantic cod fishery, which could yield up to 1.35–1.75 million tons, has netted less than 600,000 tons in recent years. Similar calculations for other fisheries provide a startling overall picture of some 11 million tons of potential catch lost each year because of fishery mismanagement. (See Table 4-3.)

Although the Atlantic cod fishery now appears to be slowly recovering, the Peruvian anchovy fishery is not. The shifts in the current off Peru's coast can directly and dramatically affect this fishery, yet it seems clear that overfishing from the mid-sixties through the early seventies doomed it to collapse even without any change in the current. (See Figure 4-1.) During seven of the eight years from 1964 through 1971 the anchovy harvest exceeded 9.5 million tons, the level identified by a team of FAO fishery biologists as the maximum sustainable yield of the fishery. The subsequent plummet to around 4 million tons, and then to just 1.5 million, makes it questionable that these stocks will ever recover to the level of two decades ago.

As early as 1973 C.P. Idyll, a leading fishery biologist, observed "there is some reason to fear that the world's greatest stock of fish may have been irreversibly damaged."[12] Marine biologist David Fluharty believes a catch of 9.5 million tons is too high even for the fishery's good years, when the current is normal. And he suggests that the anchovy quota must be adjusted on a year-to-year basis according to conditions if its yield is to be maximized over the long term.[13]

The collapse of this anchovy fishery, once the world's largest, has been costly. Peru lost two export commodities—the fish meal and the guano from sea birds that depend on anchovy—that once dominated its foreign-exchange earnings. When this fishery was at its peak, in 1970, exports of its products earned Peru $340 million, roughly a third of its foreign exchange. The disappearance of this vitally needed source of hard currency contributed to the growth of Peru's external debt; in the mid-eighties over 40 percent of the nation's exports are required merely to service its outstanding loans. And the world has lost a major protein supplement, once used in the rations of hogs and poultry.[14]

To the north, the developments in the Alaskan king crab fishery have closely paralleled those of the anchovy. Found principally in the seas off Alaska and the nearby Aleutian Islands, the king crab became an international delicacy in recent decades. Commercial crabbing in the region by the Japanese got under way in 1930, but it was disrupted by World War II and did not resume on a meaningful scale until the fifties. The seventies witnessed rapid growth in the harvest of this species. Landings of this widely sought after seafood peaked in 1980 at 86,000 tons. By 1984 the catch had fallen to 7,000 tons, less than a tenth

the earlier level. Surveys showed a precipitous drop in the number of fertile females: One analysis in late 1982 estimated that only 27 percent of the females had egg clutches. Shocked by these findings, the Alaskan Department of Fish and Game declared an emergency closure of the fishery. The unanticipated collapse of the Alaskan king crab population startled fishers and

Table 4-3. Oceanic Fisheries That Have Been Depleted

Region	Species	Main Fishing Countries	Estimated Potential[1]	1981 Catch	Loss From Mismanagement
			(thousand metric tons)		
Northwest Atlantic	Atlantic Cod	Canada, France, Greenland, Spain, United States, Soviet Union	1,350	588	762
	Haddock	Canada, United States	100	83	17
	Capelin	Canada, Soviet Union	500	39	461
	Atlantic Herring	Canada, United States	300	224	76
Northeast Atlantic	Atlantic Herring	Denmark, Finland, E. Germany, Poland, Sweden, Soviet Union	2,000	732	1,268
Southeast Atlantic	Pilchard	Soviet Union, South Africa	700	99	601
Northwest Pacific	Salmon	Japan, Soviet Union	400	251	149
Northeast Pacific	Halibut	Canada, United States	38	15	23
	Pacific Ocean Perch	Canada, Japan	210	26	184
	King Crab[2]	United States	40	7	33
Southeast Pacific	Anchoveta	Peru	9,000[3]	1,550	7,450
Total Shortfall Due to Stock Depletion:					11,024

[1]Where a range is given by the FAO, the lower end of the range is used.   [2]Catch data for 1984.
[3]Estimated potential by FAO for conditions prevailing during the sixties.
SOURCE: United Nations Food and Agriculture Organization, "Review of the State of World Fishery Resources," Rome, July 1983.

fishery managers alike and raised questions about whether the species will ever recover.[15]

In the Western Indian Ocean, several species of fish are under pressure from India and Pakistan. The export-oriented shrimp industries in both countries are stressing shrimp stocks in the vicinity of the Persian Gulf and the Arabian Sea; Arab countries report catches down sharply from the peak a decade ago. Human activities, including the destruction of nursery areas by land reclamation and coastal pollution and overfishing, appear to be responsible.[16]

Such factors may be affecting shad in India, where the catch of the freshwater spawning fish declined by more than two thirds in three years—from 35,000 tons in 1978 to 11,000 tons in 1981. This parallels an earlier decline in the U.S. shad catch. Although on opposite sides of the globe, the same factors appear to be responsible—namely stream pollution, heavy fishing, and quite possibly rising acidity in freshwater rivers as a result of expanding fossil fuel combustion.[17]

Although overfishing has become commonplace, it is not always for the same reason. In some instances it has resulted from a lack of data on stocks,

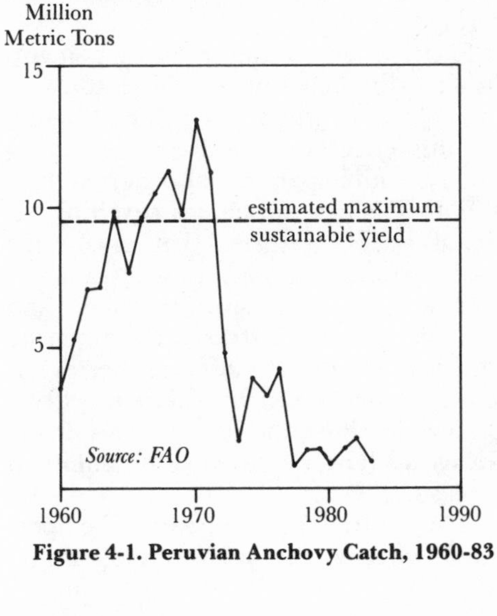

reproductive rates, and other factors needed to manage stocks intelligently. In other cases, the deficiency has stemmed from an inability to interpret available data correctly. Before the extension of offshore limits to 200 miles, there was often no national or other authority responsible for limiting the catch and establishing quotas for the national fleets working a fishery. Once collective demand exceeded the sustainable yield, the "tragedy of the commons" often followed. In still other situations, overfishing has resulted from the inability or the unwillingness of the responsible authorities to enforce quotas.

Over the last 10 years even newly developed fisheries in the more southern latitudes have quickly been fished to the point of collapse.

Whatever the cause, the past two decades have been marked by the collapse of one fishery after another. Although these collapses were initially confined to the North Atlantic, they soon spread to the North Pacific as well. Over the last 10 years even newly developed fisheries in the more southern latitudes —the Southeast Pacific, the Gulf of Thailand, the Indian Ocean, and the New Zealand coastal fisheries—have quickly been fished to the point of collapse. The net result is that no informed person can now doubt that there are limits to the growth of the catch in any fishery. What is not always clear is whether a particular year-to-year decline is the result of natural forces, such as climatic variation, or of overfishing. Worse still, a natural decline induced by changes in water temperature, for example, can itself trigger overfishing, particularly if the catch is already too close to the sustainable yield.

Scientists are now looking closely at the interaction between stocks as it

Figure 4-1. Peruvian Anchovy Catch, 1960-83

becomes clear that the complex inter-play among species makes it difficult, if not impossible, to manage a given stock effectively in isolation. A 1983 FAO cir-cular observed that "big fish eat little fish, but large individuals of small spe-cies can eat small individuals (including eggs and larva) of larger species." It is not uncommon in a fishery with several species for the fall in the catch of one to be followed by a rise in that of another. But this may or may not be a simple cause-and-effect relationship, since the stock of any particular species can vary in response to natural forces.[18]

A 1983 report from the International Center for Living Aquatic Resources Management observes: "Dangerous shifts in species composition are occur-ring on many fishing grounds as more valuable stocks diminish and fishermen shift to smaller species that are lower on the food chain. Irreversible changes may be taking place reminiscent of those oc-curring in the California sardine fishery or the Peruvian anchoveta fishery in which heavily fished stocks have been greatly reduced resulting in lasting eco-logical changes."[19]

Determining the maximum sustaina-ble yield of each fishery is a useful start-ing point for better management of this world resource, but it is of little use on its own. It must be species-specific, recognizing that it is not possible to maximize the harvest of species at all lev-els on the oceanic food chain. In an anal-ysis of the krill fishery in Antarctica, John R. Beddington and Robert M. May point out that "clearly the guiding principle cannot be maximum sutainable yield for each species. The maximum sustainable yield of baleen whales is achieved by leaving their food (krill) entirely alone. For krill, the maximum sustainable yield would be achieved by eliminating whales and other animals that compete with human beings for this food supply. To regulate harvesting by specifying maxi-mum sustainable yield for both prey and

predator species would be to try to have one's cake and eat it too."[20]

Decisions about where to maximize harvest on the food chain face fishery managers everywhere. They are fash-ioned by a combination of biological, economic, and social constraints. The most basic question is whether to maxi-mize the harvest of the larger species high on the food chain (usually prime table species) or that of the smaller spe-cies, which are valued primarily for the production of fish meal. Economics often dictate the answer. Peru, for exam-ple, converted its huge anchovy harvest of over 10 million tons per year in the late sixties and mid-seventies to fish meal because there was simply no mar-ket for such a vast quantity of anchovies as food.

In looking at the resources of the North Sea, the choice can be put rather explicitly. K.P. Andersen and Erik Ursin ask: Do we want the food resources of the North Sea to end up "on the dining table in the form of cod fed with living fish or in the form of chicken fed with fish meal?" Among other things this choice involves an assessment of the rel-ative efficiency with which cod and chicken convert small fish further down the food chain to a highly valued food form.[21]

Further complicating management, fishers alone cannot maximize the sus-tainable yield when given, for example, the influence of waste discharges by in-dustry, municipalities, and agriculture. Whole fisheries can be destroyed by na-tional energy policies that encourage coal burning that leads to acid rain and acidification of freshwater lakes and streams. Chemical stress of the marine environment directly affects fisheries but it is not always easy to isolate its effects on yields since the stress takes many forms, such as increased vulnerability to disease.

All too often there appears to be oper-ating what might be described as an overfishing syndrome. Once the catch of a fishery begins to decline, those directly dependent on its yield begin to suffer financially, making responsible authorities reluctant to intervene and restrict the catch still further. In an effort to maintain their catch, fishers deplete the dwindling stocks even further, which can push the resource past its breaking point and lead to a total collapse. Often restrictions are precisely what is needed if the resource is to be saved.

The risk associated with severe stock depletion is that there is no assurance the stocks will replenish themselves. The collapse of the fisheries listed earlier and the resulting annual reduction of the seafood harvest by some 11 million tons represent a costly loss from the marine resource base, one that exceeds the tonnage produced by fish farmers by a substantial margin. Occurring at a time when the world demand for protein is increasing steadily, it makes future rises in seafood prices almost inevitable.

THREATENED ESTUARIES

Estuaries play a role in the earth's aquatic food system that is far out of proportion to their size. Defined as that part of the aquatic environment "where the flow of the river meets the flood of the tide," an estuary is an intermediate zone between the inland world of fresh water and the salt-water oceans that cover most of the earth.

Most fish spawn either on the continental shelf or in coastal estuaries. Aquatic animals such as oysters, clams, and bay scallops spend their entire lives in estuaries. These areas are also part of the migration route for anadromous species (those that spawn in fresh water but spend most of their lives at sea), such as salmon and striped bass, and the catadromous species such as eels (for which

the reverse is true). Other species breed in the estuary itself. But perhaps even more important, the sheltered waters of estuaries serve as nurseries for young fish. If they are altered in ways that make them unsuitable for spawning and for sustaining a rich range of aquatic life, the quantity and diversity of marine protein supplies will be reduced accordingly.[22]

The complex mutual dependence of people and estuaries is expanding as populations and economies grow. As the rising demand for basic foodstuffs and timber leads to more land clearing, there is more soil erosion and hence heavier flows of silt into estuaries. The clearing of land for construction of homes, factories, and highways also adds pressure. Much of the soil is carried to the mouths of rivers and streams, where it muddies the water and reduces the amount of sunlight reaching submerged aquatic vegetation. As this dwindles, the food supply for many aquatic organisms is reduced.

Increased flows of plant nutrients are also damaging estuaries. A sevenfold increase in world chemical fertilizer use since 1950, a doubling of human sewage during the same period, and the switch to synthetic detergents are all contributing to the overload of nutrients in estuaries, which in turn multiplies the algal blooms on a scale that alters the marine environment. As the greatly increased numbers of algae die and settle to the bottom, their decomposition absorbs the dissolved oxygen from the water—oxygen that fish and other aquatic animals require to survive. Beyond a certain point, fish are actually asphyxiated.

Another source of estuarine stress is the influx of toxic materials from industry and agriculture. Synthetic chemicals and heavy metals can interfere with the reproductive processes of aquatic organisms and reduce the habitability of the environments they contaminate. Not infrequently, they render seafood inedible.

There are literally thousands of estuaries where the world's rivers meet its oceans but a relatively small number account for most of the spawning activity. The principal breeding area for the eastern coast of the United States, for example, is the Chesapeake Bay, a 200-mile-long body of water formed by the retreat of glaciers and the subsequent rise in sea level that inundated the lower Susquehanna River Valley some 15,000 years ago.

Sometimes referred to as a "protein factory," this rich estuary is losing its productivity. Dwindling stocks of key species that contribute to the Bay's rich harvest have raised concern about its continued ability to supply fish, oysters, and crabs as abundantly as in the past. These clear signs of deterioration led the U.S. Government in the mid-seventies to launch the most exhaustive study ever undertaken of a major estuary. After several years and the expenditure of some $27 million, the study concluded that the Bay was indeed deteriorating, that the deterioration was human in origin, and that all the causes could be remedied with the cooperation of the three states responsible for managing the Bay's watershed. Although some 150 rivers and streams flow into the Chesapeake, just 8 account for 90 percent of the fresh water entering the Bay and the Susquehanna alone accounts for close to half the total.[23]

One of the most obvious alterations in the Chesapeake is the extensive loss of submerged aquatic vegetation as suspended sediment, particularly in the upper reaches of the Bay, built up. This decline, under way since the sixties, accelerated during the seventies and affected all types of vegetation. The Virginia Institute of Marine Science concluded in a 20-year study of the Chesapeake's vegetation that "this estuarine system has been undergoing an environmental stress of major proportions."[24]

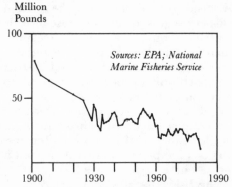

Figure 4-2. Chesapeake Bay Oyster Catch, 1900-83

Another principal conclusion of the U.S. Government's study was that the number of blue algal blooms in the upper Bay had increased roughly 250-fold since the fifties, leaving large areas without any dissolved oxygen. These changes in the Bay's chemistry have steadily reduced the harvest of prized species such as shad, oysters, and striped bass (locally known as rockfish).[25] The population of menhaden, which feed on the algal blooms, increased, but unfortunately this is an inedible, low-value fish used largely for fish meal. In the late nineteenth century the Bay each year yielded over 100 million pounds of shucked oyster meat. By the early eighties the annual harvest had fallen below 30 million pounds. (See Figure 4-2.) The decline in the catch of shad was equally precipitous, falling from more than 17 million pounds per year around the turn of the century to less than 2 million pounds in the early eighties. (See Figure 4-3.)

A similar situation with striped bass— nearly a 90 percent drop in the catch over the last decade—and an even more alarming decline in stocks of this fish, prized by chefs and recreational fishers alike, led the U.S. Congress in 1984 to consider legislation that would ban fishing for stripers altogether until

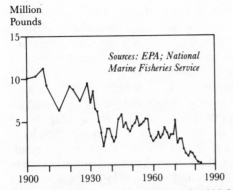

Figure 4-3. Chesapeake Bay Shad Catch, 1900-82

stocks recovered. Although the act did not pass, the state of Maryland in late 1984 banned all fishing for striped bass, including that for sport, for up to four years beginning in 1985.[26]

Restoring the Bay will require an expenditure of roughly $1 billion by the states of Maryland, Pennsylvania, and Virginia. Land use planning and the adoption of practices to control soil erosion will be needed to reduce the influx of both silt and agricultural chemicals. Stringent controls on industrial and municipal waste discharge are equally necessary.[27]

Since the findings of the government study were published in 1983, another threat has come to light: the rising acidity of the water in the streams that feed the Bay. A scientific team from the Smithsonian Institution has been analyzing the Rhode River watershed, one of the smaller rivers that feeds into the Chesapeake. They report that between 1972 and 1978 the pH level fell from 6.3 to 5.8. Scientists regularly detect strong acid pulses in the streams following heavy rains. There is some doubt about whether the larval young of freshwater spawners such as striped bass or perch could survive under these acidic conditions.[28] If this is the case, then saving the Chesapeake Bay may be yet another reason to reorient U.S. energy policies away

from the use of fossil fuels toward much heavier investments in energy efficiency and the use of renewable energy sources.

Estuaries in industrial countries are not the only ones adversely affected. Researchers at Istanbul's Technical University on Turkey's Golden Horn—a small estuary literally within the city of Istanbul that is fed by two small rivers, the Alibey and Kagithane—have pronounced the estuary dead. Not only are there no living organisms in the Golden Horn but the researchers fear that as sewage, silt, and industrial wastes continue to flow into the area, the Bosporus Straits and the Marmara Sea may eventually deteriorate as well.[29]

Changes in estuaries such as the Chesapeake Bay or Turkey's Golden Horn are undoubtedly occurring in varying degrees throughout the world. The threat elsewhere has received far too little attention to date. But the extent of the damage in the Chesapeake, now so thoroughly documented, may get scientists and governments in other areas to focus on these invaluable resources. Information gathered from the detailed study of the Bay can be used to design research programs for other estuaries and shape responses needed to restore these waters to health.

FISH FARMING

Fish farming is not a new concept. In China, where it may have originated as long as 4,000 years ago, the domestication of fish followed closely after that of livestock. Although fish farming, or aquaculture (which also includes seaweed in some countries), has been practiced for at least a few millennia and in scores of countries, world output totals just 9 million tons, roughly one seventh of the oceanic catch.[30]

Over the past decade and a half, however, aquaculture's potential has been considered by national economic policymakers, international aid agencies, farmers, and corporate investors. Two resource-related developments are responsible: the increasingly evident limits to the yield of natural oceanic and freshwater fish stocks, and the depletion of oil reserves and associated rise in price of the liquid fuels so essential to distant-water fisheries. These pressures, in conjunction with the establishment of 200-mile offshore Exclusive Economic Zones by more than 100 countries, have drawn attention to fish farming as an alternative source of protein.

Worldwide, aquaculture provides roughly one sixth of the seafood consumed directly.

Incomplete data make it difficult to determine exactly how rapidly fish farming is expanding. Since fish are grown for home consumption in backyard ponds by Third World villagers, there is no market point at which to gather information. Difficulties in measurement closely resemble those associated with trying to gauge output from home gardening or fuelwood use. In addition, country data sent to FAO, which compiles and publishes figures on fisheries, often fail to distinguish between "capture" fisheries and fish farming. And because in some countries the industry is relatively new, there is no established data gathering system. This particular deficiency plagues even statistically sophisticated countries like the United States, where the yields of new initiatives in catfish and crawfish production are hard to document.

China, with an estimated annual aquacultural output of just over 4 million tons, is far and away the world leader. (See Table 4-4.) This total consists of 800,000 tons of finfish, 1.8 million tons of shellfish, and 1.4 million tons of seaweed. Japan ranks second, with about a million tons—roughly one third each finfish, shellfish, and seaweed. Given the rapid strides in U.S. fish farming during the early eighties, a 1985 survey is likely to show the United States moving into the top ten aquacultural producers. The continental distribution of world aquacultural output is highly uneven, with Asia accounting for over half the total and Europe and North America ranking a distant second and third. In most of Latin America, fish farming is still in an embryonic stage. In Africa, it is just starting.

India's fish farmers, netting some 800,000 tons of finfish per year, narrowly edge China for world leadership in this particular category. (See Table 4-5.)

Table 4-4. Aquacultural Output, Ten Leading Countries, 1980

Country	Production
	(metric tons)
China	4,012,102
Japan	976,140
India	848,973
South Korea	481,480
Soviet Union	340,000
Philippines	285,502
Indonesia	199,297
France	198,375
Spain	194,460
Taiwan	183,673
All other	987,361
World	8,707,363

SOURCE: Aquaculture Development and Coordination Programme, *Aid for Aquaculture Development in the Third World* (Rome: Norwegian Agency for International Development, UNDP, and FAO, 1982).

In both cases carp is the main type of finfish cultivated. In South Korea, seaweed dominates the output, while Soviet fish farmers confine their attention almost entirely to finfish. In Europe, the main products are mussels and oysters. The Netherlands, for example, produces 100,000 tons of mussels each year, enough to provide each of its citizens with 10 kilograms. U.S. aquacultural output is among the most diversified of any country, including both omnivorous species such as trout and herbivorous feeders such as catfish. In 1982, catfish accounted for a good half of the U.S. aquacultural yield of 180,000 tons.[31]

Worldwide, aquaculture provides roughly one sixth of the seafood consumed directly. Of the total finfish output of some 3.7 million tons, an estimated four fifths is accounted for by carp, the mainstay of both the Chinese and Indian aquacultural economies. In both these countries, the aquacultural sector provides more than one fourth of total fish consumption. In the Philippines it accounts for about one tenth of the fish supply. In the United States, nearly all the rainbow trout, most of the catfish and crawfish, and 40 percent of the oysters are harvested from fish farms.[32]

The vast majority of the world's aquaculturalists are also agriculturalists. In part this is because aquaculture requires land and farmers own most of the area that is suitable. There are also mutual efficiencies to be gained from the integration of agricultural and aquacultural production. Many Third World farmers efficiently combine the production of pigs or poultry, particularly ducks, with that of fish by using the animal waste to fertilize the fish ponds. Such a system means that the feed consumed initially by pigs or ducks yields much more animal protein in operations that also produce fish than when the pigs or ducks are grown in isolation. But the gains do not

Table 4-5. Aquacultural Output By Type, Leading Countries, 1980

Type	Country	Production
		(metric tons)
Finfish	India	830,201
	China	813,320
	Soviet Union	340,000
	Japan	249,397
	Indonesia	177,500
	Philippines	151,612
	Taiwan	127,974
	Bangladesh	65,000
	United States	55,646
	Romania	41,325
Shellfish	China	1,757,960
	South Korea	284,749
	Japan	298,231
	France	173,000
	Spain	170,000
	Thailand	111,673
	Netherlands	98,489
	United States	74,165
	Malaysia	63,412
	Italy	49,764
Crustaceans	Indonesia	21,797
	India	17,009
	Thailand	9,923
	Taiwan	7,017
	United States	5,596
Seaweed	China	1,440,822
	Japan	426,044
	South Korea	195,663
	Philippines	132,730
	Taiwan	11,175

SOURCE: Aquaculture Development and Coordination Programme, *Aid for Aquaculture Development in the Third World* (Rome: Norwegian Agency for International Development, UNDP, and FAO, 1982).

stop there: Frequently when the fish pond is drained for harvesting, the sludge from its bottom is gathered and spread on adjacent fields as organic fertilizer.[33]

Another form of agricultural/aquacultural integration involves land use rotation between the two activities. In the southern United States, for example, catfish farmers frequently alternate between a crop of catfish and one of soybeans. This cuts the production costs of soybeans since the nutrient-rich residue on the land after a year of intensive catfish farming substantially reduces outlays for chemical fertilizer.[34]

A variation of this approach is practiced by crawfish producers in Louisiana and Texas. Since the herbivorous crawfish frequently feed on rice straw and since land that can be flooded to produce rice can also be flooded to produce crawfish, farmers commonly plant rice on the land from March to August. After this is harvested the rice paddy is again filled with water and stocked with crawfish that feed on the rice stubble.[35]

Traditional aquaculture, like traditional agriculture, is an extensive activity using relatively large amounts of land and water and little in the way of additional energy inputs. Indeed, fish farmers have usually done little more than stock fish in confined areas. However, as demand for marine protein has driven prices upward and as land has become scarce, aquaculture has embarked on a path remarkably similar to that of agriculture. Normally this has involved fertilizing the ponds in some way, using organic waste or chemical fertilizer, but more recently it has evolved into the direct feeding of fish with balanced rations, including high protein concentrates, similar to those used with livestock and poultry.

Data for both carp and catfish indicate similar responses to the varying inputs used. For example, when ponds are regularly fertilized, carp yield 390 kilograms per hectare per year. (See Table 4-6.) Under the same regime channel catfish produce 370 kilograms per hectare. When fish are fed grain or grain by-

products, usually in pellets, the output increases severalfold. If the grain is supplemented with high-quality protein, such as soy meal or fish meal from less valuable fish, the yield per hectare then jumps to three tons or more for both carp and catfish. Virtually all commercial catfish farmers in the United States now use these high-quality supplements.

Another technique used to maximize output is called polyculture—the cultivation of several fish that have different food habits. Chinese fish farmers commonly combine grass carp that feed on grass and other vegetation, silver carp that need phytoplankton, bighead carp that eat zooplankton, and common carp that feed on insects. Israeli fish culturalists have also adopted this system, growing common carp, silver carp, and mullet together, a combination that yields roughly 30 percent more than does any single species. In the United States, research at Auburn University found that a combination of channel catfish and hybrid buffalo fish yielded 4,200 kilograms

Table 4-6. Annual Fish Farming Yields of Common Carp and Channel Catfish With Varying Intensity of Cultivation

	Common Carp	Channel Catfish
	(kilograms per hectare)	
Fertilized ponds	390	370
Feeding grain or grain by-products	1,530	—
Feeding grain plus high-quality protein supplement feeds[1]	3,300	3,000

[1]Commonly fish meal from trash fish or soybean meal.
SOURCE: R.T. Lovell, R.O. Smitherson, and E.W. Shell, "Progress and Prospects of Fish Farming," in *New Protein Foods*, Vol. 3.

Table 4-7. Efficiency of Grain Conversion to Meat by Various Animals

	Grain/Meat Conversion Ratio
Beef cattle in feedlot	7.5 to 1
Pigs	3.25 to 1
Chicken	2.25 to 1
Rainbow trout	1.5 to 1

SOURCE: Hans Ackefors and Carl-Gustaf Rosen, "Farming Aquatic Animals," *Ambio*, Vol. 8, No. 4, 1979.

per hectare, an increase of 50 percent over the 2,800 kilograms per hectare from the catfish alone.[36]

One of the attractions of fish farming is the high efficiency with which fish convert vegetable matter to meat. Beef cattle in American feedlots require roughly 7 pounds of grain to produce a pound of meat. (See Table 4-7.) Pigs, by comparison, need 3.25 pounds of grain to yield a pound of pork; broilers need 2.25 pounds for a pound of chicken. Catfish, by contrast, require only 1.7 pounds of grain to produce a pound of fish. Fish are more efficient converters than farmyard species for two reasons. One, they are cold-blooded and thus do not need to consume large amounts of energy to maintain a high and steady body temperature. And two, because they live in the water, fish do not require much energy for locomotion. Together, these give fish a marked advantage in feed conversion.

In the United States, where carp are considered too bony to be a prime table fish, the channel catfish dominates, with output exceeding that of trout by a factor of four in recent years. American catfish output, less than 3,000 tons as recently as 1970, reached 62,400 tons in 1983. (See Table 4-8.) The rapid growth in catfish farming in the lower Missis-

sippi Valley is one of the world's aquacultural success stories. As the efficiency of production has increased, catfish have evolved into a widely consumed food item, much as poultry did a generation ago when advances in the industry transformed chicken from a luxury food for Sunday dinner to a daily fare.

Although there are considerable benefits to be gained from combining fish farming with that of crops and livestock, fish can also be farmed on a small scale wherever the physical resources are available. The most basic need is land that can be used for a pond, preferably over soil with sufficient clay to hold water. Fish farmers also need a source of water and some source of feed, which can range from naturally occurring plant growth in the pond to animal manures or grain products with high protein supplements.

Fish farms vary in size from several square meters to hundreds of hectares. The millions of fish farmers in east Asian countries, such as China, the Philip-

Table 4-8. United States: Aquacultural Production of Catfish, 1970–83

Year	Production
	(metric tons)
1970	2,600
1971	5,100
1972	8,300
1973	9,000
1974	7,700
1975	7,300
1976	8,600
1977	10,000
1978	13,700
1979	18,500
1980	21,100
1981	27,500
1982	45,200
1983	62,400

SOURCE: Paul Hurt, U.S. Department of Agriculture, private communication, April 4, 1984.

pines, and Indonesia, typically have less than 1 hectare each. Catfish producers in Mississippi usually average more than 50 hectares per farm. The national area varies widely, from China's 740,000 hectares to the relative newcomer the United States, which has roughly 100,000 hectares devoted to fish production. In Mississippi, which dominates the U.S. production of catfish, farmers used some 26,500 hectares—just over 100 square miles—for catfish ponds in 1983.[37]

The ability of fish farming to satisfy animal protein needs at a low cost depends in large part on the development of species that feed low in the aquatic food chain. Recognizing this, the research program at the International Center for Living Aquatic Resources Management in the Philippines has focused its efforts on species such as tilapia, carp, mullets, milkfish, clams, and oysters—all species that feed on aquatic vegetation. Over the long term the future of tropical aquaculture appears to reside in these species.

Aquacultural expansion faces the same land, water, and energy constraints that agriculture does.

The scientific base for a productive, flourishing aquaculture does not yet exist, for the systematic application of science to the breeding, nutrition, disease control, and rearing practices of aquatic organisms is still in the early stages. In contrast to livestock husbandry, which is based on several species that were domesticated thousands of years ago, many species of fish have been artificially cultivated only within the last generation. Because marine biologists have not been able to get some commercial species to reproduce in captivity, fish farmers are still largely dependent on the gathering of eggs or the capture of

fingerlings. As scientific advances in aquaculture unfold, countless new opportunities will undoubtedly develop.

That fish farming is destined to expand seems clear. How fast it will do so is less certain. It is a form of animal husbandry and as such must compete with the production of beef, pork, poultry, eggs, and milk for the use of land, water, labor, fertilizer, and feedstuffs. Fish farming will succeed only in those situations where it can compete with these other forms of food production. But in a world where pressure on resources is mounting, aquaculture should also be seen as means of tapping some currently unused resources. For example, fish can be farmed on low-lying land that is not suitable for crop production. To the extent that fish farming uses such resources or is integrated with livestock or crop production to the mutual benefit of both, it is bound to expand more rapidly. It is also a way of converting organic waste directly into animal protein. And it even creates additional jobs.

One of the constraints on aquacultural growth is land availability. A World Bank fisheries study observes that some countries, such as China, have only a modest potential for additional expansion. Others—the Philippines, Thailand, or Sri Lanka, for instance—can expand the area devoted to fish farming several-fold.[38] As a general matter, aquacultural expansion faces the same land, water, and energy constraints that agriculture does.

Most of the projections of future aquacultural output have proved to be exceedingly optimistic. In 1978, for example, the National Academy of Sciences in the United States anticipated that world output by the year 2000 would reach 50 million tons, of which 1 million tons would be produced in the United States. Given the impressive U.S. progress since then, this country may come close to the million-ton figure, but growth in this field elsewhere is only a fraction of that projected in the Academy study.[39]

Although fish farming is practiced in many countries, it is still a fledgling industry. For most species, genetic improvements through breeding that would permit various species to exploit the favorable conditions provided by aquaculture are still in the early stage. Advances in disease control and in fish nutrition are likely to be impressive in the years ahead. All told it looks as though growth in fish farming will continue and probably accelerate as demands on the earth's food-producing resources intensify.

SALMON RANCHING

In fish ranching, as opposed to farming, fish are kept in captivity only for the early part of their life. Anadromous fish (which spawn in freshwater streams but spend most of their lives in salt water) with a strong homing instinct are well suited for this type of aquaculture. Species such as salmon or ocean-going trout are hatched and confined until they reach the smolt stage (about two years old), at which time they are released for their journey to the ocean, where they will stay until they are mature and return to spawn.

Fish ranching differs from fish farming in several ways. While farming involves many species, commercial fish ranching has to date been broadly successful with only one: salmon. This does not rule out commercial possibilities with other species, but thus far they have been ranched on a limited scale. The second main difference lies in feeding. Whereas farmers must provide all the food for the fish they rear, either directly or indirectly, this is not the case with salmon. Researchers estimate that only 1 percent of a salmon's growth occurs while it is in a hatchery. For the two, three, or four years it is at sea, the predatory salmon forages on its own.

Before the modern era, salmon apparently thrived in streams and rivers throughout the northern hemisphere's higher latitudes. With modernization, however, their access to many streams and rivers was often blocked by dams, as in the U.S. Pacific Northwest and in the Baltic Sea. Some rivers—such as the Thames in England, where the salmon disappeared in the nineteenth century—became so polluted that they were no longer habitable. In other instances merciless overfishing led to the salmon's demise. The combined result is that this popular seafood source disappeared from many sites where it was once abundant.

In the late twentieth century a better understanding of the salmon's life cycle and a strong commercial demand for this tasty fish have led to the restocking of many streams. More than two centuries have passed since the 1763 discovery in Germany that salmon eggs could be fertilized in captivity. This, coupled with an awareness of the salmon's homing instinct, set the stage for modern ranching. Salmon hatcheries, usually publicly supported, and commercial salmon ranching are both based on the near-legendary homing instinct of this fish. Even when released in an unnatural setting, salmon manage to find their way back some two to five years later when it's time to breed.

Researchers at the University of Washington's hatchery regularly observe this genetically programmed behavior: "Instead of coming back to big deep rivers such as the Sacramento, the Columbia, the Fraser and the Yukon, to which many of their relatives are accustomed, Chinooks returning from the sea to their 'home' at the University must enter Puget Sound, turn left, enter the Lake Washington ship canal and pass through the locks either with the ship traffic or by way of the fish ladder along

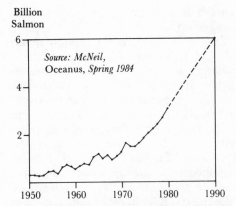

Billion
Salmon

Source: McNeil,
Oceanus, Spring 1984

Figure 4-4. Release of Juvenile Salmon into the
North Pacific, 1950-80, With Projections to 1990

the south bank. Then, after a three-and-
a-half mile trip through the congested
industrial area along the shores of Lake
Union, they must turn left again, climb a
small ladder and enter a collecting pond
on the campus." Not only does this
unerring homing instinct ensure that the
salmon return to their birthplace, it also
means they are exceedingly easy to harvest when they arrive.[40]

The only countries with extensive
salmon hatcheries and annual releases of
this fish are Japan, the Soviet Union, and
the United States. The Japanese now release over a billion salmon smolts each
year in rivers and streams on the islands
of Hokkaido and Honshu. After feeding
in the areas south of the Bering Sea, the
Aleutian Islands, and the Gulf of Alaska,
the salmon return to the rivers where
they were released. In the fall of 1982,
the Japanese harvested 28 million
salmon—one for every four Japanese.
Soviet salmon ranchers are not far behind: The smolts released are expanding
by roughly 100 million per year and the
goal is to release 3 billion annually by
the end of the century. The Soviet
salmon are released in the many small
streams of Sakhalin Island and the Kam-
chatka peninsula. By 1990 the three
countries together are expected to release 6 billion smolts into the North Pacific. (See Figure 4-4.) In addition, Canada and Sweden are also actively
engaged in salmon breeding.[41]

Japan appears to have a substantial
lead over both the Soviet Union and the
United States in the scale of its operation. (See Table 4-9.) An estimated 90
percent of the salmon that spawn in Japanese rivers and streams today originated in that nation's hatcheries. Indeed, the number of salmon now
breeding in these areas appears to far
exceed the number that spawned there
naturally prior to human interference.[42]

Both the Soviets and the Japanese
sometimes practice what is aptly described as terminal harvesting in addition to the more conventional high-seas
drift-net harvesting. Instead of catching
the salmon with boats they either place
nets across the streams or in some cases
simply net the fish by hand. If the processing factories are adjacent to the
hatcheries where the smolts are released,
the salmon on their return journey
upstream are channeled into specially
devised diversion chutes from which they
are manually transferred to a conveyor
belt that leads into the processing plant.

The great attraction of salmon hatching and ranching is that the investment
in feeding is limited to the one or two

Table 4-9. Estimated Harvest From
Salmon Ranching, By Country, 1984

Country	Quantity
	(metric tons)
Japan	108,000
Soviet Union	64,000
United States	21,000

SOURCE: Worldwatch Institute estimates based on
data from William J. McNeil, Oregon Aqua-Foods,
Springfield, Ore., private communication, October
30, 1984.

seasons it takes between the time of hatching and the point when the tiny smolts are ready for their long feeding migration to the sea. There is no need to invest in fishing trawlers or other energy-consuming harvesting equipment. And, as noted earlier, the salmon consume only minute quantities of feed in this early stage of life.

The Japanese, for example, calculate that for each kilogram of juvenile salmon released from hatcheries they get 80 kilograms of mature salmon returning. Steady progress in improving the health and vigor of the juvenile salmon that are released has raised the share returning at maturity to over 2 percent at hatcheries in both Hokkaido and Honshu. In the natural state, only an estimated 1 percent of the smolt return as adults, for many things can happen to the small salmon as they move toward the sea, including being eaten by larger fish. The 1 percent rate of return is considered the minimum for a commercially viable ranching operation.[43]

One concern that always follows the domestication or semidomestication of any species is the loss of genetic diversity. Some fishery experts in the United States at least are worried about this possibility in hatchery-reared stocks generally, and specifically in competition with native stocks.[44]

For salmon ranching to be an attractive investment, those who operate the hatcheries must of course have exclusive authority to harvest the fish returning to them. In the United States, three states —Alaska, California, and Oregon—now permit this. In Alaska, for example, once the returning salmon enter the harvest area they become the property of the corporation that released them. With this right assured, some 17 corporations are now engaged in salmon ranching in that state.[45]

Success with salmon ranching in the northern hemisphere has led to the introduction of salmon into the southern oceans where they do not naturally occur. Chinook salmon smolts from the University of Washington stock were released in Chile in 1980. The percentage that returned as adult chinooks two years later greatly exceeded the expectations of the marine biologists conducting the experiment. It is hoped that salmon released along the southern Chilean coast will feed on the enormous stocks of krill in the oceans around Antarctica, converting what is now a very low-value seafood source into a much tastier, more widely demanded one. The success of this initial introduction into the southern oceans has raised high hopes not only in Chile but in the Malvinas (Falkland) Islands and New Zealand as well.[46]

Norwegian scientists have also been highly successful at producing salmon smolts. But Norway is far from the salmon's natural feeding grounds and many salmon would probably be lost to the numerous North Atlantic fishing boats. So the Norwegians have opted to farm salmon rather than ranch them. Thus the salmon are fenced in, usually in pens within natural enclosures such as fjords. In 1982, Norwegian salmon farmers produced nearly 15,000 tons, many of which were exported to foreign markets. Given the favorable commercial prospects, Norway's producers hope to boost output to 25,000 tons by 1985.[47]

In Scotland, farmers grow salmon in large floating cages usually located in sea lochs. For them, the disadvantages of having to feed the fish throughout an entire life cycle are offset by the much lower rate of loss of the newly hatched fish. While Canada, France, and the Soviet Union are either experimenting with salmon ranching in the North Atlantic or planning to do so, Norway and Scotland are apparently sticking with farming.[48]

Salmon ranching has made great strides in recent years. The number of smolts released from hatcheries promises to overtake the number spawned naturally. If the growth that has been under way since the early seventies continues, the harvest could eventually exceed the historic highs of a half-century ago. Marine biologist William J. McNeil, who has worked with salmon for three decades, believes that "salmon ranching represents a visible step in a transition from a hunting to a farming economy in the oceans."[49]

FISHERY PROSPECTS

Substantial growth in the world fish catch in the years ahead depends in part on whether now-depleted oceanic fisheries can recover. Of the 11 fisheries that the FAO lists as severely depleted, only the North Atlantic cod has partly recovered. The most recent catch was 762,000 tons, roughly half the estimated potential. There is reason to doubt whether some of the others will ever recover. The Alaska king crab fishery in the Bering Sea was closed in late 1983, for example, but marine biologists do not expect to learn before the end of this decade at the earliest whether it will recover.

When the vast Peruvian anchovy fishery collapsed, many thought its recovery would be only a matter of time. Unfortunately, more than a decade has passed since its collapse but the anchovies have not returned in great numbers. Although the fishery has sustained a catch of 1–3 million tons per year recently, it is but a shadow of its former self. A 1983 FAO assessment comments that "the early recovery of the anchovy fishery is only a very remote possibility."[50]

The fish that tend to be depleted first are the higher value ones, the predatory species such as salmon, cod, and tuna

that are nearer the top of the aquatic food chain. As these are overfished, harvesting and production capacity is not usually left idle; it shifts to other, less desirable species. The Canadian fisheries minister described this process in great detail in 1977 concerning that country's fisheries: "In a consistent pattern, one stock after another has been fished down. In each case the sequence began with an explosive increase in fishing effort by overseas fleets, resulting first in a rapid increase in catch, but followed invariably by a drastic decline. At this point the fleets shifted their attention to other fish, working their way through the traditional species to less desirable and therefore previously untouched stock. And in the devastation of our Atlantic fisheries, Canada has been the loser from the outset."[51]

For the Third World, the Exclusive Economic Zones have helped offset the technological advantage in fishing that some larger industrial countries enjoyed.

Perhaps the most important single development in oceanic fisheries over the last decade has been some shift from distant-water fishing, frequently represented by factory ships and their associated fleets, toward local fishing, as more and more countries extend their Exclusive Economic Zone to 200 miles offshore. For the Third World, these new zones have helped offset the technological advantage in fishing that some of the larger industrial countries had enjoyed in the competition for seafood products. In looking at the future of oceanic fisheries, William Warner, author of *Distant Water*, observes that "the one constant, the one certainty, is that the richest meadows of the sea—the continental shelf and slope waters that are home to 85 percent of the world's harvestable fish—are now a staked plain. Almost everywhere, moreover, the staked lines that nations draw out 200 miles fully encompass this plain. The fishing commons of the oceans have been enclosed."[52] With this enclosure, responsibility for managing and protecting fisheries has been fixed. Whether it will be wisely discharged remains to be seen.

Any assessment of future prospects for the world fish catch must separate capture fishing and fish farming. While the world is slowly recognizing that the oceanic catch of economically useful fish may be very close to a sustainable maximum, there are extensive opportunities for expanding fish farming, particularly where land and water resources are abundant. Even as a certain amount of money is being withdrawn from distant-water oceanic fisheries, the funds spent on fish farming and ranching are increasing.

As the scientific underpinnings of fish culture broaden, farmers, corporations, governments, and international development agencies are stepping up their investment in fish production. It is estimated, for example, that farmers in the United States have invested some $400 million in catfish production facilities. In developing countries, the World Bank, the Asian Development Bank, and the Inter-American Development Bank are all increasing the farming share of their fishery sector loans.[53]

The recent spate of investment in salmon ranching by both governments and corporations is impressive and welcome. A review of the salmon harvest over the past half-century shows the catch peaking in the late thirties, just before World War II, when nearly 350 million salmon were harvested. (See Figure 4-5.) During the next decade the harvest fell to 170 million, less than half the earlier peak. Overfishing, stream obstruc-

tion by dams, and pollution were beginning to take their toll. Between 1950 and 1970 the catch remained remarkably stable at this reduced level. Since 1970, however, it has been moving steadily upward. The principal factor, in addition to quotas imposed on the catch, has been the enormous growth in the release of salmon smolt into the North Pacific from Japan, the Soviet Union, and the United States.[54]

Although it has taken 45 years, extensive research, and substantial funds, the world is finally catching as many salmon as it did in 1940. That is the good news. The bad news is that world population has increased from 2.2 billion in 1940 to 4.7 billion in 1984, thus reducing the salmon catch per person by more than half. Nonetheless this is progress: If the salmon fisheries had not been rebuilt, the per capita catch today would be only a quarter of the 1940 level.

The rebound in the world salmon fishery during the seventies and early eighties is mirrored in the price of this fish. From 1967 to 1979, the U.S. price of salmon—driven by rising incomes interacting with short supplies—increased a phenomenal sixfold. (See Figure 4-6.) As the catch has rebounded since the mid-seventies and as per capita income growth has slowed, salmon prices have

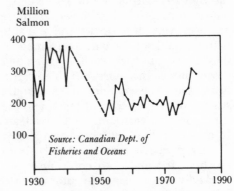

Figure 4-5. Harvest of Salmon in the North Pacific, 1930-80

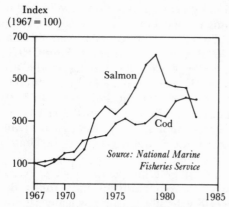

Index
(1967 = 100)

Salmon

Cod

Source: National Marine
Fisheries Service

1967   1970   1975   1980   1985

Figure 4-6. Index of U.S. Prices of Cod and Salmon, 1967-83

turned downward, declining by some 45 percent between 1979 and 1983.[55]

Analysts projecting a substantial continuing growth of the world fish catch toward the end of this century usually expect there will be widespread use of currently underutilized species such as squid and Antarctic krill. There is little question that the stocks of these two species can support a substantially larger sustained catch. But biologically adequate stocks are only one of the conditions that must be satisfied if the projected increase in the world catch is to materialize.

A review of the world squid catch shows considerable growth from 1970 through 1979, from 932,000 to over 1.5 million tons. Since then, however, there has been very little growth. (See Table 4-10.) Squid are heavily consumed in only a few countries, such as Japan and those along the northern Mediterranean. One consequence is that squid stocks are overfished near Japan and the east central Atlantic and Mediterranean. In other locations, stocks of this widely dispersed species have scarcely been touched. If squid is to contribute to a markedly larger end-of-century world fish catch, a taste for it will have to be developed among people who now con-

sume little of this seafood.

Even more formidable obstacles confront efforts to expand world consumption of krill, the small shrimplike crustaceans that are concentrated in vast stocks around Antarctica. Although they are not all that difficult to catch they are costly to harvest because they are located far from principal population centers. Catching a ton of krill requires roughly a ton of oil. Since it is not a high-value seafood product, both the energy equation and economics of doing so are questionable.[56]

Beyond the poor economics of catching krill there is again a problem marketing a form of marine protein for which there is little demand. Both the Soviet Union and Japan, the leading harvesters of krill, are finding it hard to make a palatable product that is attractive to consumers. Unless this hurdle is overcome the krill catch may never increase far beyond current levels, let alone reach

Table 4-10. World Catch of Squid, 1970–82

Year	Quantity
	(thousand metric tons)
1970	932
1971	910
1972	1,150
1973	1,070
1974	1,074
1975	1,182
1976	1,207
1977	1,229
1978	1,328
1979	1,513
1980	1,529
1981	1,354
1982	1,567

SOURCE: United Nations Food and Agriculture Organization, *Yearbook of Fishery Statistics* (Rome: various years).

the tens of millions of tons that some enthusiastic marine biologists have projected. (See Table 4-11.)

Another way to boost the world fish catch would be to move down the oceanic food chain. Rather than catching the predators at the top of the chain, such as salmon, the fishing industry could harvest species at intermediate levels—members of the herring family, for example. Although this is technically possible, the shift in consumer tastes it would require would not come quickly or easily.

Not all the factors influencing the future fish catch are within the control of those responsible for managing fisheries. Stocks of several species, such as the striped bass along the U.S. Atlantic Coast, are being reduced by pollution of the estuaries in which they spawn. Increasingly, the survival of breeding stocks of many key fish will be determined by the local and national governments responsible for controlling pollution. Although the Thames in the United Kingdom and the Potomac in Washington, for example, are far cleaner today than they were a decade or two ago, pollution in other key rivers and estuaries

Table 4-11. World Catch of Antarctic Krill, 1974–82

Year	Quantity
	(thousand metric tons)
1974	22
1975	40
1976	3
1977	123
1978	143
1979	333
1980	477
1981	448
1982	530

SOURCE: United Nations Food and Agriculture Organization, *Yearbook of Fishery Statistics* (Rome: various years).

has worsened. At the same time that the Potomac River got cleaner as a result of the stringent pollution controls, the Chesapeake Bay into which it empties became far worse.

In looking ahead, it seems unlikely that the world fish catch will grow dramatically or that the fall in per capita fish consumption under way since 1970 will be reversed. Any future growth in the catch is likely to be hard earned— whether it comes from fish farming or from expanding the oceanic catch. All indications are that the falling per capita catch of the last 15 years will continue over the next 15, further reducing marine protein consumption per person.

This brings us to the central issue of any assessment of a food source: How will the inability of the fish catch to expand apace with population affect nutrition? A study on the Philippines by the International Center for Living Aquatic Resources Management reports that "per capita fish consumption decreased 47 percent from 1970 to 1980. The gap between supply and demand is generally widening and prices seem to be moving upward in a predictable but rather striking fashion. Many believe a nutritional crisis of serious proportions is emerging."[57] This precipitous decline reflects not so much a dropoff in the catch as it does a decade of exceptionally rapid population growth, a decade when the number of Filipinos among whom the fish catch had to be divided increased by one third.

One of the most comprehensive assessments of the future of fisheries was done by FAO and published in *Agriculture: Toward 2000*. In projecting supply and demand for the end of this century, FAO analysts assumed that the demand for table fish will reach roughly 100 million tons and that the demand for fish meal and other nonfood products will remain at least at the 20-million-ton level of recent years. Together these add up to an end-of-century demand for fish of 120 million tons. On the supply side, the outlook is not bright. Even with reasonably optimistic assumptions, this U.N. organization does not think the catch will exceed 93 million tons, well below the projected demand. The analysts expect rising seafood prices will choke off the excessive demand, bringing it into balance with the much more modest supply.[58]

The bottom line of the FAO analysis is rising fish prices through the rest of the century and in all probability beyond. This may be annoying for Western consumers who consider salmon or Alaskan King Crab legs a delicacy. But it will be much more than annoying for those in the Third World whose livelihoods depend on fishing and for whom fish is the principal animal source of protein. The scenario is particularly disturbing because the projected price rises of ocean-based food resources closely parallel those for grain and other agriculturally based food staples.

5

Protecting Forests from Air Pollution and Acid Rain

Sandra Postel

Over the past decade, scientists have amassed considerable evidence that air pollutants from the combustion of fossil fuels, both oil and coal, and the smelting of metallic ores are undermining sensitive forests and soils. Damage to trees from pollutants such as gaseous sulfur dioxide and ozone is well documented. Recently, acid deposition—more commonly called acid rain—has emerged as a growing threat to forests in sensitive regions. Acid deposition refers to sulfur and nitrogen oxides that are chemically transformed in the atmosphere and fall to earth as acids in rain, snow, or fog, or as dry acid-forming particles. Although this new hazard of the industrial age is known to have killed fish and plants in hundreds of lakes in Scandinavia and eastern North America, its links to forest

This chapter appeared as Worldwatch Paper 58, *Air Pollution, Acid Rain, and the Future of Forests.*

damage remain circumstantial. Yet studies of sick and dying trees in Europe and North America make the connection impossible to ignore.

Temperate forests have a long history of stress and acidification, a history that provides a critical backdrop for considering the new strains of air pollution and acid rain. Since the end of the last continental glaciation 10,000–15,000 years ago, soils have slowly formed from the sterile layers of gravel, sand, and silt left by the retreating ice. Pioneering plants, animals, and microorganisms aided this soil development, helping form an intricate cycle of nutrient uptake and release. Death and decomposition of these inhabitants, then as now, generated acids in the soil. Where acids developed faster than other natural processes could neutralize them, the soils gradually acidified, a process that continues today.

Centuries of human use and abuse of forest ecosystems have added to this natural acidification. Many temperate forests in Europe and North America are now recovering from decades of intense burning, grazing, and timber cutting. The spruce-fir forests of New England and the Adirondacks, for example, had nearly all been clear-cut for pulp by the early twentieth century. Logging was often followed by burning that destroyed the forest floor. As these forests recover, soil formation processes naturally increase the soil's acidity.[1]

The atmosphere receives about as much sulfur from human activities as it does naturally from oceans, swamps, and volcanoes.

Air pollutants and acids generated by industrial activities are now entering forests at an unprecedented scale and rate, greatly adding to these stresses carried over from the past. Many forests in Europe and North America now receive as much as 30 times more acidity than they would if rain and snow were falling through a pristine atmosphere. Acting alone or together, several pollutants—including acid-forming sulfates and nitrates, gaseous sulfur dioxide, ozone, and heavy metals—appear to place forests under severe stress. Needles and leaves yellow and drop prematurely from branches, tree crowns progressively thin, and, ultimately, trees die. Even trees that show no visible sign of damage may be declining in growth and productivity.

Although Americans must travel to isolated mountain peaks in the Northeast to see massive tree disease and death, the loss of West Germany's woodlands is now a potent political and emotional issue among that nation's citizenry. "Waldsterben"—literally forest death—has become a household word. A survey in the summer of 1983 showed that West Germans were more concerned about the fate of their forests than about the Pershing missiles to be placed on their land later that year.[2]

Scientists cannot yet fully explain how this forest destruction is occurring. Weakened by air pollutants, acidic and impoverished soils, or toxic metals, trees may lose their resistance to natural events such as drought, insect attacks, and frost. In some cases the pollutants alone may cause injury or slowdowns in growth. The mechanisms are complex and may take decades of additional research to understand completely. But their cumulative effect is becoming frighteningly clear.

THE PATHWAYS OF POLLUTION

A variety of pollutants are implicated in the forest damage and growth slowdowns now occurring, but most can be traced back to sulfur and nitrogen oxides emitted during the burning of fossil fuels and the smelting of metallic ores. Coal and oil contain sulfur and nitrogen that are released into the atmosphere as gaseous oxides during combustion. The quantity of pollutants emitted depends on the sulfur and nitrogen content of the fuel and, for nitrogen oxides, on the temperature and efficiency of combustion. The sulfur content of coal, for example, varies from less than 1 percent to as much as 6 percent. As a result, burning a metric ton of coal may release 3–60 kilograms of sulfur. Smelting, a process of separating a metal from its ore, also releases large amounts of sulfur dioxide into the atmosphere when the ore contains sulfur. Common metals such as copper, nickel, lead, and zinc are smelted largely from sulfur-bearing rocks.[3]

Over the past century, fossil fuel and smelting emissions have altered the chemistry of the atmosphere at a rapid pace. Today the atmosphere receives about as much sulfur from human activities as it does naturally from oceans, swamps, and volcanoes—on the order of 75–100 million tons per year. Yet most of these emissions occur on just 5 percent of the earth's surface, primarily the industrial regions of Europe, eastern North America, and East Asia. In these areas, energy combustion and smelting add 5–20 times more sulfur to the atmosphere than nature does. The smelter of the International Nickel Company near Sudbury, Ontario, for example, annually spews out more than twice as much sulfur as Mount Saint Helens discharged during its recent most active year of volcanic eruptions. Emissions of nitrogen compounds are harder to estimate, but the ones from human sources also far exceed those from natural sources in many industrial areas. In the United States, human sources are thought to account for 75–90 percent of nitrogen oxides in the air.[4]

Fossil-fueled power plants, industrial boilers, and nonferrous smelters lead the list of sulfur dioxide (SO_2) emitters. The relative contribution of these sources can vary substantially in different countries. (See Table 5-1.) Electric utilities account for two thirds of these emissions in the United States, for example, and in West Germany, they account for over half. In contrast, Canada's electric utilities contribute only 16 percent of SO_2 emissions, while about a dozen smelters emit nearly half. Motor vehicles add little to sulfur emissions, but their internal combustion engines are the biggest source of nitrogen oxides (NO_X) in most industrial countries. In the United States, Canada, and West Germany, cars

Table 5-1. Sulfur Dioxide and Nitrogen Oxide Emissions in Selected Countries[1]

Emissions and Sources	Sulfur Dioxide			Nitrogen Oxide		
	United States	Canada	West Germany	United States	Canada	West Germany
	(million metric tons/year)					
Total Emissions	24.1	4.77	3.54	19.3	1.83	3.0
	(percent)					
Emissions by Sector	66	16	56	29	13	31
Electric Utilities						
Homes, Businesses	3	4	13	4	5	5
Industries	22	32	28	22	20	19
Smelters, Misc.	6	45	—	1	1	—
Transportation	3	3	3	44	61	45
Total	100	100	100	100	100	100

[1]1980 figures for United States and Canada; 1978 for West Germany.
SOURCES: U.S. and Canadian data from Environment Canada, *United States-Canada Memorandum of Intent on Transboundary Air Pollution: Executive Summaries* (Ottawa, Canada: 1983); West German data from Federal Minister of the Interior, "The Federal Government's Reply to the Interpellation of the Deputies: Air Pollution, Acid Rain and Death of Forests," Bonn, August 25, 1982, translation from the German by U.S. Congressional Research Service.

and trucks account for roughly half of NO_x emissions, while utilities generate a third or less and industries about a fifth.

Pollution from fossil fuel combustion dates back well over a century, to the Industrial Revolution. Coal used to heat homes and fuel factories generated a pall of smoke and haze that hung persistently over many cities in Europe and the United States. As the number of factories and homes grew, the problem worsened and many cities had to begin controlling urban smoke. But emissions of sulfur and nitrogen oxides, along with other combustion pollutants, continued to rise. Sulfur dioxide emissions began to increase rapidly in Europe after 1950 when many countries turned to high-sulfur oil. By 1970, annual SO_2 emissions had climbed to 50 million tons, two-and-a-half times the level at mid-century. Similarly, SO_2 emissions in both the United States and Canada rose by 40 percent between the early fifties and mid-sixties.[5]

Severe pollution episodes that resulted in scores of deaths in Donora, Pennsylvania, in 1948, London in 1952, and New York City in the early sixties drove home the hazards of polluted city air. Spurred by these threats to human health, as well as by a rising tide of environmental awareness, many countries enacted pollution control laws that mainly targeted sulfur dioxide and particulate concentrations in the air. SO_2 emissions were first reduced primarily by switching from high-sulfur to lower-sulfur fossil fuels. In the seventies, some countries began requiring new plants to install equipment for removing sulfur dioxide from smokestack emissions. As a result, the SO_2 being added to the atmosphere in North America peaked in the mid-sixties and since then has fallen by 14 percent in the United States to about 24 million tons per year. In Canada, sulfur dioxide emissions have dropped back to mid-fifties' levels of about 4.8 million

tons per year. They have also stabilized or declined slightly in Europe, though the levels vary from country to country.[6]

Government policies have paid far less attention to nitrogen oxides. This gas was not considered as a great a health hazard, and since it was odorless it caused much less of a nuisance than sulfur, with its rotten egg smell. Uncontrolled discharges from power plants, and especially the burgeoning use of automobiles in the last three decades, set NO_x on a rapidly rising path. Nitrogen oxide emissions are harder to estimate than sulfur dioxide, since they are determined by factors other than just the nitrogen content of the fuel. But they also are thought to have risen dramatically over the last several decades, possibly doubling in Europe between the late fifties and early seventies. In West Germany, for example, NO_x emissions rose by 50 percent between 1966 and 1978. North America shows similar trends: Since the fifties nitrogen oxide emissions have roughly doubled in the United States and tripled in Canada.[7]

One consequence of the drive to purify urban air over the last couple decades has been construction of tall smokestacks to better disperse pollutants into the atmosphere. These stacks sent pollutants traveling hundreds of kilometers before returning to the earth's land and waters, which may explain how extensive forest declines can be unfolding far from major industrial and urban centers. The International Nickel Company's 380-meter "superstack," for example, replaced three shorter stacks in 1972. Measurements have since shown that virtually all the sulfur and 40 percent of the heavy metals added to the atmosphere by this plant travel more than 60 kilometers from the smelter.[8]

Unlike industrial emissions of carbon dioxide, which accumulate in the atmosphere, virtually all the sulfur and nitrogen oxides that go up eventually come down in one form or another. Some return essentially unchanged as gases. Some are deposited in dry form on surfaces such as leaves and needles, where reactions with moisture can form acids. The longer the oxides remain in the atmosphere, the more likely they are to undergo oxidation to sulfuric and nitric acid, the constituents of acid rain. Under certain conditions, some of the nitrogen oxides react with hydrocarbons to form ozone. Further complicating the matter, ozone can in turn speed up the transformation of sulfur and nitrogen oxides to acid-forming sulfates and nitrates.[9]

In light of these interactions, trying to single out one pollutant as the cause for forest damage would be difficult. Trees in a given location can be affected simultaneously by several pollutants in a variety of ways. Moreover, each pollutant may affect the formation and fate of others. If ozone helps form acid rain, trees dying primarily from acid rain are dying indirectly and in part from ozone. Recent publicity focused on acid rain has tended to ignore its common origins and interactive effects with these other damaging pollutants. Divorcing acid rain from the complete pollution picture in this way could lead to ineffective strategies to control it and, more importantly, may prevent other damaging pollutants such as ozone from getting the attention they deserve. Nonetheless, acid deposition is of special concern because of its pervasiveness, its insidious ways of inflicting damage, and its potential long-term consequences.

Although acid rain was recognized over a century ago, only in the last three decades has the phenomenon become widespread. In broad areas of eastern North America and northern and central Europe, the annual pH of rain and snow now averages between 4 and 4.5. The pH scale, commonly used to express acidity, ranges from 0 to 14, with any-

thing less than 7 considered acidic. The scale is logarithmic; a decrease of one unit means a tenfold increase in acidity. (Vinegar, with a pH of about 3, for example, is 100,000 times more acidic than baking soda, which has a pH of 8.) Rain falling in preindustrial times is thought to have been in the range of 5.6, slightly acidic from interactions with natural carbon dioxide in the atmosphere. Precipitation in many industrial regions is now 10–30 times more acidic than would be expected in a pollution-free atmosphere.[10]

The precise mechanism by which acid deposition may be damaging forests is not known. Sulfates and nitrates raining down as acids have drastically different effects on different forest stands, and even on different tree species in the same forest stand. Incoming acids affect interactions between the soil and living biomass of an ecosystem in complex and varying ways. Soil structure and composition, vegetation type, climate, and elevation are only some of the natural determining variables. Yet research over the last decade has uncovered some common effects of acidity that point to several pathways by which acid deposition can threaten forests.

Trees derive their nutrition primarily from elements such as calcium, magnesium, and potassium that are weathered from minerals in the soil. Acid deposition adds to the soil hydrogen ions that displace these important nutrients from their sites, where they are bound to soil particles. Soils with a pH of 5 or more are seldom in danger since they have plentiful calcium carbonate (the constituents of lime) or silicates (which have abundant calcium, potassium, and/or magnesium) that effectively neutralize the acid ions. But soils with lower pH levels have fewer of these buffering agents, so incoming acids leach calcium and magnesium from them. Large areas of the southeastern United States, of the

Appalachian, Adirondack, and New England mountain ranges, of the Canadian shield of eastern Canada, and of Scandinavia, for example, are underlain by slightly acidic, poorly buffered soils that are especially susceptible to this process. Although soil changes generally take place over a long period of time, studies in Sweden suggest that substantial leaching of nutrients from sensitive soils can occur in just a decade.[11]

Of all the pathways by which air pollutants can affect forests, changes in the soil are the most foreboding.

Sulfates and nitrates, the other key constituents of acid deposition along with hydrogen ions, can initially have a fertilizing effect on many soils and for a time may actually boost tree growth. Forests in Scandinavia and portions of West Germany seem to have shown this effect. Yet this enhanced growth is short-lived, for eventually these "fertilizer" supplies exceed the forests' capacity to use them. Sulfate saturation usually precedes nitrate saturation, but excess quantities of either or both simply pass through the soil, carrying vital nutrients with them. With forest productivity closely tied to nutrient availability, this leaching of soils by hydrogen, sulfate, or nitrate ions eventually reduces forest growth.[12]

Research also has shown that heavy metals—either mobilized in the soil or introduced from the atmosphere—may be involved in the forest damage now occurring. Dr. Bernhard Ulrich, a soil scientist who has studied damaged beech and spruce forests in the Solling Plateau of West Germany for nearly two decades, hypothesizes that as soils become increasingly acidic, aluminum— which is normally harmlessly bound in soil minerals—becomes soluble and toxic. The free aluminum attacks the root system, making a tree less able to take up moisture and nutrients and to protect itself from insect attacks and droughts.[13]

Trace amounts of heavy metals can also enter the forest from the atmosphere. Combustion of fossil fuels, smelting, the burning of leaded gasoline, and refuse incineration are major sources of trace metals in the air. In the United States, field and laboratory research at the University of Vermont suggest that heavy metals and acid deposition act synergistically on forest systems, stunting the growth not only of trees, but of mosses, algae, nitrogen-fixing bacteria, and fungi that are essential to a forest's health. Between 1965 and 1980, metal concentrations have markedly increased in the soils on Camels Hump, a site of massive spruce dieback in Vermont's Green Mountains. Lead concentration doubled, while that of copper rose by 40 percent and zinc by 70 percent. These metals are brought into the forest with the rain and fog, which in the Vermont mountain peaks have average acidities 100 times greater than "pure" rain. Researchers at the Oak Ridge National Laboratory in Tennessee have analyzed tree cores and found higher metal concentrations in recently formed wood. These cores, taken from southern Appalachian trees, showed concentrations of zinc, copper, chromium, and aluminum generally high enough to be toxic.[14]

Of all the pathways by which air pollutants can affect forests, changes in the soil—whether by nutrient leaching, accumulation of heavy metals, or mobilization of toxic aluminum—are the most foreboding. In sensitive ecosystems these changes may be irreversible, thus harming not only mature trees now standing, but the seeds and seedlings that will become the forests of the next generation. Young trees in the beech forest studied by Dr. Ulrich in West Germany have great difficulty regenerating, apparently because of acidity in the upper soil layers. The number of spruce and maple seedlings on Camels Hump in Vermont has declined by about half over the last two decades, and the number of spruce seedlings in the higher elevations of New York's Whiteface Mountain has dropped by 80 percent.[15]

Sulfur and nitrogen oxide gases can also enter trees directly through their leaves or needles, much as carbon dioxide is taken in for photosynthesis. These pollutants can alter the trees' metabolism and ability to produce food, and thus its productivity and growth. Forestry experts at the 1982 Stockholm Conference on Acidification of the Environment reported that tree growth can apparently slow when average yearly sulfur dioxide concentrations run as low as 25–50 micrograms per cubic meter, levels that prevail over large portions of Europe.[16] For comparison, the national annual ambient air quality standard for sulfur dioxide in the United States is 80 micrograms per cubic meter, and the European Economic Community (EEC) standard is 80–120. Thus air quality levels established to protect human health appear too lenient to protect the health of forests.

Dry sulfate and nitrate particles deposited on moist foliage can form acids that leach nutrients from leaves and needles much as they are leached from soils. West German scientists have found magnesium and calcium deficiencies in the needles of declining spruce trees in the Black and Bavarian forests of southern West Germany. They suggest that acid deposition, aided by ozone that first attacks the needle's outer surface, is weakening trees through the foliage as well as the soil.[17]

Ozone by itself has been found to damage trees when concentrations of 100–200 micrograms per cubic meter last six to eight hours a day for several days. This is roughly two to three times greater than natural background levels on a typical summer day. In many rural areas of Europe, average daily concentrations are regularly in this range, and peak levels can be up to 10 times natural levels. (See Table 5-2.) Acute stress from these episodic peaks may worsen damage caused by high average concentrations. Some scientists studying the pattern of spruce and fir dieback in the Black Forest and the state of North Rhine Westphalia contend that ozone is

Table 5-2. Summer Ozone Concentrations, Selected European Countries

	Upper Daily Average	Peak	Increase of Daily Average over "Natural" Levels[1]
	(micrograms per cubic meter)		(percent)
Netherlands	80–130	500	180
West Germany[2]	100–150	400–500	200
United Kingdom	90–165	200–500	210
Belgium	—	300	—
France	70–120	—	160
Norway	—	200–300	—

[1]The midpoint of the upper daily average range is used for this calculation; "natural" ozone concentration assumed to be 60 micrograms per cubic meter. [2]Daily average figures for West Germany are from the Black Forest; the peak values are frequently recorded in rural areas. Peaks in Black Forest typically are 110–180 micrograms per cubic meter.
SOURCE: Environmental Resources Limited, *Acid Rain: A Review of the Phenomenon in the EEC and Europe* (London: Graham & Trotman Ltd., 1983).

an important factor, and possibly the leading cause there.[18]

No single hypothesis can account for the varying patterns of forest destruction observed. A reasonable explanation for the decline on one site may appear infeasible for another. Although these complexities frustrate the search for a clear-cut cause and effect, they are not surprising. Apart from their unique pathways of destruction, air pollutants are most simply understood as a biological stress. Just as stress is manifest in human beings differently—for example, as ulcers or high blood pressure—air pollution stress on trees shows up in a variety of ways depending upon the tree species, soil type, and the specific pollutants involved. Pollution-induced stress weakens a biological system and makes it more susceptible to harm from natural stresses. In the Appalachians, strong evidence exists that the growth of trees has become more closely tied to temperature and rainfall over the past few decades, a sign of increased stress.[19] Droughts may have triggered the fir dieback in West Germany in the late seventies and the spruce decline on Camels Hump in the mid-sixties. Insect infestations and root fungi have been linked to forest damage in the United States and Europe. Yet these natural factors alone seem insufficient to explain the sustained patterns of dieback and decline. Whether as a predisposing stress or a primary cause, air pollutants appear to figure prominently.

THE SIGNS OF DESTRUCTION

In just a few years, forest damage has spread with frightening rapidity through portions of central Europe. Trees covering more than 5 million hectares—an area nearly half the size of East Germany

—now show signs of injury linked to air pollutants. No nation has better documented the destruction within its borders than West Germany, where forests cover 7.4 million hectares—roughly a third of the nation's land area. Following an extensive survey in 1982, the Federal Minister of Food, Agriculture and Forestry estimated that 8 percent of West Germany's forested area was damaged. Just a year later, more thorough investigation found damage on over 2.5 million hectares—34 percent of the nation's forests. (See Table 5-3.) A third survey conducted in the summer of 1984 apparently confirms that the destruction is worsening: Half the trees are reportedly damaged. Visible injury typically takes the form of yellowing and early loss of needles, deformed shoots, deteriorating roots, a progressive thinning of tree crowns, and, in its severest stages, tree death. The symptoms appear on trees of various ages and in forests of both single and mixed species.[20]

The destruction appears worst in the heavily wooded West German states of Bavaria and Baden Württemberg, home of the famed Black Forest. Nationwide, the 1983 survey showed that three quarters of the fir trees were affected, up from 60 percent in 1982. Damage to spruce, the most important species for the forest products industry, had risen from 9 to 41 percent, and a similar increase was evident with pine. These three conifer species, which together represent two thirds of West Germany's forests, are the most severely struck. But damage has also been found among hardwood species such as beech and oak. Since most trees in the advanced stages of decline are removed from the forest, more have been affected than even these alarming survey results indicate. Dr. Georg Krause of the Land Institute for Pollution Control in Essen stated in 1983 that "hardly anyone in Germany denies the great danger to forest ecosystems."[21]

In neighboring Czechoslovakia, forest damage covers an estimated half-million hectares. Trees on some 200,000 hectares are believed to be severely damaged, and those on 40,000 hectares in the Erz Mountains reportedly have died. Dead and dying trees are plainly visible northeast of Prague in the Krokonose National Park, which has 34,000 hectares of forest, mostly populated with spruce. Not only are the spruce dying, they reportedly stopped regenerating in the park's mineral soils several years ago. Further north, in Poland, another half-million hectares of forest are affected. Researchers in Katowice, near Krakow, say that fir trees are dead or dying on nearly 180,000 hectares and that spruce trees in areas around Rybnik and Czestochowa, also in the industrialized southern region, are completely gone. Environmental scientists warn that by 1990 as many as 3 million hectares of forest may be lost if Poland proceeds with its present industrialization plans, which call for increased burning of the nation's high-sulfur brown coals.[22]

Forest damage in other European countries may not be as well documented, but collectively the accounts support the growing evidence of unprecedented forest devastation. An estimated 400,000 hectares of forest are affected in Austria. Acute damage to pine trees was found in areas of the Netherlands in the spring of 1983, and pine and fir over a wide area in the eastern part of the country are now losing needles prematurely. Some 12 percent of East Germany's forests are believed to be affected, and specialists in Romania have noted that 56,000 of that nation's 6.3 million hectares of forests have been damaged by industrial emissions. In parts of Switzerland, 25 percent of the fir trees and 10 percent of the spruce reportedly have died within a year. Various accounts also claim that trees are suffering from air pollution in France, Italy, the United Kingdom, and Yugoslavia.[23]

In the late autumn of 1983, early signs of tree injury began to emerge in northern Europe as well. Sweden, whose dying lakes first brought international attention to acid rain, now appears to have forest damage. Symptoms similar to those of the declining forests of central Europe have been reported by public and private foresters primarily in the southern and western portions of the country. Spruce and pine show the most

Table 5-3. West Germany: Forest Damage, 1982–83

Species	Area Showing Damage		Portion of Forest Affected	
	1982	1983	1982	1983
	(thousands of hectares)		(percent)	
Spruce	270	1,194	9	41
Fir	100	134	60	76
Pine	90	636	5	43
Beech	50	332	4	26
Oak	20	91	4	15
Others	32	158	4	17
Total	562	2,545	8	34

SOURCE: Der Bundesminister Fur Ernahrung, Landwirtschaft und Forsten, "Neuartige Waldschaden in der Bundesrepublik Deutschland," Bonn, October 1983.

injury. Although official estimates of damage are not yet available, early indications are that 10 percent of the timber stock in certain regions may be affected. In southern Norway, spruce apparently are also showing injury. And a rare environmental report from the Soviet Union's Communist Party paper *Pravda* recently revealed that vast areas of forest are dying from air pollution near the automobile-manufacturing city of Togliatti, about 1,300 kilometers east of Moscow. According to *Pravda,* nearby forests along the Volga River may soon resemble a wasteland.[24]

Unable to attribute this widespread destruction to natural events alone, scientists turned their attention to air pollutants, primarily to sulfur dioxide and the acids into which it transforms. Scientists surveying West Germany's forests found that damage was greater on west-facing mountain slopes exposed to more rain and fog and thus probably to more acid deposition. The needles of ailing conifers in portions of Bavaria near the Czechoslovakian border contained more sulfur than those of healthy trees. Yet injured trees elsewhere have not shown this effect. Moreover, forests are suffering on both acidic and alkaline soils and in areas where atmospheric concentrations of sulfur dioxide are low. Consequently, attention is broadening to consideration of the combined effects of gaseous sulfur and nitrogen oxides, heavy metals, and ozone.[25]

According to *Pravda,* nearby forests along the Volga River may soon resemble a wasteland.

Although forest destruction of this same magnitude is not visible in North America, trees are suffering there as well. In the United States, forest damage is most evident in the mountain ranges of the East, where field and laboratory studies have documented not only tree disease and death, but also sustained slowdowns in growth. From the Appalachians of Virginia and West Virginia northward to the Green Mountains and White Mountains of New England, red spruce is undergoing a serious dieback, a progressive thinning from the outer tree crown inward. Damage is most severe in the high-elevation forests of New York, Vermont, and New Hampshire. By the spring of 1984, researchers had detected serious spruce damage as far south as North Carolina's Mount Mitchell—the highest peak in eastern North America—and tree deaths were expected to be identified in other areas soon thereafter. Because of high precipitation rates and the ability of conifers to intercept cloud moisture, many of these high mountain forests receive three to four times more acid deposition than those at lower elevations. In addition, the soils of some of these forests have shown a marked increase in lead concentration over the past two decades, believed to come almost entirely from the atmosphere.[26]

Detailed documentation of red spruce decline has come from research on Camels Hump in the Green Mountains of Vermont. There, with the benefit of two detailed tree inventories spanning the period 1965–79, researchers have found that seedling production, tree density, and basal area have declined by about half. In 1979, over half the spruce on Camels Hump were dead. A 1982 survey throughout the Appalachians has led researchers to conclude that spruce are declining over a wide area in a variety of forests. So far, no such decline is evident in commercially valuable stands found at lower elevations in northern New England and Canada. Yet in light of the large wood-volume declines on Camels Hump since 1965, botanist Hubert Vogelmann of the University of Vermont warns that "if such losses in only a few years are representative of a general decline in forest productivity, the economic consequences for the lumber industry will be staggering."[27]

Studies on three varieties of pine in the New Jersey Pine Barrens provide the most convincing evidence to date that acid deposition may reduce tree growth. Analysis of tree rings shows that these pines have undergone a dramatic reduction in annual growth over the past 25 years, a pattern of decline not evident elsewhere in the 125-year tree ring record. Growth rates corresponded closely to the acidity measured in nearby streams, which in turn is a good index of the acidity of rain. With other factors such as drought, fire, insect pests, and ozone apparently not responsible, acid rain emerged as a likely cause. The researchers concluded that no other events in the trees' growth history are "as widespread, long-lasting, and severe in their effects."[28]

Although acid deposition's link to tree injury is still debated, scientists have firmly documented tree disease and death from ozone and other pollutants in the family of "photochemical oxidants." Ozone forms from nitrogen oxides reacting with hydrocarbons (produced mainly by automobile engines) in the presence of sunlight. Its formation and concentration are often closely tied to weather patterns and geography: A highly concentrated mass of pollutants mixing under sunny conditions is a ripe setting for ozone's creation.

Ozone has killed thousands of pine trees in the San Bernardino Mountains east of Los Angeles, California, a city now infamous for its yellow-brown photochemical smog. Tree injury was evident as early as mid-century as air pollutants from the growing urban area were carried east by marine winds. As pollution has worsened over the past three decades, losses of the stately ponderosa and Jeffrey pines have increased dramatically. Researchers discovered

that 4–6 percent of these trees in higher elevations died over a six-year period. Losses have been greater in the western part of the mountain range, which receives more pollution. Moreover, the growth rings in ponderosa pine cores show that annual radial growth declined 38 percent over 1941–71 compared with 1910–40, a decline attributed to the rise in air pollutants. In areas receiving the highest ozone doses, the marketable volume of 30-year-old pines declined by 83 percent. The researchers concluded that "this reduction in growth, along with air pollutant caused tree mortality, combine to limit production of timber in the San Bernardino Mountains."[29]

Similar damage from ozone appears to be occurring in the Appalachians. Estimates now are that 4–5 percent of the eastern white pines are dying in the southern Appalachians and the Blue Ridge Mountains and north into Pennsylvania and Ohio. Both here and in the San Bernardinos, damage is exacerbated by insects attacking trees that are weakened by air pollutants. Along with tree mortality, studies of Appalachian pines have also shown substantial growth slowdowns.[30]

High levels of ozone and other gaseous pollutants are also a problem in some developing countries. Urban areas situated in valleys surrounded by mountains, such as Mexico City, Guatemala City, and Caracas, are becoming heavily polluted from automobile emissions. Trees are dying along heavily traveled corridors in Mexico City, and uncontrolled burning of leaded gasoline is of increasing concern in Guatemala City and Malaysia. In some of these regions, unfortunately, governments are encouraging polluting industries to move to outlying areas or to build higher smokestacks—precisely the strategies believed to have worsened acid rain in the rural areas of industrial countries.[31]

Yellowing and early loss of needles, dieback of tree crowns, and ultimately tree death are obvious signs that forests are suffering. And as indicated, measurements of tree rings on weakened trees have shown in many cases that these visible symptoms are accompanied by substantial and sustained reductions in growth rates. But even more disturbing is that growth and productivity can be declining in trees that show no visible symptoms at all. Tree-ring measurements on tens of thousands of trees from Maine to Alabama have shown growth rates 10–40 percent lower than expected over the last two or three decades. These declines are evident in a half-dozen softwood species, including some of great commercial value in the southern United States. Having documented this "hidden injury" for white pine growing in the Appalachians, researchers at the Virginia Polytechnic Institute and State University concluded that it is "highly probable that growth loss in forests subjected to low-level and long-term exposures to air pollutants may be occurring unnoticed and/or unevaluated."[32]

The ultimate severity and extent of tree damage throughout the world is an open and urgent question. As forests not yet showing injury remain exposed to acid deposition and high pollutant concentrations for longer periods of time, the damage may well spread. Moreover, if growth slowdowns are occurring unnoticed, air pollutants may be quietly undermining the productivity of large areas of temperate forests.

ECONOMIC AND ECOLOGICAL COSTS

Many of Europe's forests are intensively managed conifer stands that yield large timber volumes from a comparatively small area. Although they have only one fifth the forested area of North America,

the countries of Western Europe harvest about half as much wood as Canada and the United States combined. Collectively they account for 15 percent of the world's industrial wood harvests, even though they have only 4 percent of its forests.[33]

As with agricultural crop production, the economic gains of intensive forestry are made at the risk of greater vulnerability to outside stresses, a vulnerability obviously compounded if the species being grown is sensitive to the stress. Since planted trees are purposely managed and valued for timber production, damage to them results in a direct economic loss. With plantation forestry and more-intensive forest management becoming more common worldwide, both the likelihood and potential economic effects of forest damage are increasing.

Foresters expect the death of the younger trees to significantly disrupt the wood market.

West Germany's spruce and fir forests are typically managed in even-aged stands, with trees harvested at 80–130 years of age. Although damage first appeared on older trees, spruce and fir of all ages are now affected. Foresters expect the death of the younger trees to significantly disrupt the wood market. In the summer of 1983, when forest damage was still placed at 8 percent, the reported value of the trees that had been lost was about $1.2 billion. Spread equally over a 10-year period, these losses translate into about a 5 percent decline in annual timber production, worth about $200 million per year.[34] With damage now reportedly covering half of West Germany's trees, the value of this annual timber loss is bound to rise.

Because a growing portion of the planned annual harvest in West Germany consists of dying trees, over the next few years the harvest may reach three times the normal level, and the dumping of valuable wood on the market will undoubtedly depress timber prices. Even under the optimistic assumption that the ongoing destruction ceases and that the damaged forests can be restored, future wood harvests will likely be reduced as a result of the present overcutting. Dr. H. Steinlin, Director of the Institut fur Landespflege at Albert-Ludwigs University in Freiburg, expects that from the late nineties into the first quarter of the next century, West Germany will be less self-sufficient in timber.[35]

The economic and ecological reality of these tree deaths has led West German forest researchers to visualize a very different forest in the future and to begin planning alternative management strategies. In Bavaria and other severely damaged areas, for example, soils are being limed in an attempt to counteract acidity. But without plowing lime into the soil—a prohibitively expensive task for such large areas—mineral soils cannot be restored beyond the surface. This strategy, therefore, is not an ultimate solution. Moreover, liming does nothing to reduce stress caused by ozone and gaseous sulfur dioxide. In a 1983 *Journal of Forestry* editorial, a German professor of forest policy, the president of the German Forestry Association, a Regensburg forester, and a former U. S. Fulbright Visitor to West Germany joined together to note that "air pollution is now the problem that concerns West German foresters most. The results of 200 years of forest management seem to be extinguishable within the next 10 years. . . . Only a few people think about an all-too-possible scenario: central Europe without forests."[36]

In the United States, more than half the sawtimber comes from the harvests of just a few species—notably Douglas fir and ponderosa pine in the West and loblolly, longleaf, shortleaf, and slash pines in the South. Between the mid-sixties and the late seventies, the forest industry increased its annual planting and direct-seeding of commercial species two-and-a-half times. Total U.S. plantings in 1978 were over 800,000 hectares, a substantially greater area than is annually planted for industrial wood in the tropics. Roughly 85 percent of the U.S. softwood timber harvest comes from the South and the Pacific coast area. Yet because Pacific forest industry lands cannot sustain current harvest levels, the U.S. Forest Service projects no increases in softwood supplies there until well into the next century. In contrast, supplies from the South are expected to rise by nearly 50 percent by 2030, and timber companies increasingly are turning to the South's favorable growing conditions.[37]

Recent studies of southeastern forestlands show a substantial slowing of growth over the last decade in the South's two most important species economically: loblolly and slash pine. The reductions are evident throughout a broad area of Alabama, Georgia, and South Carolina. Whether acid rain or other pollutants are responsible is uncertain, yet there is clearly cause for suspicion. Roughly 10 percent of the annual forest growth in the eastern United States occurs in areas of high sulfate deposition—over 40 kilograms per hectare annually. Over 75 percent grows in areas receiving annual sulfate doses of 20–40 kilograms per hectare.[38] Soils in many parts of the Southeast are susceptible to acidification, and acid deposition may reduce soil fertility to the point that tree productivity begins to decline. According to one 1983 study of the economic effects of acid rain, a 5 percent growth slowdown in southern softwoods would translate into an annual loss of timber sufficient to build about one tenth of new U.S. homes each year. Scientists have noted the "urgent" need to test managed forest species for sensitivity to both nitric and sulfuric acids, and that such tests must allow enough time to measure effects that appear only after several years or decades of exposure.[39] Studies have already linked ozone to reduced growth in several pine species.

These findings of pervasive growth slowdowns have greatly heightened concern in the U.S. forest products industry. Until about mid-1984, concern over the possible effects of air pollutants or acid rain had taken a back seat to such visible problems as infestations of spruce budworm, pine beetles, and gypsy moths. Yet the prospect of economic losses from long-term growth reductions has led the industry to step up its research efforts. Acid rain and air pollutants are among the factors being studied, although the industry does not feel enough is known about the problem at this time to warrant costly pollution control measures. Producing paper and other forest products consumes large amounts of energy, and additional pollution controls for power and manufacturing plants would raise production costs. Yet if the industry becomes convinced that acid rain or other pollutants are behind even small dropoffs in forest productivity, support for controls could follow. Dr. Ely Gonick, senior vice-president of International Paper, the nation's largest private forestland holder, points out that paper mills are highly capital-intensive and thus are "captives of their geography. They depend on a very long and continuing supply of reasonable cost wood to survive economically. If acid rain damaged that supply, then the mills could fail and jobs would be lost."[40]

In Canada, damage to vegetation surrounding sulfur-emitting smelters has long been evident, but so far no firm evidence exists of slower growth due to regional air pollution or acid deposition. Yet more than half of Canada's productive forest lies in the eastern part of the country, where precipitation is acidic and soils have little buffering capacity. With 1 out of every 10 Canadian jobs dependent on the forest industry, and with annual forest products valued at more than $20 billion, Canadian officials are understandably concerned about acid deposition's potential to damage their timber supply. According to Dr. Raymond Brouzes of Environment Canada: "A reduction in tree productivity as small as 1 percent or even .25 percent per year would result in a significant reduction in total wood production if compounded over the life-span of a tree. Such a reduction could have serious implications on the fibre supply and economic well-being of the forest-based industries."[41] Dr. F. H. Bormann of Yale University adds, "The danger is that by the time a 15 to 20 percent loss in productivity has been documented degradation will be irreversible."[42]

Canada already faces severe consequences from former neglect of its forests. Poor management practices and inattention to regeneration have left Canada's timberlands in a sorry state. Hoping to ease this trend, the provinces of Ontario and New Brunswick have established tenure agreements with private forestry companies, encouraging them to invest in public forestland and thereby increase timber supplies and future yields. Dr. H. Krause, forest resources professor at the University of New Brunswick, notes that improved management practices in that province are projected to eventually more than double its present yearly average incremental timber growth. Yet he follows with an as-yet-unanswerable query: "Will this increased management input be counteracted, in the future, by continuing acidic deposition?"[43]

Acid rain tends to be associated with the industrial world, but it has now been measured in many developing countries as well. Large portions of Brazil, southern India, Southeast Asia, and eastern China are underlain by the type of soils most susceptible to acidification. Threatening levels of soil acidity have reportedly been measured in some of these areas.[44] Trees are being planted in these and other developing regions to meet not only growing industrial wood demands, but critical needs for fuelwood and charcoal. Yet the ambitious industrialization plans of many of these countries—in which fossil fuels typically figure prominently—raise the possibility of acid deposition eventually countering some of the gains expected from plantation forestry.

One special concern for Third World plantation forestry is the potential acid rain has of inhibiting the functioning of soil microorganisms. These minute creatures appear to play key roles in successfully establishing tree plantations on degraded lands, where much Third World planting is taking place. Nitrogen-fixing bacteria, for example, are behind the hardiness and partial nutrient self-sufficiency of legumes, a family of trees increasingly chosen for fuelwood plantations. These bacteria and other important microorganisms may not function as well under the altered soil conditions brought about by acidification. Devoting large areas to monoculture plantations of fast-growing trees appears necessary to lessen the Third World's growing fuelwood crisis. Yet unless soils are protected from increased acidification, vital wood supplies may diminish.[45]

In addition to a worldwide growth in plantations, attempts to profitably increase short-term wood production have entailed a greater use of intensive harvesting practices that may cause long-term declines in forest productivity. Researchers at the Hubbard Brook experimental forest in the White Mountains of New Hampshire found that losses of calcium, potassium, and nitrogen during the 10 years following an experimental clear-cut of their hardwood forest were, respectively, over 3, 7, and 11 times greater than in an adjacent uncut forest. For calcium and potassium, the losses represented over half the amount stored in the forest ecosystem. In whole-tree harvesting, the branches, leaves, and twigs are removed from the forest along with the trunks. Leaves and twigs are especially rich in nutrients, which, if left in the forest, would return to the soil as the biomass decomposed. Clear-cutting combined with whole-tree harvesting may export two to three times more nutrients from a forest than a clear-cut where only the trunks are removed would. The Hubbard Brook researchers point out that it might take 60–80 years for their experimental hardwood forest, from which no wood was removed following the clear-cut, to return to precutting conditions. Whole-tree harvesting no doubt would postpone recovery even further. Cutting again before full nutrient recovery would over time probably degrade the forest's productivity.[46]

Unfortunately, few studies have examined the effects of acid deposition combined with these intensive forestry practices. Yet taken together, they increase the likelihood of long-term declines in forest productivity. Scientists at the 1982 Stockholm conference on acidification noted that "in areas of intense acidic deposition these (nutrient) losses added to those associated with logging, particularly whole-tree harvesting, may jeopardize the ability to sustain yields."[47] Dr. Gilles Robitaille of Canada's Laurentian Forest Research Centre emphatically echoes this concern: "We strip cut, cut by diameter and clear-cut ....We recover the trunks, branches, foliage, needles—everything. Nothing is left on the ground to break down and improve soil quality. Along comes the acid rain which leaches the remaining nutrients from the soil. What is left to regenerate the forest?"[48]

Beyond the direct economic losses in forestlands intensively managed for marketable timber, the changing ecology of the natural forest system brought about by acid deposition and air pollution may have severe consequences as well. From an ecological point of view, acid deposition and pollutants are relatively new stresses, and knowledge of complex forest systems is too limited to predict how forests ultimately will respond to them. Yet scientists with the Norwegian Interdisciplinary Research Programme on Acid Precipitation conclude after eight years of study that in susceptible areas the issue seems to be "a question of proportion and time required rather than whether any ecological effects appear or not."[49]

No apparent resource constraints will by themselves limit the discharge of sulfur and nitrogen oxides in the foreseeable future.

The world's forests are now the subjects of an ecological experiment of unprecedented scale and untestable outcome. Where pollutants remain at relatively low levels, many forest systems will continue to absorb them without major damage to the soil, microorganisms, or trees. Yet as chronic stress increases, ecological theory predicts a staged decline that in extreme cases could end in complete ecosystem collapse. This has occurred around high-emission sources such as the smelters at Sudbury, Ontario, and Copperhill, Tennessee.[50] The forest decline spread-

ing in central Europe could be the beginning of such a complete collapse on a much broader scale. Even if pollution remains at today's levels, forests and soils continually exposed to this degree of stress may in time lose their resistance. Moreover, long before the ecosystem ceases to function, other resources that depend on a well-functioning forest will be affected. The consequences do not stop at the edge of the woods; they ripple to groundwater, streams, and lakes that receive acids and metals that break out of the forest cycle. Our intimate connections to these forest systems ensures that we will not escape feeling the effects of their demise.

CURBING FUTURE EMISSION LEVELS

Coal is much more abundant than oil and will be the primary polluting fossil fuel in the decades ahead. About 660 billion tons are now technically and economically recoverable, which at today's rates of production would last well over two centuries, compared with roughly four decades for oil. Moreover, some 10 trillion tons of coal—equal to more than 800 times the world's annual use of energy—are known to exist and may ultimately be recovered.[51] Thus, no apparent resource constraints will by themselves limit the discharge of sulfur and nitrogen oxides in the foreseeable future. Emission levels will depend on such factors as the rate of economic growth, energy prices, the competitiveness of alternative energy sources, automobile use, and, of course, pollution control measures—all factors subject to much uncertainty. Yet current trends suggest that atmospheric pollutants and the acidity of precipitation will increase in much of the industrial and developing world.

Sulfur dioxide emissions in North America and the European Economic Community will not greatly increase over their existing high levels, and in some countries they are likely to decline. (See Table 5-4.) In the EEC, less use of fuel oil (with an average sulfur content of 2.5 percent) and greater use of coal (with an average sulfur content of 1.5 percent) will help keep SO_2 levels from rising. More importantly, a majority of EEC member countries are now committed to reducing their sulfur dioxide emissions by 30 percent or more over the next decade. Assuming they take action to fulfill their promises, the levels in Western Europe could substantially decrease. In North America, pollution controls on new power plants in the United States and commitments by Canada to halve sulfur discharges should prevent SO_2 emissions from rising very much. However, without further reductions in the United States—which emits five times as

much sulfur dioxide as Canada—emissions in eastern North America will remain high.

In contrast to these somewhat optimistic trends, SO_2 emissions in the Soviet Union and Eastern Europe—already among the most heavily polluted regions in the world—are projected to rise by a third as a result of increased burning of high-sulfur coal and lignite. By the year 2000, Eastern Europe's emissions are expected to be double those of the United States, even though the region is only one seventh as large. As in the EEC, the discharges could be less than projected if the Soviet Union, East Germany, and Bulgaria fulfill commitments made in 1984 to curb them.[52]

Nitrogen oxides, on the other hand, are expected to rise nearly everywhere. In the European Community, NO_x emissions, which are thought to have increased 40–50 percent since the early seventies, are projected to climb another 5–21 percent before the century is out. (The range reflects different assump-

Table 5-4. Sulfur Dioxide and Nitrogen Oxide Emissions, 1980, With Projections for 2000

Country or Region	Sulfur Dioxide			Nitrogen Oxides		
	1980	2000[1]	Change	1980	2000	Change
	(million metric tons)		(percent)	(million metric tons)		(percent)
United States	24.1	26.6	+10	19.3	24.1	+25
Canada	4.8	4.5	−5	1.8	2.4	+33
EEC	18.6	19.0	+2	9.2	11.1	+21
Soviet Union[2]	25.5	34.6	+36	—	—	—
Eastern Europe[2]	40.7	55.3	+36	—	—	—

[1]Projections do not take into account commitments made by more than a dozen nations in 1984 to reduce sulfur dioxide emissions. If acted upon, these commitments would significantly reduce projected SO_2 emissions from every region except the United States and Eastern Europe.   [2]Estimates are for 1982 and 2002; estimates for nitrogen oxide emissions not available or reliably estimated.

SOURCES: U.S. and Canadian data from Environment Canada, *United States-Canada Memorandum of Intent on Transboundary Air Pollution: Executive Summaries* (Ottawa, Canada: 1983); EEC data from Environmental Resources Limited, *Acid Rain: A Review of the Phenomenon in the EEC and Europe* (London: Graham & Trotman Ltd., 1983), (2.5 percent growth scenario); Soviet Union and East European data from N. H. Highton and M. J. Chadwick, "The Effects of Changing Patterns of Energy Use on Sulfur Emissions and Depositions in Europe," *Ambio*, Vol. 11, No. 6, 1982.

tions about the rate of economic growth.) This expectation is mainly attributed to utilities burning less oil and more coal, since coal combustion generates more nitrogen oxides than an equivalent amount of oil combustion, and to the expected increase in cars traveling EEC highways. In the absence of additional controls in the United States, nitrogen oxide emissions from utilities there have been projected to increase 55 percent. This estimate assumes a higher growth in energy demand than now seems likely, however, so actual NO_x increases will probably be somewhat lower. Canada's biggest increase will come from vehicles, whose emissions are projected to rise by 50 percent to roughly 1.7 million tons, or over 70 percent of total NO_x emissions.

In most areas where acid rain is now a problem, sulfur dioxide is responsible for about 70 percent of the acidity and nitrogen oxide for about 30 percent. (There are notable exceptions, such as areas in the Pacific and Rocky Mountain regions of the United States, where nitrogen oxides contribute a much greater share to precipitation acidity.)[53] But the rapidly rising emissions of NO_x and steady or declining addition of SO_2 suggest that in many areas nitrogen oxides will play an increasingly important role in the creation of acid rain over time. Moreover, since chemical reactions involving NO_x lead to ozone, the levels of ozone in areas conducive to its formation will increase as well. Given ozone's known toxicity to plants and trees, along with evidence that it helps form acid deposition and may make trees more susceptible to acid deposition's effects, reducing nitrogen oxides should clearly be part of any control strategy to protect forests.

Although estimates of future emissions in Third World countries are not readily available, trends suggest that air pollution and acid rain will worsen in many of them. Precipitation acidity is not widely monitored in developing countries, but rain with a pH of 4.5 or below has been measured in cities in China and India. Industrialization plans for many of the most populous Third World countries call for vast increases in coal burning, following essentially the same path taken by today's industrialized countries early in the century. China's annual coal output, for example, increased more than 20 times between 1949 and 1982, and is now up to 666 million tons, almost as much as in the United States. If its plans to increase per capita energy consumption are fulfilled, the nation will be burning some 900 million tons of coal each year by the turn of the century.[54]

Similarly, Brazil's consumption of coal has been rising at an average rate of about 10 percent per year, and steel, cement, and paper companies are switching from oil to coal. India expects to increase coal production to 325 million tons by 1995, roughly 2.6 times greater than 1982 levels. Sulfur dioxide emissions from coal and oil have nearly tripled there since the early sixties and were estimated at 3.2 million tons in 1979—slightly less than current emissions from West Germany. Dr. C.K. Varshney of Jawaharlal Nehru University's School of Environmental Sciences sees problems from acid rain as "very much in the making in the country. . . . The current pace of development is bound to promote acidification of the environment."[55]

Without efforts to brake these rising emissions around the world, destruction caused by acid rain and air pollution two decades from now may dwarf that evident today. Government policies are ignoring the fact that damage to forests, soils, and lakes is an added cost of fossil fuel combustion that is not taken into account in the prices consumers pay. Society is in effect subsidizing fossil-fuel-generated electricity, motor vehicle use, and metals production by allowing free use of the environment to absorb the resulting pollution. Such an "externality," so called because the social costs are external to the private costs, means a portion of the real cost of these activities is hidden. Since costs appear lower than they really are, more of these activities take place than is optimum for society. Where the environment can no longer assimilate combustion's pollution, these external costs are now becoming visible in the form of acidifying lakes and dying forests.

Correcting this inherent market failure requires that those fostering the pollution begin paying for it—either through technological controls, emissions taxes, sales taxes (for example on motor vehicles), or other means. National energy and environmental strategies are not adequately doing this, and they are insufficient to prevent air pollution and acid deposition damage from worsening in the future. Only a handful of countries now require power plants to control sulfur dioxide emissions with effective technologies. The majority still rely on low-sulfur fuels and dispersion through tall smokestacks to control pollution. The former will prove inadequate for the long term, and the latter only transfers a portion of the pollution damage from urban to rural areas.

The United States, West Germany, and the Netherlands are among the nations that have taken some concrete action in recent years. New power plants in these countries are required to install flue gas desulfurization (FGD) equipment, often called "scrubbers," which is the most widely used technology for reducing sulfur dioxide. FGD reduces SO_2 emissions by 80–95 percent and typically adds 10–15 percent to electricity generating costs. Achieving substantial pollution reductions in the near term, however, requires that the practices of existing plants be controlled. West Ger-

many was the first to begin tackling this politically difficult and more expensive task. With heightened concern over spreading damage to the nation's forests, the West German Bundestag passed legislation in July 1983 calling for tight controls on the largest 150 of its 1,500 existing plants—those over 300 megawatts.[56] Although U.S. Congressional committees have had before them some dozen proposals to curb emissions from existing sources, political divisions over the regional distribution of costs and benefits from such measures have so far prevented their passage.

Destruction caused by acid rain and air pollution two decades from now may dwarf that evident today.

Efforts to control nitrogen oxide emissions also have far to go if existing levels are even to be capped, let alone reduced. Nitrogen oxides are harder to control than SO_2 since they result not only from nitrogen contained in the fuel, but also from the oxidation of nitrogen present in the air. Both utilities and industries could halve NO_X emissions with combustion modifications costing roughly 1 percent of electricity generating costs. So far, however, little attention has been given to even these modest controls. More stringent controls would require technologies such as selective catalytic reduction, which treats flue gases for nitrogen oxides as scrubbers do for sulfur dioxides. These systems can reduce NO_X by 90 percent and typically cost 5–8 percent of generating costs, roughly half as much as scrubbers.[57]

Japan stands alone in requiring that power plants substantially reduce nitrogen oxides along with sulfur dioxide, primarily a response to the nation's health-threatening urban smog problems. To meet the required 73 percent NO_x reduction, Japanese power plants usually must go beyond combustion modifications and apply selective catalytic reduction, which has barely been tried elsewhere. Equipment to desulfurize flue gases has been installed in over a thousand Japanese plants of various sizes and types—utilities, industries, and smelters—compared with at most 200 in the United States. Moreover, the Japanese plants use a regenerative system that yields marketable by-products—elemental sulfur, sulfuric acid, or gypsum—rather than the hundreds of thousands of tons of wet sludge produced annually from the "throwaway" desulfurization process used in most U.S. plants. A ready market for sulfur materials initially made this option especially attractive, and with land for waste disposal extremely scarce, the cost of sulfur recycling was factored into electricity costs. Indeed, pollution control accounts for roughly 25 percent of the total cost of coal-generated power, and Japan's electricity costs are among the highest in the world. Yet the nation appears willing to foot this bill for the benefits of improved air quality. Writes Dr. Jumpei Ando of Chuo University, "From high buildings in Tokyo one can now see Mt. Fuji 100 kilometers away."[58]

Some promising technologies now on the horizon will expand options for controlling emissions from both new and existing plants. Besides improvements in flue gas desulfurization, two technologies that control both sulfur and nitrogen oxides during combustion look attractive. Fluidized bed combustion (FBC) involves burning crushed coal on a bed of limestone suspended by an upward injection of air. The limestone reacts with the sulfur dioxide as the coal burns, reducing SO_2 emissions by 90 percent or more. As with scrubbers, the resulting wastes must either be disposed of or made into marketable sulfur pro-

ducts. Because combustion is carried out at a lower temperature, nitrogen oxide emissions are 15–35 percent lower than from a conventional boiler.[59]

FBC is now being tried at some 30–40 plants in the Netherlands, Sweden, the United States, and West Germany. Most facilities using it have capacities of less than 40 megawatts (many are under 5 megawatts), but several in West Germany have capacities of 100 megawatts or more. Sweden's success with the technology at a 15-megawatt plant has led it to consider building a 330-megawatt commercial-scale combustor. Among the pilot plants in the United States is a 20-megawatt plant in Kentucky that, under the direction of the Electric Power Research Institute, is a prototype for a 600-megawatt demonstration unit. Also, a Minnesota utility signed a contract in the summer of 1984 for the first conversion of a conventional coal-burning boiler into a fluidized bed unit. The retrofitted plant is expected to begin operating in 1986, with a generating capacity of 125 megawatts.[60]

Another promising technology—the limestone injection multistage burner (LIMB)—merits support. It combines combustion modifications for NO_x control with injection of limestone into the combustion chamber for control of SO_2. LIMB's main advantage lies in retrofitting: For a capital cost much less than that of scrubbers, LIMB can apparently remove 50–70 percent of both sulfur *and* nitrogen oxides from existing plants. Preliminary analyses for a LIMB retrofit at a 105-megawatt plant in Ohio show capital costs of $50–90 million, compared with $177 million for a scrubber, and operating costs only half that of a scrubber. Though the technology is still being developed, pilot-scale tests make it look promising.[61]

As noted, motor vehicles are the leading source of nitrogen oxide emissions in most industrial countries. They are also a leading source of hydrocarbons, the other ingredient needed to form ozone. Cars manufactured in the United States now have catalytic converters that cut hydrocarbons by 96 percent and nitrogen oxides by 76 percent over previous levels. Other modifications allow substantial gains in fuel efficiency along with pollution reductions, despite the tendency for converters to decrease combustion efficiency. Japan's standards for automobile NO_x emissions are even stricter than those in the United States. Although European countries have made some progress in controlling automobile pollution, the large reductions possible with catalytic converters are not yet being achieved. In June 1984, the European Economic Community's environmental ministers agreed to introduce lead-free gasoline by 1989. Since catalytic converters require lead-free fuel, this move paves the way for stricter auto emission controls. So far, however, EEC members have been unable to agree on the stringency of such controls or the timetable for implementing them. As nations such as West Germany and Switzerland individually take action, others may be induced to follow their lead.[62]

Few would argue that Japan's high pollution control costs have seriously undermined its competitiveness in global markets.

Requiring those fostering air pollution to begin controlling and paying for it will raise the price of energy and products to industries and consumers. But this in turn will encourage more-efficient use of energy and materials. Few would argue that Japan's high pollution control costs have seriously undermined its competitiveness in global markets. With the exception of extremely energy-intensive industries, such as aluminum smelting, most Japanese industries have accommodated the higher energy costs by using energy more efficiently. The nation's per capita energy consumption in 1982 was 2.7 times lower than in the United States and roughly 1.5 times lower than in Denmark, Sweden, the United Kingdom, or West Germany.[63]

Industrial countries that rely on fossil fuel combustion for the near future must begin making it compatible with the preservation of their forests and other natural systems. This will be expensive, but by no means prohibitively so. Even with costly flue gas scrubbers, new coal plants can generate electricity more cheaply today than any other widely available energy source except hydropower. A decade from now, coal burned cleanly will in most cases still be less expensive than nuclear power and other conventional sources. But by then several renewable energy sources may be economically competitive, and the range of energy options will have greatly expanded.[64]

Developing countries are in a position to avoid the pollution problems for which industrial countries are now paying dearly. The renewable energy technologies now emerging alongside the large-scale centralized power grids in the industrial countries can be at the heart of Third World energy strategies just now taking shape. Where coal remains the best option, controlling sulfur and nitrogen oxide emissions is clearly essential and vastly cheaper if done from the start. Moreover, by taking advantage now of the breathing room conservation and increased energy efficiency provide, long-term energy plans can incorporate the new pollution control technologies and broader range of energy options that are fast becoming technically and economically viable.

CAN FORESTS THRIVE IN A COMMONS?

What is now unfolding in the forests of industrial countries is a tragedy of the commons on a grand scale.[65] Less-polluted air would clearly benefit all nations, but most feel that acting to curb their own emissions, without guarantees that other nations will do likewise, will incur greater costs than it yields benefits. The dilemma derives partly from a complicated and imbalanced trade in air pollutants. All but a few countries export at least half the sulfur dioxide they emit. Where it ends up depends largely on wind and weather patterns. At one end of the spectrum are the Scandinavian countries, where sulfur emissions are comparatively low and where 75–90 percent of the sulfur deposited is imported. (See Table 5-5.) At the other extreme is the United Kingdom, the largest emitter in Western Europe, which exports nearly two thirds of its emissions and imports only 20 percent of its depositions.

The data have wide error margins around them, but they do portray the general sulfur pollution patterns in Europe. (Data for Eastern Europe are particularly questionable; emissions given for these countries are probably low.) In some cases countries with modest domestic emissions receive as much sulfur per unit area as the heaviest emitters. Austria, for example, has a greater density of deposition than Great Britain, even though it emits only one tenth as much sulfur. Although much less is known about transfers of nitrogen oxides and ozone, obviously these pollutants cross borders as well.

International cooperation is essential in controlling such a wholesale continental pollutant trade. The possibility that a nation's own control efforts may prove fruitless because of uncontrolled emissions from its neighbors is a major barrier to action. Attempts to achieve multilateral cooperation, though faltering, are being made. An important, though mostly symbolic advance came in 1979 with the signing of the Convention on Long-Range Transboundary Air Pollution, an agreement reached within the forum of the United Nations Economic Commission for Europe (ECE). Unfortunately, the Convention required little concrete action toward reducing emissions from its signatories, although it did pave the way for cooperation in research, monitoring, and information exchange. It strengthened the Cooperative Programme for Monitoring and Evaluation of Long-Range Transmission of Air Pollutants in Europe, which gathers data on the transport and deposition of pollutants. The Convention also was the first time that East European nations entered into an environmental pact with those of the West. Emissions from Eastern Europe are especially high, and large quantities spill over into Austria, Scandinavian nations, and West Germany. Their cooperation is thus essential to reducing pollution levels over the continent as a whole.[66]

Until recently, the United Kingdom and West Germany were strongly allied in discouraging both the ECE of the United Nations and the European Economic Community from initiating strict controls. Yet West Germany's forest damage brought about a dramatic and unexpected reversal of that nation's position. In June 1983, members of the ECE met in Geneva to discuss the transboundary pollution problem. For the first time, West Germany broke ranks by supporting a Scandinavian proposal calling for each ECE member to reduce sulfur dioxide emissions by 30 percent by 1993. Joining West Germany in supporting the proposal (put forth by Finland, Norway, and Sweden) were Austria, Canada, Denmark, the Netherlands, and

Table 5-5. Estimated Sulfur Emissions and Depositions in Europe

Country	Annual Emissions	Average Monthly Depositions[1]	Density of Average Monthly Deposition	Share of Deposition Imported
	(thousand metric tons)		(kilograms/ hectare)	(percent)
Western Europe				
Austria	220	34.1	4.1	85
Belgium	410	16.1	5.3	58
France	1,450	121.2	2.2	48
Greece	170	25.3	1.9	63
Ireland	130	6.5	0.9	72
Italy	1,540	113.2	3.8	30
Luxembourg	20	1.1	4.2	73
Netherlands	240	17.3	4.7	77
Spain	1,050	58.3	1.2	37
Switzerland	60	14.1	3.4	90
Turkey	330	41.6	0.5	58
United Kingdom	2,130	84.7	3.5	20
West Germany	1,750	115.8	4.7	52
Eastern Europe				
Bulgaria	390	34.6	3.1	56
Czechoslovakia	1,690	130.1	10.2	63
East Germany	2,000	77.8	7.4	36
Hungary	860	46.7	5.0	58
Poland	1,250	133.0	4.3	58
Romania	1,000	79.7	3.4	64
Yugoslavia	420	109.3	4.3	49
Northern Europe				
Denmark	230	10.9	2.5	64
Finland	290	29.3	0.9	74
Norway	70	25.5	0.8	92
Sweden	260	47.2	1.0	82

[1]The calculated deposition figures are for winter months and may vary in other seasons. Density figures are given to allow better deposition comparisons since countries vary greatly in size. Obviously, loadings may vary considerably within a given country.

SOURCES: Emissions figures adapted from N.H. Highton and M.J. Chadwick, "The Effects of Changing Patterns of Energy Use on Sulfur Emissions and Depositions in Europe," *Ambio*, Vol. 11, No. 6, 1982; deposition figures and calculations based on data in Environmental Resources Limited, *Acid Rain: A Review of the Phenomenon in the EEC and Europe* (London: Graham & Trotman Ltd., 1983).

Switzerland—all nations with growing concern about acid rain and pollution damage. Dissent from France, the Soviet Union, the United Kingdom, the United States, and the nations of Eastern Europe prevented the proposal from being adopted at the meeting. Instead, the Commission issued a noncommital statement to reduce emissions where feasible. The United States stood alone in refusing to sign even this mild document. Although pressured at home and by neighboring Canada to take steps to combat acid rain damage, the Reagan administration maintains that action is unwarranted until the problem is better understood.[67]

Within the European Economic Community, policies receiving unanimous support from all 10 member countries become binding. The EEC has in fact established Community-wide ambient sulfur dioxide standards with which its members must comply. In early 1984, the EEC's policymaking arm, the European Commission, developed a proposal calling for substantial emission reductions from large existing power plants. The plan requires that by 1995, total annual emissions of sulfur dioxide from these sources be reduced by 60 percent over 1980 levels; nitrogen oxides would have to be cut by 40 percent. Though a worthy effort, the proposal does not yet have the unanimous support needed for it to become Community policy. Greece, Italy, and the United Kingdom have so far balked at setting emission limits at the Community level. Yet a number of British Parliament members are now calling for Britain to support the EEC directive, so its chances of adoption appear to be increasing.[68]

The best prospect for coming to grips with the transboundary nature of long-distance pollutant transport appears to be for nations to pursue bilateral and multilateral agreements among themselves. In late March 1984, nine European countries and Canada formed what quickly became known as the "30 percent club," for their commitments to reduce 1980 levels of sulfur dioxide emissions by at least 30 percent over the next decade. Canada, France, Norway, and West Germany promised reductions of 50 percent. Several other nations—notably including Bulgaria, East Germany, and the Soviet Union—joined the club at a sum-

mer meeting in Munich. As of September 1984, 16 nations were committed to substantial SO$_2$ reductions. (See Table 5-6.) Pressure is mounting on the United States and the United Kingdom, which are the biggest sulfur emitters in North America and Western Europe, to take similar action. Although other threatening pollutants, such as nitrogen oxides and ozone, have taken a back seat to sulfur dioxide, the international community may soon find that formal commitments to control them are essential as well.

National leaders have rarely made great political gains by attacking the problems of the next generation or the

Table 5-6. Commitments to Sulfur Dioxide Reductions, September 1984

Country	Promised Reduction Over 1980 Levels	Year Reduction to be Achieved
	(percent)	
France	50	1990
West Germany	50	1993
Canada	50	1994
Norway	50	1994
Denmark	40	1995
Netherlands	40	1995
Austria	30	1993
Finland	30	1993
Sweden	30	1993
Switzerland	30	1993
Belgium	30	1993
Lichtenstein	30	1994
Luxembourg	30	1993
Soviet Union[1]	30	1993
East Germany[1]	30	1993
Bulgaria[1]	30	1993

[1]Commitment is to reduce sulfur dioxide exports.

SOURCES: The Swedish and Norwegian NGO Secretariats on Acid Rain, "10 Countries Sign Acid Rain Pact," *Acid News*, May 1984; "Munich Conference Lays Groundwork for Sulfur Reduction Accord," *World Environment Report*, July 11, 1984.

country next door. Some nations, typically those most obviously victimized, have begun to respond to the severity of the threat that lies before them. Others, such as the United States, have been unwilling to act without irrefutable scientific proof of acid rain's and air pollution's damaging effects—proof that may require decades of additional research. If in the meantime the consequences become irreversible, a late-course correction strategy will fail—no matter how much better scientists understand the problem.

BEYOND THE FOREST

The emerging threat to the world's forests clearly raises the potential economic and ecological consequences of acid rain and air pollution. Yet decisions to take action need not—indeed should not—rest upon what is happening there alone. Forest destruction is but an addition to a litany of consequences rooted in the combustion of fossil fuels in power plants, factories, and automobiles. As discussed in Chapter 1, possibly the most serious long-term consequence of fossil-fuel combustion is the buildup of carbon dioxide in the atmosphere. And ozone levels in many agricultural regions are now high enough to damage valuable crops. In the United States, ozone is lowering the productivity of corn, wheat, soybeans, and peanuts, with losses valued at $1.9–4.5 billion each year.[69]

Vast areas of fertile farmland now regularly receive rain that is highly acidic. Although acid rain's effects on crops vary, soybeans and corn have shown lower yields when grown under the acidic conditions now typical in the eastern United States. Lakes and streams continue to acidify in northern Europe and eastern North America, killing fish and plant life. Acid rain and gaseous sulfur and nitrogen oxides are known to damage a host of everyday materials including paint, paper, textiles, and building stone. Corrosion of copper and lead plumbing pipes by acidic groundwater threatens to contaminate household tap water. Aluminum and other heavy metals mobilized in acidifying soils and leached into underground drinking water supplies also threaten human health. Like damage to forests and soils, these effects are insidious and thus hard to measure, but the potential economic loss and human suffering they may cause is staggering.[70]

Because acid rain, ozone, and the buildup of carbon dioxide in the atmosphere are problems with a common origin, they can also have common solutions. Yet most existing and proposed strategies address isolated issues, rather than strive for the integrated solutions that are needed. Placing desulfurizing scrubbers on smokestacks, for example, will reduce sulfur dioxide and thereby control acid rain. But this technology will do nothing to help crops suffering from ozone, nothing to ensure that rain two decades from now will not be just as acidic from nitrogen oxides, and nothing to slow the rate at which carbon dioxide is increasing in the atmosphere. Technological controls for specific pollutants must be part of any plan to reduce emissions substantially in the immediate future. But funds are limited, and the time available for reversing these threatening trends grows ever shorter. These problems of common origin must be tackled simultaneously and at their core.

Using energy more efficiently, recycling more paper and metals, and generating more power from alternative energy sources are rarely considered in strategies to reduce air pollution or acid rain. Yet they are among the most effective and least costly ways that exist. Sul-

fur dioxide and nitrogen oxide emissions were lower in 1980 than they
would have been without the impressive
energy efficiency gains made during the
seventies. Although two oil price hikes
helped spur these energy savings, nations can achieve much greater efficiency
—and thus further reduce pollution—in
the coming decades, as documented in
Chapter 7. Installing desulfurizing
scrubbers on plants producing a total of
35,000 megawatts of power would cost
$5–10 billion, for example; cutting sul-
fur dioxide by saving 35,000 megawatts
through adoption of efficiency standards
for common household appliances
would cost less than 1 percent of this.
Moreover, emissions of nitrogen oxides
and carbon dioxide would be reduced at
no extra cost.[71]

**The question is no longer whether
proof of damage is irrefutable, but
whether forests are sufficiently
threatened to warrant action.**

Similarly, recycling common materials
rather than discarding them attacks acid
rain, ozone, and carbon dioxide buildup
in two ways—directly, by reducing pollution at the production factory, and indirectly, by reducing energy demand
and thus pollution emitted at the power
plant. Each ton of copper produced by
Canada's smelters generates an average
of 2.7 tons of sulfur dioxide. Because
one third of Canada's 1980 copper supply came from recycled scrap rather than
sulfur-laden ore, one million fewer tons
of sulfur dioxide entered Canada's atmosphere—equal to 21 percent of the
nation's sulfur dioxide emissions that
year.

In virtually all nations, recycling has
barely scratched the surface of its potential. Worldwide only about one fourth of

the paper and less than one third of the
aluminum used is recycled. In contrast
to copper production, the feedstocks for
these common materials contain little or
no sulfur, but the benefits from recycling
them are nonetheless dramatic: Each ton
of paper made from waste paper rather
than new wood reduces energy use by a
third to a half and air pollutants by as
much as 95 percent. Aluminum produced from recycled cans rather than
from virgin ore cuts emissions of nitrogen oxides by 95 percent and sulfur dioxide by 99 percent.[72]

Generating more power from the
wind, photovoltaic solar cells, and other
renewable energy sources is central to
what has been called a "CO_2 benign"
energy strategy.[73] Added to increased
energy efficiency and recycling, these alternative energy sources round out a
strategy that is not only CO_2 benign but
"acid rain and ozone benign" as well.

In the near term, however, the most
cost-effective gains will come from further squeezing the sponges of energy
efficiency and recycling. Together they
will not only reduce pollution; they also
offer a bridge to the mid-nineties when
several renewable energy sources should
be economically competitive. As noted
throughout this volume, conservation,
recycling, and alternative energy sources
also provide a myriad of other benefits
besides cutting air pollution. Collectively they greatly alter the cost-benefit
calculations that are inherent in decisions about whether and how to protect
forests, lakes, and crops and to prevent
carbon dioxide from warming the
planet.

The biosphere is not infinitely resilient. What is happening in the industrial
world's fields and forests are signs that
fossil fuel combustion has ecological
limits, and that exceeding them exacts a
price. Unless energy and environmental
strategies begin to reflect this, today's
threats are bound to become tomor-

row's catastrophes. Given the rapidity with which the forest destruction has unfolded, the relevant question is no longer whether proof of damage from air pollutants or acid rain is irrefutable, but whether the forests are sufficiently threatened to warrant action. Undoubtedly, West German foresters would answer with a resounding yes. But the real test is whether nations so far spared severe losses will muster the political will to take action to avoid them.

6

Conserving
Biological Diversity

Edward C. Wolf

If Charles Darwin were writing today, his masterwork would probably be known as *The Disappearance of Species*. In 1859, publication of Darwin's *The Origin of Species* sparked an intellectual revolution. A century and a quarter later the planet is losing its living diversity at unprecedented rates. As human populations grow and as societies modernize, land degradation, forest cutting, coastal development, and environmental stresses such as acid rain are accelerating the extinction of plant and animal species. Resources that undoubtedly hold great potential for agriculture and new biotechnologies are being irretrievably lost.

The millions of different plants, animals, and microorganisms on earth today are products of a natural evolution stretching unbroken through 3.5 billion years.[1] Throughout this time, plants and animals have tended to produce more offspring than the environment can sustain, so only those whose inherited characteristics allow them to reproduce successfully will survive. Changes have

accumulated and compounded, species have adapted to environmental change, and the result is a multitude of living forms generally well suited to the conditions they face.

People have long exploited the genetic variability within species to create the food surpluses that make modern urban civilization possible. Human selection of crops and livestock is as old as the cultivation of food grains, which began at least 10,000 years ago. Neolithic farmers coaxed our most important crops and livestock from the wild relatives of those plants and animals millennia ago.[2] Since then, breeders' efforts to assemble desired genetic traits from different crop varieties, or in some special cases between species, gradually enabled the development of the high-yielding wheat, rice, and hybrid corn that sustain modern societies.

Given the vast areas planted to the few major cereal species, the genetic variability within each species is needed to keep agriculture resilient. Modern breeding programs depend on unique genes to provide resistance to new plant diseases. And wild relatives of commercial crops ranging from tomatoes to wheat have provided genetic material worth billions of dollars in higher crop yields. Recent recognition of the past and potential contribution of the genes of wild relatives to major crops has earned them the label "the newest resource."[3]

The contribution of such genes has often been limited by the difficulty of making viable crosses between wild and domesticated species. Today's revolution in the sophistication of biotechnologies and the science of genetics is slowly breaching biological barriers, raising the prospect that useful traits may soon be transferred between species that could never before be crossed by conventional breeders. As it becomes easier to use the wild relatives of cultivated plants, inventories of the distribution and properties of little-noted plants and animals will be needed. Genetic material from all sources will appreciate in value, and the fruits of efforts to bend new species to human uses may mark a turning point as important as the domestication of plants and animals by our Neolithic ancestors.

At another level of diversity, intact ecosystems play a central role in maintaining conditions that favor life on earth. Natural assemblages of species make critical contributions on a local scale, moderating the water flow within watersheds, buffering against damaging floods, cleansing urban air of pollutants and particulates, and sustaining the natural populations of predatory birds and insects that help keep crop pests in check. Natural ecosystems provide these services most efficiently when undisturbed. When key species are eliminated, vital services are disrupted. The cascade of consequences can lead to outbreaks of virulent pests, the demise of commercial species, and costly engineering projects that attempt to replace once-natural processes.[4]

Control functions, it now appears, operate at the global level as well. The cycling and global abundance of elements as common as carbon and as rare as iodine—both essential to human survival—are regulated by certain key ecosystems and regions. Atmospheric scientist James Lovelock, originator of the Gaia Hypothesis that the earth's total community of living organisms modifies conditions to create an optimal environment for life, emphasizes our ignorance of "planetary control systems . . . associations of species which cooperate to perform some essential regulatory functions." According to Lovelock, large-scale disturbance of natural communities in the tropics or the offshore continental shelves may jeopardize the regulation of such critical substances as atmospheric oxygen, with unknown implications for earth's habitability. And not all regions or natural communities contribute equally to these functions; Lovelock cautions that "what we do to our planet may depend greatly on where we do it." Although the impact of our interventions at all these levels cannot be predicted with confidence, humanity's ability to extinguish species clearly rivals the natural forces that have molded the history of life.[5]

ASSESSING EXTINCTIONS

Extinction is forever. This truth was not assailed even when researchers at the University of California at Berkeley announced last June that they had cloned genes from the pelt of an extinct animal known as the quagga, a relative of the horse. Unfortunately for those envisioning the imminent resurrection of passenger pigeons and dodos, researchers only expect the gene fragments to help un-

State of the World—1985

ravel the quagga's relationship to zebras and horses, which will solve an evolutionary riddle but not disclose extinction's secret.[6]

When Charles Darwin speculated on the quagga's kinship in The Origin of Species, herds of this partly striped mammal still roamed the plains of South Africa. Twenty years later, the quagga had been hunted to extinction. It joined a litany of such losses due to hunting and overharvesting that coincided with European exploration. Since then, the pace of species loss has accelerated as populations and human settlements have expanded worldwide. (See Table 6-1.)

Scientists who study the ebb and flow of life generally distinguish two types of extinction. In the first, a plant or animal species is transformed over a number of generations into a physically distinct descendant by natural selection. This in a sense denotes biological "success": The species gradually adapts to its changing environment. The second—terminal extinction—is the outright elimination of a species, an evolutionary dead end. Fos-

sils attest that most of the animals that once roamed the earth have no living descendants; only a few of the myriad branches of the tree of life have endowed our world with its present array of plants and animals.

The earth's history has been repeatedly interrupted by wide-ranging episodes of terminal extinctions that have earned the name "mass extinctions." These occasional contractions of life forms define the boundaries of geologic ages and signify global changes of the past. There have been six such large-scale losses in the last 500 million years; one of the most severe, at the end of the Permian period about 240 million years ago, may have exterminated 95 percent of all living species in the oceans.[7]

Biologists and paleontologists are struggling to provide coherent explanations for these mass extinctions, and the scientific community is far from universal agreement. Current hypotheses build on evidence that some of these events can be correlated with asteroid impacts, one of which coincided with the disap-

Table 6-1. Estimated Acceleration of Mammal Extinctions

Time Period	Extinctions Per Century	Percent of Present Stock of Species Lost[1]	Principal Cause
Pleistocene (3.5 million years)	0.01	—	Natural extinction
Late Pleistocene (100,000 years)	0.08	0.002	Climate change/Neolithic hunters
1600–1980 A.D.	17	0.4	European expansion/ hunting and commerce
1980–2000 A.D.[2]	145	3.5	Habitat disruption

[1]Assumes that present stock of 4,100 mammal species is close to that throughout the recent evolutionary past. [2]Assumes that one fifth of the 145 threatened mammals of the Americas and Australasia listed by the IUCN's Mammal Red Data Book disappear by 2000.
SOURCES: Author's estimates based on data from Dr. Paul Martin, University of Arizona, Tucson, private communication, October 15, 1984, and International Union for the Conservation of Nature and Natural Resources, The IUCN Mammal Red Data Book (Gland, Switzerland: 1982).

pearance of dinosaurs 65 million years ago. David Raup and John Sepkowski of the University of Chicago, analyzing the marine fossil record, point out that widespread extinctions seem to occur roughly every 26 million years. This has prompted speculation that periodic cosmic events, perhaps comet showers associated with an as-yet-undiscovered sister star of the sun, have disrupted life on earth with repeated cataclysms.[8]

Despite the controversy, a few things are known with certainty about mass extinctions. First, none occurred abruptly: Hard-shelled marine species seem to have been lost at these times at a rate of about 1.2 species per 1,000 years. Even the rather sudden loss of the dinosaurs was spread over two million years.[9] Second, life does not bounce back rapidly from mass extinctions. Each was followed by a biological lag of several million years before new species emerged to reestablish the previous level of diversity. And third, humans caused none of the great extinctions of the distant past.

That was true until the late Pleistocene era, which ended 10,000 years ago, when many of the dominant large mammals in North America and Europe disappeared. Although a changing global climate probably played a part, the demise of woolly mammoths and sabertoothed cats has been ascribed to the appearance of Neolithic hunters. Early tribes may have hunted the great creatures using fire drives, inadvertently creating the prairies of the Great Plains in the process.

Ten thousand years is a long time in human terms, a span beyond the duration of governments, beyond even the records of written history. But in the history of life it is an instant, far too short to fill biological gaps adequately. As George Gaylord Simpson notes in *Fossils and the History of Life*, "The late Pleistocene extinctions have not been followed by a rise in originations—not only be-

cause the extinctions were so limited in kind and extent, but also because there clearly has not been enough time since then for the origination of distinctly new species in nature."[10]

Against this backdrop, the current contraction of biological diversity is cause for alarm. And while complete disappearance is most serious, other losses merit attention. Unique races and populations can also be extinguished; such diminishment of genetic variety within a species must be counted a biological loss, for the pool of further evolution is gradually drained.

Diminishment of genetic variety within a species must be counted a biological loss, for the pool of further evolution is gradually drained.

Extinction rates and their consequences would be known with more confidence if scientists had a complete inventory of life on earth. Unfortunately, our lists are far from exhaustive. About 1.5 million living organisms have been scientifically described. Flowering plants, fish, amphibians, reptiles, birds, and mammals total about 290,000, of which plants alone account for 85 percent.[11] Yet from the patterns and distribution of species already investigated, scientists suspect that between 5 million and 10 million species remain undescribed, and estimates as high as 50 million have been made.

This wealth of life is distributed far from equitably among different regions. From forest surveys and samples of study plots, it is clear that the tropics host a richer array of trees, flowering plants, insects, birds, and higher animals than earth's cooler regions. Costa Rica's La Amistad Park, for example, which is smaller than Rhode Island, is home to more bird species than inhabit all of North America. Of the 250,000 named species of flowering plants, more than a third are native to tropical America. The richest of tropical life zones are the rain forests. Covering just 7 percent of the earth's land surface, rain forests may harbor more than 40 percent of all living plants and animals. As might be expected with such a high concentration, many species are restricted to small areas and highly dependent on others for food, pollination, or protection during critical phases of their life cycles.[12]

Researchers have recently turned to the least-known zone of this little-known region—the canopy of tropical forests—and found it to be a far richer province of life than ever imagined. Adapting mountain climbing equipment and techniques to the great rain forest trees, and using biocides that selectively kill canopy insects in a small study plot, scientists working in Peru have uncovered evidence that estimates of tropical species must be multiplied manyfold. Based on the new survey, entomologist Terry Lee Erwin of the Smithsonian Institution believes the number of insect species alone may total close to 50 million.[13]

Far from engendering complacency about disappearing species, the new findings make exinction rates even more critical. The research illustrates that many tropical species are more highly localized, and thereby more vulnerable, than anyone previously believed. Four out of five of the insects Erwin collected are new to science. His results so far reveal that nearly 9 out of 10 tropical insects are restricted to a particular type of forest, and as much as 13 percent exist on only one species of tree.[14]

Since species lists are incomplete, patterns of resource and land use must be used to judge the seriousness of recent pressures on biological diversity. Rates of forest clearing in the tropics, the health of certain key indicator ecosys-

tems, and changing patterns of natural catastrophes provide useful proxies for more precise measures of species loss. The peculiarities of tropical forest biology—the high proportion of endemic species and their complex interactions—have prompted tropical biologists to rely on rates of forest cutting for rough approximations of plant and animal extinctions. Biologist Thomas Lovejoy of the World Wildlife Fund used this approach to estimate species extinctions for *The Global 2000 Report to the President,* showing that 15–20 percent of living species could be pushed to extinction by the year 2000 under the range of deforestation estimates contained in the report. Lovejoy stressed that insects and plants would suffer the most.[15]

The richness of tropical forest species today may be due in part to natural contractions the forest zone has experienced in its evolutionary past. Advancing glaciers and cooler climates during the ice ages are thought to have caused tropical forests to retreat into climatically stable "refuges." With the gradual creation of "islands" of forest in a sea of grassland more tolerant of an ice-age climate, isolated populations of forest species gradually diverged, ultimately becoming fully distinct species. These newly diverse varieties spread as forests recovered in a more benign climate, progressively enriching the set of species of the whole tropical zone.[16]

The existence of these species-rich refuges means that the biological impacts of forest clearing cannot simply be extrapolated from deforestation rates alone. Lovejoy and his colleague Eneas Salati conclude that "the relationship between the percentage of Amazonia deforested and the percentage of Amazonian biota threatened with extinction depends, therefore, on the extent to which deforestation is aimed toward or away from refugia."[17] Unfortunately, these well-endowed zones have not been thoroughly mapped in the Amazon, and their locations in other tropical regions are even less known. Until species-rich refuges have been identified, mapped, and protected, deforestation will continue to be a particularly deadly form of Russian roulette.

Although islands of forest are created when land is cleared for timber or agriculture, the ultimate effect is quite different from previous contractions. First, diversity of species is closely related to the amount of undisturbed habitat available. As a forest is reduced to islands or refuges, many animal species disappear faster than new species arise. Second, as populations are localized into smaller fragmented areas, they become vulnerable both to the effects of inbreeding, which diminishes inherent genetic variation, and to chance fluctuations or disease epidemics that can quickly wipe out small populations.[18] Because patterns of tropical development are haphazard, undisturbed forest remnants today are far smaller than the natural refuges of the past, too small to allow new species to form.

The status of the mangrove forests of the world's coastal areas is a second important indicator of how species are faring—in this case, in adjacent ecosystems both on- and offshore. These partially submerged forests line coasts and rim estuaries in the tropics and subtropics, where they stabilize shorelines and provide shelter and spawning grounds for many economically important fish and shellfish species. Though mangroves are often cut as coastal areas develop, forest losses are difficult to assess since few inventories have been conducted. The mangrove area on tropical coastlines may have been cut by a third already; one estimate puts the annual toll from forest cutting and degradation at 260,-000 hectares. A 1983 survey by the International Union for the Conservation of Nature and Natural Resources (IUCN)

identified 20 plant and 89 animal species known to be at risk of extinction in mangrove forests and pointed out that "in the majority of the countries containing mangrove resources, both the types of plants and animals associated with mangrove forests and the distribution and extent of the mangrove plant communities are poorly known."[19]

A third proxy for estimates of species loss is the pattern and extent of natural catastrophes, which regularly disrupt forestlands and can considerably reduce biological diversity. The "natural" event of recent years that has perhaps had the greatest effect on living diversity was the massive forest fire that blazed for three months in early 1983 in Indonesian Kalimantan on the island of Borneo. Over 3.5 million hectares of forest burned: 800,000 of primary forest, 1.4 million of commercially logged woodland, 750,000 of second-growth forest that sustained shifting cultivators, and 550,000 hectares of peat swamps. This charred area, nearly the size of Taiwan, is a single loss equal to nearly two years of human-caused deforestation throughout Southeast Asia.[20]

Large fires were previously unknown in tropical moist forests; any area that gets five times as much rain as falls on New York City or London should surely be difficult to ignite. But drought caused by the anomalous climatic patterns labeled "El Nino" dried the forest; as trees dropped their leaves in an effort to conserve moisture, a ready tinder accumulated on the forest floor. Shifting cultivators started small burns to clear cropland; lightning probably ignited fires as well. Once small fires spread out of control, brush and damaged trees left standing by selective commercial logging intensified the blaze. The fire in Kalimantan was not a stress to which the region's species had adapted, and the biological losses were severe.[21]

Close examination reveals some im-

portant human causes of this natural catastrophe. The ranks of cultivators in
Kalimantan had recently been increased
by 10,000, resettled as part of Indonesia's massive "transmigration" program meant to reduce the overpopula-
tion of Java and Bali. Both farmers and
loggers directly promoted the fire's
spread. Researchers at the University of
Hamburg suggest that changes in the
turbidity of coastal waters due to soil
erosion in Southeast Asia may have altered regional atmospheric currents,
contributing to the drought. Thus human-caused deforestation on the subcontinent may have inadvertently triggered the "natural" catastrophe in the
forests of the Malaysian archipelago.[22]

**Deforestation on the sub-continent
may have inadvertantly triggered
the "natural" catastrophe of the
Malaysian archipelago.**

The constellation of factors implicated in Kalimantan's conflagration
hold lessons for other tropical regions.
In particular, the Brazilian Amazon also
hosts large-scale resettlement schemes
and timber concessions; a disruption of
the area's hydrological cycle that fostered drought conditions could make a
similar catastrophic fire possible. As discussed in Chapter 1, new research indicates that the forest cutting in Brazil may
already be affecting the region's hydrology; even forest clearing that steers
clear of the species-rich refuges could
compromise the region's biological future by increasing the likelihood of massive "natural" disasters.[23]

Although there are some who question these rates of tropical deforestation
and other ecological change, there is virtually no dissent from biologists concerning the effects of large-scale disrup-

tion of primary forests. Reviewing the
various estimates of forest disruption,
the peculiarities of tropical biology, and
the records of previous extinctions in the
history of life, Daniel Simberloff of
Florida State University puts the prospective loss of tropical species well
within the class of mass extinctions that
have punctuated earth's history half a
dozen times in the last 500 million years.
It may be the first such extinction to
affect so widely the plants, insects, and
invertebrates that sustain higher life. It is
without a doubt the first mass extinction
to which humans will have to adjust.[24]

At the news that widespread extinctions are already occurring, some will
wonder why losses of insects, plants, and
even vertebrates should concern us.
They should remember that the emergence of flowering plants—bearing
abundant edible seeds, roots, tubers,
and fruits—may have laid the foundation
for the emergence of humanity. As biologist Lynn Margulis observes, "the actual steps that led to the origination of
seeds and fruits are not known, but that
evolutionary innovation changed the living world by producing an environment
in which man and other mammals could
survive."[25] As discussed in the next section, the potential uses of higher plants
are far from fully exploited; reversing
the evolutionary tide that cast us ashore
seems unwise indeed.

THE FOUNDATIONS OF
AGRICULTURE

The genetic diversity within the handful
of crop and livestock species that feed
humanity—so-called germplasm resources—holds much of the potential for
improving agricultural performance. At
the same time, great opportunities lie in

broadening the base of species that provide our food and fiber. An agriculture sufficient to feed a world population expected to double in the next 40 years will need and use both kinds of diversity.

Increasing harvests rest on a foundation of genetic diversity that has provided the range of variation for improving crops to date. Throughout most of history, the selection and breeding of superior plants was done by individual farmers working from the limited stocks in their fields, augmented by occasional spontaneous crosses with wild relatives nearby. Cultivated crops, though single species, contained an incredible array of genetic types adapted to local circumstances.

In industrial countries, few farmers can spare the time or land for plant breeding. The selection of high performance crops today is done by government scientists and by private companies who sell specially bred seed to farmers for planting. Farmers have traded their independence from the market for higher performance and larger harvests; as a result, a few successful varieties are planted on millions of acres.

Fifteen years after a devastating epidemic of Southern Corn Leaf Blight cut the U.S. corn harvest by 15 percent and alerted the nation to the genetic vulnerability of its crops, a visitor to the wheat fields of the Dakotas or the corn fields of Iowa can still see row upon row of uniform plants stretching to the horizon. Yet under this uniformity lie forms of diversity not available to most of the world's farmers. The many varieties under study by the private plant breeding industry, the widely available information on pest outbreaks and weather conditions worldwide that constitutes an "early warning system," and a seed industry that can transport varieties quickly to areas that need them all protect American farmers from fatal vulnerability.[26] These safeguards have come at

a substantial price: U.S. farmers now spend over $4 billion each year on seeds, and while the cost per ton of grain harvested has declined in real terms over the past three decades, the cost per harvested acre has doubled. (See Table 6-2.)

In a 1972 report on genetic vulnerability, the National Academy of Sciences listed reserve stocks, land held out of production, crop insurance, and the ability to convert corn and soybean acreage back to wheat suitable for human diets as other important margins of protection against a large-scale crop failure in the United States. Such "invisible diversity" reflects the affluence of Americans in this field but contributes little to the security of most the rest of the world's farmers.[27] Most developing countries have negligible reserve stocks, little or no surplus cropland, no system for insuring crops, and a much larger reliance on cereal grains for food than North America. Many Third World nations must opt for lower yields and less crop uniformity in order to get the extra margin of resistance to disease that planting a wide range of locally adapted varieties affords.

Until recently, international assistance aimed at boosting harvests in the developing world placed more emphasis on increasing yields than on maintaining stable harvests. The semidwarf varieties of wheat and rice developed by the international agricultural research centers two decades ago—varieties that channel more energy into grain production than into plant growth—have increased harvests substantially. But progressive farmers' adoption of modern varieties and increased irrigation has enabled them to harvest two or more genetically uniform crops each year. This has led to serious pest damage and hastened the replacement and loss of many locally adapted varieties of rice that could hold traits useful to plant breeders. During

Table 6-2. Seed Costs in U.S. Agriculture, 1950–83

Year	Seed Purchased[1]	Seed Cost Per Ton of Grain Produced[1]	Seed Cost Per Acre Harvested[1]
	(million dollars)	(dollars)	(dollars)
1950	2,100	15.79	6.25
1955	2,006	14.54	6.02
1960	1,629	9.00	5.13
1965	2,088	11.34	7.15
1970	2,183	11.67	7.55
1971	2,407	10.11	8.02
1972	2,404	10.54	8.31
1973	3,297	13.85	10.43
1974	3,637	17.82	11.30
1975	3,665	14.72	11.11
1976	3,855	14.94	11.68
1977	3,824	14.37	11.31
1978	3,781	13.70	11.46
1979	3,905	12.89	11.48
1980	4,050	15.00	11.88
1981	4,342	13.04	12.30
1982	4,154	12.29	11.87
1983	3,468	16.67	11.84

[1]Calculated in constant 1983 dollars.
SOURCES: Worldwatch Institute estimates based on data from U.S. Department of Agriculture (USDA), Economic Research Service (ERS), *Economic Indicators of the Farm Sector: Income and Balance Sheet Statistics, 1982* (Washington, D.C.: U.S. Government Printing Office, 1983); USDA, *Economic Indicators of the Farm Sector: Production and Efficiency Statistics, 1982* (Washington, D.C.: U.S. Government Printing Office, 1984); USDA, ERS, *World Indices of Agricultural and Food Production, 1950–83* (unpublished printout) (Washington, D.C.: 1984).

the late sixties and the seventies, serious damage to rice harvests due to pests and disease outbreaks in modern varieties

was reported in India, Indonesia, the Philippines, South Korea, South Vietnam, Sri Lanka, and Taiwan.[28]

For the 800 million farmers of the Third World, monocultures remain the exception, not the rule, although among farmers who have adopted modern methods this approach is becoming more common. According to geneticist T.T. Chang, head of the International Rice Germplasm Center in the Philippines, many Asian rice farmers "intentionally plant a mixture of different varieties in the same field to forestall epidemics." Thai farmers plant the modern semidwarf varieties on part of their land during the dry season and sow traditional varieties during the monsoon season. They have thus established a system that allows them to take advantage of the productivity of irrigated modern varieties during dry months and the stability of the traditional varieties in the wet season when pest outbreaks are common. This strategy of hedging against likely environmental or climatic damages amounts to "the most effective long-lasting means of stabilizing yields," according to Chang.[29]

By the early eighties, 10 of the world's 13 international agricultural research centers had begun to focus on germplasm conservation as a vital element of their strategy to boost food supplies. In countries and regions where there are few commercial or national plant breeding efforts, new crop varieties are developed and distributed from the centers. Their efforts to collect and catalogue traditional crops and the wild relatives of such crops in developing countries may be even more important over the long run. Locally adapted varieties, called landraces, offer an unexploited ocean of potentially useful genes for crop breeders, but unless they are collected when high-performing varieties replace them, they quickly disappear. Botanist Garrison Wilkes points out that "the technological bind of improved varieties is that they eliminate the resource on which they are based."[30]

Gene banks in Third World countries are likely to outnumber those in industrial nations by the end of the eighties.

For a decade, collecting and conserving crop germplasm has been coordinated worldwide by one of the 13 international centers, the International Board for Plant Genetic Resources. IBPGR has overseen field collection of crop varieties and the establishment of gene banks that store at low temperatures the seeds and cuttings of most major food and commodity crops. Though the first and largest gene banks were in the United States, Western Europe, Japan, and the Soviet Union, germplasm is now stored in many Third World countries as well. (See Table 6-3.) Gene banks there are likely to outnumber those in industrial nations by the end of the eighties.[31]

One specific benefit these offer the Third World is a measure of insurance against age-old natural and social catastrophes. Stresses like the severe drought in Africa and regional wars in Central America and Southeast Asia can force people to eat the seed that should be saved for planting. Traditional rice varieties lost in Kampuchea during the seventies, for example, were restored from holdings of the International Rice Research Institute in the Philippines.[32]

Although the establishment of germplasm collections is a positive development, it signals that "the centers of genetic variability are moving from natural systems and primitive agriculture to gene banks and breeders' working collections with the liabilities that a concentration of resource (power) implies," points out Garrison Wilkes.[33] One result has been the emergence of political disputes over the control of germplasm. In November 1983, the U.N. Food and Agriculture Organization (FAO) adopted a nonbinding "International Undertaking on Plant Genetic Resources" at its twenty-second biennial conference. The agreement proposed establishing a coordinated network of national, regional, and international centers for base collections of plant germplasm and putting existing gene banks under FAO auspices.[34]

Controversy erupted around the proposal's endorsement of the principle of "free exchange of germplasm." At issue was whether elite breeders' stocks, the product of long and costly commercial breeding efforts, should be exchanged among countries on the same basis as wild species and traditional cultivated varieties that had never undergone deliberate scientific selection for their traits. The United States, Japan, and the

Table 6-3. Number of Samples of Major Crops Held in Gene Banks in Industrial and Developing Countries, 1983

Crop	Industrial Countries[1]	Developing Countries[1]
	samples (countries)	
Wheat	246,700 (7)	87,000 (3)
Rice	50,800 (3)	148,500 (11)
Maize	40,900 (4)	36,450 (4)
Sorghum	42,900 (3)	37,000 (4)
Barley	127,500 (7)	47,500 (4)
Millet	4,300 (3)	34,500 (2)
Potato	20,600 (4)	21,400 (2)
Soybean	14,350 (3)	15,900 (2)

[1]Includes short-, medium-, and long-term storage facilities.
SOURCE: Adapted from D. L. Plucknett et al., "Crop Germplasm Conservation and Developing Countries," *Science*, April 8, 1983.

countries of Western Europe felt the FAO proposal undermined economic interests and contravened laws that made some breeders' stocks proprietary material in their countries. Its advocates, such as Colombia, Cuba, Libya, and Mexico, countered that the breeders in industrial countries currently had free access to the genetic resources of developing countries that they then developed into commercial varieties to be sold back to the Third World at considerable profit.

There are actually few restrictions on the exchange of germplasm, particularly for breeding purposes, and the growing ranks of gene banks in the Third World should allay fears that the West hopes to "corner the market" on crop germplasm. Many countries urgently need to develop plant breeding programs to work with stored material and to adapt to national needs the varieties supplied by the international agricultural research centers. Although private seed companies are seeking markets in some developing countries, it is still ministries of agriculture, not private companies, that distribute improved seed to farmers in most of the Third World.[35]

The debate on gene banks and who controls them tends to obscure the fact that existing collections for major crops are largely complete. Evaluation and use of collected germplasm and an effort to preserve landraces and wild crop relatives where they still exist are the critical needs of germplasm conservation; by casting doubt on the status of the existing system, the FAO proposal may actually slow progress toward these goals.

Though national gene banks and the collections of the international agricultural research centers include vast numbers of varieties already, numbers alone do not guarantee conservation. Seed must be periodically regenerated, and varieties assessed for their agronomic qualities. Seed that is left for too long

before being grown out or that is improperly stored will lose its viability. According to William L. Brown, former Chairman of Pioneer Hi-Bred International, more corn germplasm may be lost from poorly managed gene banks than from fields that collectors have not yet visited.[36]

The idea of setting aside parks for crop relatives and landraces may seem like an impossible luxury in countries where farmland is already at a premium, but this may be the least costly and most advantageous way to ensure the future contribution of presently uncollected genetic resources. Gene banks in effect "freeze" evolution. Allowing crop populations to grow naturally and to adapt to pest attacks, competitor species, and weather and climate fluctuations keeps them dynamic in an evolutionary sense and fosters new gene combinations. Donald Duvick, Pioneer Hi-Bred's director of plant breeding, maintains that "the concept of 'gene parks' where crop species in the broadest sense can co-evolve with their pests seems to be the only way to conserve genetic variability in any truly wide-scale evolutionary sense. Gene parks would not take the place of gene banks; they would be logical (and biological) adjuncts to them."[37]

BEYOND CONVENTIONAL SPECIES

The 30 or so most familiar domesticated plants and animals are by no means the only species with useful traits. Charles Darwin speculated that the plants and animals of unexplored regions could be bred deliberately to reveal "a standard of perfection comparable with that acquired by the plants in countries anciently civilized."[38] As new technologies for breeding and improving species emerge, unconventional livestock and plants are likely to make a growing contribution to the world's food security.

Among the most promising candidates for enhancing animal husbandry are species used by traditional cultures throughout the world. Although countries in the temperate zone know cattle, horses, pigs, and sheep, the familiar breeds of these animals perform poorly in the heat and humidity of the tropics. Animals like the banteng of Indonesia, the mithan of southeast and central Asia, and the yak that is native to high altitudes of the Tibetan plateau offer a hardiness and adaptation to harsh environments that cattle cannot match. They can also breed with cattle, producing exotic hybrids like Indonesia's madura, which can run as fast as a horse, and yakows, which combine the hardiness of yaks with the higher milk production of cattle.[39]

Another step removed from these exotic but already domesticated species are wild animals related to domestics, whose potential contribution to food supplies is virtually unknown. A primitive bovine called the kouprey, which wanders the rugged war-torn border between Thailand and Kampuchea, is even larger than domestic cattle and may be resistant to rinderpest, a devastating livestock disease. Though the kouprey is on the brink of extinction, occasional reports suggest that some may still exist in the wild. Less threatened, though hardly less exotic, the piglike babirusa of Indonesia has an extra stomach sac that may be a rumen, allowing the animal to forage and thrive without the grain and high-quality feed that hogs require. Since they tame easily, babirusas may prove to be a valuable source of animal protein in poor rural areas where grain cannot be spared for feed.[40]

A technological revolution in the livestock industry of the industrial world may make the use, and indirectly the conservation, of these unconventional species far quicker and more widespread than otherwise possible. Artificial insemination and in vitro fertilization can cross parents from different continents. Freezing and transporting embryos and implanting them in surrogate mothers may permit introduction of some species to countries where quarantine regulations bar the entry of adults. Researchers at the University of Florida, for example, hope to import babirusa embryos from Indonesia and implant them in domestic pigs to study the animal's potential for domestication.[41]

Wild species are poorly documented, knowledge of valuable hybrids is spotty, and no one agency coordinates worldwide efforts to improve livestock species or conserve their wild relatives. According to the United Nations Environment Programme (UNEP), "animal genetic resources have been seriously neglected by comparison with plant genetic resources."[42] Attempting to fill this gap, UNEP and FAO recently launched an annual bulletin on animal genetic resources, and the Board on Science and Technology for International Development of the National Research Council in the United States has supported a series of projects on unconventional animals and farming systems. The surface has barely been scratched on this subject of enormous potential benefit to rural families throughout the Third World.

Paralleling researchers' interest in unconventional livestock, plant scientists are investigating staple crops and vegetables that have been planted for millennia but overlooked in recent generations. One such crop is quinoa, which once complemented corn as a staple of the Inca empire in the South American highlands. Recent surveys have found that the plant, still grown by traditional highland communities, has a high protein content and an amino acid balance that compares favorably with milk. Its exceptional drought resistance and productivity on saline and alkaline soils suggest that quinoa may once again become an important crop in marginal areas.[43]

Amaranth, a staple food of the Aztecs, is now being studied in Mexico, Africa, India, Southeast Asia, and the United States. Amaranth seed comes closer than any of the major cereal grains to providing people with a full supply of amino acids, and the leaves are edible as a green vegetable as well. In 1981 the International Board for Plant Genetic Resources surveyed the status of amaranth germplasm and implemented a global plan of collection and preservation, for current holdings in the United States, India, and Nigeria are far from complete.[44]

The oil price increases of the seventies focused attention on the plant kingdom as a potential source of substitutes for fossil fuels and petrochemicals. The search has already begun to pay off. Jojoba, a succulent plant native to the desert of the American Southwest, bears seeds that can be pressed to yield an industrial oil comparable in quality to sperm whale oil. The cost of jojoba oil has declined steadily, and output is expected to reach a million gallons by 1990 in the United States alone. *Vernonia galamensis,* a plant native to east Africa, is a natural source of epoxy acid, a material used in the manufacture of polyvinyl chloride. The U.S. market for epoxy oils is estimated at $100 million, and a U.S. Department of Agriculture plant exploration officer who evaluated this vernonia has suggested it be cultivated in Zimbabwe, where it might become a substantial export crop and an important source of foreign exchange. Though these examples seem inconsequential beside the world's vast flows of lubricating oils and petrochemicals, they represent substitutions that will become common in the years ahead.[45]

A new commercial crop from the world's arid areas is guayule, a wild shrub that produces a rubber virtually indistinguishable from natural rubber. Among the plant's virtues are its ability to thrive in water-short desert areas and its potential role as a second line of defense against the genetic uniformity of the world's crop of rubber trees in Brazil, Indonesia, and Malaysia. Guayule promises a new source of export earnings to countries seeking productive uses of arid lands.[46]

Despite humanity's dependence on a variety of tree species for fuelwood, fodder, building materials, and medicines, the genetic resources of forest species have never been systematically evaluated. Although the wild relatives of some crops like grain sorghum and rye can survive and even thrive on disturbed land, slower-growing trees with intricate ecological relationships often succumb to environmental disturbance, and valuable forms can be lost.

Conservation of tree genetic resources will require the creation of forest preserves. Although many tree seeds can be preserved in gene banks, regenerating seed and evaluating the useful properties of mature trees can take decades. Natural stands that have desirable characteristics such as drought resistance are often highly localized, so populations must be surveyed and useful gene pools preserved. The National Research Council published a systematic review of fuelwood species in the tropics in 1983, but thus far no one has offered to coordinate a worldwide effort to identify and preserve useful tree germplasm. Meanwhile, valuable gene pools disappear as land is cleared, urban areas expand, arid lands are degraded, and forests are disrupted throughout the world.[47]

BIOTECHNOLOGY AND DIVERSITY

Riding a wave of scientific discovery and financial enthusiasm, developers of gene splicing and other biotechnologies have announced a new era in which a diversity of species and genes will supply a host of goods and services. Some applications of biotechnology can capitalize on the variability within life forms; others may intensify the pressures that modern agriculture has brought to bear on wild relatives and traditional varieties of crops, hastening their disappearance. Yet if practitioners see that a commitment to the conservation of living diversity will serve their interests and ensure the future of this nascent industry, earth's myriad species may become more secure.

Some of the researchers in applied biotechnology are well aware that much of the future potential of their work depends on access to the rich genetic diversity in nature. Dr. Winston J. Brill of Agracetus notes: "The accelerated destruction of the gene pool is doubly ironic. It is caused primarily by the clearing of land in the tropical rain forest for farming. Moreover, it is happening at the dawn of an age in which such genetic wealth, until now a relatively inaccessible trust fund, is becoming a currency with high immediate value."[48] Useful as such a perception is, it overlooks the fact that traditional varieties and the wild relatives of cultivated crops, the gene pools most likely to prove immediately useful in biotechnological applications, are threatened more by the spread of modern crop varieties to existing fields than by the clearing of new land.

The unique potential of the biotechnologies stems from the insight that underlying nature's diversity is a unity in the way genetic material encodes and expresses the instructions for growth and development. The genes that make up the chromosomes of wheat and of humans are made of the same building blocks and operate according to similar rules. There is nothing new about manipulating genes; as mentioned earlier, breeders have introduced and eliminated genes from domesticated species for thousands of years. Biotechnologies enable scientists to sidestep sex, to alter heredity more quickly and with more precision than natural breeding permits. In some cases this involves manipulating genetic material itself; in others, scientists work with complete cells to cross the barriers that prevent reproduction between distinct species, changing the context in which genetic material is expressed without rearranging the genes themselves.

Gene splicing techniques may foster the conservation of species by making exotic and endangered species directly valuable.

Gene splicing techniques may foster the conservation of species by making exotic and endangered species directly valuable. The most widespread application of this technology so far has been the insertion of genes for desired substances into bacteria, whose metabolism can be commandeered to produce interferon and other valuable chemicals in large quantity in fermentation tanks. Given the thousands of plant and animal species that produce useful drugs or chemicals, gene splicing may encourage the preservation of useful genetic varieties while reducing the pressure to harvest plants indiscriminately to supply a desired substance.

One technique that can assist the conservation of threatened plants by making it easier to screen them for useful properties is tissue or cell culture. With this method, a single plant cell stripped of its rigid cell wall can be multiplied into a mass of undifferentiated cells called a callus, which is then induced to grow into a mature plant. The technique allows thousands of cells from a single plant to become "parents" of a new generation. While in the single-cell or tissue stage, cultures can be easily screened for traits such as resistance to herbicides and disease toxins. An astonishing feature of tissue culture is that the process releases genetic variation in plants derived from the same parent; cultured plants could in some cases help reconstitute genetic variation in rare or overharvested species.[49]

Tissue culture also offers a way to produce plant compounds whose genetic instructions are too complex to be spliced into bacteria. An endangered flower from Madagascar, the rosy periwinkle, supplies two drugs valuable in treating leukemia and Hodgkin's disease. At the University of British Columbia, cultured cells of the rosy periwinkle are being grown in 100-liter batches, and their anticancer compounds are being isolated. If the technique is a commercial success, it will offer a compelling reason for conserving the species in the wild: The genetic diversity of wild populations is likely to harbor individual plants that produce more effective or more easily extracted forms of the drugs.[50]

Despite tissue culture's advantages in quickly selecting useful plant varieties, some of the most important cultivated plants cannot yet be consistently regenerated in a laboratory. Standard techniques do not exist to regenerate wheat, corn, or soybeans. A more fundamental difficulty with tissue culture is the problem of selecting useful agronomic traits at the single-cell or tissue level. Some of the most important traits of crop performance are characteristic only of whole plants and cannot be identified in

a petri dish. Selecting useful plants still requires that they be grown out, a process that takes land, labor, and time.[51]

While tissue culture can elicit genetic diversity from the cells of a single plant, a technique called protoplast fusion allows the genetically distinct cells of two species to be combined into one. Protoplast fusion merges two plant cells from which the cell walls have been removed. When plants are then regenerated, the result is an interspecies hybrid that could not be produced by conventional breeding. Curious combinations like the "pomato" have been produced, but the complex genetics involved in combining distinct species seldom results in a viable hybrid with useful traits. Protoplast fusion may be more useful for combining genes from related species that do not interbreed successfully; the technique could speed the introduction of useful traits from wild relatives into crops, providing yet another incentive to collect and conserve wild varieties.[52]

The most powerful technique of plant biotechnology is recombinant DNA, or gene splicing. The ability to introduce specific genes into plant cells depends on the identification of useful genes in other species, the cloning of copies in bacteria, the transfer of the new material into cultured plant cells using an infective bacteria or virus, and the regeneration of a transformed adult plant. In principle, genes from almost any source could be transferred into plants this way; in practice, identifying useful traits that will be expressed in their new cellular environment in just the right way is perhaps the most difficult step. As two prominent plant scientists point out, the techniques themselves do not help answer the most basic question: "What genes can we transfer into plants that will improve a crop species?"[53]

Recombinant DNA increases the likelihood that traits like disease resistance or drought tolerance will be transferred from wild species into cultivated crops. As with the other biotechnologies discussed, substantial roadblocks remain. No bacteria or virus has yet been found that can transfer DNA reliably into the most important members of the grass family, which include the world's major cereal grains. Improvements in corn, wheat, and rice will only come from conventional plant breeding for some time to come.[54]

The holy grail of plant biotechnology is the transfer of genes for nitrogen fixation from bacteria to plants so that nonlegumes like corn or wheat can thrive without artificial fertilizer. The process is dauntingly complex. Seventeen separate genes of the bacterium *Klebsiella pneumoniae* encode the instructions for nitrogen fixation; although these genes have been successfully transferred into a variety of yeast, whose cells resemble those of higher plants more than bacteria, the yeast cannot fix nitrogen. The nitrogen fixation carried out by *Rhizobium* bacteria in the root nodules of legumes is even more complicated, and less likely to be successfully integrated into the metabolism of plant cells.[55]

Although it seldom captures headlines, engineering the microorganisms that coexist with plants holds more immediate potential for improving agriculture than splicing the genes of crops themselves. This approach capitalizes on the extensive knowledge of how to manipulate microbial systems and on the fact that microorganisms are far simpler than plants. Some important opportunities lie in improving the nitrogen-fixing ability of rhizobia, transferring the ability to fix nitrogen from rhizobia into bacteria that might be induced to attach themselves to corn roots, and enhancing the ability of some soil microorganisms to isolate soil chemicals that can promote bacterial and fungal diseases. Combining conventional plant breeding with the genetic manipulation of plants'

symbiotic bacteria may be the best way to quickly use the natural genetic diversity of both.[56]

The use of microbes and the direct manipulation of higher organisms are both being applied to animal husbandry as well. Since almost all the methods of applying biotechnology to animals could be used on humans, this raises widely discussed ethical questions. Biotechnologies likely to be applied to animal husbandry range from the design and production of new vaccines to the actual transfer of genes between species, yet the technologies with the greatest implications for biological diversity involve engineering the normal reproductive process.

Building on the accomplishments of artificial insemination, the most common new techniques speed the pace and extend the reach of genetic change in livestock. Embryo transfer can turn prize cows into "superovulators," generating 40 or more calves a year without actually having to give birth. Although this compresses the time in which a herd can be improved with the genetic traits of superior parents, it also hastens the elimination of unidentified, potentially useful genetic traits from a herd. Cryogenic techniques first used 30 years ago to store bull semen for artificial insemination are now being used to freeze viable sperm, unfertilized eggs, and even embryos themselves. A particular genetic constitution can be stored indefinitely, transported worldwide, and used when needed, much as plant germplasm is conserved and used today. The transfer of embryos into surrogate mothers, in some cases mothers of entirely different species, even provides a new way to propagate some endangered species in zoos.[57]

All these techniques are currently expensive and rely on sophisticated technology. Not all animal species are suited to such manipulations; while domestic animals have been bred for thousands of years for their reproductive hardiness, wild species often prove infertile in captivity. Nonetheless, the ability of breeders to produce and transport embryos to order will generate a worldwide business that has been estimated at $1 billion a year by the end of the eighties. The potential market for biotechnology products in the livestock industry—$7.5 billion in 1981—is growing by 15–20 percent each year.[58]

Constraints on fresh water and electricity supplies may slow the development of biotechnology in the Third World.

Most of the research and all the commercial development of biotechnology has taken place in industrial countries, but many developing countries are realizing that the new technologies could help them solve some of the health, energy, and agricultural problems that slow their development. Several institutions have been proposed to speed the application of biotechnology to the needs of poor countries and train scientists from the Third World; the best known is the international biotechnology center of the United Nations Industrial Development Organization (UNIDO). First proposed in 1981, the center was intended to broaden the focus of biotechnology research, which until then only addressed the problems of industrial countries.[59]

India and Italy have been chosen to host two "campuses" of the UNIDO center, and other countries may be able to affiliate their national biotechnology programs with the training and research efforts of the center. Unfortunately, although Italy has provided funds, other prospective donor countries (France,

Japan, the United Kingdom, the United States, and West Germany) have so far been reluctant to support the project, reportedly wary of stimulating competition in a field in which they have a decided technical lead.

On a more modest scale, a network is already in place to encourage the conservation and use of microbiological resources within the Third World. Sponsored by UNESCO, the United Nations Environment Programme, and the International Cell Research Organization, this Microbiological Resource Center (MIRCEN) network was created to "preserve microbial gene pools and make them accessible to developing countries." The 12 MIRCEN centers, from Guatemala to Thailand, produce catalogs and maintain collections of important microbial strains. Brazil, Kenya, Senegal, and the United States host centers with a primary focus on nitrogen-fixing bacteria; others conduct research and training in applied biotechnology. The informal MIRCEN network, already effective in the Third World, provides a foundation for technology transfer that the controversial UNIDO center seems unlikely to replace.[60]

Even if industrial countries can be induced to share their expertise with developing countries, constraints on fresh water and electricity supplies may slow the development of biotechnology in the Third World. The Organisation for Economic Co-operation and Development (OECD) found that the scarcity and high cost of water prompted the closing of two Israeli beet sugar factories. OECD concluded that "the introduction of processes based on biotechnology may depend on other technologies concerned with the production of fresh water."[61] Since most of the laboratory equipment used in the sophisticated work of splicing, transferring, and expressing desired genes also requires electricity, uncertainties in its supply or overtaxed national electrical grids could also compromise the development of national biotechnology programs in many poor countries.[62]

Helping the Third World to overcome the constraints that impede biotechnology may be in the long-run interest of the commercial biotechnology industry of the United States, Europe, and Japan. Many of the likely applications of biotechnology in developing countries—providing fuel substitutes for oil and fuelwood, improving the performance of crops, upgrading the quality of food—can reduce the pressures of overharvesting and environmental degradation that currently threaten the very genetic resources of wild populations that the industry needs to draw on. Few of these wild gene pools, the raw material for future medicines, foods, and fuels, are likely to survive intact where people must struggle to provide basic needs.

Since the first laboratory experiments involving genetic engineering a decade ago, the possible release of genetically engineered organisms into the environment has been the focus of considerable debate, making it difficult to speculate too much on the technology's eventual impact on efforts to conserve biological diversity. In the mid-seventies, the city council of Cambridge, Massachusetts, voiced concern over the possible inadvertent escape of engineered microbes from the laboratories where they were developed; a careful appraisal of the risks involved defused the early fears. A second, more intractable phase of the debate was inaugurated with the first planned release of genetically modified bacteria in 1983.

A project by University of California researchers to field-test engineered bacteria that could retard the formation of frost on potato plants was halted by a federal court order in May 1984. Since the original injunction, two tests by University of California scientists and three

by private companies have been postponed pending an assessment of the environmental impact of releasing genetically engineered organisms. Aside from disputes over whether the National Institutes of Health (which has informally regulated recombinant DNA research since 1974) should conduct the environmental review, and over which other federal agencies have authority to regulate biotechnology in the United States, a more fundamental question has been raised over just how to assess the potential environmental implications of the new technology.

Scientists disagree about the impact of releasing genetically engineered organisms. Advocates point out that plants or microorganisms in which single genes have been altered cannot be compared to introduced pests, such as the fungus that causes Dutch elm disease or the Gypsy moth; they argue that spliced genes are ruled by the same biological laws that govern genes introduced by conventional plant breeding. Opponents emphasize that even slight genetic changes can alter the checks and balances that ordinarily keep natural populations in check.[63]

Researchers are unsure even of what questions to ask in evaluating the environmental impacts of engineered organisms; there are few ways to predict or anticipate the complex ecological effects on which regulators must base their decisions. Biologists who study ecology, physiology, and evolution must work beside geneticists and biochemists to evaluate the risks. Unfortunately, the pace of development of biotechnology is likely to outstrip our understanding of ecological complexities.[64]

These questions about releasing the progeny of genetic engineering serve to remind us that biotechnology is being introduced to a world of biological complexity. Laboratory researchers are just beginning to recognize "the difference between the open field and the fermentation tank," writes Winston Brill of Agracetus. He cautions that to understand the role of microbiology in agriculture, "one must begin to explore the subtle question of the interaction of microorganisms with one another and with the biosphere as a whole."[65] As these connections become better understood, a biotechnology attentive to natural history may provide some of the most powerful tools to reduce the pressures on genetic resources and enhance the value and conservation of wild species.

SETTING CONSERVATION PRIORITIES

"We cannot manage the biosphere in detail," points out George Woodwell, Director of the Ecosystems Center at the Marine Biological Laboratory at Woods Hole. Acknowledging the limits to our understanding of living systems may be the first step toward conserving biological diversity. Although the exact mechanisms of extinction may elude us, we know enough to abandon the idea that mass extinctions in coming years are inevitable. Efforts to slow extinctions—particularly in the tropical forests, where the greatest number are at the highest risk—and to rein in the forces that endanger species will conserve both biological and human opportunities.[66]

The goal of a conservation strategy must be to ensure that evolution continues. Allowing for the play of natural forces by which both wild and domestic species evolve will maintain gene pools and retain genetic traits that may prove valuable in the future. Aside from the biological wisdom of protecting species' capacity to adapt, it makes sense to preserve a constellation of species and genes for human needs we cannot anticipate. The world population, now doubling every 40 years, demands that plant breeders select traits that increase yields and harvests. Yet when human populations are stable or growing only slowly, diversity within a crop—a patchwork of varieties—may better suit human needs. The availability of that diversity will depend on conservation choices made now.

Present knowledge about species losses and ecosystem functions, though incomplete, is sufficient to target conservation efforts and to anticipate likely changes. The emerging science of conservation biology, the branch of biology that deals with the loss of diversity, is rapidly enriching this knowledge. A guiding discipline is "conservation genetics," which studies the potential of species to survive and evolve in parks and managed areas. Scientists can estimate the size of animal populations that will preserve a desired amount of genetic diversity and can foresee biological losses. For example, one study of the population genetics and ecological needs of large animals suggests that even the largest protected areas are unlikely, without intensive management, to sustain viable populations of predators such as the wolf and mountain lion as well as large mammals including elephants, virtually guaranteeing their extinction in the wild within the next century. Recognizing the kinds of species unlikely to survive in the wild, managers can better allocate scarce conservation funds between efforts to slow the demise of some species and to maintain others that seem able to adapt.[67]

Much of the information needed to set conservation priorities can be had rather cheaply. Conservationist Norman Myers suggests that a systematic biological inventory of the remaining tropical forests could be completed by the end of the eighties at a cost of just $5 million a year.

In a project with an annual budget of $40,000, researchers Richard Evans Schultes and Mark J. Plotkin of Harvard University's Botanical Museum are compiling a comprehensive index of the plants used by native peoples of the Amazon and the Atlantic rain forest of eastern Brazil. By highlighting plants with known physiological effects, the work could become an essential reference for biotechnology companies seeking potential new products. This pioneering research provides a model for similar surveys in other regions, a rationale for conserving little-known plants, and a basis for a more secure future for native peoples.[68]

Since Darwin's time, biologists have known that species become rare before they become extinct and that, once rare, species are vulnerable to disappearance. Discounting or ignoring rarity makes us accomplices to extinction. Protesting this shortsightedness, Darwin noted that to accept rarity but express surprise at extinction "is much the same as to admit that sickness in the individual is the forerunner of death—to feel no surprise at sickness, but, when the sick man dies, to wonder and to suspect that he died by some deed of violence."[69]

Inventories of rare and endangered species can thus illuminate pressures and suggest preservation priorities. On a global scale, the most important lists have been compiled by the International Union for the Conservation of Nature and Natural Resources. *Red Data Books* have been published for birds, mammals, amphibians and reptiles, plants, and, most recently, invertebrates. These volumes, which provide samplings of species known to be endangered in different regions rather than exhaustive lists, guide national and private preservation efforts. IUCN currently lists 145 mammals, 437 birds, and 69 amphibians and reptiles from selected groups known to be endangered or threatened in various regions. In addition, the organization provides data on 250 of a suspected 20,000–25,000 threatened plants and on over 400 threatened invertebrates to illustrate the pressures on those groups.[70]

Endangered species (those prone to disappearance over all or most of their natural range) and threatened species (whose populations are declining and considered likely to become endangered) are identified according to broader criteria than ever before. Categories introduced in the IUCN's invertebrate book include "commercially threatened" species whose numbers are depleted by overharvesting, and "threatened communities" or complexes of species that are jeopardized by the same forces and that must be protected as a group. A number of countries over the last decade have taken steps toward listing endangered species, many in response to the Convention on International Trade in Endangered Species of Flora and Fauna. Although this is an important development, few national lists are sufficiently detailed, and fewer countries provide legislative protections as strict as those in Canada, the Soviet Union, or the United States.[71]

Discounting or ignoring rarity makes us accomplices to extinction.

In 1973, the Endangered Species Act mandated listing and extended U.S. Government protection to species considered "endangered." Listing and management have been pursued simultaneously, waxing and waning according to administration priorities since the law was enacted. During the first decade of protection, the U.S. Office of Endangered Species favored the listing and protection of vertebrates over insects, mollusks, and plants. By 1984, nearly 60 percent of the species receiving federal protection as endangered or threatened were vertebrates, while of those being considered for listing, plants and invertebrates outnumbered vertebrates nine to one. (See Table 6-4.) In May 1984, the U.S. Department of Interior broke with the past and identified 876 invertebrates deserving immediate listing or further study.[72]

Future efforts to protect species and to prevent rare ones from slipping toward extinction will depend on a deeper understanding of the biology of rarity and extinction and a sense of how human interactions with the biosphere affect them. One ambitious study, started in 1979 in the Amazon Basin near Manaus, Brazil, hopes to reveal the kinds of changes in biological diversity that can be anticipated as a consequence of development patterns. The Minimum Critical Size of Ecosystems project, sponsored jointly by the World Wildlife Fund-U.S. and the Brazilian National Institute for Amazonian Research, was initiated to investigate how species' numbers would change in patches of primary forest as surrounding land was cleared by ranchers for livestock.

The study was made possible by a Brazilian law requiring that half the land in

Amazonian development projects be left in trees. Scientists arranged with ranchers to set aside the necessary forest in reserves ranging in size from 1 to 10,000 hectares. The remaining primary forest in the area was cut and burned to establish cattle ranches. Burning degrades much of the area and isolates remnant forest patches. Both the outright destruction and the isolation lead to a decline in forest species. The Minimum Critical Size project studies these forest fragments to learn what happens when the habitat of a species shrinks below the size needed to sustain it.[73]

This new brand of ecological research attempts to understand not just an underlying biological system but the way that system is affected by changing land uses. The project will yield results over several decades, for the species changes in the largest forest fragments are expected to occur far more slowly than in the patches of a few hectares. Results should provide a sharper sense of the biological consequences of land clearing in Amazonia, and the relative survival of species in the various forest fragments will confirm conservation priorities in the size and location of protected areas. Yet researchers caution that all the conclusions are ecosystem-dependent: The study will shed light on change in the

Table 6-4. United States: Listing of Endangered or Threatened Species, 1984

Category	Endangered	Threatened	Total	Under Consideration for Listing
	(number of species)			
Vertebrates[1]	152	34	186	363
Invertebrates[2]	28	6	43	401
Insects	7	6	13	475
Plants	63	11	74	2,588

[1]Includes mammals, birds, reptiles, amphibians, and fishes.   [2]Excludes insects.
SOURCES: Michael Bender, U.S. Department of Interior, Fish and Wildlife Service, Office of Endangered Species, private communication, July 30, 1984; Defenders of Wildlife, *Saving Endangered Species: A Report and Plan for Action* (Washington, D.C.: 1984).

forests of Amazonia, but the lessons from Brazil may not apply in Zaire or India.

No effort is likely to contribute as much to the conservation of living diversity as the creation of parks and other protected areas where complete living communities can continue to evolve. Given the pace of land-use change in industrial and developing countries alike, the absolute size of areas set aside now is critically important for the future. A 1982 listing by the United Nations reported just under 400 million hectares protected in national parks and preserves, slightly more than half as much as planted to cereal crops worldwide. During the seventies, the number of park areas tripled. Different ecological zones, however, enjoy vastly different degrees of protection. And the amount of land safeguarded in a particular country says nothing of the ecological significance of the areas preserved.[74]

A little more than a quarter of the world's area in parks is in "biosphere reserves," areas of special ecological importance designated as part of a worldwide network coordinated by UNESCO's Man and the Biosphere program. Although the UNESCO system is far from complete, it is the foundation of a preservation strategy based on the great variety of the world's ecosystems. A logical place to focus efforts to protect the greatest biological diversity in the smallest area is the species-rich "refuges" described earlier in this chapter. The government of Brazil has created over eight million hectares of preserves in Amazonian areas known to be refuges. Though similar pockets of forest area have been identified in tropical Africa, they are not yet the target of conservation efforts.[75]

One grave threat to existing protected areas may be shifts in global climate associated with increased dependence on fossil fuels. Temperature and moisture changes would affect the distribution of tropical vegetation and alter ecosystems; some park areas might become unsuitable for the species they were intended to protect. To these global climatic factors must be added the local effect that disrupting large areas of natural forest has on efforts to keep small forest remnants intact.[76]

Some ecologists argue that existing and prospective parks are insufficient to protect a critical share of the world's tropical forests. Ira Rubinoff, director of the Smithsonian Institution's Tropical Research Institute, has proposed a worldwide system of tropical moist forest preserves to protect 10 percent of remaining tropical forests, which would be about 100 million hectares. He sees this as the minimum area needed to preserve existing forest types and keep forest management options open. Only about 4 percent of Africa's forests, 2 percent of Latin America's, and 6 percent of those of tropical Asia are protected; not all of these are rain forests.[77]

In a somewhat parallel fashion to the redefinition of parks, the concept of gene banks must be broadened. Efforts to identify the genetic resources of natural populations are as critical as better management and use of the germplasm collections in which seeds and plant material are stored. "In situ" gene banks should be established to complement artificial collections. In addition, certain kinds of "invisible" gene banks must be investigated; for example, since seeds of many plants survive in the soil long after their parent plants have been harvested, valuable genetic resources can be lost by uncontrolled soil erosion on agricultural land and cleared forestland.[78]

The success of future efforts to conserve biological diversity rests to a large extent on whether they can be reconciled with development policy. The World Bank took an important step in this direction in 1984 by adopting environmental guidelines for its lending program; the Bank has committed itself to refuse to finance economic development projects that will cause irreversible environmental deterioration, including species extinctions. National development efforts should reappraise the value of their remaining wild areas, which are too often considered blank spaces on the map. Hundreds of thousands of hectares of forests have been cleared by farm families participating in massive transmigration and land settlement programs in Indonesia and Brazil, despite indications that most of this land cannot be continuously cultivated once the forest is cleared. Addressing the underlying causes of pressure on forests—in these cases, population growth that has outrun economic opportunities in other regions —is the only way options for the sustainable uses of forests will be preserved.[79]

Many of the most ambitious efforts to protect biological diversity recognize that conservation goals will be thwarted until the value of biological resources is more widely acknowledged. One sure way to focus international attention on this issue is to require financial support. Ira Rubinoff proposes financing the system of tropical forest reserves with a progressive tax voluntarily assumed by the 43 countries whose per capita income exceeds $1,500. He maintains that this $3-billion annual investment by the industrial countries would be an investment in future world security for rich and poor nations alike.[80]

Nicholas Guppy, writing in Foreign Af-

fairs, argues forcefully that much destruction of tropical forests has resulted from a long-standing underpricing of tropical timber in comparison with other uses of tropical forestland. He advocates pricing this resource closer to its value by creating an Organization of Timber Exporting Countries, made up of the 17 nations that hold 92 percent of the export trade in tropical timbers and 90 percent of remaining tropical forests. Guppy anticipates that a price rise would reduce demand for tropical forest products and, through a system of taxation, generate revenues sufficient to cover the estimated annual costs of $75–219 billion for human settlement, reforestation, and improved management of forest resources—costs far greater than either that of managing forest reserves or current levels of aid to tropical development.[81]

These examples from the tropics hold a lesson that applies anywhere: Biological resources will only be conserved when their prices reflect their intrinsic value. The growing demand for genetic diversity in agriculture and the emerging applications of biotechnologies suggest that elusive values will come into sharper economic focus in the years ahead. Evolution has progressed unmanaged for 3.5 billion years, but its future path is certain to be shaped by human forces. In the words of Sir Otto Frankel, "we have acquired evolutionary responsibility."[82] It would be a tragedy if our failure to exercise this responsibility left the next Darwin with nothing to write about.

7

Increasing
Energy Efficiency

William U. Chandler

Ancient prophets tried to predict the future with geomancy, a method of divination by drawing dots at random on paper. Energy forecasts, notoriously inaccurate, have been likened to this approach. For all their flaws, however, studies of energy futures continue to command attention. They help define the "state of the world" by exploring where current trends will lead. They influence visions of the energy future, affect research and development expenditures, inhibit or encourage investment in energy supply systems, and thus become battlegrounds for the future itself.[1]

The trends that energy forecasters now draw on paper can affect the entire planet, from Latin American debt to global climate. The higher the predicted demand for energy, the higher the cost of building systems to meet it. The greater the predicted demand for coal,

An expanded version of this chapter appeared as Worldwatch Paper 63, *Energy Productivity: Key to Environmental Protection and Economic Progress*.

the greater the urgency of averting forest destruction by acid rain and climatic change from carbon dioxide buildup.[2] The wider the error in projected demand, the greater the waste of scarce resources and the worse the failure to provide for human needs.

The energy events of the seventies caused great upheavals in world energy markets—caused, in effect, a conservation revolution. Like the Green Revolution in agriculture, conservation allowed a brief respite from shortages. It has produced an oil glut, price declines, and time to adjust. But the world of the mid-eighties has relaxed, as it did after the Green Revolution, failing perhaps to make permanent the gains won. A sanguine outlook pervades the energy community as forecasters again draw curves of energy growth bending toward the tops of their graphs. Some suggest a tripling of demand by 2025.[3] If these visions become reality, the world will pay an enormous economic and environmental price.

THE BURDEN OF ENERGY DEMAND

Not since the early seventies have analysts so complacently projected a high energy demand future. Alan Manne of Stanford University attributes this, especially the similarity of most official energy demand projections, to "the herd instinct that operates within the community of energy analysts."[4] Nevertheless, the consensus is that worldwide commercial energy demand will increase from about 300 exajoules (EJ) in 1983 to 485 EJ by the year 2000. (Commercial energy excludes dung and firewood, which total approximately 50 EJ. An exajoule is the equivalent of 163 million barrels of oil, or almost 1 quadrillion BTU.) The physical magnitude of this scenario numbs the mind. If this comes to pass, the oil output of two new Saudi Arabias will be needed. In addition, the coal production of the world will almost double, and three times as many rivers must be impounded behind hydroelectric dams. Widely cited projections conclude that by the year 2025 the world will need four-and-a-half times the hydropower and three-and-a-half times the coal used today, along with a total of 365 large nuclear power plants. Moreover, they typically forecast a 125 percent increase in energy demand by then.[5]

Among the consequences of using so much energy would be greater risk of acid rain, carbon dioxide-induced climate change, species extinction, water degradation, human dislocation, and capital shortages and debt—connections discussed at length in Chapters 1, 5, and 6. Tripling coal use, for example, could triple total sulfur dioxide emissions and in 40 years cause serious acid rain problems in areas all over the globe. And the radical development of hydroelectric power would seriously affect freshwater environments: Fish and mollusk species would be eradicated, fertile bottomlands destroyed, forests inundated, and water supplies warmed, depleted of oxygen, and loaded with silt.[6]

The economic prospect of a high energy demand future is similarily unappealing. Much Third World debt has been incurred to finance energy imports. Foreign payments for oil consume the largest share of total export earnings for many countries, including half those of Japan and Brazil. Expensive hydroelectric and nuclear energy systems have added to this reservoir of debt. Moreover, meeting world energy demand is expected to consume over 7 percent of all capital investment for the rest of this decade.[7]

Just using the most efficient lights in the United States would save a third of U.S. coal-fired electric energy.

This picture of the future is as alterable as it is unattractive. Energy demand projections are a function of modelers' expectations about prices, environmental regulations, and the ability of the world to respond to energy conservation's potential. They represent these analysts' conceptions of how the world works, not necessarily of how it could work. All serious projections are made with models that expose the assumptions that determine their results. One role of models, in fact, is to make transparent the energy supply, demand, and policy consequences that nations face.

Most models of worldwide energy demand are, by necessity, macroeconomic. That is, they concentrate on broad trends in population, economic output, energy prices, and the interrelationships among these factors. The high energy demand future that they describe can be contrasted with the high conservation potential consistently demonstrated in economic-engineering models and analyses, such as those that show the specific possibilities of efficiency in steel-making or automobiles. The world has barely cut into the conservation potential. Industry, transportation, and housing remain inefficient. Conservation possibilities are so great that economic growth could resume without large increases in total energy use. Simply by slowly adopting existing measures, the world could cut the projected energy demand growth rate of 2 percent per year almost in half.

The global conservation potential can be illustrated in energy portraits of a small number of nations. Some 15 coun-

tries, containing about 65 percent of the world's population, are responsible for about 80 percent of all commercial energy use. (See Table 7-1.) Among these are developing countries such as Brazil, China, and India—nations that have a legitimate claim to greater total energy use. Industrial countries, on the other hand, can substantially raise industrial output, passenger and freight transportation, and household services without greatly increasing energy demand. A single decision in either the United States—to raise automobile fuel economy to 40 miles per gallon—or the Soviet Union—to produce steel as efficiently as Japan does—would save as much energy as Brazil now consumes. Just using the

Table 7-1. Energy Consumption in Selected Countries, 1982

Country	Population	Commercial Energy Consumption[1]	Per Capita Energy Consumption	Energy Imports as Share of Exports[2]
	(million)	(exajoules[3])	(gigajoules[3])	(percent)
Argentina	28	1.7	61	11
Brazil	127	4.0	32	52
Canada	25	9.7	395	11
China	1,008	17.9	17	n.a.
France	54	8.5	156	33
East Germany	17	3.8	231	n.a.
India	717	4.9	7	81
Italy	56	6.2	110	41
Japan	118	15.8	134	48
Mexico	73	4.2	58	−76
Poland	36	5.0	138	20
Soviet Union	270	55.0	204	−77
United Kingdom	56	7.7	152	14
United States	232	75.1	324	36
West Germany	62	11.5	187	23
Total	2,879	232.0	80	—
World Total	4,585	300.0	65	

[1]Commercial energy consumption figures are Worldwatch extrapolations from 1981 data. [2]A negative figure indicates the percent of exports earned from oil sales. [3]An exajoule is one billion billion joules; a gigajoule is one billion joules, which approximately equals 1 million BTUs.
SOURCE: World Bank, *World Development Report 1984* (New York: Oxford University Press, 1984.)

most efficient lights in the United States would save a third of U.S. coal-fired electric energy.[8] Effecting such savings will require great political skill and dexterity. But conservation's benefits—savings in capital, foreign exchange, environment, and health—will put nations that realize its potential at an advantage. Conversely, the pressures of shortages of capital, foreign exchange, and environmental amenities are likely to force people everywhere to conserve energy.

INDUSTRIAL EFFICIENCY GAINS

Industry has provided the largest efficiency gains of any energy-using sector since World War II. A combination of technological improvements and shifts from less-efficient coal to natural gas and oil provided industrial countries with an annual rate of conservation improvements of over 1 percent even as energy prices declined. This rate tripled in Western nations after the energy crisis of 1979. Despite the gains, however, an enormous potential for cutting energy costs still remains in existing plants, and builders of new production facilities can choose equipment and processes that are considerably more efficient than those already in use.

Industrial processes consume more of the world's commercial energy than either transportation or housing. Only in Western Europe does the category of residential and commercial buildings sometimes edge out industry as the most energy-intensive sector. In some countries, particularly the centrally planned economies of the Soviet Union and Eastern Europe, the share allocated to industry approaches two thirds of all energy consumed.[9] Production of basic materi-

als—especially iron and steel, aluminum, paper, chemicals, and concrete—consumes the most. Eighty percent of U.S. industrial energy, for example, is used in the manufacture of these goods. In contrast, agriculture, which is included under the industrial heading, accounts for only 6 percent of sectoral demand.[10]

Japan provides a model of industrial energy efficiency, having made major gains since the early seventies. The energy intensities of chemical and steel production have dropped by 38 and 16 percent, respectively, since 1973, and energy use per unit of output has fallen in every major industry since 1975. The Japanese spent between $25 million and $125 million per year throughout the seventies on energy efficiency in steel production alone. These investments typically paid for themselves in just two years.[11]

The French industrial sector also ranks among the most energy-efficient, and, like Japan, made large improvements after 1973. Energy intensity in textiles, building materials, rubber and plastics, and mechanical construction fell by more than 30 percent, an annual rate of improvement of more than 3.5 percent. Energy efficiency in paper and steel production increased at more than 2.5 percent per year over the same period.[12]

In the United States, total industrial energy use fell by 6 percent between 1972 and 1981 while output in paper, aluminum, steel, and cement increased by 12.8 percent. Thus, the energy intensity of the production of these basic materials fell by 17 percent. As elsewhere, the largest stimulus was higher energy prices, and the major steps taken to cut energy use were "housekeeping" in nature, not requiring substantial capital investments. Other industrial nations that have cut industrial energy intensity include Italy, where energy use in the manufacturing sector declined by 37 percent per unit of output between 1973 and 1981 (5.8 percent per year). West Germany has cut industrial energy intensity at a rate of 2.9 percent per year since 1950, thus making gains even while energy prices declined.[13] During this time, U.S. industry also made gains despite declining energy prices, though they were smaller than after the energy price increases of the seventies.

The iron and steel industry exemplifies the global progress made and the potential remaining. Steel-making is both an energy-intensive and a massive enterprise, with annual production totaling about 700 million metric tons. The process consumes 15 percent of all energy used in Japan and the Soviet Union, and over 9 percent of all energy used in Brazil. Altogether, steel manufacturing absorbs about 6 percent of world commercial energy use.[14]

Eighty-six percent of the world's steel is made in 15 countries, with nearly two thirds manufactured in China, Japan, the Soviet Union, the United States, and West Germany. The least efficient major manufacturers are China and the Soviet Union, with China, in fact, using over twice as much energy per ton of steel produced as the most efficient large producers. (See Table 7-2.)

Italy and Spain rank highest in energy efficiency in steel manufacturing because they are major recyclers. They produce steel using the electric arc, or "recycling," furnace, which uses virtually 100 percent scrap. Recycling enables producers to save up to two thirds of the energy used to produce steel from ore. These two nations partly owe their high rate of recycling, however, to steel-scrap imports from the United States, West Germany, and elsewhere. The world steel recycling rate, despite an abundance of scrap and the advantages of its use, averages only 25 percent, a rate that could be doubled or perhaps tripled.[15]

Steel-making can be made more ener-

Table 7-2. Energy Use in Steel Manufacturing in Major Producing Countries, Ranked by Efficiency, 1980

Country[1]	Production[2]	Energy Used Per Ton[3]
	(million metric tons)	(gigajoules[4])
Italy	25	17.6
Spain	12	18.4
Japan	107	18.8
	43	21.7
Belgium	13	22.7
Poland	18	23.0
United Kingdom	17	23.4
Brazil	14	23.9
United States	115	23.9
France	23	23.9
	15	24.7
Soviet Union	150	31.0
Australia	8	36.1
China	35	38.1
India	10	41.0
World	700	26.0
Best Technology		
Virgin Ore		18.8
Recycled Scrap		10.0

[1]These 15 countries account for 84 percent of world steel production. [2]Steel production figures represent averages for years 1978 through 1981. [3]Energy totals are for crude steel production, including ironmaking. [4]A gigajoule equals one billion joules, approximately 1 million BTUs.
SOURCES: Andrea N. Ketoff, "Italian End-Use Energy Structure," and Hugh Saddler, "Energy Demand and Supply in Australia," presented at Global Workshop on End-Use Energy Strategies; other countries from U.N. Economic Commission for Europe and World Bank.

gy-efficient both by improving existing facilities and by switching to more-efficient furnaces. An assessment of investments available to the U.S. steel industry suggests the lucrative potential of conservation the world over. Upgrading conventional furnaces yields high average rates of return: 25 percent per year for continuous casting, 31 percent for waste-heat recovery, and 43 percent for more-efficient electric motors. Switching to the electric arc furnace can yield a 57 percent rate of return. In one study of U.S. industry, Marc Ross of the University of Michigan estimated that investments such as these could cut the energy required per ton of steel by a third by the year 2000.[16]

The Soviets recycle little steel and rely heavily on the inefficient open hearth furnace. This technology was used to make some 87 percent of U.S. steel as recently as 1960; having been replaced by the basic oxygen and the electric arc furnaces, it now is used for only about 8 percent of output. Although it has also almost disappeared from Western Europe, the open hearth furnace accounts for 55–60 percent of production in Eastern Europe and the Soviet Union, where the electric arc furnace provides less than 13 percent of the steel.[17]

China and India also still rely heavily on the open hearth furnace and take little advantage of heat recovery opportunities. Developing countries overall could save at least 10 percent of the energy they use in existing steel facilities by spending only $2–4 billion, according to a World Bank study. This investment would pay for itself in energy savings in just one year.[18]

Though installing new steel-making plants provides an opportunity for improving efficiency, it is an uncertain one. The rate of improvement will depend on the rate of demand for steel—a factor difficult to predict not only because of the uncertainty in the global economy but because the industrial market economies presently have about 50 percent excess capacity. Much of the growth in demand, however, is expected in developing countries, and it would be surprising if they did not build their own production facilities. Such plants would provide

steel made with cheaper labor, more-efficient capital, and lower energy costs, freeing them from foreign-exchange burdens.

The great potential for conservation in the steel industry may, unfortunately, be long delayed. The United Nations Economic Commission for Europe recently forecast that the world's largest steelmaker, the Soviet Union, would fail to reduce the energy intensity of its production below 26 gigajoules per ton before the end of the century. This would only match the current world average and would still be 44 percent higher than Japan's rate today.[19]

Energy conservation in the steel industry clearly depends on energy price. To the extent that market pricing of energy has conveyed the message that energy is precious and expensive, market-oriented countries have conserved. Theoretically, centrally controlled countries could at a stroke mandate the improvement of energy efficiency to any desired level. Studies of these economies, however, show that economic systems never operate so simply, and that complex quota and allocation systems often defeat the best of intentions.[20] In other countries faced with higher energy prices, state-owned corporations have usually performed better, as exemplified by Nippon Steel Corporation and Siderbras of Brazil. And competition has created additional pressure to save not only energy but labor and materials as well. Privately owned minimills using the electric arc furnace constitute a dynamic new force for conservation. Major changes like these are difficult factors to anticipate and thus include in models of future production.[21]

The macroeconomic models in vogue today implicitly assume that conservation will not work well. Most are based on the belief that the United States, for example, will not reach the current Japanese level of efficiency in steel for 35 years. They assume that the Soviet Union, China, and India will not match today's performance by the Japanese until after the year 2050. Yet the modelers also assume that half the world economic output in the year 2000 will be generated by new facilities. Soviet steel-making capacity, for example, is projected to double. And current plans in Brazil call for 50 percent more steel-making capacity by the year 1990.[22] Since growth implies new industrial equipment, there is no good reason why the facilities cannot be at least as efficient as the Japanese steel industry is today.

Indeed, even the Japanese steel industry could economically be 20 percent more efficient. Only a quarter of its steel is formed in electric arc furnaces. Most industry experts expect the minimill to capture a much larger share of the world steel market. Furthermore, if two major constraints on the minimill—the lack of cost-effective technology for rolling thin metal sheets and the need to remove impurities from recycled scrap—are overcome by new technology, minimills may soon produce any type of steel desired. If this happens, a real revolution may take place in steel production. Today's dominant steel-makers, already suffering from high energy and labor costs and low productivity, could find themselves far less competitive.[23]

The prospect for energy efficiency in steel-making, according to some observers, is dimmed by the current economic climate. Staggering from a recession and bad management, the industry cannot afford to invest in conservation, its managers claim, much less in totally new capacity. This perspective overlooks several basic facts, however. First, when new capacity is needed, conservation investments save capital. Steel mills built around the electric arc furnace, for example, cost only $350–550 per annual ton of steel capacity, compared with $1,500–1,700 for conventional mills

using basic oxygen furnaces. Even if the minimill plant cannot obtain scrap and requires a special iron ore reduction facility, the capital cost per annual ton of production totals only $500–900. Adding labor and energy savings to these capital cost reductions gives an overall cost advantage of the minimill in excess of $100 per ton of steel produced.[24]

The macroeconomic models in vogue today implicitly assume that conservation will not work well.

To assume the world steel industry will forgo the energy-saving minimill in new steel production is to assume that its captains are less than skillful. In countries as technically sophisticated as Brazil, the expertise and technology for achieving the highest levels of efficiency in steel-making exist locally, as they do for other energy-consuming industries.[25] Furthermore, new capacity can outperform the old and capture its markets. This mechanism is already at work, as evidenced by the success of the minimill. To counter this competition, even the major U.S. steel-makers are investing in energy- and cost-saving measures.

Aluminum production is another energy-intensive process, requiring 1 percent of the world's commercial energy. The main draw is for electricity to smelt aluminum from alumina. The efficiency of this technique varies widely around the world. Energy-poor countries such as France are the most efficient, while those with cheap electricity, especially hydroelectric power, use up to half again as much per unit. (See Table 7-3.) The world average is in the range of 16,500 kilowatt-hours per ton. All nations could reduce the rate to 13,000 kilowatt-hours per ton if they applied the best available and economically practicable technology. Recycling, moreover, can cut energy requirements by 90 percent. The world aluminum recycling rate is only 28 percent and could be doubled or tripled.[26]

An entirely new, non-electric process of producing aluminum—by coking

Table 7-3. Electricity Use in Aluminum Smelting in Major Producing Countries, Ranked by Efficiency, 1981

Country	Share of World Production[1]	Electricity Used Per Ton
	(thousand tons)	(kilowatt-hours)
Italy	300	13,300
Netherlands	300	13,300
France	450	13,500
Brazil	300	14,000
West Germany	800	14,500
Japan	700	14,900
United States	4,300	15,400
Australia	400	16,100
Norway	700	18,000
Soviet Union	2,000	18,000
Canada	1,200	20,000
World	15,900	16,500
Best Technology		
Virgin Ore		13,000
Recycled Scrap		1,600[2]

[1]Average primary production for years 1980–82.
[2]Electric energy-equivalent.
SOURCES: Worldwatch Institute, derived from Aluminum Association, *Aluminum Statistical Review for 1983* (Washington, D.C.: 1984); David Wilson, *The Demand for Energy in the Soviet Union;* S. Y. Shen, *Energy and Materials Flow in the Production of Primary Aluminum;* U.N. Economic Commission for Europe; Jose Goldemberg et al., "Brazil: End-Use Strategy," and Rolf Bauerschmidt, "End-Use Energy Strategy for Federal Republic of Germany," presented at Global Workshop on End-Use Energy Strategies. World average from U.N. Environment Programme, "Energy and Resource Conservation in the Aluminum Industry," *Industry and Environment,* August/September 1983.

bauxite in a blast furnace—has been developed by the Mitsui Alumina Corporation of Japan. Announced in 1981, the process has been patented in Japan, where a commercial-scale plant is under construction now, and patents are pending in nine other industrial countries.[27] This technology could not only cut energy costs, it could completely change the current trend toward moving aluminum production to hydroelectric-rich countries in the developing world.

The world now produces about 16 million tons of aluminum, requiring the equivalent of 14 percent of world baseload hydroelectric generating capacity. If demand for aluminum doubles by the year 2000, as analysts from the World Bank and the Organisation for Economic Co-operation and Development (OECD) project, electrical demand for production would increase 50 percent, even if energy intensity is reduced to today's most efficient level of smelting ore. A rate of improvement of 1.6 percent per year in aluminum production energy efficiency is needed to attain this best-technology level by the end of the century. Most analysts, however, assume only one third this rate of improvement, which is what the world has averaged since 1955. The change realized will depend strongly on electric energy prices and demand for aluminum. As demand increases, more efficiency improvements will be made. On the other hand, electric energy subsidies will reduce conservation.[28]

Assessing efficiencies in the pulp and paper, chemicals, and cement industries is more complex because they encompass greater diversity in product and process. Many energy-saving opportunities are common among them, however. Two techniques typify large, across-the-board savings opportunities: upgrading electric motors and improving heat recovery, including insulation and steam generation using waste heat.[29]

Electric industrial motors consume over 80 percent of all electric energy used in U.S. industry, and a remarkable 40 percent of all electricity used in Brazil. Howard Geller of the American Council for an Energy-Efficient Economy has demonstrated the value of improving the ubiquitous motor. His analysis suggests that investing in more-efficient motors and motor speed controls in Brazil would save 10,000 megawatts by the year 2000, or over 17 percent of projected new demand for generating capacity.[30]

Motors can be made more efficient in two ways. First, using higher quality steel along with better design reduces energy losses due to heating and magnetization of the core. More-efficient motors cost only 25 percent more than the average new motor, an investment that in new applications yields a "profit" of between 40 and 200 percent per year, depending on usage rates and electric costs. Most motors are rebuilt rather than replaced, however, because new, highly efficient motors cost four times more than remanufactured units. Despite this differential, in Brazil the energy savings obtainable by replacing motors in need of rebuilding with new ones would provide a rate of return on the extra investment of 10–50 percent per year. Motors can also be improved by adding variable frequency drives to match the speed of heavy industrial motors with the desired power output. Research sponsored by the Electric Power Research Institute estimated that the use of these devices in the United States could save over 7 percent of all electricity used.[31]

Papermaking involves considerable pumping of liquids, for which electric motors are largely used. In the United States, replacing electric motors with more-efficient ones would typically provide a 47 percent return on investment. Changing to new pulping and lime regeneration equipment would provide 20–40 percent returns.[32] Some of the equipment used in papermaking in the United States is 50 years old but remains in service because of rapidly growing demand for paper. If demand growth for paper slows, this inefficient equipment could be retired.

The products of the paper industry are becoming "so commonplace, abundant, and cheap that they are almost invisible to consumers."[33] The industry, however, is far from "invisible" in energy use. In the United States, where one third of the world's paper is made, the industry requires a tenth of all industrial energy and ranks just behind chemicals, steel, and oil refining in energy use.

Paper recycling, fortunately, saves about one third of the energy used to make paper from virgin fibers, counting the wood waste used in American paper mills. The United States, however, recycles only 25 percent of all paper consumed, compared with 50 percent in Japan and the Netherlands. Energy requirements for U.S. paper production could be cut by at least 15 percent by recycling as extensively as do the Japanese and Dutch. Since the United States uses over half a percent of the world's commercial energy making pulp and paper, the absolute savings would be substantial.[34]

Chemical processing is the world's fastest-growing industry and it already is the largest industrial energy user in the United States. U.S. chemical output grew 50 percent between 1972 and 1981, but at the same time energy efficiency increased 24 percent. Chemical production in West Germany grew 840 percent between World War II and 1982, while energy use by this sector grew only 300 percent. Energy intensity, moreover, has declined rapidly since 1979. Just as in the paper industry, pumping of liquids and heating with steam are required. Investments by the chemicals industry in electric pumps, heat recovery devices, and cogeneration offer rates of return of 43, 15, and 18 percent per year, respectively.[35]

The production of plastics and synthetic materials dominates the chemical industry in terms of energy use. Significantly, oil is the raw material for these products. U.S. production of olefins for plastics and synthetic materials requires 3.5 percent of all oil used in the country. Only small amounts of plastic are recycled, although this process recovers virtually all the energy embodied in them. Burning waste plastic, the most common method of energy recovery, returns only half the energy used in its manufacture. Recycling is unfortunately impeded by the fact that post-consumer plastic scrap is difficult to sort and recover. Some chemical products are more easily recyclable. Antifreeze, a major synthetic product, could be recovered and purified. Tires also can be rather easily recovered, and making them with reclaim-rubber uses only about 10 percent as much energy as manufacturing them from virgin synthetic fibers.[36] A major policy measure that all countries could implement is to ensure the recyclability of materials. This might include the banning of certain plastic packaging.

A major policy measure that all countries could implement is to ensure the recyclability of materials.

Cement, an intermediate product in the manufacture of concrete, is the world's most widely used construction material. Its production requires much heating and grinding, but large energy savings can be obtained by grinding and mixing the silicates, calcium, and aluminates in a new dry process rather than in a slurry. The old wet process requires more than 7.6 gigajoules per ton, and switching to the dry process saves nearly a quarter of that. The United States now produces half its cement with this more efficient process, and as a result average energy consumption per ton is down to 6.5 gigajoules. Although new cement-making capacity throughout much of the world uses the dry technique, the Soviet Union continues to rely primarily on the inefficient wet process; institutional resistance is apparently delaying the adoption of the dry process. Australia has not changed either and as a result averages 7.2 gigajoules per ton of cement produced. The energy requirements of both wet and dry processes can be improved by preheating the kilns with recovered waste heat. West European nations combine the dry process with heat recovery and as a result use 25 percent less energy than the United States.[37]

The importance of a comparatively small number of conservation initiatives in industry is underscored by a simple comparison. The Soviet Union is expected by the year 2000 to increase its consumption of coal for the manufacture of iron and steel by more energy than Brazil uses today for everything. Simply making the Soviet iron and steel industry as efficient by the year 2000 as the Japanese are now would reduce this increase by four fifths.[38] Most scenarios assume the Soviets will do no better in this area than the current world average by the end of the century. But because they also assume that the Soviets will double steel production capacity by then, implicit in their forecasts is the installation of technology 20 percent less efficient than the Japanese now use and 40 percent less efficient than available technology that is economical at current world energy prices. Perhaps because the Soviets enjoy energy abundance and do not use market pricing for energy they have little incentive to conserve. But failing to do so will cost them dearly in lost opportunities to sell oil and earn foreign exchange. They also supply most of the fuel for their East European allies, and any inefficiency in the Soviet Union drives up the cost of supplying these countries.

Worldwide, improvements may slacken, but probably not as much as assumed by most macroeconomic modelers. They project industrial efficiency in the Eastern bloc and developing countries will improve far slower than in the OECD, and that the OECD will improve at only about 0.8 percent per year. To reach economical levels of efficiency by the year 2000, a rate of improvement in industry everywhere of more than 2.3 percent per year is needed. The modelers, then, may be encouraging the world to invest far more in energy supply than is warranted.

SAVING OIL IN TRANSPORTATION

Although the transportation sector uses less energy than industry, it uses oil almost exclusively. Thus automobile fuel economy, mass transit, and efficient freight hauling offer the largest oil savings. Private cars consume about 7 percent of the world's commercial energy, or 17 percent of the oil used each year. The United States, in fact, uses 10 percent of the world's oil output as gasoline for motor cars and light trucks.[39]

The transportation sector uses 20–25 percent of energy delivered to consumers throughout Western Europe, North America (including Mexico), and Brazil. In Eastern Europe and the Soviet Union, however, the figure is only 7–13 percent, chiefly because fewer people own cars. Automobile ownership and use is strongly related to income everywhere, even in countries as different as Australia and Japan. Japanese use of energy

for transportation is similar to other OECD countries, despite the fact that the nation is small, densely populated, and ideal for mass transportation.[40]

Affluence, automobile ownership, and fuel efficiency are important issues in both rich and poor countries, even where renewable energy resources are abundant. This fact is evident in Brazil, a country so dramatically divided by income levels that Brazilian physicist Jose Goldemberg describes it as "a Belgium inside an India." Car ownership has increased substantially in the last two decades, growing at 7 percent annually even during the last five years, despite the deep recession and high energy costs. Still, the number of cars per person remains only 15 percent as high as in the United States, leaving considerable room for expansion, and ownership among the relatively rich can be expected to continue growing. Even a moderate increase over the rest of the century would double auto fuel demand by the year 2000, given the current levels of fuel efficiency.[41]

Opposing scenarios can be drawn for meeting the challenge of transportation fuel needs. The options range from pursuing all-out efforts to develop alternative fuels to fashioning a future free of automobiles. Brazil, again, offers a microcosm of a larger body of conflicting forces and alternatives. To meet part of the expected twofold increase in fuel demand for cars, the nation plans to double national oil production. Supplying the remainder with alcohol would require 16–20 percent of the total land area committed to crop production in 1980. Goldemberg and his colleagues conclude "these are formidable requirements which are probably impossible to achieve in reality."[42] Even today's alcohol fuel output, which meets about 3 percent of Brazilian total energy needs, apparently has caused serious social and environmental stresses.[43] Alternatively, improving automobile fuel economy both would extend oil supplies long enough to develop renewable energy sources safely and would make the use of renewable energy feasible.

The fundamental importance of auto fuel economy can be seen by contrasting current efficiency levels with the technical and economic potential. Fuel economy around the world averages about 21 miles per gallon (8.9 kilometers per liter), though it varies widely. (See Table 7-4.) The U.S. automobile fleet, not surprisingly, is the world's least efficient, and the newest American models rate only slightly better than the world average for existing cars.

A simple calculation illustrates the profound importance of raising these ratings. If by the year 2000 American cars were as efficient as the Japanese (assuming saturation in car ownership), 5 percent of world oil use would be saved. Doubling auto fuel efficiency worldwide would permit twice as many cars without increasing energy consumption, or it would allow savings of about 8 percent of world oil output. Achieving this should cost less than $20 per barrel saved; the alternative, producing gasoline or alcohol fuel, will cost $40–60 per barrel.[44]

The potential to do even better than this is great. Automobile fuel economy can be improved far beyond current Japanese levels. Indeed, several major manufacturers have produced prototype cars that obtain up to 93 miles per gallon. Models that get 78 miles to the gallon have been built by General Motors (a two-passenger car) and Volkswagen (a four- to five- passenger model).[45]

The trade-offs between ways to meet automobile fuel demand can be illustrated by returning to the case of Brazil. If the country chooses to concentrate on alcohol fuels, and if its cars are no more efficient at the end of this century than they are today, over twice as much fuel

Table 7-4. Automobile Fuel Economy, Selected Countries, 1982

Country	Autos	Fleet Average	New Cars
	(million)	(miles per gallon[1])	
Australia	6.3	19	24
Brazil	9.7	20	24
Canada	10.6	18	27
France	17.8	27	32
East Germany	2.4	27	32
Italy	17.7	24	31
Japan	39.0	31	30
Soviet Union	8.0	26	29
United Kingdom	15.6	22	28
United States	125.4	16	22
West Germany	23.2	22	28
Other	77.0	n.a.	n.a.
Total	353.0	21[2]	25[3]

[1]Actual mileage on the road. Data may not be strictly comparable due to differing national testing methods. [2]Based on 80 percent of the cars in the world. [3]Based on 70 percent of the new cars in the world.

SOURCE: International Energy Agency, *World Energy Outlook* (Paris: OECD, 1982); International Road Federation, *World Road Statistics 1978–82* (Washington, D.C.: 1983); United Nations Economic Commission for Europe, *An Energy Efficient Future: Prospects for Europe and North America* (London: Butterworths, 1983); Motor Vehicle Manufacturers Association, *World Motor Vehicle Data Book, 1983* (Detroit, Mich.: 1983).

will be needed. This would equal six times the current level of alcohol fuel production. If within the next five years, however, Brazil required all new cars to get 31 miles per gallon, projected consumption would grow by "only" 43 percent. This level of fuel economy in new cars could reportedly be achieved in short order without major capital investments in Brazil's auto industry. If Brazil mandated a new-car fuel economy of 47 miles to the gallon, fuel demand would by the year 2000 be slightly lower than today.[46]

Many options can be incorporated to achieve these high fuel economy levels. Reducing auto weight can save 25 percent of the energy used in the typical car. Engineering more-efficient engines can yield another 20 percent improvement, as can the installation of efficient continuously variable transmissions (CVT). General Motors and Fiat both will soon begin production of the CVT in France. Simply installing the most efficient tire available on the market today would improve the fuel economy of most cars by 1–3 miles per gallon.[47]

Rolf Bauerschmidt of the University of Essen has shown how West German fuel consumption could be cut by a fifth by the year 2000 while the auto fleet grows by 12 percent. He assumes that new cars will mainly be diesel-fueled vehicles getting 36 miles per gallon. Gasoline-powered cars would not grow in number but would become more efficient, achieving 29 miles to the gallon. These goals are easily within the realm of technical feasibility, though they may require government intervention. He also assumes that travel by train will double, a more uncertain prospect. Rail passenger-travel remains at about the same level as just after World War II, and the service, though excellent and improving, is heavily subsidized.[48]

Where transportion systems are inadequate or nonexistent, there are even greater opportunities to use mass transit to cut or avoid growth in energy use. Traveling by train is inherently more efficient than using a private car. In West Germany, for example, railroads use only one fourth as much energy as cars to move people an equal distance.[49] The autobus is comparable in efficiency. No mode of passenger transportation, however, is more efficient than van or car pools.

Technical improvements are also pos-

sible in mass transit systems. East European trains, for example, perform more efficiently than West European ones. If Soviet railways achieved a similar technical level of efficiency, savings of 50 percent could be made.[50]

Developing countries face a particularly difficult task in providing transportation services. Strapped with debt and under pressure from the International Monetary Fund to cut domestic expenditures, budgets for providing additional bus services have been reduced, and rail services are frequently out of the question because of their high initial capital cost. But failing to provide mass transportation costs dearly if, as often happens, the lack of service is made up privately with motor cars.

Nigeria illustrates this dilemma. The lack of transport services is evidenced by the use of only half a barrel of oil equivalent per capita in transportation in 1980, less than a sixth the level in West Germany. One Nigerian analyst projects this will rise to 3.2 barrels of oil equivalent per capita by 2010. Wide use of mass transit would greatly reduce this projection, but the current service is so poor that it strongly encourages the purchase of automobiles. Potential passengers are deterred by buses filled to crushing levels. Many already commute four hours per day on mass transit and, despite crowded roads, find private transport more convenient when they can afford it. Most cars carry only two passengers, though average capacity is five. Yet roads are so crowded in Lagos that in 1978 legislation was enacted that permitted vehicle use only on alternate days. Predictably, the law was circumvented by those who could afford second cars.[51]

An alternative that reduces congestion, saves energy, and cuts government transportation costs is the jitney. Jitneys are comparatively small vehicles that offer shared rides along major routes.

Small fleets of these taxicabs, vans, or trucks are usually operated by private owners. Though problems sometimes arise in regularity of service and in neglect of less profitable routes, these are generally outweighed by large increases in low-cost transportation service. Profit-making private jitneys often operate at full seating capacity, usually during rush periods. Although they have the potential for lowering the efficiency of public transport by skimming the most profitable routes, they can also reduce governments' need to buy large vehicles to meet rush-hour demand. These large vehicles would be used either at less than full load—or not at all—during most of the day. Thus jitneys can save commuters the energy and capital costs inherent in private cars and can save governments some of the high capital and operating costs of mass-transit vehicles. Studies report the successful operation of jitney services in a dozen cities around the world, from Hong Kong to Buenos Aires.[52]

It falls to governments to ensure that auto fuel efficiency, the single most important energy policy in the world, is achieved.

Most countries face trade-offs in the movement of freight, which often burns up more energy than passenger transport. The Soviet Union, in fact, uses 75 percent of all transport fuel moving freight. This fuel use can be reduced by both shifts from truck to rail as well as increased efficiency of transport trucks, which carry half or more of the freight in the United States, Europe, and Brazil.[53] Soviet freight is mostly carried by rail, which is why the country has the highest freight transport efficiency, though the use of coal in locomotives instead of diesel fuel makes them less efficient than

would otherwise be expected. Replacing Soviet gasoline-powered trucks with diesel units would also bring improvement.

Freight transport over the road is expected to grow in most major countries, so the importance of increased efficiency of transport trucks is central. U.S. truck transport is inefficient due to poor aerodynamics and poor load factors, which has historically been due to a bad regulatory policy that required many truck operators to return empty to their destinations. Technical improvements such as airfoils, however, can improve efficiency by 6 percent, with turbocharging adding 12 percent and radial tires 10 percent. In Brazil, a doubling of efficiency of trucks is considered feasible. This would permit at least twice as much road freight transport without any increase in fuel consumption.[54]

A basic problem in both the United States and Brazil is the decline of railroads. In Brazil they are poorly managed and inefficient, while using the U.S. rail system is slower than sending freight by highway, due to poorly maintained rail beds and poor freight transfer systems at switchyards. A major shift back to rail would be costly and is unlikely without the impetus of much higher fuel costs or government intervention. Developing countries, however, will probably want to give priority to rail transport over highway construction. Water transport is far more efficient than either rail or truck, if waterways already exist. The construction of waterways to compete with rail has not always been an effective use of capital, but in Brazil, water transportation along the Amazon to the industrialized south probably presents a better alternative than construction of either rail or highways.[55]

Worldwide, the future of oil use depends most on the future of transportation, especially the automobile. Because saving oil can help secure the future of the automobile as well as relieve economic and environmental pressure, it is only prudent to seek the highest economically achievable rates of fuel efficiency. Governments will play a major role in the future of transportation because generally they alone possess the resources to provide alternative transportation and because they can legislate fuel economy. They will also greatly affect freight transportation energy use, albeit less directly. Fuel economy levels of 30 miles per gallon are achievable everywhere by the end of the century; levels of 50 miles per gallon are attainable shortly thereafter. But the world will not realize this important potential if governments adopt a hands-off attitude.

Although market signals for energy prices are vital to increased fuel economy, the market alone will not bring about economically feasible levels—for two main reasons. The first is that consumers do not consider fuel economy as a top priority when buying cars unless fuel prices are increasing rapidly. Second, when an oil emergency does occur, automakers cannot quickly supply efficient cars. Typically, five years are required to re-tool to make new cars more efficient.

Thus, the market alone cannot guarantee future energy efficiency or even promote completely rational economic behavior in the short term. It falls to governments to ensure that auto fuel efficiency, the single most important energy policy in the world, is achieved. To effect this, a combination of market pricing, fuel taxes, and efficiency regulations will be required.

Buildings and Appliance Efficiency

Energy use in buildings around the world ranges between extremes. In most industrial countries, oil, gas, and electricity warm or cool air, heat water, provide light, refrigerate food, and run appliances such as ranges, washing machines, and televisions. In developing countries, wood or dung is the principal fuel, used mainly for cooking. More-efficient stoves would both reduce wood waste and improve the quality of life in these areas, but their use is somewhat problematic. Measures for halving energy use in industrial nations include improving and replacing appliances, especially furnaces and air conditioners, and reducing heat loss from poorly insulated buildings.

The opportunities for conservation are greatest in North America and Western Europe, where rates of energy use in the buildings sector reflect both the climate and high income levels. These countries have a long way to go before completely adjusting to the energy price increases of the seventies. Nonetheless, improvements since 1973 in the OECD countries in this region have been impressive. (See Figure 7-1.) Denmark, the most improved of these nations, has reduced energy use in buildings by 32 percent, an impressive record considering that the area of buildings heated increased by 23 percent over the period. Canada and the United States also show major reductions—19 and 16 percent, respectively. France, Sweden, and West Germany registered smaller percentage reductions, but they started from a more efficient base.[56]

The Swedes managed most of their savings with capital investments, while 75 percent of the improvements in the other countries resulted from no-cost or low-cost changes such as turning down thermostats. Lee Schipper of the Lawrence Berkeley Laboratory reports that technical efficiency of Swedish houses far exceeds that of the United States, even after adjustment for climate. Swedish homes, on average, have twice the insulation values of homes in the north-

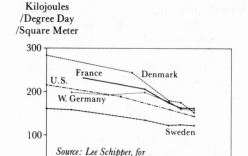

Kilojoules
/Degree Day
/Square Meter

Figure 7-1. Efficiency Improvements in Residential Space Heating in Selected Countries, 1970-82

ern state of Minnesota.[57]

The potential for improving the heat-saving capability of homes even in cold climates can be readily illustrated. C.A. Ficner has compared costs in Canada of energy options in new homes of conventional design, energy-saving design, active solar heating, and passive solar heating. A typical new house in Canada costs $80,000 to build and $800 per year to heat. By spending an additional $3,000 to build a thermally tighter structure, the cost of energy could be cut to $100 per year. The additional construction cost would add $450 per year in interest and principal to typical mortgage payments, giving an overall cost of $550. Thus net annual savings would total $250. In contrast, passive- and active-solar homes cost $92,000 and $100,000 to build. Their "heating" costs would total $2,200 and $3,300 per year.[58]

Conservation is the clear winner. Its importance is clear also: Almost 40 percent of all Canadian end-use energy goes into buildings. Half of this could be saved, an amount equal to 50 percent more than is supplied by hydropower in Canada. The benefits of energy conservation go far beyond the annual dollar savings to the houseowner, however. Reduced energy demand means reduced

energy facility construction costs. The energy-efficient home would save society $7,000 in capital costs compared with a conventional house, even allowing for the additional cost to the homeowner.[59]

Similar benefits abound in the home appliance market. Energy cost savings to homeowners, coupled with some strong policy measures, have increased efficiency since 1972 in the United States. Appliances for space heating, water heating, air conditioning, and refrigeration require three fourths of the energy used in U.S. buildings, with 42 percent going for space heat alone. Typical new gas furnaces now are about 70 percent efficient, having improved slightly over the last decade. New gas-fired systems, however, are 94 percent efficient. These employ heat exchangers that remove heat from flue gases by condensing them. Unfortunately, consumers usually choose less efficient units.[60] (See Table 7-5.)

The seasonal efficiency of central air conditioners has improved by over 25 percent in the United States since 1972.

Table 7-5. Efficiency of Typical U.S. Household Appliances Versus Best 1983/84 Models

	(percent)
Electric Heat Pump	53
Gas Furnace	50
Gas Water Heater	73
Electric Water Heater	35
Central Air Conditioner	84
Room Air Conditioner	64
Refrigerator Freezer	55
Freezer	73

SOURCE: Howard S. Geller, "Efficient Residential Appliances and Space Conditioning Equipment," in ACEEE, *Doing Better, Vol. E.*

Room air conditioners have also improved, by about 17 percent. The improvements occurred most dramatically between 1981 and 1982, presumably to meet Californian minimum appliance efficiency standards.[61]

Water heaters use 14 percent of the energy consumed in the U.S. buildings sector. But the efficiency of electric water heaters, which represent a third of the market, declined between 1972 and 1980—by about 2 percent. (No data have been collected since that time, unfortunately, as a result of Reagan administration policy.) Typical natural-gas-fired water heaters are only 48 percent efficient at point of use, compared with 80 percent for new pulse-combustion models. A new pulse-unit water heater would save over $115 per year in fuel in the average U.S. home.[62]

Refrigeration units in Japan, even adjusted for smaller size, are twice as efficient as U.S. refrigerators. The Japanese refrigerators do not sacrifice frost-free features or other conveniences to attain efficiency. Rather, they have more-efficient compressors, better design, and better insulation. A U.S. concern is that the Japanese could capture a sizable share of their market, just as the Japanese automakers did. This prospect is uncertain for several reasons, including the difficulty of making international comparisons, due to inconsistent testing methods, for all appliances. Nevertheless, the apparently higher efficiency of the Japanese refrigerator at least suggests the threat to U.S. manufacturers.[63]

More-efficient appliances cost more to purchase, but they quickly pay for themselves. A highly efficient furnace may cost an additional $1,000, but it can yield an annual return on investment of 15 percent over an average model due to an efficiency improvement of 50 percent or more. A gas-fired water heater with an improvement of 33 percent over the average model in the United States costs up to $110 more, but it yields a rate of return of 35 percent per year. A refrigerator/freezer now on the market with an improvement of 20 percent yields an annual return of 52 percent. It costs only $60 more than models with average efficiencies.[64]

Refrigeration units in Japan, even adjusted for smaller size, are twice as efficient as U.S. refrigerators.

An Oak Ridge National Laboratory study in the southern United States showed that, even if an existing central air conditioning unit is not worn-out, replacing it can pay for the extra cost in only five years. Significantly, it was shown that many air conditioning units are oversized, which leads to much energy waste from cycling losses. Oversized units cost more to buy as well as to operate. Replacing the average worn-out unit with a properly sized efficient one pays for itself in 6–12 months in the southern United States and in 18–36 months in the mid-Atlantic states.[65]

Lighting in the United States costs about $30 billion in electricity each year, and consumes 25 percent of all electric power output. New ballasts to stabilize the current in the circuits of fluorescent lights can reduce energy costs by 20–25 percent, and replacing incandescent bulbs with small fluorescents can cut consumption by an estimated 75 percent. A recent article in the Electric Power Research Institute's *EPRI Journal* suggests that half the electricity used for lighting could be saved in the United States—420 billion kilowatt-hours per year. If accomplished, the savings would represent 0.5 percent of all world commercial energy, and 35 percent more electricity than the entire annual hydroelectric power output of the United

States. This potential is greater than the hydroelectric output of Central and South America, Eastern Europe, and the Soviet Union combined. As the *EPRI Journal* put it, "[This energy] could be saved through energy-efficient strategies, all without imposing any hardships on productivity, safety, or esthetics."[66]

Commercial buildings use about one eighth of the energy consumed in the United States. Because lighting represents 40 percent of the peak electrical requirements for these buildings, peak loads on utilities could be cut sharply with lighting energy conservation. Lights contribute much of the heat that must be removed by air conditioning. In fact, air conditioning is often required in these buildings in cold weather to remove the heat generated by excess lighting. Audits and small investments in improvements in commercial buildings could yield electricity savings of 30 percent in lighting, 25 in space heat, 20 in air conditioning, and 15 percent for water heating.[67]

Swedish homes use 30–50 percent less heat than American homes. The Swedes enacted performance standards for residences in the mid-seventies and offered incentives for conservation investments. Efficiency levels often exceed the requirements, though the standards may have increased awareness and accelerated the overall improvement. The analysts attribute the improvement to loans totaling more than $850 million made available for efficiency investments; to cooperation between homeowners, builders, and the government; to a national commitment to quality housing; to price increases; and to the new standards. They also noted that improvements were greater in homes built by those who inhabited them, as opposed to those who built homes to sell.[68]

The scope for saving energy in this sector is broad even where energy use in buildings is comparatively low, such as

the Soviet Union. The low usage is due in part to smaller living spaces, but also to the efficiency that is afforded by central heating systems. Many people live in cities in multifamily dwellings, permitting very efficient district heating. It also makes cogeneration possible, and the Soviets take good advantage of this opportunity. The United Nations has estimated, however, that an additional 20 percent savings could be attained in Soviet buildings by the year 2000. The study underscores the importance of conservation by noting that an increase of about 42 percent in total energy use by this sector is likely even if these savings are achieved, based on an assumption of rising living standards.[69]

The U.N. study also concluded that conservation could hold buildings-sector energy demand in Western Europe to a rise of only 5 percent. Other research suggests a reduction in absolute energy use is possible. A Lawrence Berkeley Laboratory study estimates that with no change in energy prices, demand for energy per household in North America and Western Europe should remain constant. That is, increased demand for services as incomes grow would be offset by efficiency improvements. The authors point out, too, that demand for most major energy services, or appliances, in these areas is saturated, and that the faster incomes grow, the sooner people can and will replace existing models with energy-efficient ones.[70] With rising prices and rising incomes, efficiency would improve faster.

In relative terms, Denmark, France, and West Germany have been most successful in improving efficiency in buildings, and the reason appears to be a concerted and balanced commitment at the highest national levels to bring about energy savings. In the absence of balance, subsidies for conservation in the buildings sector in the form of direct grants have not been good policy. Billions of dollars worth of grants in Canada and the United Kingdom, for example, were not supplemented with information programs and were thus less effective than they might have been.[71] More fundamentally, a policy that assures rational energy pricing, backed with efficiency regulations in cases of classic market failure, offers the best hope of energy conservation in residential and commercial buildings.

Improving energy efficiency in residences in developing countries presents a different but no less important problem. Fuelwood and charcoal provide two thirds of all energy used in Africa and a third of that used in Asia. Wood, in fact, supplies the equivalent of 5.5 million barrels of oil per day, 80 percent of which is used for cooking. Indeed, one of the worst problems facing the developing world is the shrinking availability of fuel for cooking. As fuelwood becomes less available, the burden of collecting and transporting it, which usually falls on women and children, greatly adds to an already heavy work load. The widening circle of firewood collection, moreover, adds to the deforestation and soil erosion caused principally by lumbering, agriculture, and drought.[72]

The challenge is to improve the efficiency of cookstoves without adding to the work load, straining limited household budgets, diminishing sociocultural values, or reducing the utility of the cooking fire.[73] The fire is often simply an arrangement of three stones that support a cooking pot. Long, uncut branches or dung cakes are fed in from the unsheltered sides. The fire often serves as the center of family activity, though it rarely is needed for heat. Frequently, however, it is the only source of light.

Because the first step to more-efficient wood use is to shelter the fire from the wind, the social and lighting functions of the fire can be compromised. Moreover, if the fire is enclosed in a stove, extra work is required to cut the wood to fit. The attraction of energy conservation, then, is partly offset by the loss of some amenities and the need for more work. But if a new stove cuts fuel consumption by half or a fourth, as some suggest, then the time and effort of collecting fuel is greatly reduced. If the stove has a chimney, moreover, cooks are exposed to far less smoke and living spaces are made more comfortable. Lighting can be replaced with kerosene, but at additional expense.

One serious problem with stoves is that locally made versions often deteriorate to the point where they no longer save fuel. This is common where clay is used for construction. Reinforcing the clay or using scrap metal or ceramics to build the stove can improve performance. Another serious problem is that poor design leads to a mismatch between pots and the cooking holes into which they fit. Related difficulties are the failure to include enough cooking holes and the uneven distribution of heat among them, so that the cook is forced to spend more time preparing meals. Better design can solve these problems. Projects in El Salvador, Kenya, and Nepal have provided experience that will permit better design and production.[74]

The key to saving firewood and dung are low-cost, prefabricated stoves that are both durable and simple to use and service. The solution of technical problems alone, unfortunately, will not be sufficient, for the women who would most benefit from improved stoves usually cannot buy them. Until women share more control of family purse strings, this problem is not likely to disappear.

POLICIES FOR AN
ENERGY-EFFICIENT FUTURE

Two drastically different visions of the world energy future have come into focus. On one hand, energy demand models based on history indicate that global demand will more than double by the year 2025. On the other, analyses based on energy conservation show how demand could be held to a much smaller increase, stretching nonrenewable energy supplies and facilitating the use of renewable resources. Both visions have claim to validity, and the one that comes to pass will depend on conscious policy choices.

David Rose of the Massachusetts Institute of Technology attempted to reconcile these pictures by applying the widely respected energy demand model created by Jae Edmonds and John Reilly of the Institute for Energy Analysis. Rose obtained energy demand results that differed by 100 percent depending on the amount of conservation assumed. But his study did not report the crucial impact that conservation had on energy prices—or the crucial effect that prices had on demand. Worldwatch therefore asked Edmonds and Reilly to run their model using conservation improvements consistent with the potential demonstrated in this chapter.[75]

Two scenarios were created for Worldwatch and contrasted with a third done previously for the U.S. Department of Energy (DOE). (See Table 7-6.) Most of the basic assumptions for economic growth, consumer price response, and some 30-odd other factors were the same in all three: The world's economy and population were assumed to grow until 2000 at annual rates of 3.2 and 1.2 percent, respectively. The only assumption that differed significantly among the scenarios was the amount of energy conservation realized.

The Worldwatch Available Technology Scenario incorporated efficiency improvements rapid enough to make all countries by the end of the century as efficient as the most efficient countries today. It also assumed that the world economy would by the year 2025 be using the most efficient and economical energy-using devices currently available. The annual improvement rates required to achieve these goals are 2 percent in industry and transportation and 1.5 percent for buildings until the year 2000, and then 1.2 percent for all sectors thereafter. In the Worldwatch New Technology Scenario, the higher rates of improvement are assumed to continue through new developments until the year 2025. The reference case, from the Department of Energy, assumes that efficiency will improve at only a 0.8 percent rate.[76]

The conservation contribution in the two models prepared for Worldwatch was impressive: The Available Technology Scenario saves 175 exajoules annually in the year 2025, an amount equal to 60 percent of current world commercial energy use.

The environmental importance of such an improvement can be seen in the quantity of sulfur produced under the different assumptions. Acid-rain-forming sulfur emissions would, without controls, increase by 165 percent under the high energy scenario. Application of available conservation measures could hold these releases to a 35 percent increase. Emissions control technologies still would be required, but their cost would be drastically reduced. It is likely that sulfur emissions are not the sole culprit in acid rain, but the link is strong enough to raise serious concern about rising emissions. Acid rain now threatens forests, aquatic life, and building materials throughout eastern North America and Europe. Without conservation and sulfur emissions controls,

Table 7-6. World Energy Consumption and Carbon Dioxide and Sulfur Emissions in 1984, With Alternative Projections for 2000 and 2025

Scenario	Assumed Annual Energy Efficiency Improvement	Annual Energy Use	Annual Carbon Dioxide Emissions[1]	Annual Sulfur Emissions
	(percent)	(exajoules)	(billion tons)	(million tons)
1984 (estimated)	2.3	300	5.0	100
Year 2000				
DOE Medium	0.8	460	7.2	170
Worldwatch Available Technology	1.8	360	5.8	120
Worldwatch New Technology	1.8	360	5.8	120
Year 2025				
DOE Medium	0.8	675	10.3	265
Worldwatch Available Technology	1.2	500	7.9	170
Worldwatch New Technology	1.8	450	7.0	135

[1]Measured in terms of carbon.
SOURCE: Worldwatch Institute and J. Edmonds et al., *An Analysis of Possible Future Atmospheric Retention of Fossil Fuel CO₂* (Washington, D.C.: U.S. Department of Energy, 1984). Assumptions are described in Notes 76 and 78.

this threat could double.

The conservation scenarios would reduce carbon dioxide emissions as well. Scientists agree that far-reaching changes in global climate will occur if atmospheric concentrations reach 600 parts per million, roughly double the pre-industrial level. The DOE scenario would increase the concentration to 440 parts per million from the 340 level of the early eighties, whereas the Worldwatch scenarios would hold it to 410–420. Even decreasing the present level of carbon emissions significantly by using biomass energy on a massive scale

would hold the carbon dioxide concentration only to 400 parts per million. The conservation scenarios would, however, reduce the buildup sufficiently to provide time to find a way to minimize fossil fuel combustion.

The New Technology Scenario would save 225 exajoules a year. This projection is considered less likely, however, for unlike the first one it rests on further technological developments. To attain even the more plausible Worldwatch conservation scenario, efficiency must continue to improve at recent rates until the end of the century. Energy use per unit of output declined at about 1 percent per year between 1960 and 1978, but then dropped 2 percent yearly after 1979.[77]

The difference between the high and the low energy futures would have important economic and environmental consequences. Oil production equal to the current output of Saudi Arabia and Venezuela would be saved. Coal amounting to 40 percent more than the entire world uses today would be saved. Energy worth $2 trillion would be saved in the year 2025, almost $300 per person. In comparison, the cost of energy saved would, throughout the period, average only about half the cost of new energy supplies.

The potential for improvements in the world's major uses of energy can be contrasted with the target rates assumed in the Worldwatch Available Technology Scenario. For the world steel industry to match the current Japanese level of efficiency by the end of the century, for example, it will have to raise energy efficiency at an annual rate of 2.3 percent. But if by then it is to save as much energy as present costs already justify, it will have to increase efficiency at almost 4 percent a year. Meeting economically feasible levels of efficiency in aluminum, chemicals, and cement production requires improvement rates of 1–3 percent per year. And if the world by the year 2000 is to record auto fuel economy as high as the Japanese now register, it will have to increase energy efficiency at an annual rate of 2.3 percent. Getting 45 miles per gallon by 2025 means efficiency will have to rise at about 2 percent a year. Last, to reach currently economical levels of energy use in buildings will require improving at 1.5 percent per year between now and the year 2025. Of course, if energy prices increase any at all, more conservation will be needed.

These rates are not directly comparable to the rate of change in the use of energy per unit of economic output, but they are telling indicators of the potential for reducing the energy intensity of the world economy. Steel, aluminium, chemicals, paper, and cement production consume most of the energy used in industry. Cars and trucks burn up most of the energy used in transporation. And furnaces, appliances, and lights account for most of the energy in buildings. So these uses hold a good deal of the technical and economic potential for energy conservation.

The role of energy prices in these scenarios is crucial, if also complex and surprising. It is complex because energy demand rises as prices fall, yet energy prices rise as demand rises. The effect of price is further complicated by conservation that occurs not as a result of price increases but of technical innovation. The role of price is surprising because even though price incentives bring about conservation, lower energy costs resulted from the two Worldwatch scenarios than from the DOE projection. Oil, for example, would cost $52 per barrel in 2025 in the Worldwatch Available Technology future, compared with $57 in the DOE future. Conservation occurs both as a result of price pressure and technical innovation. The modelers actually intervened to keep prices up, but not as high as if conservation had worked less well. They performed the policy equivalents of promoting conservation with taxes, regulations, information programs, incentives, research and development, and leadership. The natural result was both lower energy prices and lower energy demand.[78]

Some pessimism is warranted, however. The policies that would bring about maximum energy conservation are clearly not in place. Over half the world operates in a system without price signals that communicate the value of energy. Where energy is allocated or rationed it usually is used inefficiently. In market economies, energy use is encouraged by tax credits for energy production, by subsidies for declining and inefficient energy-using industries, and by price controls. Many facets of the energy market in OECD countries are protected from market mechanisms. Electric power, for example, is a regulated industry, and consumers pay a price far below electricity's marginal value. The auto industry, the product of which is a major energy consumer, is sheltered and subsidized and functions as a virtual monopoly in most countries.

Six policy tools can influence the intensity of energy use: energy price, efficiency regulations, capital availability, information, research, and leadership. Price is by far the most important. The least energy-efficient economies are those that have virtually told people that energy is not precious and can be used liberally. They impose price controls and subsidies that distort market signals and lead to waste. Canada, Norway, the Soviet Union, the United States, and the oil-producing developing countries, to greater or lesser degrees, belong to this category.

Some countries have recently reduced energy subsidies. The United States and Canada have eliminated the most important consumer subsidy, oil price controls, but continue to control the price of large quantities of natural gas. The World Bank has used its leverage to encourage the elimination of price subsidies wherever it could (particularly those for gasoline), even denying loans in some instances to Egypt, Mexico, and Venezuela, partially because these countries subsidized energy prices. Recently, Brazil, Indonesia, the Ivory Coast, South Korea, and Turkey have moved to eliminate or trim measures that encourage energy waste.[79]

The most efficient nations are those that not only have accepted the reality of market prices but also bill energy consumers for the external costs of energy. These governments impose taxes to charge energy users for the burden to society their consumption represents, including the burden of environmental damage and of needing foreign exchange to import oil. France, Italy, Japan, and West Germany generally pursue these policies. They typically impose taxes on oil, for example, that increase the purchase price.

Energy price increases have stimulated more conservation than any other factor—witness the doubling of efficiency improvement rates following the two price hikes of the seventies. A detailed analysis of why energy use changed in the United States after 1973 reinforces this conclusion. Eric Hirst led a study at Oak Ridge National Laboratory that estimated the country now uses almost 20 percent less energy than it would have if policies had not changed. Price rises caused two thirds of the conservation response in the United States. Hirst and his coauthors suggest that the remaining third may be due to a variety of government measures such as automobile fuel economy standards.[80]

Jae Edmonds points out, however, that energy scarcity alone may not be enough to encourage a level of conservation consistent with a low energy future. The widespread belief that an oil glut will persist for years has already diminished conservation efforts and may continue to do so. Price increases, moreover, will have little effect in centrally planned nations insulated from price signals or in regulated markets such as that for electric power. And as the world depends more on electricity, the role of markets in determining energy prices will diminish.[81]

There is the further problem of market failure. The classic case is the appliance bought by a landlord who does not pay the energy bill for operating it. The landlord has every incentive to buy the least costly furnace or water heater, not to pay more for one that will save energy costs. The tenant who will pay the energy bill has no say in the choice of appliance. Another example is the case of the more efficient but slightly more expensive automobile. Manufacturers could improve the fuel economy of their cars by 10–30 miles per gallon at an additional cost of $100–300 per vehicle. They balk at doing so, however, fearing that the slightly higher purchase price will decrease sales. Consumers typically pay more attention to the purchase price of items than to potential life-cycle energy costs.

Market pricing and the removal of energy consumption subsidies are prerequisites for an energy-efficient economy.

New technological developments will be necessary to attain the more-efficient Worldwatch scenario. Promising areas for research lie in the development of new materials for making lighter automobiles, ceramics for lighter engines, high-temperature sensing and control systems, large heat pumps, and entirely new industrial processes. Industry support for research varies widely by category, with the iron and steel and the paper industries spending relatively very little. U.S. Government support for energy conservation research has declined precipitously because of Reagan administration cuts. But as the Worldwatch Available Technology Scenario suggests, the greatest opportunity for conservation lies in putting known measures into practice. Innovations of this type will depend heavily on the spread of information on their value and availability.[82]

Many countries in both East and West

have implemented a variety of energy conservation information and assistance programs. Efficiency labeling of energy consuming products such as automobiles, tires, furnaces, and refrigerators has been a very useful government function in Sweden, the United States, and Western Europe. Other measures such as voluntary efficiency goals, efficiency audits, and grant programs have a mixed record of achievement, but many deserve continued support. The success of these programs seems to depend on national leadership, for they are taken most seriously when popular leaders elevate their importance.

In summary, nothing substitutes for realistic energy pricing policies. Market pricing and the removal of energy consumption subsidies, therefore, are prerequisites for an energy-efficient economy. Taxing energy use, however, could provide governments with a supplemental solution, one that would help resolve several problems: Conservation would be encouraged, alternative energy supply fostered, and deficits financed. A portion of the tax revenues would be required to protect low-income groups from the negative effects of the tax.

Regulatory policies can provide a minimum level of efficiency where markets fail or do not exist. The obvious targets for minimum performance standards are automobiles, furnaces, water heaters, air conditioners, and heat pumps. Automakers, for example, should at least be required to increase fuel economy to 30 and 45 miles per gallon by, respectively, the end of the century and the year 2025. Minimum performance levels might also be required for industries in centrally planned economies, although the complexity of such standards as well as redundancy makes them undesirable in market economies. The standards chosen for all items should be based on marginal energy costs, including the environmental and other external costs of energy. As Clark Bullard of the University of Illinois suggests, regulatory policy seldom can take society beyond the economically desirable levels, and indeed should not do so.[83] Nevertheless, regulations can provide an insurance policy against failure.

Policymakers are thus presented with the task of making energy policy on numerous fronts. Many industries, services, and, finally, people will be affected in complex, sometimes conflicting ways. But the most important policies reduce to a few manageable items, and the most important benefits clearly are worth the effort.

Leaders can think of conservation in many ways. They can see it, for example, as a way to improve trade balances by either reducing the need to import energy or freeing up extra fuel for export. Conservation can be considered a way to promote economic growth by cutting capital requirements for energy and thus making funds available for more-productive economic investments elsewhere. And they can view conservation as a preventive for catastrophic climate change or forest damage as a result of carbon dioxide, acid rain, and all the other environmental problems caused by energy use.

The risk of failure, whether from undue pessimism or failure of will, is great. The risk includes overbuilding energy facilities, overstressing energy capital budgets, and overburdening the environment. It is a risk that need not be borne.

8

Harnessing Renewable Energy

Christopher Flavin and Cynthia Pollock

Amid falling oil prices and laissez-faire energy policies in some countries, renewable energy development might be expected to lag badly. In fact, worldwide reliance on renewable energy sources has grown more than 10 percent per year since the late seventies, chiefly due to a surge in the use of hydropower and wood fuel. Solar collector sales have leveled off in many countries, but the use of wind power is growing at an unprecedented pace, thanks largely to the stunning development of wind farms in California. Over 5,000 turbines were installed in 1984 alone, setting the stage for wind power to be a significant energy source in many countries. In Brazil, one of the largest countries in the Third World, alcohol from sugarcane provides 43 percent of automotive fuel. Technological advances continue across a wide spectrum of new energy sources.

Boosting the prospects for some renewable energy sources is the mounting evidence that coal and nuclear power are not the long-run alternatives to oil that many had hoped. The growing evidence of damage to forests and crops from acid rain and air pollutants documented in Chapter 5 suggests that the need for expensive pollution control technologies will constrain growth in coal use. In the United States, nuclear power's financial problems are worsening, burdening utilities with $15-billion worth of canceled plants and another $100 billion tied up in plants under construction. Although these two sources will continue to be major contributors to the world energy budget, their potential is clearly limited.

Improved energy efficiency, as indicated in Chapter 7, is the most economical and least environmentally disruptive of the alternative energy strategies being pursued, and it deserves the highest priority on national agendas. Technologies that tap renewable energy sources must therefore be compatible with the less energy-intensive systems that are likely to develop in many parts of the world. Although efficiency will in a sense limit the size of the market for new energy sources, it is unlikely to seriously constrain the renewables industry in the near future. The market for replacing outmoded and uneconomical fossil-fuel-based systems is enormous, providing roles for both efficiency and renewables.

Some of the progress in renewable energy technologies in the past decade has been stimulated by government-sponsored R&D. These efforts are modest, however, dwarfed in most countries by continuing support for nuclear power and fossil fuel technologies. And in some cases they have been misdirected —with heavy expenditures, for example, on the development of large wind machines when smaller units developed commercially for a fraction of the cost have turned out to be far more successful. But generally the public funds have been well spent and have paved the way for private industry.

One sure sign that renewable energy has come of age is the increasingly tough questions the industry must face. In the United States, the issue of whether renewable energy tax credits should be extended beyond 1985 has become a major political question, brought to the fore by the several hundred million dollars of tax subsidies that went to wind farms alone in 1984. As with new energy sources in the past, tax subsidies have given the renewable energy industry a needed early boost, but such subsidies are only justified if they lead to rapid commercialization of an economical energy source. Tax credits should and probably will be withdrawn when they are no longer justified.

The environmental and social consequences of renewable energy projects also require serious evaluation. Massive hydropower projects being built in some developing countries may not be worth their economic and ecological costs. Some alcohol-fuel programs threaten to tie up valuable agricultural land and further disenfranchise the rural poor. Land-intensive wind farms and solar thermal power technologies are expected to result in land-use battles in some parts of the world. There are trade-offs to be made in the development of any energy source, and renewables will realize their promise only if these concerns are addressed early.

The four renewable energy sources and technologies discussed in this year's *State of the World* are at varying stages of commercialization. Hydropower has long been economical and is widely used. Solar water heating and alcohol fuels are economical in certain circumstances and steady progress is being made. Solar thermal power technologies are more problematic, but evidence is increasingly persuasive that some will be feeding electricity into the world's utility grids within a decade. Alcohol will soon be the main automotive fuel in Brazil, but it has found only limited use in most other countries.

HYDROPOWER

Falling water currently provides nearly one quarter of the world's electricity. A major stimulus to the industrial revolutions in North America and Western Europe, hydropower was overshadowed by the growth in fossil fuel use during the half-century of falling oil prices. More recently, the search for less expensive, indigenous energy sparked a boom in the use of this traditional source. Thousands of hydroelectric projects are under construction on four continents, but conflicts surrounding the economic and environmental merits of this strategy are far from resolved. Most of the large hydro projects are in the Third World, and many threaten to inundate valuable cropland, destroy rare species, and displace indigenous peoples.

Table 8-1. Countries Obtaining More Than Half Their Electricity From Hydropower

Proportion of Total Electricity Capacity That Is Hydroelectric	Countries
90–100	Bhutan, Ghana, Laos, Norway, Uganda, Zaire, Zambia
80–89	Brazil, Iceland, Luxembourg, Mozambique, Nepal, Rwanda, Switzerland
70–79	Cameroon, Congo, Costa Rica, Malawi, Sri Lanka
60–69	Afghanistan, Angola, Austria, Colombia, Ethiopia, Ivory Coast, Mali, New Zealand, North Korea, Paraguay, Tanzania
50–59	Bolivia, Canada, Central African Republic, Chile, Dominica, Egypt, Gabon, Honduras, Kenya, Peru, Portugal, Sudan, Surinam, Sweden, Uruguay

SOURCES: World Bank, Energy Department, "1981 Power/Energy Data Sheet for 100 Developing Countries," Washington, D.C., March 1984; United Nations, *Yearbook of World Energy Statistics 1981* (New York: 1983).

Some half-dozen nations around the world rely almost exclusively on water for their electricity and dozens more generate over half their power at dams. (See Table 8-1.) During the past five years, 10 countries have increased their hydroelectric capacity by over 57,000 megawatts—the equivalent of 57 large nuclear reactors. (See Table 8-2.) Developing countries get over two fifths of their electricity from hydropower, and a 1982 World Bank survey found that 10 nations planned to add more than 5,000 megawatts each from 1980 through 1995. At a time when new orders for coal and nuclear plants have slowed, the pace of dam construction has accelerated. Brazil, Canada, the Soviet Union, and the United States have the largest construction programs, but plans for future dams are centered in the Third World, where electricity demand is growing most rapidly.[1]

Large dams, the cheapest source of electricity in most areas where they can be used, are going up at an unprecedented pace. The Hoover, built in the United States in 1936, was the first to exceed 150 meters in height. By 1980, just 65 large dams had been constructed; 44 more are due to be completed before the end of 1990—26 in Latin America and Asia alone.[2]

The use of electricity in developing countries, though tempered by recent economic problems, is growing far faster than in industrial nations. Large foreign debts and sluggish economic performance may slow dam construction, which is very capital-intensive, but the World Bank expects hydro capacity in the developing world to double in the eighties.[3] Once dams are built, electricity can be generated without fuel imports, reducing foreign-exchange needs. But many hydro projects cost billions of dollars and create debt problems of their own until construction loans are repaid.

China and Brazil have the largest and most ambitious hydro blueprints. While China has the greater potential, Brazil is building more rapidly; its hydroelectric capacity is expected to double by 1993. In China, the 10,000 megawatts of hydro capacity under construction in 1980 were enough to expand the country's hydroelectric output by more than half. The ambitious government plan envisions building 10 major hydroelectric facilities by the turn of the century, each

Table 8-2. Countries With Major Hydroelectric Additions Between 1978 and 1983

Country	Operating Capacity		Capacity Increase	Increase
	1978	1983		
	(megawatts)			(percent)
Brazil	22,000	34,035	12,035	55
Canada	41,898	51,512	9,614	23
Soviet Union	47,500	55,889[1]	8,389	18
United States	70,989	78,968	7,979	11
Japan	26,099	33,313	7,214	28
Norway	17,000	21,290[1]	4,290	25
France	18,675	21,300	2,625	14
Mexico	4,541	6,500	1,959	43
India	10,832	12,561[1]	1,729	16
Argentina	2,935	4,646	1,711	58
Total	262,469	320,014	57,545	22

[1]Capacity in 1982.

SOURCE: Worldwatch Institute, based on World Bank, U.S. Department of Energy, and personal communications with embassies, consulting firms, and utility representatives.

consisting of several large dams. The Three Gorges project being considered for the Chang Jiang (Yangtze) River would produce up to 13,000 megawatts of power.[4]

The largest hydroelectric project currently being built is on the Paraná River between Paraguay and Brazil. Itaipu—"singing rock" in the Guarani Indian dialect—will have almost twice the capacity of the previous record holder, the Grand Coulee. (See Table 8-3.) The first two generators started operating in October 1984, and when completed in the early nineties, 18 generators will produce 12,600 megawatts of power. The cost is estimated at $18 billion. Five miles long and half the height of the Empire State building, the dam is regarded as one of the world's premier engineering achievements. Brazil and Paraguay are to manufacture 85 percent of the equipment, though the project was designed and financed by corporations and banks from around the world. The electricity produced at Itaipu will be owned

equally by the two countries, but tiny Paraguay will sell almost all its share to the rapidly expanding cities and industries of southern Brazil.[5]

Industrial countries with plans for major hydro expansion include Austria, Canada, the Soviet Union, and the United States. Austria intends to expand its hydroelectric capacity by 45 percent between 1982 and 1995; the Soviet Union has five large dams slated for completion during the eighties; and in the United States, where 8,000 megawatts of capacity have been added in the past five years, 23 states plan to harness more hydropower by 1991.[6]

Many of the large hydro projects being built in the United States and the Soviet Union are intended only to meet peak power demand. Water is released when power use is high and then electric pumps refill the reservoir at night when demand is low and electricity is cheaper. In the United States, 16 percent of total hydroelectric capacity is derived from pumped-storage facilities. Although the practice results in a net energy loss, it saves consumers money.[7]

In Canada, where almost 70 percent of the nation's electricity comes from falling water, several major projects will be completed by 1985. By diverting the rivers emptying into James Bay and building three large dams, Hydro-Quebec obtained 10,300 megawatts of power. The company markets an additional 5,225 megawatts from the recently built Churchill Falls Dam under an agreement with the provincial government of Newfoundland. Hydro-Quebec sells most of this power in Canada, but about 15 percent of its revenues are earned from sales to the United States. In 1984 Canada exported some $1.5-billion worth of electricity, and trade is expected to reach $5 billion by 1989. Utilities in New York and throughout New England, which currently depend on expensive oil and nuclear plants, have already signed multiyear contracts with Hydro-Quebec.

Electricity produced in western Canada is exported to California, and an agreement between Manitoba and six Northern Plains states is imminent.[8]

Growing international sales of hydropower confirm that falling water can profitably produce electricity for distant cities. First employed in Sweden in 1952, high-voltage transmission lines enable long-distance transport of electricity. A 1,700-kilometer line, the longest in the world, was inaugurated in Zaire in 1984. Ghana, Laos, Mozambique, Uganda, and Zambia all export hydroelectricity to their energy-thirsty neighbors.[9] And the wealth of untapped hydropower in Nepal could fuel the industrial growth of India to its south, where development is constrained by insufficient electricity.

One alternative to international trade in electricity is for energy-intensive industries to move to areas with inexpensive power sources. Aluminum smelters require more electricity per ton of prod-

Table 8-3. Largest Hydroelectric Plants, Operating or Under Construction, 1984

Plant	Country	Rated Capacity Upon Completion	Expected or Actual Completion Date
		(megawatts)	(year)
Itaipu	Brazil/Paraguay	12,600	1990
James Bay	Canada	10,269[1]	1985
Guri	Venezuela	10,000	1986
Tucurui	Brazil	8,000	1985
Grand Coulee	United States	6,494	1942
Sayano-Shushensk	Soviet Union	6,400	1984
Corpus Posadas	Argentina/Paraguay	6,000	1988
Krasnoyarsk	Soviet Union	6,000	1973
Churchill Falls	Canada	5,225	1971
Bratsk	Soviet Union	4,500	1964
Ust-Ilim	Soviet Union	4,500	1978
Yacyreta-Apipe	Argentina/Paraguay	4,050	1988
Cabora Bassa	Mozambique	4,000	1974

[1]Combined output of La Grande 2,3,4.
SOURCES: T.W. Mermel, "Major Dams of the World-1983," *Water Power & Dam Construction*, August 1983; Hydro-Quebec, *Annual Report 1983* (Montreal: 1983).

uct than any other commodity, encouraging producers to move to sparsely populated river basins where power is cheap. Northern Quebec, the Brazilian Amazon, Siberia, and southern Australia have all recently become attractive places to do business. Large hydroelectric dams are still starting up service in these areas for $1,000 per kilowatt or less. A more typical construction cost for a hydro plant is $1,500 per kilowatt, almost double that of a coal plant but only 50–75 percent as much as a nuclear facility. Countering these high investment costs is the fact that hydro plants have at least twice the life expectancy of thermal generating units, their operating costs are extremely low, and fuel costs are zero.[10]

Small hydro plants can economically supply many rural areas with electricity people would otherwise be unable to afford.

Technologies are also available to harness the energy of smaller rivers and streams. Very small turbines and generators, with an output of several megawatts or less, are the most suitable for many applications, especially in developing countries. Today two billion people are without reliable electricity; most will not be reached by utility grids during their lifetimes. Even in countries like Zaire and Brazil with immense hydro potential, large projects will not reach the majority of rural people for many decades. Small hydro plants can economically supply many rural areas with electricity people would otherwise be unable to afford. And water previously harnessed for other purposes—flood control, irrigation, or municipal drinking supplies— is being routed through turbines to enhance its productivity. Likewise, dams

that have been allowed to deteriorate over the years are being repaired: Thousands could be retrofitted on the tea plantations of Sri Lanka alone.

China leads the world in small hydropower development: Over 90,000 generators installed since 1952 supply more than one third of the electricity in rural areas. Communities and individuals are given technical assistance and encouraged to install, manage, and reap the profits of a generating facility. The bulk of the projects are undertaken at the community level using local skills and resources. At least 60 factories, employing over 8,000 people, produce the components of small plants. The average generating capacity per site has risen to 80 kilowatts and is growing rapidly. According to one manufacturer in Hangzhou, East China, his 7-kilowatt unit can be built and installed in less than a month. In 1983, China completed 1,150 small hydropower stations, adding an aggregate generating capacity of 400 megawatts.[11]

Because China has actively developed small hydro technology and others have not kept pace, its hydro equipment is now being used in a number of countries. Turbines are exported to Canada, Pakistan, Peru, the Philippines, Sri Lanka, and the United States. The largest export deal to date is with Colombia: The contract is for 60 generating plants, valued at $50 million, and includes installation assistance and the training of Colombian staff. Payment will be in commodities—cotton, sugar, coffee, cocoa, leather, and plywood—which is an interesting example of the growing technical cooperation between developing countries.[12]

In rural Pakistan, where electricity is used primarily for lighting, a 10-kilowatt hydro plant provides enough power for about 100 families (compared with just 2 families in the United States). The use of local materials, voluntary labor, and communal administration has kept the costs of hydroelectric facilities surprisingly low—$350–500 per kilowatt. Several dozen plants are already operating and an even greater number are planned or under construction. A more typical cost for small-scale hydro projects in the United States is $2,000–3,000 per kilowatt. Reductions are clearly possible, however, as turbine technologies are standardized and packages are tailored to the needs of developing nations. Likely adaptations include using sturdy local materials that require minimal maintenance and forgoing the use of sophisticated technologies to control water and electricity flows.[13]

Small hydro development in the United States is being encouraged by the Public Utility Regulatory Policies Act of 1978, which requires electric utilities to purchase power from small, independent suppliers. In most states the utilities must pay for the electricity at its "avoided cost" of production, a great stimulus to hydro development. The New England River Basins Commission estimated in 1980 that the potential of the region's 8,200 existing or former dam sites equaled about 7 percent of the area's generating capacity.[14] Not surprisingly, permit applications to reserve potential development sites flooded the Federal Energy Regulatory Commission, reaching a peak of 1,856 in 1981. (See Table 8-4.) Despite this early interest, the number of licenses issued annually did not reach the level widely predicted. Only 138 projects—with a total

capacity of 272 megawatts—were in operation as of February 1984. Another 164 projects, which would add 300 megawatts, were under construction.

Environmentalists and community leaders in New England and the Pacific Northwest have rightly questioned the desirability of damming all potential sites. Building several small projects in a watershed is probably justified in many cases, although parks, wilderness areas, and scenic rivers should be protected. A growing number of river basins, however, are threatened with overdevelopment. For example, more than 45 applications have been filed for hydro projects on the Salmon River in Idaho. If all of these were developed, fish and other aquatic life could be irreparably harmed.[15]

Although no mechanism exists in most European countries for selling privately generated electricity to state utilities, there are still opportunities to derive power from mountain streams. An upgrading program recently begun in France calls for the installation of 27 small hydro turbines at nine existing dams on the River Var. The first units, commissioned in 1984, are designed to provide 10 percent of Nice's power. An inventory of sites in Czechoslovakia revealed that 15,000 small hydroelectric stations in operation in 1930 had fallen into disuse. The preliminary survey indicated that 10,000 of the plants, each under 100 kilowatts, could be economically renovated. The overhauling will be subsidized by the state and managed by

Table 8-4. United States: Permits and Licenses for Hydroelectric Plants, 1978–83

	1978	1979	1980	1981	1982	1983	Total
Preliminary Permit Applications	36	76	501	1,856	944	624	4,037
Preliminary Permits Issued	2	13	138	578	750	416	1,897
License Applications	25	33	86	100	267	260	771
Licenses Issued	21	10	75	66	55	88	315

SOURCE: Idaho National Engineering Laboratory, "Hydroelectric Development History and Future Trends," prepared for the U.S. Department of Energy, January 1984.

public and private agencies.[16]

The costs and benefits of hydropower development must of course be carefully weighed. Too often dams have been constructed without sufficient planning, leading to unforeseen and unwanted consequences. Inadequate fish handling facilities have eliminated access to essential spawning areas, reservoirs have expanded the breeding grounds for snails that spread schistosomiasis, and the recreational benefits attributed to artificial lakes are often less valuable than the wildlife and white-water river activities they replace. In addition, large projects often displace indigenous peoples, whose cultures and life-styles are irrevocably altered even if they receive new land in return for their flooded homeland.[17]

The flooding of Lake Brokopondo in Suriname in 1964 created the first large reservoir in a rain forest and a noxious stench that persisted for years. Instead of razing the forest and earning millions of dollars of foreign exchange for the lumber, 570 square miles of trees disappeared under water. Their subsequent decomposition produced acids that corroded the dam's cooling system and intolerable amounts of hydrogen sulfide. Unfortunately, the experience has been repeated even in the most recent projects. Water hyacinth, a plant that spreads rapidly in impounded reservoirs, is another unwanted result of some hydro developments: It clogs turbines and robs other aquatic life of essential nutrients.[18]

One of the most persistent problems associated with hydroelectric developments is the failure to maintain stable watersheds. As described in Chapter 3, deforestation of riverbanks often results in accelerated erosion and rapid sedimentation of waterways and reservoirs. Numerous examples exist of dams whose lifetimes were cut short, sometimes by more than half, because of unanticipated siltation. Hydroelectric facilities are too expensive and watersheds too valuable to allow this to continue. A reservoir that is filling rapidly with sediment is not a renewable energy source. Better planning and detailed environmental assessments can mitigate most of these problems. Comprehensive watershed-management programs should be formulated before dam construction is begun. If the potential environmental impacts are evaluated early in the planning process, unsound projects can be scrapped before they become failures.

Throughout the world, hundreds of thousands of megawatts of hydroelectricity have already been harnessed, but the remaining potential is enormous. The 1980 World Energy Conference predicted that global hydroelectric output would quadruple between 1976 and 2020. And the World Bank, based on its 1982 survey, estimates that installed hydroelectric capacity in 100 developing countries will almost triple between 1980 and 1995. Yet even after this increase, only two thirds of the economically feasible hydro potential will have been captured.[19]

Although large-scale hydroelectric development in industrial countries appears to be slowing, a growing number of developing countries are investing huge sums of money in both large- and small-scale projects. With careful planning and an eye toward social and environmental impacts, the long-term productivity that would justify these investments can be realized.

NEW DIRECTIONS IN SOLAR WATER HEATING

Since the early seventies, solar water heating using flat-plate collectors has been one of the best publicized renewable energy technologies. Although sometimes overshadowed by more dazzling innovations, both commercial and residential solar heating continue to grow. In many areas of Australia, Greece, and Israel, most homes heat their water with solar collectors. Among larger countries, Japan and the United States do the most solar water heating, and each supports a solar industry with sales of several hundred million dollars a year.

The Israeli Government expects 60 percent of the country's hot water to be heated by solar collectors by 1990.

Although the sun has been used to dry crops and heat homes for millennia, modern solar water heating dates from 1891, when a flat-plate collector was patented in Baltimore, Maryland. California engineer William Bailey developed the first commercial system in 1909. His "Day and Night" collector consisted of a glass-covered box with a metal absorber plate and copper tubing. The tendency of hot water to rise circulated the heated water to a separate storage tank. By 1918, some 4,000 systems had been sold. The availability of cheap natural gas in California in the twenties caused the collector market to collapse, but solar heating became popular in Florida. By the late thirties, 50,000 systems had been installed in the Miami area, covering the roofs of four out of five new homes.[20]

After the oil price increases of the seventies, solar water heating again became popular. The technology has changed only modestly: Air, water, or another fluid circulates from the collector to a tank, carrying the sun's heat to where it is needed. In Israel and Japan, "passive" systems that incorporate both a collector and tank and rely on natural circulation predominate. Most American systems, on the other hand, are pump-driven, with a separate indoor storage tank.

Solar collectors are most popular in areas where fuel costs are high and sunshine plentiful. Israel, with 320 days of annual sunshine and virtually no oil reserves, has installed over 500,000 systems, enough to meet 40 percent of the country's hot water needs. Israeli collectors are locally designed and relatively simple, with most single-family homes needing just a 150-liter storage tank. Electricity is used as a backup, but the typical household spends only $25 a year on supplemental water heating.[21]

Israel's solar systems are successful in part because they sell for only $600, less than a fifth the average price in the United States. Since 1980, the Israeli Government has also offered modest solar tax credits, and solar water heating is required on all new homes and apartment buildings less than seven stories high. The government expects 60 percent of the country's hot water to be heated by solar collectors by 1990. Israeli universities, research institutes, and private companies are international leaders in this technology and have developed a substantial export market in Europe, the Middle and Far East, and North and South America. One Israeli company has installed 400,000 systems in 22 countries.[22]

In Europe, solar water heating is most popular in Greece. The Energy Ministry estimates that there are 100,000 small domestic systems in place, as well as hundreds in hotels. Approximately 250,000 square meters of collectors have been installed. On many Greek Islands simple rooftop collectors are used on the great majority of houses. France also has about 250,000 square meters of solar collectors, most of them the more expensive pumped-circulation designs.

An extensive program of government support aims to have two million square meters installed by 1990, enough to heat water for over 400,000 houses.[23]

The European Economic Community assists with the financing of solar hot water systems on much of the continent. This, together with government incentive programs, has led to limited use of the technology in Italy, the United Kingdom, and West Germany. About 20,000 British homes have solar-heated water. In Eastern Europe, all the members of COMECON now have plans to use solar hot water. Among the most active programs are those of Czechoslovakia and Romania, where hundreds of apartment buildings are solar-heated. Bulgaria plans to install 30,000 square meters of collectors by 1985.[24]

In Japan, as in Israel, the use of solar-heated water predates the 1973 oil embargo. According to one estimate, prior to the use of gas- and oil-fired water heaters in the late fifties, 38 million Japanese homes had solar collectors. Since the early seventies, rising petroleum prices and a program of special government grants and loans have led to a revival of solar water heating. Japan now has about four million solar hot water systems in place, serving over 10 percent of its houses. Approximately 500,000 systems are installed each year, and the goal for 1990 is to have seven million. Also planned are 6,500 apartment and office building systems and 1,900 for factories. The Tokyo city government is adding solar heating to schools, hospitals, and other government buildings. Most Japanese collectors are passive models with gas or electric backup. Prices average about $700 per system, competitive with the cost of conventional heating.[25]

Australia's collector industry is one of the world's strongest. Over 100,000 homes have solar hot water systems, making Australia the third largest per capita user, behind Israel and Japan. Costs of less than $1,000 make collectors economical in the rural "outback" where fuels must be trucked long distances. Australian solar companies have steadily improved their collector designs and are major collector exporters.[26]

Many other countries have made some use of solar heating. China had 80,000 square meters of collectors in place in 1980. South Korea also has collectors on many rooftops. In India and Nepal, hundreds of government-run institutions such as schools and hospitals are being fitted with solar heating systems. China, India, Mexico, and several Middle Eastern countries are among those now conducting research on solar heating at national universities and research institutes.[27]

Although affordable energy sources are badly needed in most developing countries, a domestic water-heating system other than a wood or charcoal fire is beyond the means of the vast majority of people. In an attempt to get around this problem, the government-run Central Mortgage Bank in Colombia is financing a solar heating project for 1,000 families in Medellin and Bogota. One indication of the potential market in developing countries is the fact that the U.S. Solar Corporation had by 1984 signed licensing or direct sales agreements with companies in Belize, Brazil, India, Iraq, Panama, Peru, the Philippines, Saudi Arabia, South Korea, and Yemen.[28]

In some parts of the United States, solar water heating is widely used and has a well-developed industry to support it. Centered largely in Arizona, California, and Florida, the U.S. industry has produced over 1.5 million square meters of solar collectors annually in recent years, representing about $700–800 million of annual sales. (See Figure 8-1.) Over one million systems, spanning about 11 million square meters, have been installed since the early seventies.

About half these are low-temperature systems that are widely used in California and Florida to heat swimming pools. Solar heating supplies about 20 trillion BTUs each year, most of it from the more efficient medium-temperature systems used for household water heating. The U.S. Department of Energy projects that solar water heating will grow tenfold by 1990.[29]

So far, just a few hundred thousand Americans use solar-heated water. Collectors have not become as popular as many in the industry expected. And since 1980, the sale of low-temperature pool systems has fallen more than 50 percent, due to market saturation and a change in California law prohibiting tax credits for such systems. The million or so square meters of medium-temperature solar collectors sold annually since 1981 are sufficient for 100,000 homes each year and an equal number of commercial and industrial systems. Industry leaders believe that the economic recovery of 1984 boosted sales, although figures are not yet available to confirm their impression.[30]

The American collector industry consists of about 250 companies, mostly relatively small manufacturers and component suppliers. Leading are is a solid core of 10 manufacturers that shipped over half the collectors sold in 1983. Ventures into this industry by Fortune 500 companies have met with limited success. Exxon, for example, sold its solar hot water subsidiary in 1981.[31]

The typical U.S. solar hot water system—with pump-driven collectors and a large capacity—costs about $4,000. Consequently, sales depend on federal tax credits and similar credits available in 29 states. But these tax breaks are useful mainly to the wealthy. Substantial use of solar collectors by low-income people has only occurred where financial assistance or community self-help programs are available. The Tennessee Valley Authority, for example, has supported the installation of 5,000 systems with no- and low-interest loans. Pacific Gas and Electric and the Long Island Lighting Company have similar programs. In Colorado's San Luis Valley, where half the population is below the poverty line, one quarter of the homes have solar collectors, thanks to a community program that installs locally built systems for a few hundred dollars.[32]

Although most systems used to be sold by small contractors and specialty stores, large retail chains and even door-to-door sales staff have entered the business. Sears Roebuck and Company now markets collectors in some stores and plans to expand their availability. Some smaller companies are opening up new retail outlets and distributorships each month. Extended payment plans and tax credits ease the consumer's financial burden, making collectors an attractive purchase.[33]

Large commercial and industrial systems are the most rapidly growing use of solar collectors in the United States. Hotels, laundries, food processors, and many other businesses require extensive amounts of hot water, and most have

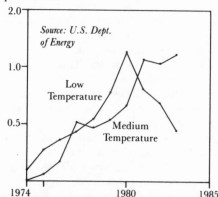

Million Square Meters

Source: U.S. Dept. of Energy

Low Temperature

Medium Temperature

1974   1980   1985

Figure 8-1. Solar Collector Manufacturing in the United States, 1974-83

seen their natural gas and electricity bills soar in recent years. Large orders enable manufacturers to gear up production lines and minimize marketing costs. The biggest system yet was installed at the Packerland meat-packing plant in Green Bay, Wisconsin, in 1984. It cost $30 million and includes 10,000 square meters of solar collectors.[34]

The Packerland project is a product of the "Solar Utility Program" developed by American Solar King, a Texas-based company. It is intended to assuage the reluctance of many firms to invest considerable sums in energy projects, a business with which they are unfamiliar. American Solar King agrees to sell a company hot water at 20 percent less than the price of heating it with gas, designs and builds the collector system, and raises the needed capital from third-party investors. For the host company there is virtually no risk. The Packerland project alone used more than a tenth of the medium-temperature collectors manufactured in the United States in 1984 and allowed American Solar King to quadruple its manufacturing capacity. This company and others believe that the largely untapped commercial-industrial market has considerable potential.[35]

American manufacturers have made major efforts to lower costs, mainly by simplifying their systems. Since the early eighties, a growing share of the solar water heaters sold in the United States have been simple "passive" systems, many of them exported by Israeli and Japanese companies. Some American firms have obtained licenses to manufacture the foreign-designed collectors and others have developed their own natural-circulation systems. In California it is estimated that such systems now claim half the solar collector market. Although some cost about as much as the typical active system, others are available for $1,000 or less. Low cost and reliability

are finally being combined by many manufacturers, and this could lead to far greater use of solar collectors.[36]

Sears Roebuck and Company now markets solar collectors in some stores.

Costs can be further reduced by technological advances. Researchers report that although the best collectors have improved little in the past five years, average systems are more efficient and last longer. Optical properties, thermal stability, and surface uniformity have all improved and the real price of collectors has been halved since 1977. Most manufacturers have switched to the use of low-iron glass on their collectors, an improvement that boosts the transmission of sunlight by 10 percent. Required testing and certification of these systems in many states has ended the horror stories that accompanied some faulty early installations.[37]

Advanced collector designs and materials may eventually yield even better performance at a lower cost. The design that has received the most attention so far is the vacuum tube solar collector, which has found limited use in Europe, Japan, and the United States. Vacuum tube collectors are efficient and work well in cold weather, but they are fragile and expensive, and will probably be confined to specialty markets.[38]

Plastic thin-film solar collectors may be the next step in solar water heating. First developed by Brookhaven National Laboratories in the United States in 1979, the "solar sandwich" has several layers of plastic film suspended by lightweight steel. The collectors weigh only a tenth as much as metal or glass ones and are much less expensive to produce. A New York-based company has turned the Brookhaven design into a commercial system that it plans to sell for $760. If the performance and longevity of these collectors is sufficient, the result could be greatly expanded use of solar water heating.[39]

Although the past decade has seen unprecedented progress in solar water heating, the enormous potential of this energy source has only begun to be tapped. Properly designed and built systems are clearly economical where the weather is sunny and fuel prices are high. Developing countries and the rapidly growing sunbelt regions of Europe and the United States may one day get most of their hot water from the sun's energy. But solar heating does not make sense in every region, and policymakers should evaluate its feasibility closely before promoting its use.

SOLAR THERMAL POWER GENERATION

There are two main technologies for generating electricity from sunlight. Photovoltaic cells, discussed at length in *State of the World-1984,* are made of silicon; they directly convert sunlight to electricity. Solar thermal power technologies produce electricity in much the way conventional coal- and oil-fired plants do. They capture the sun's heat and use it to produce steam that spins a turbine and a generator. Although these technologies have not been developed as rapidly as photovoltaics, recent advances suggest that they have substantial potential.

Solar thermal power technologies are designed to concentrate the relatively diffuse energy of the sun and use it to heat a fluid to well above the boiling point of water. To accomplish this, large areas must be covered with durable solar collectors. The steam or hot water produced can be used directly in a district heating system or industrial complex or indirectly to generate electricity. Because it is often difficult to place such facilities near a big energy user, the latter is generally more practical.

One approach is to install individual solar concentrating devices—either parabolic troughs or dishes—that collect heat. These can be attached to individual power generators or they can pipe hot fluid to a circulating water system that is hooked up to a central generator. A second technology being developed is a solar central receiver that uses a large array of mirrors to concentrate sunlight on a single receiving device. The intense heat turns water or some other fluid into steam that runs a turbine. The last approach, in many ways the simplest, is a solar pond—a large expanse of saline water that is carefully controlled so that the captured heat is kept at the bottom and insulated by upper layers of water. The hot water can be siphoned from the pond's lower areas to generate electricity.

All three approaches—described in some detail in this section—are at similar stages of development: Several experimental systems are operating, testing is under way, and more advanced and larger systems are being designed and built. (See Table 8-5.) The research is being done in just a few areas of the world—the southwestern United States, Australia, the Middle East (principally Israel), and southern Europe—because the technologies work best in desert or Mediterranean climates with clear air and intense sunshine.

Parabolic troughs, the first solar thermal power technology, consist of rectangular, concave mirrored collectors that focus sunlight onto a thin pipe running across the collector. A fluid inside the receiver tube, usually oil, is heated to

Table 8-5. Large Solar Thermal Electric Systems, Operating or Planned, 1984

Project	Location	Technology	Operating Capacity	Expected or Actual Completion Date
			(kilowatts)	(year)
Solar 100	California	Central Receiver	100,000	*
Denby Lake	California	Solar Pond	48,000	1988
Luz	California	Trough Collector	41,800	1986
Carissa Plain	California	Central Receiver	30,000	*
Roan	California	Trough Collector	15,000	1985
Solar One	California	Central Receiver	10,000	1982
Mysovoye	Soviet Union	Central Receiver	5,000	1983
Bet haArava	Israel	Solar Pond	5,000	1984
La Jet	California	Dish Receiver	4,500	1984
Themis	France	Central Receiver	2,000	1983
CESA-1	Spain	Central Receiver	1,200	1983
Sunshine	Japan	Central Receiver	1,000	1981
Eurelios	Italy	Central Receiver	1,000	1981

*Projects on hold with no definite completion date.
SOURCE: Worldwatch Institute, based on research reports, news articles, and private communications.

above the boiling point of water, sometimes further heated by a fossil-fuel-fired boiler, and then conveyed to a heat exchanger where water is turned to steam. Since the mid-seventies, this technology has benefited from research funded by the U.S. Department of Energy. The emphasis has been on reducing costs and boosting the efficiency of small experimental systems. Parabolic troughs now provide process heat for several American factories. An estimated half-million square feet of troughs have been installed in the United States.[40]

Researchers working on second- and third-generation collectors have reduced costs to between $4,000 and $4,500 per kilowatt. Though still more expensive than conventional generating technologies, troughs may become an economical source of process heat, and perhaps electricity, in areas now dependent on oil. Companies in France, the United States, and West Germany are already trying to commercialize solar troughs. The Solar Kinetics Company of Irving, Texas, has installed a 60,000-square-foot industrial process heat system in Arizona. The Roan Corporation has signed a contract to build a solar trough generator that will feed 15 megawatts of power into the Pacific Gas & Electric grid.[41]

The most ambitious trough project to date is being constructed in Daggett, California, by Luz Engineering, an affiliate of an Israeli company. The power from the 42-megawatt system will be sold to Southern California Edison. Made possible by U.S. tax credits and special loans from the Israeli and Japanese Governments, this $60-million plant could help determine the economic viability of solar troughs.[42]

Solar dish generating systems present a greater technical challenge than troughs but are more efficient. Typically, each dish is about 20 feet in diameter, and its parabolically shaped, mirrored surface is designed to track the sun. A thermal receiver is mounted at the focal point of the dish. Efficiencies of over 20 percent and temperatures of well over 700 degrees Fahrenheit have been achieved. Experimental systems currently use a pipe to move a heated fluid to a central generator. The heat lost from transporting the fluid is substantial, but it is hoped that eventually a heat engine can be attached to each dish. Such engines use heat to expand gas in a cylinder, thereby driving a piston and an alternator. Although not yet commercialized, the high efficiency of this technology indicates that it is worth pursuing.[43]

Parabolic dish systems have been developed in Israel and the United States. Though still small and experimental, most have worked well. Efforts are now directed at reducing costs, which according to researchers at the Weizmann Institute in Israel should reach $200 per square meter. Use of plastic structural materials and synthetic reflective materials such as mylar show considerable promise. Large-scale factory manufacturing and site-assembly of the systems can also lower costs, which are projected to fall to between $2,000 and $3,000 per kilowatt.[44]

The U.S. Department of Energy has supported several test facilities, including a 25-kilowatt dish built in Rancho Mirage, California, and two 100-kilowatt multiple-dish systems. In Shenandoah, Georgia, 114 parabolic dishes with a capacity of 400 kilowatts supply heat and power to a knitwear factory. Other, smaller systems have been installed in Kuwait and in New South Wales, Australia. Carlo LaPorta of the Solar Energy Industries Association estimates that over 100,000 square feet of dish systems had been installed in the United States by the end of 1983.[45]

Dwarfing the projects completed thus far is a 700-dish system covering 320,-000 square feet that is being built by La Jet Energy Company in southern California. It will generate 4.5 megawatts of power to sell to the San Diego Gas and Electric Company. La Jet claims a cost of less than $4,000 per kilowatt, competitive with trough systems. The new facility is one of the first large solar thermal power projects to be financed by private investors, albeit with the help of government tax credits. David Halbert of La Jet expects that further cost reductions will make it possible to install 200 megawatts of dish systems in the next four years.[46]

The second major way to generate electricity from sunlight is with solar central receivers, also known as "power towers." A large array of independently tracking mirrors called heliostats focus sunlight on a central receiver. In most systems the receiver is mounted on a tower that is 50–100 meters tall. Steam or a hot fluid is piped from the receiver to a heat exchanger, turbine, and generator located on the ground. Solar central receivers concentrate sunlight 200-fold or more, yielding temperatures above 500 degrees Celsius. But efficiencies are only 20–25 percent because heat is lost over the substantial distance between the heliostats and receiver.[47]

Solar central receivers have been a major focus of government alternative energy programs since the mid-seventies. So far, six plants (listed in Table 8-5) have been built in as many countries, and there are several demonstration projects in Europe. Israeli researchers are planning a 3,000-kilowatt central receiver to be used in the manufacture of chemicals. More ambitious even than its Mysovoye project, the Soviet Union announced in 1983 plans for a 300,000-kilowatt solar central receiver backed up by a fossil fuel plant. Scheduled to be built in the southern Soviet republic of Uzbekistan, this project would dwarf all current systems.[48]

The first receivers are expensive. The largest, the 10-megawatt Solar One in southern California, cost the U.S. Government $140 million and has been the target of critics who question whether alternative energy funds would not be more effectively spent on commercializing smaller, simpler technologies. In fact, Solar One did claim a disproportionately large share of the government's solar budget in the late seventies. The project represents a significant engineering accomplishment, but analysts are divided as to its potential as an economical power source.[49]

Solar One began generating power in 1982 and entered commercial operation in 1984. It has 1,800 heliostats and a 30-story tower. With computer controls designed to keep each tracking mirror at an ideal angle and to monitor and regulate the generating system, the entire facility can be run by just one person. So far, the plant's performance has met or exceeded expectations, with a peak power output of over 12,000 kilowatts. By drawing on its storage system it has operated continuously for 33 hours and generated 74,000 kilowatt-hours in a day, enough power for 4,000 homes.[50]

Solar One's main failing is its cost: $14,000 per kilowatt, high even for a one-of-a-kind demonstration project. Making the solar central receiver an economical power source will require significant advances, many of which are now the focus of engineering research. Heliostats are the dominant expense of a central receiver system, and the technology's potential hinges largely on whether these costs can be substantially reduced. One study shows the cost falling from $375 per square meter to between $100 and $200, but that will only occur if heliostats are mass-produced on a scale that is not currently planned.[51]

Several U.S. companies have developed more-advanced central receiver designs and are seriously considering major efforts to commercialize the technology. McDonnell Douglas, in partnership with Southern California Edison and several other companies, has plans

for a 100-megawatt project called Solar 100. It would cost $550 million, occupy 280 hectares (over one square mile), and produce enough power for 50,000 homes. Rockwell International, ARCO Solar Industries, and Pacific Gas and Electric have plans for a 30-megawatt system that would circulate molten sodium for greater efficiency. Both projects were put on hold in 1984, however, because of difficulty in attracting investors. These very large and risky investments are unlikely to be made without solar tax credits, which the U.S. Congress has so far refused to extend beyond the end of 1985.[52]

Engineering studies have concluded that third-generation central receivers in sunny climates may have costs of between $2,500 and $4,000 per kilowatt. The lower end of this range would make the receivers an economically viable power source, but such projections are highly tenuous: They depend on a more advanced technology that has not yet been demonstrated and on the assumption that heliostats will soon be mass-produced. Both the heliostat production facilities and the solar plants themselves require investments of hundreds of millions of dollars, large sums to devote to an uncertain technology and market.[53]

Even under optimistic assumptions, it will be at least a decade before economical solar receiver plants can be successfully commercialized. Unlike dishes and troughs, receivers make sense only on a large scale, which creates formidable hurdles to their commercialization. One important advantage that central receivers do have is that the systems incorporate heat storage, so power can be generated during the early evening hours when electricity demand is often highest. Most of the early government demonstrations of solar receivers have ended, and the technology's future is largely in the hands of the private market, with the possible assistance of government tax policies. Solar receivers may find a substantial market after the turn of the century. Or they may turn out to have been an expensive wrong turn by government solar energy researchers.

Solar ponds, the third approach to solar thermal power generation, are the simplest technology. In 1902, a Russian scientist discovered that naturally salty ponds often have relatively high temperatures a meter or two below the surface. The water in such ponds tends to stratify, with the relatively dense, salty layers near the bottom preventing the natural convection that normally would keep the pond cool. Harry Tabor, known as the father of solar energy in Israel, proposed in 1954 that artificial salt-gradient solar ponds be built for commercial energy production. Hot water could be slowly drawn from the bottom of ponds and used for heating, water desalination, or electricity generation.[54]

Since the early seventies, researchers in Australia, Israel, and the United States have conducted research on solar ponds. By carefully controlling the salinity and by using chemicals to prevent cloudiness, temperatures above the boiling point of water have been attained. Although solar ponds are relatively inefficient, capturing only 10–20 percent of the sunlight striking them, they make up for this with their low cost and inherent storage capability. Solar ponds can generate power whenever it is most needed, regardless of whether the sun is out at the time. The engineering required is no more complicated than for a large plumbing system.

Many of the solar ponds built so far are intended to provide heat rather than power. This is the most efficient use of the technology since the ponds do not reach very high temperatures. A 2,000-square-meter pond built in 1978 in Miamisburg, Ohio, provides heat for a municipal swimming pool and recreation building. And an 800-square-meter pond heats a storage building near Flagstaff, Arizona. But these ponds can also generate power by conveying the hot water to a heat engine. Although inefficient compared with other solar-electric generators, solar ponds are also much less expensive than the other technologies discussed here.[55]

Solar ponds can generate power whenever it is most needed, regardless of whether the sun is out at the time.

In theory, solar ponds can be built almost anywhere—a natural one has even been discovered in Antarctica—but they will be most feasible in areas with unused land, lots of sunlight, and naturally occurring salt lakes, marshes, or dry lake beds. Expenses can be reduced if the pond is on impermeable ground, eliminating the need for an artificial liner. The world's first commercial-size solar pond, a 150-kilowatt system, was built in 1979 at Ein Bokek on the shores of the salty Dead Sea. Two additional ponds with a capacity of 5,000 kilowatts were completed in 1984 that provide power for East Jerusalem at 10–15¢ per kilowatt-hour. (Again, see Table 8-5.) Israeli researchers are confident that solar ponds are competitive with virtually any other power source in their fossil-fuel-short country. Projects on the drawing board could produce as much as 2,000 megawatts from solar ponds by the end of the century, increasing the country's generating capacity by 75 percent.[56]

The United States has approximately a dozen solar ponds, most of them small, experimental projects designed to test the technology or to heat greenhouses or hog barns. The best natural locations are near the Great Salt Lake in Utah and the Salton Sea in California. A study funded by the Department of Energy in the late seventies found that a 600-kilowatt solar pond near the Salton Sea was feasible. Although the U.S. Government has not pursued this, the Israeli company designing the Dead Sea project has begun working on a 48-megawatt solar pond near the Salton Sea. Southern California Edison has agreed to purchase the power—mainly at times of peak demand. The Israeli company is also considering a large project in Utah.[57]

Australia has been researching solar ponds since the sixties but only has a few small ones in operation. The most notable is a 2,000-square-meter project near Alice Springs, a remote area where energy costs are high. It produces 20 kilowatts of electricity. Other countries with experimental solar ponds include Brazil, India, Saudi Arabia, and Turkey. The success or failure of the large projects in Israel and the United States is likely to influence the speed with which other countries proceed.[58]

A study by Frost & Sullivan, a consulting firm in the United States, projects that worldwide solar-pond generating capacity will reach 400 megawatts in 2000 and 3,500 megawatts by 2010. Even with this rapid growth, it is unlikely that solar ponds will provide power in more than a few locations by the end of the century. In most areas, low-cost land, water, and salt are not available, and other solar energy technologies will probably be more feasible.[59]

Solar thermal power technologies are evolving too rapidly to make firm predictions. Based on the cost estimates now available, it seems likely that some form of solar thermal electric generation will become common in sunny regions by the end of the century. Frost & Sullivan projects that the solar thermal technologies other than ponds will provide 1,200 megawatts of power in the year 2000 and 10,000 megawatts by 2010. But solar thermal power plants are land-intensive, requiring six to eight acres per megawatt. Although this is only a small constraint in the desert regions where solar thermal power is most feasible, these systems also need lots of water, a major limitation. Parabolic dishes and solar ponds appear to have the most promise, largely because they are small technologies that can be built rapidly and in stages and are already being commercialized.[60]

ALCOHOL FUELS

A replacement for the vast quantities of petroleum that run the world's motor vehicles has been one of the most elusive goals of researchers and energy planners. From oil shale to propane, from hydrogen to jojoba oil, the list of alternatives could fill a chemist's textbook. Among the various options, alcohol fuels derived from biological materials show the most promise. Although little ethanol (ethyl alcohol) was used as a fuel in 1974, over 70 million barrels were burned in automobiles in 1984. And in Brazil, ethanol now accounts for 43 percent of automotive fuel consumption. Although no other country comes close to this, alcohol-fuel use is growing in at least a dozen nations, with everything from corn to sugar beets and cheese whey being used as a feedstock. Alcohol is likely to play a significant role in powering the world's automobiles—with major implications for national energy balances, employment, income distribution, and food availability.

Alcohol actually predates gasoline as an automotive fuel. The first internal-combustion engine burned pure ethanol and Henry Ford designed his engines to run on either gasoline or ethanol by simply adjusting the carburetor. In France, gasoline and alcohol were used about equally at the turn of the century. From World War I through the thirties, alcohol-powered cars were common in Australia, Brazil, Cuba, and various European countries, thanks in part to the influence of farmers who sought to assure markets for their crops.[61]

In Brazil, ethanol now accounts for 43 percent of automotive fuel consumption.

Alcohol production is a relatively simple process. Sugars are fermented using the enzymes produced by a kind of yeast, and the result is a combination of ethanol, water, and marketable carbon dioxide gas. Sugarcane, sugar beets, and sorghum are direct sources of the necessary sugars. Using a more complicated process, starches from corn and other grains or from cassava, a root crop, can be converted to sugars and then fermented.

In the mid-seventies, Brazil launched the world's most ambitious effort to reduce dependence on imported petroleum. The country is a major sugar exporter and ethanol derived from sugarcane is viewed as a way to reduce oil imports and prop up sugar prices, both helpful in reducing the country's $90-billion foreign debt. Beginning in 1975 the Brazilian Government's Proalcool program offered incentives for alcohol-fuel production. Since the country had excess distillery capacity and a long history of gasohol use, the new fuel caught on almost immediately.[62]

The Brazilian Government has gradually raised its commitment to alcohol fuels, providing low-interest loans, for example, to industrialists who build new sugar mills and distilleries. By heavily taxing gasoline but not ethanol, the government keeps the latter at less than $1.50 per gallon, compared with $2.40 for gasoline. Over 300 distilleries have been built and another 100 are under construction. The program relies largely on domestic technology and financing, but loans from abroad, including $250 million from the World Bank, have provided support. So far, the government has spent $4.5 billion on the Proalcool program.[63]

In 1979 Brazil's automobile manufacturers signed an agreement with the government that required them to build cars designed to run on pure alcohol. (Such cars are exempt from the country's value-added tax.) Almost three quarters of the cars sold in 1983 run on pure alcohol, and there are now over 1.2 million such cars out of a total fleet of 10 million. (See Table 8-6.) The other 9 million automobiles use a gasohol mixture that is 23 percent ethanol.[64]

Brazil produced 57 million barrels of alcohol fuel in 1984—up from 2 million barrels in 1976. (See Table 8-7.) This ambitious program, together with recent oil discoveries, has helped Brazil cut its oil imports in half since 1978. The country plans to triple production of alcohol fuel by 1993, which combined with successes in oil exploration might allow Brazil to reach its goal of importing no oil for cars by the early nineties.[65]

No program of this size is without costs. Competition between food and

Table 8-6. Brazil: Sales of Gasohol and Alcohol Vehicles, 1980–83

Year	Gasohol Vehicles	Alcohol Vehicles
1980	775,000	241,000
1981	496,000	137,000
1982	452,000	234,000
1983	212,000	590,000

SOURCE: Howard Geller, "Ethanol from Sugarcane in Brazil," in Annual Reviews, Inc., *Annual Review of Energy*, Vol. 10 (Palo Alto, Calif.: forthcoming).

Table 8-7. Alcohol-Fuel Production and Use, Brazil and the United States, 1976–84

Year	United States			Brazil		
	Production	Use	Share of Auto Fuel	Production	Use	Share of Auto Fuel
	(million barrels)		(percent)	(million barrels)		(percent)
1976	—	—	—	2.0	1.1	1.0
1977	—	—	—	6.2	4.0	3.8
1978	0.3	0.6	0.02	12.5	9.5	8.4
1979	0.5	1.2	0.05	19.6	14.1	12.2
1980	0.9	1.9	0.08	20.1	16.9	16.3
1981	1.8	2.0	0.09	23.9	16.0	16.1
1982	5.0	5.5	0.24	32.9	23.3	22.5
1983	8.9	10.3	0.45	47.7	39.0	35.7
1984[1]	10.0	12.0	0.52	57.2	47.0	43.0

[1]Estimated.
SOURCE: Worldwatch Institute, based on unpublished data from Information Resources Inc., Washington, D.C., 1984.

fuel crops is of particular concern since sugarcane is being grown on some of the country's richest farmland. A hectare of land that feeds five people if used for rice cultivation yields only enough sugarcane to run one automobile. Attempts are being made to encourage the planting of sugarcane on marginal land, but whether they will be effective given the political power of wealthy sugar growers is uncertain. The acreage devoted to subsidized export crops—soybeans used as livestock feed in Europe as well as sugar—is growing rapidly. Brazil is losing the small farms that supply local vegetable and dairy markets. Many of these farmers are being forced to move to the marginal soils of the newly cleared Amazon Basin. Brazil has millions of poor people with little chance of competing with subsidized crops in their daily struggle for food. The resulting inequalities and hardship could well outweigh the economic benefits of the alcohol program.[66]

A barrel of gasoline refined domestically from imported crude oil costs about $41 in Brazil, whereas alcohol costs $50–55 per barrel. Only a compli-cated array of government subsidies leads motorists to fill up with ethanol. Yet an analysis by Howard Geller of the American Council for an Energy-Efficient Economy shows that the extra interest payments on the country's debt that result from importing petroleum in effect cancel out oil's cost advantage. And Geller believes that the cost of producing ethanol is no higher than that of domestic oil exploration, extraction, and refining. Moreover, the alcohol-fuel program has the important secondary effect of stimulating industrial development. Sugarcane cultivation and alcohol production are labor-intensive, and about a half-million new full-time jobs have been created.[67]

In recent years smaller alcohol-fuel programs have sprung up around the world, roughly tracing the tropical sugarcane belt. Latin American countries with programs that should be able to produce sizable quantities in the future include Costa Rica, Cuba, Mexico, Nicaragua, Paraguay, and several Caribbean islands. Cuba is the leading producer outside Brazil, with the capacity to produce over three million barrels of ethanol each year.[68]

Zimbabwe is another major sugar grower that has begun using some of its cane for alcohol production. One facility now produces 200,000 barrels per year —not much by world standards, but enough to supply 12–15 percent of the country's automotive fuel and reduce the oil import bill. Additional plants are being built. Kenya also has a cane-based alcohol-fuel plant that uses a Brazilian design and was financed by European aid agencies. The Mehta plant produces 138,000 barrels of alcohol per year, but because it is expensive and unreliable, the government has delayed plans for additional plants. The World Bank is funding an alcohol-fuel facility in Mali and considering one in Zambia. Major reliance on alcohol fuels in Africa is not likely in the near future, however. The continent's massive food deficits and economic problems make it doubtful that land and financial resources should be devoted to fuel production.[69]

Several Asian countries—including China, India, Indonesia, and Malaysia— have substantial sugarcane crops that could be distilled into alcohol fuel. Indonesia has two small operating plants, and the Philippines and Sri Lanka are producing limited amounts of fuel in pilot facilities. Although alcohol-fuel use is likely to expand somewhat in developing countries, many once-ambitious programs have been put on hold in the past few years due to financial difficulties. Major efforts to imitate the Brazilian program would be difficult and possibly counterproductive. Most countries lack sufficient fertile land to expand cane production greatly without cutting into food supplies. Efforts to cultivate cassava and other tropical plants, which can be grown by small holders on marginal lands, are essential if alcohol fuel is to make a significant contribution in most of the Third World.[70]

Alcohol-fuel programs in temperate countries are of necessity far different from those in the tropics. Because sugarcane cannot be grown there, other feedstocks and production processes must be used. To date, common grain crops have been the most popular temperate-zone feedstocks. Ninety-five percent of U.S. alcohol fuel comes from corn, for example, and the rest from a mixture of wheat, barley, other grains, and agricultural wastes. The carbohydrate or starch from the grains is heated until it breaks down into simpler sugars. Research into more-efficient and cheaper ways to produce ethanol are being undertaken in major grain-producing countries such as Argentina, Australia, and France.[71]

In the United States, the use of alcohol fuel has grown rapidly since the first government incentives were enacted in 1979. Gasohol is now exempt from the 5¢-per-gallon federal gasoline tax and from similar levies in over 30 states. In addition, the U.S. Department of Energy and several state Departments of Energy and Agriculture have loan guarantee and cost-sharing programs to encourage the building of alcohol-production facilities. Based on average corn prices and the sale of the residues for livestock feed, ethanol is now produced at a wholesale cost of $1.30 per gallon, compared with 94¢ per gallon for high-octane unleaded gasoline.[72]

Ethanol production in the United States rose from 900,000 barrels in 1980 to 10 million in 1984. (See Table 8-8.) Although the goal set by Congress of 48 million barrels by 1985 will not be met, production has increased more than fivefold since 1981. Today approximately 5 percent of the "gasoline" sold in the country is actually a 1-to-10 ethanol-gasoline blend. In Indiana and some other farm states, an estimated one third of the fuel sold is part alcohol. Whereas in 1980 the "gasohol" label was proudly displayed as a show of independence from imported oil, most gasohol is now marketed as a high-octane unleaded fuel that improves engine performance. Demand has outstripped supply, and ethanol imported from Brazil serves 15 percent of the American market despite steep import duties of 60¢ per gallon.[73]

By mid-1984 there were about 150 major ethanol plants in operation, many smaller on-farm plants, and dozens of others being planned or built. Dominating the industry is Archer-Daniels Midland, one of the world's largest grain companies, but many small entrepreneurial firms are entering the business. One is the Ultrasystems Company, which is building the Dawn-Enterprises alcohol plant in North Dakota, scheduled for completion in 1985. Located in a rich barley-growing region close to abundant supplies of cheap lignite coal, the plant is designed to minimize the two dominant costs of alcohol production—feedstock and fuel. The facility will produce 71,000 barrels of alcohol each year as well as distillers' grain to be sold to livestock operations and carbon dioxide to the carbonated beverage industry. A smaller, 3,000-barrel plant in California's Central Valley uses waste from a cheese factory to produce ethanol and animal feed. Another in Vermont uses

corn as feedstock and wood pellets as fuel to produce alcohol for upstate New York fuel blenders.[74]

The prospects for alcohol fuels were enhanced in 1984 when the U.S. Environmental Protection Agency (EPA) proposed the virtual elimination of lead from gasoline by 1986. Lead has been a common additive for decades because it inexpensively raises octane and makes gasoline burn more evenly in high-compression engines. Although American cars have been designed to run on unleaded fuel since the mid-seventies, many motorists have dismantled their cars' anti-pollution devices and continue to purchase leaded gas. EPA has decided that a further crackdown is essential in order to protect public health. Studies show that ethanol added at the refinery is not only the cheapest alternative means of boosting octane, it is a way to raise the overall efficiency of the refinery. It is difficult to know how the refining industry will respond to the new standards, but demand for ethanol will probably rise and bid up prices, leading to new distillery construction. A Washington, D.C., consulting firm projects that annual ethanol use will reach 120 million barrels by the nineties, over 10 times the 1984 level. Half of U.S. automobiles could be running on alcohol blends.[75]

The U.S. alcohol-fuel industry has been criticized on a variety of grounds, including its net energy efficiency and its impact on world food prices. Historically, distilleries have relied on natural gas as a fuel. Combining this energy requirement with the fuel used to cultivate corn led some analysts to conclude that the ethanol energy yield is less than the energy input. An authoritative 1982 U.S. Department of Agriculture study largely laid these fears to rest, however, by showing a net energy yield of 1.5 to 1 for recently completed ethanol plants using modern technology. Moreover, most of

Table 8-8. United States: Production of Alcohol Fuel From Corn, 1980–84

Year	Corn Used	Area in Corn	Alcohol Fuel Produced
	(million bushels)	(thousand hectares)	(million barrels)
1980	15	57	0.9
1981	35	134	1.8
1982	80	308	5.0
1983	135	518	8.9
1984	160	615	10.0

SOURCES: Worldwatch Institute estimates based on unpublished data from U.S. Department of Agriculture.

these new facilities are fueled by coal, lignite, or wood—less-valuable fuels than the ethanol that is produced. At current fuel prices there is ample incentive to maximize the energy yield.[76]

As in Brazil, the farm sector in the United States is a strong proponent of alcohol fuels, viewing them as a way of boosting demand for corn and other grains and thus keeping prices high. The alcohol produced in 1984 required about 160 million bushels of corn—2 percent of the country's crop. Although not enough to affect food prices significantly, that will not be true for long given the rate of expansion. Major U.S. reliance on alcohol fuel derived from food grains would almost certainly have an impact on the world grain market, in which the United States is the dominant exporter. Diverting the entire U.S. corn crop (30 percent of the world total) to alcohol production would fuel just one fourth of the nation's cars. Heavy reliance on alcohol fuel will only be possible if much of the feed value of the crops can be retained in the residue left after alcohol production and if new crops and agricultural wastes are able to play an important role.[77]

Major U.S. reliance on alcohol fuel derived from food grains would almost certainly have an impact on the world grain market.

A study by the Center for the Biology of Natural Systems concludes that a shift from the corn-soybean crop mix now typical in the U.S. Midwest to a corn-sugar beet mix would allow farmers to produce as much high-protein animal feed as before and also provide feedstock for alcohol production. The Center estimates that if this scheme were adopted throughout the Midwest, the yield in 1995 would be 700 million barrels of ethanol, which is a quarter of current annual gasoline use.[78] Although it is doubtful that land and water resources are sufficient to allow such a drastic shift, rising petroleum costs should quite naturally lead to efforts to maximize the energy as well as the food yield of the world's cropland.

Researchers have only begun to explore the potential of currently underused crops as feedstocks, but many appear to have higher alcohol yields than those now used. The jerusalem artichoke is one promising possibility. This perennial grows in a wide range of soils and climates and produces sugars that can be used directly for alcohol production. It yields almost twice as much alcohol per hectare as corn, but because the jerusalem artichoke has been of little commercial importance in the past, it will take time for it to be widely cultivated. Sweet sorghum and sudan grasses are temperate-zone crops that produce sugars that can be used for alcohol production. Potatoes are prolific producers of carbohydrates and could become a fuel crop. And renewed interest in alcohol fuel coincides with the emergence of biotechnology, which may help develop new crop varieties more suited to alcohol production.[79]

Wood, grasses, and other cellulose-based materials are abundant and can be grown on much less fertile or well-watered land than most food crops. Cellulose, like carbohydrates, can be broken down into simple sugars for distillation into ethanol, but the cellulosic bonds are far stronger and cannot be dissolved by simple heating. Acid hydrolysis and enzymatic hydrolysis are the two chemical processes that researchers believe have the most promise as cellulose converters, and each is being investigated. The Soviet Union has 40 acid hydrolysis plants using wood feedstock, and Brazil is applying the same technology to convert eucalyptus wood into lignin—used for coke production—and sugars. Other countries conducting research on this approach include France, Japan, New Zealand, and the United States. Enzymatic hydrolysis, a biochemical process, is more problematic; it is being researched extensively in the United States and Canada and may soon be pilot-tested.[80]

Also important is finding ways to produce alcohol fuel using waste materials. Farms, food processors, and municipal dumps are good feedstock sources, but finding the right materials and separating them from other wastes is often difficult. In the past several years small U.S. distilleries have been set up using almond hulls, cheese whey, spoiled food, and even discarded jelly beans. Another avenue worth pursuing is the production of ethanol from algae, a one-celled aquatic organism. Several biotechnology companies working on new algae strains and production techniques claim to be near commercialization. In one interesting dovetailing of renewable technologies, a California firm plans to use waste heat from a solar electric generator to warm its algae distillery.[81]

Another alcohol—methanol—can be produced from wood and other cellulosic materials and appears to have substantial potential as an automotive fuel. Engines must be substantially modified to use this fuel, since it corrodes some materials, but in the right cars, methanol is clean-burning and efficient. Though possessing only about half the energy value of gasoline, methanol's high oxygen content allows it to be burned more efficiently. Methanol can also be produced from natural gas and coal, making it perhaps the most versatile liquid fuel being examined.[82]

Methanol is produced by gasifying dried wood and then converting methane to methanol using a catalyst. This is a well-established technology, and the

U.S. Office of Technology Assessment estimates that wood costing $30 a ton can be converted to methanol for $1.10 a gallon. Given the fuel's low energy content, this is far too expensive to make it competitive, but researchers in Brazil, Canada, France, New Zealand, Norway, the Philippines, and elsewhere are working to lower production costs. Scientists at the U.S. Solar Energy Research Institute have developed a gasifier that can double the methanol yield from wood, and Brazilian researchers report similar results. These more advanced processes have not yet been proved in commercial-sized plants.[83]

Some limited use of methanol fuel has begun. About 100 million gallons are used in U.S. automobiles each year. The ARCO Oil Company sells a blended gasoline with 5 percent methanol. The fuel has a high octane value but some people say their cars do not run well on it. In the long run, engine modifications will be required to allow automobiles to run on fuel containing more than 10 percent methanol.[84]

The California Energy Commission, in conjunction with the Ford Motor Company, has developed a fleet of 506 methanol-fueled cars that are used by 6 state agencies and 15 local governments. The autos have performed well so far, and testing by the Environmental Protection Agency shows impressively low emissions of nitrogen oxides and hydrocarbons. Engines running on this fuel do emit formaldehyde and unburned methanol, but not in quantities that appear to present health hazards. Brazil and Norway have also successfully tested methanol-fueled automobiles. But none of these cars has yet been optimized for methanol use, and researchers believe that improvements in fuel efficiency and pollutant reductions are possible. The U.S. Solar Energy Research Institute has developed an engine that converts methanol to hydrogen and carbon monoxide before burning it, giving an efficiency of 30 miles per gallon—close to the fuel economy of gasoline despite methanol's lower energy content.[85]

Methanol's advantages make it a likely automotive fuel in many parts of the world, but its future as a "renewable" fuel is more dubious. For the foreseeable future it appears that natural gas and coal will be less expensive methanol feedstocks than wood and other biomass materials. For many oil-producing countries that are currently flaring or reinjecting large quantities of natural gas for which they have no markets, the export of methanol fuel would be logical. And methanol may be the most economical synthetic fuel for countries with vast coal reserves. Only those that lack inexpensive coal and natural gas are likely to turn to biomass for methanol production.

Alcohol-fuel use will probably grow substantially. For the United States alone, Colin A. Houston & Associates of New Jersey forecasts a fivefold increase by 1995, with ethanol use going from 2 billion to 9 billion gallons and methanol from 0.2 billion to 1.8 billion gallons.[86] These projections can be considered conservative, particularly in light of tax incentives and more-stringent lead standards for gasoline.

But alcohol fuels will by no means solve the world's liquid fuel problems. Cars currently burn about 20 million barrels of gasoline each day; making a large dent in that figure will not be easy. Improved automobile fuel efficiency is without doubt the most economical way to reduce gasoline consumption. Brazil, for example, could now almost eliminate gasoline use in automobiles by doubling the efficiency of its cars—at a far lower cost than it would take to double alcohol-fuel production. In the long run, a sustainable transport system will involve a combination of more-efficient automobiles, improved public transportation, and greater reliance on renewable fuels.

OTHER RENEWABLE ENERGY HIGHLIGHTS

The accelerated development of renewable energy sources entered its second decade in 1984. Government support of renewable energy has leveled off in most countries, but the surge in private investment described in *State of the World-1984* continues. Commercial development of wind power and wood-fired power plants in particular is far exceeding earlier expectations. It is important to look beyond the four technologies discussed in detail in this chapter in order to grasp renewable energy's growing contribution.

Worldwide geothermal generating capacity reached approximately 3,400 megawatts at the beginning of 1984, up more than 20 percent from a year earlier. The United States continues to use the most geothermal energy, largely at the 1,300-megawatt Geysers project in northern California. In the Philippines, geothermal generating capacity has passed 800 megawatts and is scheduled to reach 1,700 megawatts by the end of 1985—meeting 18 percent of the country's electricity needs. In Mexico, geothermal capacity expanded in 1984 from 205 megawatts to 645 megawatts. According to geothermal analyst Ronald DiPippo of Southeastern Massachusetts University, worldwide geothermal capacity will reach 5,800 megawatts by the end of 1985, and will exceed 10,000 megawatts before 1990. In some areas, such as Central America and Indonesia, geothermal resources will be a principal source of energy.[87]

The use of wood fuel and other biomass by industry, electric utilities, and district heating systems has expanded dramatically in the past few years. In the United States alone, over 100 biomass-fueled power projects have been started since 1981, representing a generating capacity of 1,800 megawatts. The projects are spread throughout the country. Although wood fuel has long been an important energy source for the forest products industry, most of the recent projects were undertaken by independent energy producers. The Philippines has built 17 wood-fired power plants and plans to have 60 by 1990. Meanwhile, Sweden plans to use wood fuel for district heating in many of its cities. Municipal, industrial, and agricultural wastes are also serving as feedstocks for at least a score of recently begun small generating plants in the United States.[88]

Solar electric generation using photovoltaics continues to advance, though not at the same pace as a few years ago. The manufacture of solar cells grew about 20 percent in 1984, reaching 26 megawatts of peak-power capacity. Large generating plants continue to be installed and are the most dynamic aspect of photovoltaics development. The Sacramento Municipal Utility District in California has completed the first megawatt of an eventual 100-megawatt photovoltaic system. ARCO Solar has finished a 6.5-megawatt project, currently the world's largest, that provides enough power for 2,000 homes. The United Energy Corporation will complete two 8-megawatt photovoltaic projects in California in 1985, and Austin, Texas, will build a 300-kilowatt generator, the first to be financed by a utility.[89]

The U.S. photovoltaics industry is still weak financially. Earnings do not cover research and development budgets, and most companies lose money—an estimated $50 million industry-wide in 1983. Faced with limited sales growth and the prospect of soon losing solar tax credits, many companies retrenched in 1984. The two largest companies, ARCO Solar and Solarex, laid off 70 and 140 workers, respectively, trimming their marketing efforts more than their R&D programs. The Japanese photovoltaics industry, in contrast, has shown remarkable strength and appears ready to surpass the American industry within a few years. The Kyocera Company has set up offices and assembly facilities on the U.S. West Coast, part of an aggressive marketing effort. The Hoxan Company is building a 9-megawatt manufacturing plant—the world's largest—and plans to sell the resulting modules at about half the current price.[90]

Wind power is perhaps the world's most rapidly developing new energy source, and growth is centered in California. The state's wind farm boom continued strongly in 1984, with close to 4,700 new turbines installed. This brought the total capacity to 609 megawatts, almost triple the figure at the end of 1983. (See Table 8-9.) Wind farms provided California utilities with $20-million worth of electricity in 1984—enough for 40,000 homes. Total investment in this field amounted to almost $700 million.[91]

The first wind farms have been plagued by frequent mechanical failures, leaving large numbers of machines idle in windy weather. But most wind farmers appeared to be putting these problems behind them in 1984, as redesigned and rebuilt wind machines were installed and operated more reliably. The economics of wind power are also improving. The cost per kilowatt has fallen by almost half in the past three years and is now less than $1,900 per kilowatt. Although wind farms still depend on tax credits, they are likely to be economical without this support within a few years.[92]

The California Energy Commission estimates that the good wind sites in the state can harness up to 13,000 mega-

Table 8-9. California: Wind Farms, 1981-84

Year	Machines Installed	Capacity Installed	Average Capacity	Average Cost	Power Generated[1]
	(number)	(megawatts)	(kilowatts)	(dollars per kilowatt)	(million kilowatt hours)
1981	144	7	49	3,100	1
1982	1,145	64	56	2,175	6
1983	2,493	172	69	1,960	74
1984[2]	4,687	366	78	1,870	250
Total	8,469	609	72	—	330

[1]Most wind machines are installed in the last half of a given year and do not produce substantial power until the next year. [2]Preliminary estimate.
SOURCE: Mike Batham, California Energy Commission, private communication, December 11, 1984.

watts of power. If all this land were developed, the state would get roughly twice as much energy from the wind as from nuclear power. Wind farms will also have an effect on land use. Prime sites in San Gorgonio Pass produce between $12,000 and $15,000 of electricity per acre in addition to the $20–30 the land earns for cattle grazing. (Prime midwestern farmland planted in corn, by comparison, yields up to $400 per acre per year.)[93]

Although over 90 percent of the U.S. wind farms are in California, the technology is spreading rapidly. Commercial farms have been installed in Hawaii, Montana, New York, and Oregon. Internationally, Denmark, the Netherlands, and Sweden are now planning wind farms, and several other countries have major research programs. Wind farms are also being considered in some developing countries, particularly islands and coastal areas in the trade wind belt. Some developers see California as little more than a proving ground before they tap the Third World market.[94]

Renewable energy sources are expanding far faster than most energy policymakers realize. In the United States, for example, renewable energy growth has outpaced that of conventional sources since 1979 and has reached about 10 percent of the national energy budget. Nuclear power, in contrast, provides 5 percent. Yet the U.S. Department of Energy ignores or underestimates renewable energy in most of its statistical reports.[95]

Prime sites produce between $12,000 and $15,000 of electricity per acre in addition to the $20–30 the land earns for cattle grazing.

Most striking is the growing contribution of renewable energy to electricity generation in the United States. Excluding large hydropower, almost 5,000-megawatts worth of renewable electricity projects have been started since 1980, while coal and nuclear plant cancellations outstripped new orders by a substantial margin. California, where most of the new projects are concentrated, is likely to get one quarter of its electricity from renewables within five years.[96]

If there is one lesson to emerge from a decade of development, it is that efforts to make long-range forecasts about such rapidly evolving technologies are pointless. Solar central receivers have languished despite hundred-million-dollar development programs and the best efforts of engineers. Wind farms relying on small wind machines have surpassed the projections of all planners, as has the use of wood fuel. Perhaps the best thing that government planners could do would be to stop trying to pick the most promising new energy technologies in advance and instead create a level playing field on which renewable and conventional sources can compete economically. Although the exact pattern of future development is unclear, improved efficiency and renewable energy appear ready to form the foundation of a more sustainable and less environmentally disruptive energy system at the turn of the century.

9

Stopping Population Growth

Lester R. Brown

The world of the mid-eighties is a world of stark demographic contrasts. Variations in fertility among countries have never been wider. Some populations change little in size from year to year or decline slightly while others are experiencing the fastest growth ever recorded. The populations of West Germany and Hungary are slowly declining in size, for example, while those of Kenya and Syria are doubling in less than 20 years.[1]

These disparities are placing great stress on the international economic system and on national political structures. Runaway population growth is indirectly fueling the debt crisis by increasing the need for imported food and other basic commodities. Low-fertility countries are food aid donors; high-fertility countries, the recipients. Nations with low fertility are invariably the lenders; those with high fertility, the borrowers. In most countries with high fertility, food production per person is either stagnant or declining.

Population policy is moving to the top of agendas of national governments and international development agencies. In the President's foreword to the *World Development Report 1984*, the first of the World Bank's annual reports to highlight this issue, A. W. Clausen observes that "population growth does not provide the drama of financial crisis or political upheaval but its significance for shaping the world of our children and grandchildren is at least as great."[2]

FROM BUCHAREST TO MEXICO CITY

In the late summer of 1984, world attention focused on this pressing problem as the U.N. International Conference on Population convened in Mexico City. The occasion was the tenth anniversary of the U.N.'s first World Population Conference, which had been held in Bucharest. The official purpose of the Mexico City Conference, in which 149 countries participated, was to review the world population plan of action adopted at Bucharest. The contrast in the moods of the two gatherings could not have been greater.

In Bucharest there had been a wide political schism between the representatives of industrial countries, who pushed for an increase in Third World family planning efforts, and those from developing countries, whose leaders argued that social and economic progress was the key to slowing population growth. The debate had been sustained and sometimes vitriolic. "Development is the best contraceptive" became the rallying cry of many Third World representatives.

In Mexico City this division had virtually disappeared and the mood was much more somber. The Mexican capital itself was an all-too-graphic reminder of the consequences of failing to stem population growth. The influx of rural jobless in search of work had pushed the city's population to the bursting point. Crowded, congested, and polluted, the city provided visible daily evidence of population stresses. A new tone of urgency could be heard in Mexico City. No longer was it a matter of whether there was a need to slow population growth. The question was how: Which contraceptives were most effective and how could they be delivered to people who needed them? And further, how can smaller families be encouraged?

Many things have happened since Bucharest to foster this change in attitude. The costly consequences of continuing rapid population growth that had seemed so theoretical in the 1974 debate were becoming increasingly real for many. Few developing countries at the Mexico City gathering were not experiencing a deterioration of their forests, their soils, and their grasslands, as well as a wholesale alteration of their hy-

drological cycles. In most cases food deficits were larger than they had been in 1974. Despite the U.N.'s World Food Conference, held in Rome in 1974 on the heels of the population meeting, most of the Third World was having difficulty expanding food production fast enough to improve diets. More countries were facing famine in 1984 than 10 years earlier.

In Africa there had been a marked change in attitudes toward family planning, much of it occurring in the early eighties. The "frightening arithmetic" of population growth became a cliché in African capitals. It was in the national economic planning commissions that the population threat surfaced most clearly. For many planners struggling to improve living conditions, keeping up with record rates of population growth was a losing battle. Falling per capita food production was now the rule, not the exception.

The notion that development would lower fertility in developing countries, as it had in the industrial ones, was of little comfort to most Third World leaders. Economic and social gains brought population growth to a near standstill over two centuries in Europe, but no country there ever faced population increases of 3 percent per year, which yields a twentyfold increase per century. It was now clear to many in the developing world that they had perhaps two generations to halt population growth. And that one generation had already passed.

The economic development that was supposed to serve as a contraceptive was not occurring as projected. Incomes were falling in most of Africa and Latin America during the eighties. In their efforts to maintain the economic growth of the pre-1973 period, scores of Third World countries went deeply into debt. For most it was a tragic mistake. Several, including Nigeria, Peru, and the Philippines, found that over half their export earnings disappeared to service their outstanding loans. And the social improvements that were to drive the demographic transition had been replaced by social disintegration in several countries. For national delegations in Mexico City who were faced with debt-induced domestic austerity programs, the slogan "development is the best contraceptive" had a hollow ring indeed.

Third World leaders are now speaking out on the urgency of slowing population growth.

Another source of the changed attitudes about controlling population growth was the recent introduction of active government programs to do so. At the time of Bucharest, several developing countries had adopted the two-child family as a desirable social goal. But the notion of a one-child family as a serious national aim had not yet surfaced. Midway between the two conferences, China became the first country to adopt such a program. For the Chinese, it was not merely a slogan but the centerpiece of a nationwide effort replete with incentives and disincentives.[3]

During the interim between Bucharest and Mexico City, the World Fertility Survey was also largely completed. The largest social science research project ever undertaken, it analyzed in great detail the attitudes toward childbearing and family size and identified a substantial unmet demand for family planning services. It also looked at the many economic and social influences on fertility, considered the role of social gains in reducing family size, and concluded that improved education and employment opportunities for women correlated more closely with fertility decline than any other social indicator. The study

also indirectly emphasized the difficulty of quickly slowing population growth by relying solely on basic economic and social changes.[4]

Awareness that rapid population growth is a threat to improvements in the human condition is now widespread. At Mexico City, at times the only dissenting voice was that of the United States. Speaking from a position paper that was more ideological than analytical in content, members of the U.S. delegation argued that population growth was a neutral phenomenon and that the key to slowing the growth in numbers was deregulation and the unleashing of market forces. In the framework of a free enterprise system, they claimed, such forces would solve the problem. Somewhat paradoxically, the United States also pledged continuing support for family planning. Those preparing the statement apparently overlooked China's success in bringing down population growth within an economic environment that has been anything but free enterprise. They also conveniently ignored the fact that the country with the lowest birth rate in the Western Hemisphere, lower even than the United States, is Cuba, a centrally planned economy.[5]

Third World leaders are now speaking out on the urgency of slowing population growth. They range from the presidents of Brazil and Kenya to the leading industrialists of India. In Latin America, the resistance of the Catholic church is being overridden by popular opinion and by women who demand relief from incessant childbearing. The United Nations Fund for Population Activities (UNFPA) and the World Bank are being inundated by requests from African governments that want to launch family planning programs.

The first step in solving this most basic global problem is identification and awareness. Awareness must reach the point where a political response becomes feasible. Many Third World countries are now at that point, as their statements in Mexico City indicate. Perhaps the most important was that of Rafael Salas, the head of UNFPA and Secretary General of the conference. He went beyond urging a mere slowing of population growth, saying "our goal is the stabilization of global population within the shortest period possible before the end of the next century."[6]

FERTILITY TRENDS AND PROJECTIONS

World population in 1984 totaled 4.76 billion, an increase of some 81 million in a year. This growth—the result of 133 million births and 52 million deaths—means the contemporary world is still in the middle of the demographic transition, with high fertility and comparatively low mortality.[7] Behind this global generalization lie wide disparities between nations. The population sizes of a dozen countries, all in Europe, are now essentially stationary, neither growing nor declining. (See Table 9-1.) They range from tiny Luxembourg to West Germany, which may be on the verge of a long-term decline in population size. In a world where population stability is now widely recognized as a goal that is not only desirable but essential over the longer term, the achievement of zero population growth by this dozen countries containing 5.2 percent of the world's population is an encouraging beginning.

In addition, six more European countries are approaching zero population growth, with annual growth rates of 0.5 percent or less and fertility rates well below replacement level. In size, they go

Table 9-1. Countries At or Approaching Zero Population Growth, 1984[1]

Country	Annual Rate of Change	Population
	(percent)	(million)
At ZPG[2]		
Austria	0.0	7.6
Belgium	+0.1	9.9
Denmark	−0.1	5.1
East Germany	+0.1	16.7
Hungary	−0.2	10.7
Italy	+0.1	56.8
Luxembourg	0.0	0.4
Norway	+0.2	4.1
Sweden	0.0	8.3
Switzerland	+0.2	6.5
United Kingdom	+0.1	55.6
West Germany	−0.2	61.4
Total		243.1
Approaching ZPG[3]		
Bulgaria	+0.3	8.9
Czechoslovakia	+0.3	15.4
Finland	+0.5	4.9
France	+0.4	54.6
Netherlands	+0.4	14.4
Romania	+0.5	22.6
Total		120.8

[1]Excludes migration. [2]Zero population growth is here defined as within a range of plus or minus 0.2 percent change in population size per year. [3]Countries with a population growth rate of 0.5 percent per year or less with fertility below replacement.
SOURCE: Worldwatch Institute estimates, based on data in United Nations, *Monthly Bulletin of Statistics*, New York, monthly.

from Finland, with less than 5 million people, to France, with 55 million. If these six also cease growing, they will boost the share of the world's people living in countries with no population growth to a total of 7.7 percent.

The next big change in this figure is

likely to come when one of the three largest industrial countries—Japan, the United States, or the Soviet Union—reaches a stationary population. The first two, which have both slowly growing populations and fertility rates below replacement level, are moving in this direction. In fact, Japan's current population growth rate of less than 0.7 percent per year and below-replacement fertility mean that country could be at or near zero population growth by the end of the century. So, too, could the United States, if it can regain control of its borders and limit immigration to that which is legal.

This is much less likely for the Soviet Union, however. After a generation of moving downward in tandem, birth rates in the United States and the Soviet Union are now beginning to diverge—largely because of high fertility in the Soviet Union's Asian, predominantly Muslim republics. In the European Soviet Union, rates are similar to those in Western Europe, either approaching or below zero population growth. Births and deaths in this region are essentially in balance. In the Asian republics, however, fertility remains high—so high, in fact, that the demographic center of gravity is shifting eastward toward central Asia. Indeed, in the Muslim republics birth rates are higher than in several states in India.[8]

At the other end of the fertility spectrum are the Indian subcontinent, the Middle East, Africa, and Latin America. Although India has made some progress in reducing its fertility, dropping its growth rate to 2.2 percent per year, the populations of Bangladesh and Pakistan continue to expand, at 3.1 and 2.8 percent respectively. The combined number of people in these three countries—897 million in 1982—is projected to reach 2.54 billion before it stops growing. (See Table 9-2.) In the Middle East, evidence of effective family planning is virtually nonexistent. Annual population growth rates range from 3.2 percent in Iran to 3.7 percent in Syria. The proceeds from oil exports help sustain these record gains in Iraq and Iran, but the huge populations projected for the middle of the next century and beyond will materialize after most of the oil is gone, raising questions as to how these people will be supported.

The demographic prospect in Africa is equally bleak. As in most of the Third World, not only is population growth rapid, but the number of young people reaching the age when they can have children is far greater than ever before. The World Bank projects that the current populations of Ethiopia and Nigeria will increase sevenfold before coming to a halt, a century or more hence. For Nigeria, which is now home to 91 million people, the Bank projects an incredible addition of 527 million—more than the current population of the entire continent.

The projected growth for North America, all of Europe, and the Soviet Union is less than the additions expected in either Bangladesh or Nigeria.

In Latin America some progress is being made in reducing fertility. Between the early sixties and the early eighties birth rates were reduced in Brazil by 30 percent, in Colombia by 37 percent, and in Mexico by 20 percent. Declines of this magnitude in these three countries, which make up close to two thirds of Latin America's total population, are encouraging. Unfortunately, with so many people now under the age of 15 (44 percent of Mexico's population, for example), the growth momentum remains strong. World Bank demographers pro-

Table 9-2. Current Population of Selected Countries, With Projections to Stationary State

Country	Population, 1982	Population Size When Stationary State is Achieved	Change From 1982 Population
	(million)	(million)	(percent)
Bangladesh	93	454	+388
Brazil	127	304	+139
China	1,008	1,461	+45
Egypt	44	114	+159
Ethiopia	33	231	+600
France	54	62	+15
India	717	1,707	+138
Indonesia	153	370	+142
Japan	118	128	+8
Mexico	73	199	+173
Nigeria	91	618	+579
Pakistan	87	377	+333
Poland	36	49	+36
South Africa	30	123	+310
South Korea	39	70	+79
Soviet Union	270	377	+40
Turkey	47	111	+136
United Kingdom	56	59	+5
United States	232	292	+26
West Germany	62	54	−13

SOURCE: World Bank, *World Development Report 1984* (New York: Oxford University Press, 1984).

ject that Mexico's population will nearly triple before growth stops.[9]

In sum, although the population projections for the industrial countries and East Asia seem reasonable enough in terms of what local resource and life-support systems can sustain, those for much of the rest of the world do not. Most demographers are still projecting that world population will continue growing until it reaches some 10 billion, but that most of the 5.3 billion additional people will be concentrated in a few regions—principally the Indian subcontinent, the Middle East, Africa, and Latin America. For example, the projected growth for North America, all of Europe, and the Soviet Union is less than the additions expected in either Bangladesh or Nigeria.[10]

These projections of severalfold increases in the national populations for many Third World countries have an air of unreality. There is considerable disparity between demography and other disciplines such as ecology, agronomy, and, increasingly, economics. What demographers are projecting just does not mesh with what ecologists or agronomists are reporting. In all too many countries ecological deterioration is translating into economic decline that in turn leads to social disintegration. As outlined in Chapter 1, the result can be a breakdown of progress and a return to the first phase of the demographic transition: high birth rates *and* high death rates. Although this will lead to a smaller population size, it is presumably not a route to that goal that any country would choose to follow. The time has come to assemble an interdisciplinary team that can consider this process and make realistic population projections.

SOCIAL INFLUENCES ON FERTILITY

To assess the effects of various fertility-reduction practices or influences, demographers start with a base figure of 17 births per woman as maximum fertility. This is the number of children that a woman is biologically capable of bearing during her reproductive life, roughly from age 15 to 50. Few women, of course, ever have this many children. Even in developing societies with high fertility, the national average rarely reaches half the maximum theoretical potential. (See Table 9-3.)

One reason the actual number of births per woman in developing societies is well below the maximum possible is that in most countries the average age of marriage is considerably above the onset of reproductive capacity. Even in Bangladesh, where child betrothal is still practiced and where the consummation of marriage typically takes place within a few years of sexual maturity, the delay of marriage avoids at least one birth for the average woman. In countries further along the development scale and in which the average age of marriage is much higher, such as Colombia, Costa

Rica, and Sri Lanka, this practice may avoid as many as five births per woman.

Recognition of the role of later marriages in reducing fertility and slowing population growth has led many governments to raise the legal age of marriage, although such laws are difficult to enforce. Among the countries that have attempted this are China, India, and Tunisia. Compliance is usually best in countries where economic gains and social trends are naturally ·bringing about such change. In developing countries experiencing steady economic improvement, the marriage age tends to rise. In South Korea, for example, the average age of marriage for women, which was 16.6 years in 1925, reached nearly 24 by 1975, with most of the increase coming during the last two decades.[11]

Although breast-feeding was not fully appreciated in the early days of the modern family planning movement, it too plays an important role in controlling fertility. Women who are breast-feeding do not usually ovulate, a precaution taken by nature to avoid the physiological stress associated with lactating and being pregnant simultaneously. Reliable data on breast-feeding, only recently available for a number of developing countries, show that this practice makes its maximum contribution in the least developed ones, where access to infant formulas and contraception is limited. In African countries, such as Ghana and Kenya, the contraceptive effect of breast-feeding avoids over four births. The contribution of this practice is influenced both by how many women nurse and by how long they do so after each birth. In Bangladesh, for example, the average mother breast-feeds for 29 months. This uncommonly long period has historically played an important role in limiting the number of children, and still accounts for nearly seven fewer

Table 9-3. Sources of Fertility Reduction, Selected Developing Countries

Country	Maximum Fertility of Average Woman	Actual Fertility	Reduction from Maximum Fertility Due to			
			Marriage Delay	Breast-Feeding	Contra-ception	All Other Factors
			(births per woman)			
Bangladesh	17	6.0	1.2	6.8	0.8	2.3
Colombia	17	4.3	4.7	1.5	4.2	2.3
Costa Rica	17	3.2	4.7	0.8	6.9	1.5
Ghana	17	6.2	2.2	4.3	0.9	3.4
Indonesia	17	4.5	2.6	5.2	2.5	2.1
Jordan	17	7.6	3.3	2.5	2.6	0.9
Kenya	17	7.4	2.7	4.2	0.7	2.0
Lesotho	17	5.3	3.0	4.3	0.5	3.9
Mexico	17	6.3	3.4	1.8	3.4	2.0
Nepal	17	6.1	1.7	6.1	0.2	2.8
Pakistan	17	6.2	2.3	4.5	0.4	3.6
Paraguay	17	4.6	4.5	2.0	3.2	2.7
Peru	17	5.4	4.7	2.7	2.8	1.5
Philippines	17	5.1	5.0	2.6	3.0	1.3
Senegal	17	6.9	1.7	4.6	0.2	3.5
South Korea	17	4.2	4.7	3.3	2.6	2.2
Sri Lanka	17	3.7	5.0	4.3	2.3	1.7
Syria	17	7.5	3.4	2.8	2.1	1.2
Thailand	17	4.6	4.0	3.9	3.5	1.1
Venezuela	17	4.4	4.2	1.4	5.1	2.0

SOURCE: Adapted from World Bank, *World Development Report 1984* (New York: Oxford University Press, 1984), which compiled a table from World Fertility Survey data gathered during the mid- and late seventies.

births for the average Bangladeshi woman.

Unfortunately, breast-feeding is declining in many developing countries. For example, in Thailand the average nursing period declined from 22.4 months in 1969 to 17.5 months in 1979, a drop of just over a fifth in a decade. Similar patterns can be seen in other developing countries where infant formulas are promoted as an alternative to mother's milk. The growing share of women who work outside the home as modernization progresses also interferes with regular breast-feeding. Many developing country governments are seeking to counter the decline in this traditional practice because the use of infant formulas, often with unsanitary water supplies, increases infant illness and mortality. And in industrial societies breast-feeding is being encouraged by the medical community because at least some authorities feel that infants nourished this way are healthier and better adjusted than those who are bottle-fed.[12]

The contribution of contraception to the reduction of fertility varies widely within the Third World. In over a half-dozen of the countries in Table 9-3 contraception prevents less than one birth per woman, far less than either delayed marriage or breast-feeding. Yet in others contraception plays a dominant role: In Costa Rica, its use prevents close to seven births per woman. In such cases, contraception has played a major role in moderating population growth. If breast-feeding declines in frequency or in duration, as it has in so many cases, contraceptive usage should increase merely to offset the former's effect on fertility. Indeed, the slower fertility decline observed in some regions may be partly attributable to a decline in breast-feeding.[13]

As societies modernize, the factors controlling fertility change. At the broadest level, later marriage and contraception become more important and the role of breast-feeding subsides. In the final stage of the demographic transition, the mix of contraceptive practices typically shifts away from those used for spacing children to the more reliable methods, such as sterilization, used to stop having children altogether.

The social indicator that correlates most closely with declining fertility across the whole range of development is the education of women. The attainment of literacy itself brings an initial abrupt reduction in fertility. It declines further as women's average education level is progressively raised to primary school, secondary school, and then college. Paralleling this, the economic indicator closely correlated with fertility decline is women's participation in the paid work force outside the home. In societies where population growth has come to a halt, this figure commonly ranges from well over 50 percent in some West European countries to over 90 percent in some of socialist Eastern Europe for women in their working and childbearing years.[14]

CONTRACEPTIVE PRACTICES

The voluntary prevention of impregnation or conception is not new. One method still widely used, for example, even in technologically advanced industrial societies is withdrawal or coitus interruptus, a practice that goes back at least a few thousand years. Contraception can be broadly grouped into three categories: traditional practices of withdrawal, abstinence, and rhythm; modern reversible technologies of the oral contraceptive, the intrauterine device (IUD), and barrier devices such as condoms and diaphragms, which are often used in conjunction with spermicides; and surgical sterilization. Also reversible is a fairly new hormonal injection, usually marketed under the trade name Depo Provera, that is being used in some 80 industrial and developing countries, although it is not yet approved in the United States. One shot provides contraceptive protection for several months, an important consideration in areas where medical personnel and goods are in short supply.[15]

Worldwide, sterilization protects more couples from unwanted pregnancy than any other practice.

Worldwide, sterilization protects more couples from unwanted pregnancy than any other practice, largely because of its prevalence in three populous countries—China, India, and the United States. Oral contraceptives (the pill) rank second, partly because they are extensively used in so many areas, both industrial and developing. Indeed, the pill is the mainstay of family planning efforts in all but a handful of the countries where contraception is commonly used.[16]

Patterns of contraceptive use vary widely among countries and do not necessarily correspond with levels of development. (See Table 9-4.) The pill, for example, completely dominates Egypt's family planning program: 17 of every 20 contracepting couples rely on this method. And in Indonesia nearly 3 out of 5 couples using contraception take the pill. It is ironic that a modern contraceptive is so prevalent in some key developing countries at the same time that traditional approaches are so widely used in some industrial countries. In France, for example, a third of the couples protected by contraception now use traditional methods, such as withdrawal. In Poland, these older techniques also dominate the effort to limit family size. This heavy dependence on traditional methods in Poland and a number of other East European countries is in part due to the lack of modern contraceptives.

Table 9-4. Share of Couples Using Contraception in Selected Countries, By Method, Circa 1978[1]

Country	Traditional Methods[2]	Pill	IUD	Condom, Diaphragm, Spermicide	Sterili- zation	All Methods
			(percent)			
Australia	21	26	6	10	4	67
Bangladesh	3	3	—	1	1	8
Belgium	35	31	3	7	5	81
China	3	6	35	1	24	69
Colombia	9	19	8	5	8	49
Egypt	1	17	2	—	—	20
France	26	31	9	8	5	79
Ghana	—	2	—	2	—	4
India	—	—	1	3	20	24
Indonesia	4	16	6	2	0	28
Kenya	3	2	1	1	—	7
Mexico	9	15	7	4	7	42
Peru	18	5	1	7	3	34
Poland	41	2	1	13	—	57
South Korea	11	7	10	6	20	54
Spain	32	12	—	7	—	51
Thailand	4	22	4	7	16	53
Turkey	26	6	3	4	1	40
United States	6	23	6	14	19	68
United Kingdom	9	24	6	21	15	75

[1]Includes all women of reproductive age and in stable sexual union. [2]Includes withdrawal, abstinence, rhythm, and douche.
SOURCE: All data except for China from Ann Larson, "Patterns of Contraceptive Use Around the World," Population Reference Bureau, Washington, D.C., July 1981; Chinese data from Laurie Liskin et al., "Vasectomy—Safe and Simple," *Population Reports*, November/December 1983.

Most of the data in Table 9-4 were gathered from surveys, but in a few cases, such as India, the information comes from family planning service agencies and hence does not include figures on traditional or folk methods of pregnancy prevention. If survey data were available for India, they would most likely show withdrawal and abstinence playing at least a small role in reducing fertility well below the biological maximum.

India is unique in its overwhelming dependence on sterilization, both male and female, largely because of vigorous government promotion and the failure to provide other methods until recently, such as oral contraceptives. Reportedly five of every six couples protected by contraception rely on sterilization. Much of the remaining protection in India comes from the condom and IUD, although the latter acquired a bad reputation during a poorly run government campaign in the late sixties. The emphasis then was on insertion, with little attention to follow-up. As a result, many women suffered complications, including excessive menstrual bleeding and pain. IUDs are thus not as widely used in India as they are in other developing countries. Women in China, in contrast, depend heavily on IUDs, the method chosen by half the 118 million married women of reproductive age who are using contraception. Thus some 59 million Chinese rely on IUDs to avoid unwanted pregnancies. Sterilization is the second most popular method in China.

In the United States, the pill is the most widely used contraceptive, chosen by one third of the couples who use a method. Sterilization, both male and female, is a close second, promising to displace the pill soon. Most of the remaining one third or so of couples choose diaphragms or IUDs. The pattern in the United Kingdom is strikingly similar.

Cultural similarities—including a common language, the regular exchange of medical information, and the common press coverage accorded research reports in the two countries—may contribute to the contraceptive usage similarities.

The methods chosen in particular countries can change over time as governments gain experience in providing family planning services, as they understand couples' needs better, and as new technologies become available. For example, South Korea's family planning program relied heavily on IUDs until the pill was introduced in 1968, partly because for some women the IUD had undesirable side effects. Yet the IUD continued to be the dominant technology chosen until 1976, when the government realized that 85 percent of the couples using contraception were doing so to stop having children entirely. This led to an expansion of sterilization services for both men and women. Within a matter of years sterilization moved to the forefront of South Korea's family planning program, preventing more pregnancies than the pill and the IUD combined.[17]

Cultural influences also shape contraceptive usage in ways it is often hard to anticipate. In Indonesia, for instance, the IUD is quite popular on Bali, populated largely by Hindus. But on Java, with its predominantly Muslim population, it is far less widely used. Apparently Balinese women are accustomed to male child birth attendants whereas Javanese women rely on midwives and are thus reluctant to have a doctor, usually a man, insert an IUD.[18]

Sterilization, an essentially nonreversible surgical procedure, is in many ways an ideal technique for couples who are certain they do not want any more children. At one time sterilization was limited to women, but over the last two decades male sterilization (vasectomy) has become much more common. (See Table 9-5.) In three of the world's most populous countries, the number of vasectomies has in some years approached or exceeded female sterilizations. In India and the United States, vasectomies account for roughly half of all sterilizations. In China, female sterilizations (tubectomies) are more numerous, averaging some 2.5 million per year from 1971 to 1978 compared with 1.7 million vasectomies.[19]

In the years ahead, vasectomy is likely to get more attention. One indication of this is a conference that was held in Colombo, Sri Lanka, in the fall of 1982—the first international gathering ever to be devoted exclusively to the subject of vasectomy. Representatives of some 25 countries shared information on program successes and the potential long-term role of vasectomy in the worldwide effort to slow population growth. Some reported on highly successful programs; the efforts of others were just beginning.[20]

Although more women than men are sterilized in most countries, interest in vasectomy is rising in the Third World. Where medical and economic resources are scarce, vasectomies have an advantage over female sterilizations or other

methods of fertility control, once the desired family size is reached. They are a one-time procedure and are surgically somewhat simpler to perform than female sterilization. In some areas paramedics have been drawn into the program. At the Colombo meeting, A. Latif Naek of Pakistan argued that "in rural Pakistan, there is a shortage of doctors, and one has to decide on priorities. Some of the paramedics could probably do vasectomies better than physicians because they [paramedics] are trained only in that."[21] Male sterilizations are also a good way to involve men in family planning programs. M.A.B. Mustafa, a Khartoum gynecologist, observed at the conference that "about six years ago, I came to the conclusion that if family planning is to be effective in the Sudan, men must be involved and a vasectomy program included."[22]

Even while international attention is focusing more on the potential role of vasectomy, some countries that have successful sterilization programs for both sexes have noted a shift back toward greater reliance on female surgery. In part this is due to men's resistance to vasectomy and reluctance to be involved in family planning. It also stems from two new techniques for female sterilization, laparoscopy and minilaparotomy, both perfected during the seventies. A laparoscopy requires only a small abdominal incision, large enough to insert a laparoscope that is used to cut and then tie the woman's fallopian tubes. A minilaparotomy requires an even smaller incision. With both of these relatively new methods, female sterilizations, like male ones, can be performed with local anesthetic and on an outpatient basis. Because family planning programs in so many countries are oriented more toward women than men, laparoscopy and minilaparotomy have quickly become popular.[23]

Table 9-5. Estimated Number of Couples Preventing Births by Vasectomy, 1983

Country	Couples Protected by Vasectomy
China	12,000,000
India	12,000,000
United States	5,000,000
United Kingdom	1,100,000
All other	2,800,000
World Total	32,900,000

SOURCE: Laurie Liskin et al., "Vasectomy—Safe and Simple," *Population Reports*, November/December 1983.

ADVANCES IN CONTRACEPTIVE TECHNOLOGY

Since the pill was developed in the late fifties and the IUD became important in the mid-sixties, few completely new contraceptives have been introduced. However, there have been a number of important innovations in birth control technology during the 20 years. Examples include injectable steroids like Depo Provera and implantable steroid-releasing devices, the two female sterilization procedures just described, and improved means of pregnancy termination through menstrual regulation or prostaglandins.

Of course, advances in contraceptive technology are not essential to slowing population growth—as a number of countries, both industrial and developing, have demonstrated. Indeed, traditional societies maintained a stationary population size relying only on traditional techniques. But the rapid growth now confronting the world community, and the frightening rates still facing some Third World countries, argue for effective family planning programs. Their effectiveness in turn depends on providing as many different birth control methods as possible. For developing countries, the primary concerns are that contraceptives are safe, inexpensive, simple to use, and depend little on medical personnel.[24]

Beyond this pressing societal need, the varying individual situations of millions of couples around the world call for increasing the range of contraceptives available. No one method is appropriate for all couples or for any one person's entire reproductive life. In some instances the object is to postpone pregnancy until well beyond the initiation of sexual activity. In other situations contraceptives are used to space the birth of children. And sometimes, when no more children are desired, the goal is to prevent pregnancy completely.

Developing a new female contraceptive may take 10–20 years and cost up to $50 million. Reproductive physiologists estimate that it will probably take even longer to develop an entirely new male contraceptive, simply because less research has been done on the male reproductive system. Any new product must be carefully tested before it is approved by any national governments. In addition, the criteria for testing and approving new contraceptives vary from country to country. These financial and regulatory hurdles have discouraged the private sector from moving ahead as vigorously as might be socially desired.[25]

Nevertheless, although it is underfunded, research on new methods is moving ahead on several fronts. Among the public-sector agencies actively engaged in this new field are the World Health Organization; the National Institute of Child Health and Human Development in the United States; India's Council for Medical Research; the Population Council, supported by U.S. foundations and the Agency for International Development (AID); and the Program for Applied Research on Fertility Regulation and Family Health International, both supported heavily by AID. Some efforts are intended to improve existing contraceptives, others are pursuing entirely new lines of research. (See Table 9-6.) Over the next decade or so, a new generation of contraceptives is expected to reach the marketplace.

One technological advance that would greatly increase the flexibility of existing family planning programs is reversible sterilization. Surgical techniques now used for vasectomy are highly reversible but only within five years of the original operation, and sophisticated microsurgery is required. Successful reversal of female sterilization is too low to be reliable.[26]

Table 9-6. Prospective New or Improved Technologies for Controlling Fertility

Likely To Be Available by 1990
Safer oral contraceptives
Improved IUDs
Improved barrier contraceptives for women
Improved long-acting steroid injections
Improved ovulation-detection methods
Steroid implants
Steroid vaginal rings
Menses inducer to be taken for missed period

Could Be Available by 1990
Monthly steroid-based contraceptive pill
New types of drug-releasing IUDs
Antipregnancy vaccine for women
Sperm-suppression contraceptives for men
Reversible female sterilization
Simplified male and female sterilization
Self-administered menses inducer

Could Be Available by 2000
Antifertility vaccine for men
Antisperm drugs for men
Ovulation prediction techniques (for use with periodic abstinence)
New types of antiovulation contraceptive drugs for women
Drugs that disrupt women's ovum transport
Reversible male sterilization
Pharmacologic or immunological sterilization for men and women

SOURCES: U.S. Office of Technology Assessment, *World Population and Fertility Planning Technologies: The Next Twenty Years* (Washington, D.C.: U.S. Government Printing Office, 1982); George Zeidenstein, "Contraception in the Population/Development Equation," presented at the First Conference of the Asian Forum of Parliamentarians on Population and Development, New Delhi, February 17–20, 1984.

An important new contraceptive being worked on is a pill for men that would suppress sperm development. The Chinese, who are participating in this research, accidentally discovered that men in certain communities in China had uncommonly low fertility. Researchers eventually traced this phenomenon to the use of cottonseed oil that was not highly refined, and specifically to a substance called gossypol, a compound found in cottonseed. Although gossypol has some side effects, tests are under way on the safety and effectiveness of a gossypol-based male pill. Another male contraceptive that could be on the market before the end of the century is an antifertility vaccine, which would also greatly broaden the range of male contraceptive options.[27]

For women, there are potential advances on several fronts, including barrier methods, hormonal contraceptives, and in some instances a combination of the two. One such combination, steroid vaginal rings, may well be available before 1990. Another approach with considerable potential is a self-administered menses inducer, in effect a very early abortion, which might be on the market by 1990. At the forefront is a subdermal implant developed by Population Council scientists that will be marketed under the trademark NORPLANT. Consisting of six tiny silicone rubber capsules, this implant can be inserted under the skin of a woman's upper arm or forearm. Within 24 hours it starts providing protection against pregnancy and continues to do so for at least five years. But it can be removed quite easily if a return to normal fertility is desired. Some 7,000 women in 14 countries have participated in field research, demonstrating the implant's effectiveness in a broad range of social settings. The Population Council has licensed a Finnish pharmaceutical firm to develop and market the implant, with the stipulation that the company must make a major distribution effort in developing countries.[28]

These initiatives and prospects of new

birth control methods in the next few decades are encouraging. Unfortunately, worldwide expenditures on reproductive research and contraceptive development are minuscule, so small that they almost get lost in the global R&D budget. Even with the most generous accounting, they total less than $200 million per year. If we are to meet the challenge, especially in developing countries, of slowing and eventually halting population growth, far more must be done to provide couples with the widest possible range of contraceptive technologies.

TWO FAMILY PLANNING GAPS

There are two major family planning gaps: one between the demand for family planning services and their availability, and another between the societal need to slow population growth quickly and the private interests of couples in doing so. Neither will be easy to narrow. The first requires far greater expenditures on family planning services—an increase in local clinics, trained personnel, information, and services. The second gap can be eliminated only through intensive public education efforts that help people understand the social consequences of continuing excessive population growth.

Ten years ago, at the World Population Conference in Bucharest, the assembled governments took a bold step toward reducing the gap in availability of family planning services. They agreed it was the basic human right of couples to plan their families and to have access to the services needed to do so. Agreeing to this point and making the services available were, however, two different

things. A May 1977 Worldwatch Paper noted that "more than half the world's couples go to bed each night unprotected from unplanned pregnancy."[29] In the seven years since, the share of couples that are now unprotected has undoubtedly declined. But it is still substantial—only about two fifths of all Third World couples use contraceptives. Excluding China, the figure is substantially less.

Worldwide expenditures on reproductive research and contraceptive development are so small that they almost get lost in the global R & D budget.

The World Fertility Survey reported that half of all women interviewed in the developing world said that they wanted no more children. (See Table 9-7.) This is the good news. The bad news, according to a World Bank study, is that "many couples who say they want no more children do not use contraception—usually because they have poor access to modern services."[30]

In Latin America, 61 percent of the women surveyed in Mexico, 69 percent in Colombia, and 75 percent in Peru indicated that they wanted no more children. The share of married Asian women in this category was consistently rather high—50 percent in Bangladesh, 49 percent in Indonesia, 68 percent in Thailand, and 77 percent in South Korea. Only in Africa did a decided minority of the women have this view—20 percent in Ghana, 25 percent in Kenya, and 27 percent in the Sudan. Even in Africa, these numbers dwarf the proportion of women actually practicing contraception, suggesting that the desire to limit family size far outstrips the availability of family planning services.

Table 9-7. Share of Married Women Aged 15–49 Who Want No More Children, Selected Developing Countries, Circa 1980

Country	Percent
Bangladesh	50
Colombia	69
Costa Rica	55
Ecuador	59
Egypt	58
Ghana	20
Indonesia	49
Ivory Coast	12
Kenya	25
Mexico	61
Pakistan	50
Peru	75
Philippines	59
South Korea	77
Sri Lanka	67
Syria	44
Sudan	27
Thailand	68
Tunisia	56
Venezuela	56

SOURCE: World Bank, *World Development Report 1984* (New York: Oxford University Press, 1984).

There is another set of numbers that says a great deal about the inadequacy of current family planning efforts: the share of women who report that they want to practice contraception but who either lack ready access to services or cannot afford them. (See Table 9-8.) This group requires no urging or further education on the advantages of family planning. They are women who are convinced of the need to limit their family size.

In Kenya, for example, 8 percent of the women report an unmet need for contraceptive services, versus 7 percent who already use contraception. So merely making services more available in Kenya could double the number practicing family planning. Similarly, in Thailand, where 53 percent of the women already rely on contraception, an additional 14 percent report they would do so if affordable services were conveniently available. Expanding the family planning program in Thailand would raise the number of women using contraception by nearly a quarter and could reduce the crude birth rate by at least a few points, moving that country even closer toward eventual population stability. And in Bangladesh, which has one of the highest percentages of unmet need for contraception, 26 percent of all married women would use contraception if given the opportunity to do so. This figure is especially significant because it is three times as large as the 8 percent reporting current contraceptive use.

One step governments can take to increase the availability in many countries is to eliminate existing restrictions on contraceptive use. For example, when Turkey repealed a law banning sterilization, it opened up a whole new area in the country's family planning program. And when the Indian medical community finally agreed the pill could be promoted, some 23 years after it had first been introduced in the country, Indian couples had a valuable new contraceptive for spacing their children and a useful complement to the sterilization programs that currently dominate the national family planning program.[31]

Another important initiative is greater reliance on paramedics. At the Colombo conference on the role of vasectomy, Phaitun Gojaseni of Thailand observed that "we need wide coverage for a family planning program, and paramedics are better than nothing."[32] Although the medical profession sometimes resists, more and more governments are recognizing that getting the brakes on population growth quickly will require the ex-

Table 9-8. Unmet Need for Contraception Among Married Women Aged 15–49, Selected Developing Countries, Circa 1980

Country	Percent[1]
Bangladesh	26
Colombia	16
Costa Rica	8
Ecuador	20
Egypt	17
Ghana	6
Indonesia	12
Kenya	8
Mexico	18
Nepal	24
Pakistan	22
Peru	27
Philippines	20
South Korea	23
Sri Lanka	24
Syria	11
Sudan	8
Thailand	14
Tunisia	14
Venezuela	16

[1]Average of high and low estimates.
SOURCE: World Bank, *World Development Report 1984* (New York: Oxford University Press: 1984).

tensive use of paramedics or "barefoot doctors."

All too often women who are denied access to contraceptive services turn to abortion to limit the size of their families. Indeed, in many countries the extent of reliance on abortion, legal or illegal, is an index of this family planning gap. Where services providing safe, reliable contraceptives are widely available and easily affordable, induced abortion rates are typically much lower than elsewhere. In other countries, abortion has become an important birth control technology—not for avoiding pregnancies but for avoiding births.

Roughly a tenth of the world's 4.76 billion people live in countries where abortion is totally prohibited. About one fifth live where abortion is permitted only to save a woman's life. And for roughly one quarter of the world abortions are legally available on at least limited grounds, such as threat to the woman's health, adverse social conditions, or extreme economic circumstances. As a rule, these conditions are interpreted rather liberally. In the remaining countries, which contain close to half the world's people, abortion is freely available.[33]

Although there is no systematic international reporting of data on either induced or spontaneous abortions, scholars such as the late Christopher Tietze have assiduously collected numbers on induced abortions for many countries. (See Table 9-9.) According to figures gathered by the Centers for Disease Control in Atlanta, abortions in the United States, which climbed steadily following legalization by a Supreme Court decision in 1973, appear to have leveled off since 1980.[34]

In Latin America, abortion is widely practiced, though mostly illegally. In Cuba, however, where it is legal, the number of abortions apparently approaches that of live births. In some East European countries, such as Hungary, abortions exceeded live births from 1959 through 1973. A similar situation existed in Romania from the late fifties through 1966, when abortion was sharply restricted. In the Soviet Union, a 1974 estimate by the International Planned Parenthood Federation cited 230 abortions for every 100 live births, indicating some 70 percent of all Soviet pregnancies ended in abortion.[35]

The small share of international aid that is devoted to family planning highlights a major problem in reducing this gap in availability of birth control. Popu-

Table 9-9. Incidence of Legal Induced Abortion, Selected Countries, 1980

Country	Abortions	Abortions per 100 Live Births
	(number)	
Bulgaria	128,500	98
Canada	65,100	18
Cuba	104,000	76
Czechoslovakia	103,500	44
East Germany	80,100	35
England & Wales	128,600	20
France	171,300	21
Italy	220,300	34
Japan	2,250,000	120
Poland	145,600	22
Romania	404,000	99
Sweden	33,100	36
Tunisia	20,500	10
United States	1,583,900	43
West Germany	108,900	18

SOURCE: Christopher Tietze, *Induced Abortion: A World Review, 1983* (New York: Population Council, 1983).

lation assistance amounts to less than 2 percent of total foreign aid (about $490 million out of $38 billion in 1981), a rather paltry sum given the high social costs of failing to slow population growth in much of the Third World. In the early eighties, the United States was providing about half the governmental assistance in family planning, a reflection of its traditional leadership on this issue. Back in 1971, however, the U.S. contribution accounted for 81 percent of government aid. Fortunately, other industrial governments, such as Canada, Japan, West Germany, and those of several Nordic countries, are now playing a much more prominent role.[36] (See Table 9-10.)

Not surprisingly, the lion's share of the international family planning budget goes to Asia, the region with half the world's people. Of the top seven recipient countries, Egypt is the only exception to this pattern. Many African family planning programs are newly launched and although the total population assistance they receive is relatively small in international terms, it is substantial in per capita terms. Kenya, for example, receives 36¢ per capita and Zambia re-

Table 9-10. Population Assistance, By Donor, 1981

Donor	Amount
	(million dollars)
Government	
Australia	3.3
Belgium	0.8
Canada	14.0
Denmark	8.5
Finland	3.1
Italy	1.0
Japan	33.4
Netherlands	13.2
New Zealand	0.5
Norway	32.4
Sweden	30.7
Switzerland	1.4
United Kingdom	13.1
United States	193.4
West Germany	22.5
Others	2.4
Total	373.9
Organization	
World Bank	77.3
Ford Foundation	7.6
Rockefeller Foundation	4.9
Other Private Donors	27.4
Total	117.2
World Total	491.1

SOURCE: Barbara K. Herz, "Official Development Assistance for Population," World Bank, Washington, D.C., unpublished, September 1983.

ceives 25¢, levels that compare favorably in per capita terms with the major recipients in Asia.[37]

Most of the funding for family planning programs in the Third World comes from indigenous sources, however. This is particularly true for large countries like China and India, where assistance from abroad averages 1¢ and 4¢ per capita respectively. Such foreign assistance does nonetheless play a strategic role because it comes in the form of hard currency, permitting the purchase of equipment and contraceptives not otherwise available. It also frequently brings with it technical assistance that is sorely needed—whether it be statisticians helping design a census or doctors who can train local medical staffs in such procedures as laparoscopy.

The gap between the desire to limit family size and the means to do so is a measurable one. The second family planning gap—between the family size desired by couples and that which is desirable from a societal point of view—may present little problem in some countries. But in others it may be very difficult to deal with. In family planning, as in many other areas, the untrammeled pursuit of individual interests can wreak social havoc. This is the justification for such things as compulsory vaccinations, traffic speed restrictions, and pollution controls.

Most of the funding for family planning programs in the Third World comes from indigenous sources.

In noting the differences, in some cases wide, between the family size commonly desired by individual couples and that which is tolerable from a societal point of view, the World Bank observes

that "there is a balance between the private right of procreation and social responsibility."[38] Each society must seek that balance in light of its own circumstances. China, for example, determined from detailed projections of population growth and future supplies of land, water, energy, and jobs that it is in the social interest to reduce the average number of children per couple to well below two. The result is the world's first one-child family program.

The provision of information can play an important role in bridging the gap between privately desired family size and the smaller, socially desirable size. For individuals, this can take the form of information about family health and welfare. For governments, it may be population/resource projections, which show how future population growth will affect per capita supplies of essential resources. And ecological research can help raise public understanding of the relationship between the carrying capacity of local biological systems and the demands of both present and future populations. It can point out, for example, that beyond a certain point rising fuel needs can lead to deforestation.

Sometimes this exercise of projecting population/resource relationships into the future can have a dramatic effect on childbearing decisions. Among other things it shifts the very personal question of whether or when to have children from the traditional focus of providing security in old age to the more relevant one of how the number of children a person has will affect the quality of life of those children a generation hence. This subtle but important shift has been instrumental in gaining acceptance of the one-child family program in China.

One of the demographic difficulties that many governments will have to contend with over the next several decades is the momentum inherent in the age structures of populations now dominated by young people, those born since 1970. In a number of societies children under 15 constitute close to half the total population. (See Table 9-11.) This enormous group of young people will reach reproductive age by the end of the century. Even if these countries were to achieve replacement fertility by then— roughly 2.1 children per couple—the dominance of young people would lead to a doubling of population in many Third World countries. In a few, such as Kenya and Libya, if replacement fertility were reached this year the current population would still increase 2.1 times before growth would stop. Unfortunately, none of these demographically young countries is even close to reaching replacement fertility.[39]

The difficult decisions that more and more governments will face will be in the trade-off between family size and living standards. The more children there are in the average family, the lower the quality of life for society as a whole. Many countries are now moving into a period where a failure to sharply reduce family size is already leading to a decline in per capita consumption of food, energy, and water. A generation ago, when population pressures in developing countries were far less than they are today, the rapid growth resulting from large families simply meant a slower rate of overall improvement. Today, in all too many cases it means a deterioration in living conditions.

Beyond the costs calculated earlier of getting family planning services to those who have already expressed a desire for them, the cost of eliminating the second family planning gap—that is, reducing the desired family size to that which is socially optimal—also needs to be estimated. This will require far more than a simple expansion of family planning services. It demands a research program that will help governments to understand better future trends and relation-

Table 9-11. Share of Population Under Fifteen in Selected Countries, 1984

Country	Share
	(percent)
Nigeria	48
Algeria	47
Bangladesh	46
Mexico	44
Ethiopia	43
South Africa	42
Egypt	39
Turkey	39
India	39
Thailand	39
Indonesia	39
Brazil	37
China	34
Poland	25
Soviet Union	25
Spain	25
Japan	23
United States	22
United Kingdom	21
West Germany	18

SOURCE: Population Reference Bureau, *1984 World Population Data Sheet* (Washington, D.C.: 1984).

ships between population size and resource availability, between the demands of future citizens and the sustainable yields of life-support systems. A handful of industrial and developing country governments have begun this exercise. All have undertaken national year 2000 studies (or, in the case of Mexico, a proposed Year 2010 study) that will assess population/resource relationships.[40]

In addition to the research component of eliminating the second family planning gap, information needs to be disseminated to effect changes in attitudes toward family size. Finally, to the extent that changing perceptions of future conditions do not bring about the needed reduction in family size, governments will need to use incentives and disincentives. Perhaps a score or more countries now use incentives of one form or another, ranging from a one-time $10 payment for a vasectomy in India to preferred access to schools and jobs for only children in China. Whatever the cost of bridging this second family planning gap, it is not nearly so great as the costs of failing to do so: slowed social and economic progress and, in some countries, hunger, malnutrition, disease, and outright starvation.

COMPONENTS OF SUCCESS

Successful family planning programs vary widely in their composition and thrust but all have certain characteristics in common. In many developing countries success has been markedly facilitated by a head of state who both understands the multidimensional population threat and is committed to doing something about it. Not only must this concern exist, but enthusiastic, highly visible public support is especially helpful.

Closely related to this commitment at the top is the setting of goals and the allocation of responsibility for achieving them. The fixing of responsibility, essential for successful management of any program, is particularly important with population policy. Regular monitoring of the program is also usually essential. During the late seventies, for example, President Suharto of Indonesia instituted quarterly meetings with the provincial governors to review the family planning programs. These discussions permitted a timely sharing of information that helped overcome obstacles that had developed at the local level. And the very fact that the meetings were convened demonstrated Suharto's personal concern with the population issue.[41]

A successful program requires strong public support. This can be achieved in various ways. Apart from demonstrated enthusiasm by political leaders, projections of population alternatives can help clarify choices, giving substance to the urgency of dealing with the issue. This information can be used in public education programs, as the Chinese have done, to create an awareness of the issue commensurate with its gravity.

Some countries have effectively used support by well-known athletes, television celebrities, and actors to promote family planning or have worked small-family themes into popular soap operas. The use of respected members of society, such as popular political leaders or prominent intellectuals, to inform the public of the social costs of rapid population growth often stimulates awareness. Such efforts are sometimes essential if social acceptance of family planning and national population policies is to be established quickly.

Experience has repeatedly shown that the programs that work best are grass-roots ones, staffed by local people, by leaders from within the community. Their advice is typically more acceptable than that of an outsider brought in specifically to promote a program. Services should be readily available geographically and economically. If couples wishing to control their fertility have to travel more than an hour to reach a family planning service center, they are likely to be discouraged from doing so. If services are too costly, they go unused.

The family planning programs that work best are those that offer the entire panoply of services—the more contraceptives offered, the more likely couples will find a method that meets their needs. For personal or medical reasons some contraceptives may not be acceptable. With a wide range to choose from, satisfaction and therefore continuation of use are far more likely. Sterilization, for both men and women, is an important component. Countries where it is illegal are severely handicapped in trying to reach population stability. Those with the most successful programs also back up their contraceptive services with abortion, if desired, in the case of contraceptive failure. In virtually all of the dozen or so countries that have stopped population growth, abortion has been readily available.

Success of a family planning program and a population policy should no longer be measured just by contraceptive usage rates. The issue is not whether fertility is declining, or declining faster than it was before, but whether it is declining fast enough to sustain improvements in living standards. Against this backdrop, just providing family planning services may not be enough. To succeed, a program may have to be an activist one that reaches out and contacts people, that takes information and services to each household. Merely opening a family planning service center in a community, which may have sufficed 15 years ago, may no longer constitute an adequate effort.

There is no universal ideal for the shape of population policies and family planning programs. Each country must tailor its educational effort, family planning services, and pattern of incentives and disincentives to its particular circumstances. This is not to say that governments should not adopt successful initiatives from other countries. But if they do not consider whether a particular program is socially and politically acceptable within their society, their efforts may be in vain.

10

Getting Back on Track

Lester R. Brown and Edward C. Wolf

If the goal of economic, environmental, and population policies is to improve the human condition, then the policies of many governments are now failing. Whether using conventional economic indicators such as economic growth and income per person or even more basic measures of individual well-being such as food consumption, the trends in many countries are not encouraging.

Social indicators tell a similar story. The increases in life expectancy registered throughout the world during the third quarter of this century are no longer occurring at all in some countries. Infant mortality rates, once sharply declining almost everywhere, are now rising in some food-deficit Third World nations. These reversals on the social front are most evident in Africa, where food is scarce, and in the debt-ridden countries of Latin America, where incomes have fallen some 10 percent since 1980.[1]

Perhaps more serious than these recent downturns is a loss of confidence in the future that exists in so many quarters. This apprehension is born of a lack of concrete progress on some of the key threats to our future. United Nations documents refer to the prospect of much

of the Third World becoming a desert if recent trends continue. In private, World Bank officials talk despairingly of social institutions deteriorating to the point that some countries in Africa may be "going back to the bush."

Few national political leaders have a vision of the future. And fewer still have a plan for translating that vision into a reality. Many are so preoccupied with day-to-day crises that they no longer have time to look ahead, no time to imagine what could be. The question that should challenge political leaders everywhere is how to get the world back on track. How can we restore the improvement in living conditions that characterized virtually the entire world during the third quarter of this century?

RETHINKING THE FUTURE

Restoring the broad-based gains in living standards will not be easy. But it is not impossible. Among other things it will require a thorough overhauling of economic and population policies and a restructuring of national priorities in the use of public resources. The cornerstone of such a reorientation is the realization that our security and future wellbeing may be threatened less by the conflicts among nations than they are by the deteriorating relationship between ourselves, soon to be five billion, and the natural systems and resources that sustain us.

The principal elements of an effort to build a sustainable society are rather straightforward. They include economic and population policies that respect the carrying capacity of local ecosystems, protect soils, and preserve biological diversity. Any strategy that aims to improve living standards will recognize the depletable nature of fossil fuels. Successful economic plans will capitalize on the abundance of labor and minimize the use of scarce capital.

Although restoring improvements in living standards is a formidable task, all the individual initiatives for doing so are reinforcing. For example, planting trees conserves soil and water, reduces the buildup of carbon dioxide (CO_2), stabilizes the hydrological cycle, minimizes flooding and drought, provides employment, and ensures a renewable source of energy. Similarly, slowing population growth makes virtually all problems much more manageable, as those countries that have reduced fertility are discovering. Increasing energy efficiency cuts down on CO_2 buildup, reduces acid rain and hence protects forests, and provides higher living standards with a given supply of energy. Recycling materials also illustrates this pattern of reinforcement: As it increases, energy requirements dwindle, air pollution and acid rain decline, pressure on forests is reduced through paper recycling, and employment increases.

A global future that provides improved living standards for everyone will not be a simple extrapolation of the recent past. It will be a complex mixture of advanced and traditional technology. The United States, for example, now uses as much firewood as India, some 130 million tons in 1981. Food production, too, will represent a complex combination—embracing both centuries-old techniques of composting and home food production on the one hand, and the latest advances in gene splicing on the other.[2]

In some important ways, a sustainable world economy will be more internationally interdependent; in others, much less so. Coping with common environmental threats such as acid rain, CO_2 buildup, and climate change will require an orchestrated response among nations far exceeding any such effort to date. Many other activities, however, will become much more localized. Countries everywhere, for example, will become much more self-sufficient in energy production, depending less on fossil fuel imports and more on indigenous supplies of renewable energy. National gene banks and plant breeding programs to help preserve each country's endowment of plant genetic resources will become commonplace. Information and technology will move across national boundaries on a larger scale, whereas materials such as food and energy will probably cross borders less. With an increase in recycling, the raw materials traded internationally may also diminish.

By some criteria, national economies will be more centralized and by others, less centralized. For example, strategies to reduce CO_2 buildup will be nationally designed and managed but the actual efforts to cope with this threat will involve a decentralization of energy systems. To cite one case, the massive thousand-megawatt, coal-fired electric generating plants will be replaced with more and more local cogeneration, much of it by industrial firms that will simultaneously produce electricity and process steam.

At present there are no good guides to the future that reasonably portray the mix that is beginning to unfold. One thing is certain: We are not moving toward the exclusively high-technology world that many had once anticipated. Information is becoming an increasingly valuable commodity, one that will play a central role in shaping the future.

A GENERATION OF ONE-CHILD FAMILIES

Earlier chapters outlined why countries with rapid population growth that wait too long before applying the brakes may find themselves in trouble. The first country to recognize this was China. After rejecting for ideological reasons the urging of a vigorous family planning program by some of their own eminent intellectuals in the fifties, the Chinese found by the seventies that they were facing potential demographic disaster.

As mentioned in Chapter 9, during the post-Mao assessment in the late seventies the Chinese undertook several alternative projections of population growth and resource demands. Even assuming that each couple would have just two children, it was clear that the population would continue to grow, because of the youthful age structure, by another 300–400 million people. Recognizing that such an increase in population would further reduce already limited per capita supplies of cropland, fresh water, and energy, the leaders in Beijing saw that it would jeopardize the hard-earned gains of the past generation. Rather than risk a fall in living standards, they decided to launch a one-child family program.

Like China, other Third World countries appear to be waiting too long before tackling their population problems.

China is unique in terms of population size, but it shares with every country the relationship between population and local life-support systems. The principal difference between China and other densely populated countries such as Bangladesh, India, Ethiopia, Nigeria, and Mexico may be that the Chinese have had the foresight to make projections of their population and resources and the courage to translate the findings into policy.

A generation of one-child families may be the key to restoring a sustained improvement in living standards.

In one Third World country after another, the pressure on local life-support systems is becoming excessive, as can be seen in their dwindling forests, eroding soils, disappearing farmland, and falling water tables. If other governments take a serious look at future population/resource balances, they may reach the same conclusion the Chinese did. And they may discover that they are forced to choose between a one-child family program and falling living standards or, in some cases, rising death rates. Given the unprecedented numbers of young people who will reach reproductive age within the next two decades, a generation of one-child families may be the key to restoring a sustained improvement in living standards. Success in striving for an average of one child per family will bring problems of its own, including a severe distortion of age-group distribution, but it may be the price many societies will have to pay for neglecting population policy for too long.

No government would launch a one-child family program for fun. Politically it is extraordinarily demanding, particularly in societies with a strong preference for sons, as the Chinese leadership can attest. Yet in some countries, the alternative may be an Ethiopian-type situation, where population growth is being checked by famine. In parts of the Third World where the average couple is now having five children, halting population growth will not be easy. Both ingrained childbearing practices and youthful populations make this a difficult task. The inherent difficulties can be seen in World Bank population projections, which show most of these nations reaching replacement-level fertility of roughly two children per couple around 2035, about a half-century from now. (See Table 10-1.) Once this level is reached, most Third World populations will still double again because of the predominance of young people.

Consider Bangladesh, for example: Though it is much smaller than China, it is one of the most crowded lands on earth. Fertility in Bangladesh is not projected to fall to replacement level until

Table 10-1. Selected Countries That May Have To Adopt a One-Child Family Goal to Avoid a Decline in Living Standards

Country	1982 Population	Assumed Year of Reaching Replacement Fertility	Population Momentum[1]	Projected Population When Stationary State Is Reached
	(million)			(million)
Ethiopia	33	2045	1.9	231
Senegal	6	2040	1.9	36
Bangladesh	93	2035	1.9	454
Nigeria	91	2035	2.0	618
Pakistan	87	2035	1.9	377
Uganda	14	2035	2.0	89
Bolivia	6	2030	1.8	22
Ghana	12	2030	2.0	83
Kenya	18	2030	2.1	153
Tanzania	20	2030	2.0	117
Zaire	31	2030	1.9	172
Zimbabwe	8	2030	2.1	62
Algeria	20	2025	2.9	119
Iran	41	2020	1.9	159
Peru	17	2020	1.9	49
South Africa	30	2020	1.8	123
Syria	10	2020	2.0	42
India	717	2010	1.7	1,707
Mexico	73	2010	1.9	199
Philippines	51	2010	1.8	127

[1]This measures the projected population growth after fertility has fallen to replacement level, due to the large number of young people. (For most Third World countries, this is roughly a doubling.)
SOURCE: World Bank, *World Development Report 1984* (New York: Oxford University Press, 1984).

2035. At that point its population would be so predominantly youthful that growth would continue until eventually there were 454 million Bangladeshis, five times the 1982 population.

Neighboring India has a more successful family planning program and is expected to reach replacement-level fertility by 2010, a quarter-century from now. Yet, like Bangladesh, it would have a rather youthful population that would continue to grow until it came to a halt at 1.7 billion. In effect, India would add the equivalent of China's population to its current numbers. For a country that is now losing some 4.7 billion tons of topsoil from its cropland each year, the prospect of another billion people is distressing, to say the least.[3]

Ethiopia—whose starving people provided the most graphic and continuing reminder in late 1984 of Third World development problems—is not expected to reach replacement-level fertility until 2045. With the momentum inherent in its age structure, the number of Ethiopians is projected to continue expanding until it reaches 231 million, seven times the current population and as many people as now live in the United States. In a country where soils are so eroded that many farmers can no longer feed themselves, this demographic projection appears unrealistic.

Nigeria, the most populous country in Africa, is in a similar situation. If it attains replacement-level fertility in 2035, its youthful population will reach 618 million, more than now live in all of Africa. In some ways Nigeria is much more vulnerable than other Third World countries because its extraordinarily rapid population growth is being supported by imports financed almost entirely by exports of oil, which will be largely depleted by 2000.[4]

Mexico may also have waited too long. Its current population of 73 million is projected to reach 199 million before growth comes to a halt. Water is already critically short, not only in Mexico City but in other parts of central and northern Mexico as well. With a near tripling of Mexicans in prospect, stringent water rationing would seem inevitable. Like Nigeria, Mexico's current population buildup is being supported by oil exports.

These population projections for key Third World countries are the official World Bank projections, but there is an air of unreality about them. Although they are sound in narrow demographic terms, they bear little relation to the deterioration of basic life-support systems and to the resulting hunger and deprivation. The key question facing political leaders in these countries is not whether the projections will materialize, but whether population growth will be checked by vigorous family planning programs or by hunger-induced rises in death rates.

The magnitude of the effort needed to halt world population growth is outlined in a recent study by the Population Institute, which analyzed the costs of providing family planning services in 12 developing countries that contain close to two thirds of the Third World beyond China. (See Table 10-2.) The starting point of the study was the announced population goals of the 12 governments. For Bangladesh, Indonesia, and Thailand, the official goal is to bring fertility down to replacement level by 2000. India hopes to achieve this by 1996. Although other governments have stated their goals differently, the desired reduction in population growth is similar. Egypt, for example, wants to bring its crude birth rate from 37 in 1982 to 20 by the end of the century. Mexico aims for an overall population growth rate of 1 percent in the year 2000, down from 2.3 percent in 1984. For Turkey, the end-of-century goal is three children per couple.

The cost of providing family planning

Table 10-2. Family Planning Costs in Selected Countries, 1985, With Projections to 2000

Country	1985	1990	2000
	(million dollars)		
Bangladesh	56	99	221
Brazil	105	126	179
Egypt	28	39	80
India	313	497	806
Indonesia	141	168	245
Kenya	9	21	48
Mexico	55	81	127
Nigeria	33	68	188
Pakistan	29	68	156
Thailand	42	47	58
Turkey	24	37	75
Zaire	14	30	65
Total	849	1,281	2,248

SOURCE: Population Institute, *Toward Population Stabilization: Findings From Project 1990* (New York: 1984).

services to achieve these goals is substantial. The study notes that the funds would come from four sources—individual couples who pay some or all of the expense of contraceptives they use, private family planning organizations, governments of the countries in question, and the international donor community. The Population Institute calculates that annual expenditures on family planning from all sources would climb from $849 million in 1985 to $2.3 billion in 2000. In these countries couples using family planning services would increase from 64 million in 1980 to 240 million in the year 2000, roughly a quadrupling.

The World Bank estimates that adoption of a "rapid" fertility decline goal (2.4 children per couple in 2000) would require 72 percent of couples to practice contraception and an annual expenditure on family planning of $7.6 billion in 2000. Adoption of such a goal, which

would require a 7 percent annual growth in family planning expenditures, would be more than offset by reduced public expenditures in other sectors. Year 2000 savings in education expenditures alone would reach $6 or more per capita in such disparate countries as South Korea and Zimbabwe.[5]

These projected expenditures over the next 15 years are not beyond reach. Yet they cover only the first gap in family planning—the provision of services. For the typical Third World country, bridging the second gap—that between desired family size and the much smaller family required to meet stated national population goals—will mean reducing average family size from today's five children to about two by the year 2000. And this may not be possible without substantial financial incentives or disincentives, such as those now being used in China to encourage one-child families. Wherever desired family size exceeds that which is consistent with the realization of population goals, substantial expenditures or penalties may be required to reconcile the two.

RESTORING SOILS

Never before has the conservation of topsoil been so directly linked to efforts to improve human well-being. Few countries will succeed in attempts to boost domestic food production at the rate demanded by population growth if soil-depleting agriculture continues. The forces that create agricultural deficits and push food prices up around the world are unlikely to be controlled if topsoil continues to be degraded and lost. Soil conservation saves fertilizer, fuel, and farmers' efforts, providing a foundation on which stable agricultural systems can be built. Long considered an obligation to future generations, soil conservation must now be seen as a key to a secure livelihood for the present generation of farmers as well.

In an effort to sustain the remarkable doubling of world food output over the past generation, farmers extended cultivation onto steeply sloping land and introduced continuous row cropping on erosion-prone rolling land. As a result, soil erosion has accelerated steadily, and it now afflicts industrial and developing countries alike. The ninefold increase in fertilizer use and the near-tripling of the world's irrigated cropland since mid-century have masked the effects of soil erosion on crop productivity. Yet as of 1984 the loss of topsoil from cropland in excess of new soil formation totaled some 25.4 billion tons. (See Table 10-3.) If this soil depletion through erosion is not soon checked, persistent pockets of famine are likely to appear.

The slowdown in the rate of growth in grain yields, described in Chapter 2, sug-

Table 10-3. Estimated Excessive Erosion of Topsoil From World Cropland

Country	Total Cropland	Excessive Soil Loss
	(million acres)	(million tons)
United States	421	1,700
Soviet Union	620	2,500
India	346	4,700
China	245	4,300
Total	1,632	13,200
Rest of World	1,506	12,200
World Total	3,138	25,400

SOURCE: Authors' estimates based on data from national soil surveys, reported levels of soil loss in major crop-growing regions, and indirect evidence including river sediment loads and reservoir siltation rates.

gests that the contribution of fertilizers and energy-intensive inputs to world harvests may face diminishing returns. As existing technologies are disseminated more widely outside industrial countries and as new technologies improve plant performance or help reduce the toll taken each year by insects and spoilage, improvements in grain yields worldwide are likely, but they will be incremental rather than exponential. Yield-enhancing technologies tend to work best on deep soils and that part of their contribution to higher crop productivity is forgone on topsoils reduced by erosion. Thus soil conservation makes the most of new technologies.[6]

Careful inventories of agricultural soils and the pressures placed on them will provide a foundation for better agricultural policies. The 1982 National Resources Inventory in the United States is the most comprehensive national soil survey ever undertaken. Based on nearly one million sample points nationwide, the survey provides a picture of soils nearly five times more detailed than an inventory done in 1977. Preliminary results show that 44 percent of U.S. cropland was losing topsoil in 1982 in excess of its soil-loss tolerance level, and that over 90 percent of the soil eroding at excessive rates is on less than one quarter of the cropland. These results attest to the need for corrective action and point out where conservation efforts can most profitably be focused.[7]

Two other major food-producing countries, China and India. have produced national estimates of excessive soil loss. A study of China's resources prepared for the Institute of Scientific and Technical Information reports that five billion tons of soil and sand are washed into rivers each year. The government of India estimated in 1976 that soil degradation affected 150 million hectares. Soil scientists working with these figures concluded that the nation's croplands were losing a total of six billion tons of soil each year.[8]

Despite considerable evidence of excessive soil erosion in the Soviet Union, the world's fourth major food producer, no comprehensive national survey has been undertaken. Perhaps the best indirect evidence of pressures on Soviet soils is the 1984 decision to fallow over 21 million hectares of cropland, the highest level since the sixties. The Soviets have decided to pull land out of production despite expected grain imports of over 50 million tons, the most by any country in history.[9]

The widespread adoption of conservation tillage methods is the most hopeful sign of progress toward stabilizing soils in the United States.

Some governments have failed to support soil conservation enthusiastically because they could not see the link between topsoil losses and land productivity. Fortunately, new analytic tools are becoming available to scientists and policymakers. A productivity index (PI) that calculates the ratio between actual and potential crop yields at various levels of soil loss has been applied to soils in the major crop-producing regions of the United States and is being tested on tropical soils in Hawaii, India, Mexico, and Nigeria. Scientists coordinating the international work on the productivity index conclude that "a knowledge of the global distribution of soils combined with estimates of erosion could, using the PI, improve estimates of the global impact of erosion."[10] But the needed inventory of the world's soils will depend on the painstaking collection of data over many years, an effort that has barely begun.

In the absence of effective government policies, the widespread adoption of conservation tillage methods is the most hopeful sign of progress toward stabilizing soils in the United States. According to a study by the American Farmland Trust, "on most of the Nation's cropland, conservation tillage is all that is necessary to control erosion."[11] Usually adopted by the farmer to reduce fuel needs and tillage costs, minimum tillage techniques that leave crop residues and stubble on the field maximize soil moisture and reduce the loss of topsoil to wind and water. The growth in U.S. acreage tilled this way has been remarkably steady, increasing almost every year since data collection began in 1972. In 1984, it reached 108 million acres, nearly one third of all the land in crops.[12] Unfortunately, minimum tillage methods are usually adopted first by more progressive farmers, not by those with the most seriously eroding soils.

Information on the progress of conservation tillage in other countries is sparse. There is some indication that these techniques are being used in major crop-growing regions of the Soviet Union, though it is difficult to judge how widespread they are. And researchers at the International Institute of Tropical Agriculture, in Ibadan, Nigeria, are investigating ways to adapt conservation tillage to tropical soils. If their research results in stable, profitable cropping systems, it may restore the agricultural stability that was lost in the humid tropics as traditional shifting cultivation systems broke down.[13]

The United States unilaterally attempts to balance the world's supply and demand of agricultural commodities by withholding land from production during times of surplus. But little or no effort has been made to coordinate the farm supply management programs that divert land with the conservation programs designed to reduce soil erosion. With farm program costs out of control and public endorsement of traditional farm price-support programs diminishing, Congress may be unable to legislate a new farm program in 1985 unless it directly incorporates soil and water conservation with supply management and price supports. In effect, public enthusiasm for soil conservation could be used to divert highly eroded cropland to other uses, such as fuelwood production or grazing. This would bring the production of key farm commodities down to a level that would allow higher prices and revive the profitability of U.S. farms.

Scores of countries have, like Kenya, become food deficit, but few have linked the shortages with the depletion of their soil by erosion.

One Third World country that has formulated an effective response to soil erosion is Kenya. With the assistance of the Swedish International Development Authority, Kenya designed a national program that by mid-1983 had trained some 1,300 agricultural officers and 3,500 technical assistants in soil and water management, established 50 tree nurseries, and distributed 127,000 fruit trees and 3.5 million fuel or fodder trees to farmers. Terraces had been constructed on 100,000 farms. Farmers themselves had constructed roughly 10,-000 kilometers of cutoff drains designed to reduce the erosive runoff of water.[14]

The Kenyan experience demonstrates that a Third World country with limited fiscal resources and a scarcity of local skills can design and implement an effective national soil and water conservation program with a minimum of outside assistance. The keys appear to be a committed leadership and local participation in the design of a program that has demonstrated economic benefits, both short-term and long-term. Kenya's program also illuminates the long-term commitment other governments must begin to make. By 1980, the program extension staff was able to bring conservation improvements to 30,000–35,000 farms per year; at that rate, it would take 25 years to stabilize Kenya's soils. Even with more staff, comprehensive soil conservation in Kenya will take at least 15 years, a period during which the country's population is expected to nearly double.[15]

Over the past generation, scores of countries have, like Kenya, become food-deficit, but few have linked the shortages with the depletion of their soil by erosion. In many countries people know that food prices are rising, but most do not know why. Understanding that lost soil means lower inherent productivity, which in turn means costlier food, is an important first step toward an international soil conservation ethic.

REFORESTING THE EARTH

One telling measure of humanity's progress toward sustainability is the extent of efforts to plant trees. Tree planting where forests have been cleared—reforestation—and where no forests have grown before—afforestation—can supply needed resources, restore ecological integrity, and help moderate climate change.

Unfortunately, forests face an onslaught of pressures that degrade their economic and ecological value. Estimates for 76 tropical countries show that their forests are being cleared 10 times more rapidly than they are replanted. Over 11 million hectares of tropical forests are being cut each year, a rate of deforestation that reduces this resource by 6 percent in a decade.[16] In the industrial countries, vast areas of forests are dead and dying in central Europe, as described in Chapter 5, and declines in forest growth are reported in eastern North America. Acid rain and other air pollutants are stressing once-productive forests beyond their ability to cope.

This situation cannot long continue. Replanting is needed to ensure the present and future supply of wood products for industry and for fuel. Many tropical countries rely on forest product exports for desperately needed foreign exchange. Industrial countries still depend on wood as a raw material, and they burn increasing amounts as fuel in highly efficient wood-fired boilers. Developing countries like Brazil are also relying more on wood, which they convert to charcoal used to smelt steel. All the traditional demands for wood products are being compounded: The number of rural households throughout the Third World that depend on fuelwood for cooking and heat continues to rise; affordable substitute fuels are not being introduced fast enough in Third World cities; and modernization efforts like China's must supply vast amounts of paper for education and communication, as well as wood for construction and energy, if aspirations are to be met.

But tree planting projects are still too few and far between to meet these economic needs. All the plantations for industrial use and fuelwood plus all the natural regrowth are far from compensating for the conversion of forests to grassland, cropland, or degraded scrub. In the tropics, where the ratio of replanting to deforestation is especially important, only 1 hectare of forest is planted for each 10 hectares cleared. Different regions have markedly different rates of forest restocking. (See Table 10-4.) Asia's low ratio, which looks like a suc-

Table 10-4. Ratio of Forest Clearing to Planting in the Tropics, 1980–85

Region	Clearing to Planting Ratio
Africa	29 to 1
Latin America	10 to 1
Asia	5 to 1
Tropics Average	10 to 1

SOURCE: United Nations Food and Agriculture Organization, Forest Resources Division, *Tropical Forest Resources*, Forestry Paper 30 (Rome: 1982).

cessful effort to reduce pressures on forests, is actually a legacy of long-sustained overharvesting. What little unexploited natural forest remains in the region is inaccessible, which slows the rate of cutting; meanwhile, severe and disruptive wood shortages have prompted the world's most ambitious tree planting campaigns, including those in China and South Korea.[17]

Perhaps more important than these regional disparities in rates, trees are rarely planted where forests are being cut. Nearly 1.5 million hectares of tropical forests are cut annually in Brazil, largely in the unique rain forests of Amazonia, yet the hundreds of thousands of hectares of plantations established each year are concentrated far away in the southern states of Minas Gerais and Paraná. The same situation prevails in Peru and Venezuela.[18]

The largest share of plantations established so far have been planted to meet industrial needs, ranging from sawlogs and veneer logs to wood pulp for the paper industry. Brazil's 2 million hectares of industrial plantations are expected to double by the end of the century. In India, over two thirds of the 3.2 million hectares planted between 1951 and 1980 were industrial plantations. Throughout the tropical countries, more than half the 1.1 million hectares of plantations established each year produce wood for industrial uses.[19]

Although the spread of plantations to fulfill industrial wood needs is encouraging, progress toward providing sufficient wood for household cooking and heating needs is far more sporadic. Although the world is not about to run out of forests, fuelwood shortages are still the most widely suffered material scarcity: Fuelwood supply and demand remain badly out of equilibrium, and unmet demand translates directly into unsustainable pressures on natural woodlands. A secure supply of domestic fuel in developing countries can only be provided if families themselves are engaged in growing and caring for the trees they will later burn.

An effort to reclaim five million hectares of degraded land in India with agroforestry projects could create jobs for two million people.

Plantations have a part to play in supplying this fuelwood, but they currently fall far short of the task. In India, only 12 percent of the 3.2 million hectares planted during 30 years supply fuelwood. According to the Food and Agriculture Organization, 21 tropical countries had no plantations for household fuelwood as recently as 1980, and 9 others listed less than a quarter of their plantations for non-industrial purposes. Even these proportions can deceive: Most of Brazil's so-called non-industrial plantations supply not household needs but wood for charcoal used by the steel industry.[20]

A few successful efforts do provide some encouragement, however. In the Indian state of Gujarat, where free seed-

lings have been distributed by the government, tree farming has become the main source of income for some farmers. In 1980, the 50 million seedlings distributed by the forestry department, enough to plant 25 thousand hectares, fell far short of the demand. In 1983, the state distributed 200 million seedlings. Even this is not enough, however. The Indian Forest Service estimates that the number of farmers engaged in tree growing must increase more than twentyfold to ensure the wood fuel needs of Gujarat's population. Although Gujarat's program has been criticized for its social inequities and its almost exclusive reliance on eucalyptus (which can deplete water supplies), it has created an interest in tree planting that will almost certainly spill over to other states.[21]

Nepal has also mounted a vigorous campaign to replant its denuded hillsides by giving its people the means to grow trees for themselves. Tree nurseries and plantations have been established in 350 villages, from which a variety of fruit, fodder, and fuelwood species are distributed. Technical assistance and funding for the program have come from the World Bank, several United Nations agencies, and a handful of national and private aid agencies. The outcome of Nepal's program will be the focus of attention throughout South Asia, since the stability of forests and watersheds in the Himalayas affects not just the Nepalese but the tens of millions of farm families downriver on the vast plains of the Ganges.[22]

Where successful reforestation programs have taken root, they invariably meet a wide range of social needs. In several regions, such efforts have helped reduce unemployment. In Minas Gerais and Espiritu Santo, Brazil, 100,000 hectares of tree plantations are put in by hand each year; other labor-intensive planting projects have been developed in Colombia, the Congo, Guatemala, Honduras, the Philippines, and Venezuela.

Combining agriculture with forestry in replanting schemes can boost employment and enhance farm productivity; the U.S. Office of Technology Assessment estimates that an effort to reclaim five million hectares of degraded land in India with agroforestry projects could create jobs for two million people.[23]

The ecological benefits of intact forests also argue for a stepped-up planting effort. Trees are essential in stabilizing soils and water supplies. Forests in the Himalayas, for example, are the master link in a chain between the monsoon and millions of farmers vulnerable to floods on the plains of the Ganges and Brahmaputra rivers. More immediately, landslides from slopes made unstable by the loss of trees directly endanger mountain communities. And hydrological disruptions where trees have been removed, ranging from heavy spring flooding to reduced water flow during dry seasons, make rural life more tenuous and fuel the exodus to Third World cities.

The few countries that have launched national mass planting campaigns have done so to restore degraded environments. In China, official goals call for increasing forest cover from 12 percent to 20 percent of the country's territory by the year 2000. The long-run target is to restore trees to one third of China's territory. To accomplish the first objective, the Chinese hope to plant trees on 67 million hectares, an effort that will approximately quadruple the current annual planting effort of all the countries in the tropics combined. Geographer Vaclav Smil, who has written extensively on Chinese environmental issues, believes these targets can only be reached with a combination of aerial seeding and mass planting on an unprecedented scale. The responsibility system, which has made trees productive assets for private profit in the Chinese countryside, may help sustain the momentum of official efforts.[24]

The country that has achieved the most rapid success with a national program may be South Korea. Beginning in the early seventies, South Korea sought to restore its tree cover. By the end of 1977 some 643,000 hectares of village woodlots had been planted in fast-growing pines, most of them on wasteland on hillsides that had been deforested over the years. In just a few years, trees were established on an area over half that in rice, the country's food staple.[25]

In Europe, Italy has engaged in extensive reforestation in recent years, much of it on marginal cropland in hilly areas that had been abandoned. Recent estimates indicate that 2–3 million hectares of land are being planted in trees in an effort to avoid excessive soil erosion. This newly forested acreage is at least three times as large as that of South Korea.[26]

Though national mass planting efforts can replace the wood that is lost as natural woodlands are cut or degraded, single-species plantings, whether in plantations or on degraded land, are no more akin to natural forests than cornfields are to the tallgrass prairie. The many values of intact natural forests—wildlife habitat, aesthetic enjoyment, a natural bank for genetic resources, and an arena in which evolution can continue—simply are irreconcilable with intensive management. Forest resources for the future should be a mosaic of single-use plantations, multiple-use natural forests, and intact undisturbed stands. Protection and innovative management of natural forests must complement planting efforts.

An especially important contribution of healthy forests to humanity's future may be their climatic role that is just being recognized. Forests turn carbon from the atmosphere into wood and foliage, but this natural accumulation has been reversed in our century. Recent research reveals that the clearing of forests —for agriculture or grazing, for example —releases enormous amounts of carbon into the atmosphere. George Woodwell and his colleagues at the Marine Biological Laboratory at Woods Hole, Massachusetts, used several methods to estimate the net release of CO_2 from forest cutting and concluded that the world's forests currently release between 1.8 billion and 4.7 billion tons of carbon each year. The higher estimate is close to the amount of carbon discharged annually by fossil fuels, roughly 4.8 billion tons. Even more startling, Woodwell found that if forest clearing continues to increase in proportion to population growth, the yearly loss of carbon from forests will reach between 7 billion and 9 billion tons early in the next century— probably surpassing the amount from fossil fuels.[27]

Although in principle the CO_2 problem is controllable, the world's forests and tree plantations are not now being managed in a way that recognizes their role in CO_2 stabilization. The total amount of carbon taken up by trees during afforestation and natural regeneration of cut forests is only a tiny fraction of the amount released by cleared woodlands and fossil fuels. To slow the buildup of CO_2 and forestall climatic changes, the deforestation of the earth must be reversed. If vigorous efforts are made, the contribution of carbon from forests can be brought under control. At the same time, reforestation and afforestation, by taking up carbon from the air and turning it into wood and leaves, can skim some of the CO_2 released by fossil fuels and transform a problem into a productive resource. Coupled with attention to energy efficiency and development of renewable energy sources, an ambitious replanting effort could go a long way toward restraining the forces most likely to drive climatic change.

More tropical plantations are being established each year in the early eighties than were planted in the late seventies—an encouraging sign. If the rate of increase continues, over 40 million hect-

ares of tree farms may stand in tropical countries by the turn of the century. Nearly 2 million additional hectares would be planted each year, roughly double present plantings. China's national reforestation strategy calls for planting 3–4 million hectares of trees each year. Coupling such efforts with those in the tropical countries might increase the annual share of carbon absorbed by new trees to 6 percent of the carbon released to the atmosphere. If other countries join China, Italy, Nepal, and South Korea and begin planting on a large scale, the share could be even higher.[28]

Ironically, the burning of fossil fuels may well constrain forest's ability to offset these fuels' effects on the composition of the atmosphere. Acid rain and air pollutants are killing forests in central Europe and apparently reducing the growth of forests throughout eastern North America, as pointed out in Chapter 5. In the southeastern United States, growth declines in economically important loblolly and shortleaf pine have already prompted the timber industry to adopt more-efficient forest management practices. Anything that diminishes growth rates also reduces the amount of carbon trees take up. Acidification and pollutant stress, already reported in China and Brazil, could undermine hopes that tree planting in the Third World can help stabilize the world's climate.

Reforestation and attempts to reverse deforestation deserve greater international support and an increased commitment from political leaders if these efforts are to provide secure livelihoods and more-abundant resources. Countries such as Brazil must reappraise official policies that encourage the establishment of wood plantations on existing cropland while providing government support and incentives for agricultural settlement and forest clearing in frontier rain forests that cannot sustain farming over the long run. International lending agencies must avoid similar contradictions in their lending policies and reshuffle their priorities. Agriculture receives 20 times more funds from international aid agencies than forestry does. Although the World Bank spent over $1 million on reforestation projects between 1968 and 1980, it financed at many times that level projects ranging from dams to road construction that destroyed forest resources.[29]

Recent initiatives provide a glimmer of hope. In the Indian state of Uttar Pradesh, the World Bank is funding a watershed reclamation project that will restore trees and terrace fields on 312,000 hectares. Coupled with policies that slow population growth, efforts like this to restore forests can enhance the resources and environmental stability that make other improvements in human well-being possible.[30]

An Energy-Efficient World

Contemporary interest in energy efficiency can be traced to the oil price increases of 1973 and 1979. Each price hike brought with it the need to recalculate the optimum investment in energy efficiency. If oil priced at $12 a barrel justified the installation of four inches of attic insulation, for example, then oil at $30 might justify six or eight inches of insulation. Investments in conservation that were uneconomical when oil was pegged at $2 a barrel might be highly profitable at $30 a barrel. In addition to economic and national security concerns, two major new reasons argue for investing in energy efficiency: acid rain and rising atmospheric CO_2.

Over the past several years the world's energy efficiency has risen steadily,

breaking the historical lockstep relation between energy use and economic growth. Progress has been particularly impressive with oil. From mid-century until the early seventies, the amount of oil used per $1,000 of gross world product increased from 1.33 barrels in 1950 to over 2.2 barrels. (See Table 10-5.)

Table 10-5. Oil Intensity of World Economic Output, 1950–84

Year	Oil Used Per $1,000 of Output[1]
	(barrels)
1950	1.33
1955	1.46
1960	1.67
1965	1.90
1970	2.17
1971	2.21
1972	2.23
1973	2.27
1974	2.13
1975	2.05
1976	2.15
1977	2.16
1978	2.14
1979	2.15
1980	2.05
1981	1.93
1982	1.80
1983	1.80
1984	1.78

[1]In 1980 dollars.
SOURCES: Worldwatch Institute estimates based on data from American Petroleum Institute, *Basic Petroleum Data Book* (Washington, D.C.: 1984); Herbert R. Block, *The Planetary Product in 1980* (Washington, D.C.: U.S. Department of State, 1981); and International Monetary Fund, *World Economic Outlook* (Washington, D.C.: May 1984 and September 1984).

After 1979, however, this figure dropped sharply, falling from 2.15 barrels to 1.78 barrels in 1984. This reduction in oil intensity is a result of both greater efficiency in oil use and the substitution of other sources of energy—coal, renewable sources, and nuclear power.

Although the world gains in raising energy efficiency have been impressive, they have been rather uneven: Some countries have achieved spectacular gains, others have made little progress. These variations can be seen by comparing the energy efficiency of steel-making, aluminum production, and auto transport. (See Table 10-6.) In the first two of these basic economic activities, Italy is the world leader. In steel production, India narrowly edges out China as the least efficient and uses 2.3 times as much energy as Italy to produce a ton of steel. For aluminum, the variations among major producing countries are somewhat less. Canada, endowed with cheap hydropower, is the least efficient. Italy is half again as efficient as Canada.

With auto fuel efficiency, the difference between the most and least efficient national automobile fleets is wide. Japan is the most efficient, obtaining an average of 31 miles per gallon. Not surprisingly, the United States brings up the rear, with 16 miles per gallon, giving a ratio of nearly two to one between the most and the least efficient national automobile fleets. For all three of these key sectors, merely getting the rest of the world up to the average level of the most efficient country would sharply reduce world energy consumption. There is no reason, however, to limit future gains in efficiency to those already achieved, since even the most efficient countries are employing some outdated inefficient technologies.

Efforts to increase energy efficiency come in stages. After the first oil price increase in late 1973, many homeowners in industrial countries responded by turning their thermostats down. The second stage involves steps that require somewhat more time, such as the addition of wall and ceiling insulation. Over the long term, the basic principles of energy architecture can be employed to produce highly energy-efficient homes. Canada has proved that commercially attractive homes can be built that are so energy-efficient they do not need furnaces. They are warmed by the heat generated by household appliances, by the body heat of their residents, and, in times of uncommonly low temperatures, by a backup electric baseboard heater.[31]

A staged approach also applies in the transportation system. At first attention focuses on the establishment of fuel effi-

Table 10-6. Range of Energy Efficiency in Key Sectors of Major National Economies, Circa 1981

	Most Efficient Country	Least Efficient Country	Ratio of Highest to Lowest
Steel Production (gigajoules/ton)	Italy 17.6	India 41.0	2.3 to 1
Aluminum Production (thousand kwh/ton)	Italy 13.3	Canada 20.0	1.5 to 1
Auto Fuel Efficiency (miles per gallon)	Japan 31.0	United States 16.0	1.9 to 1

SOURCE: Drawn from Tables 7-2, 7-3, and 7-4 in Chapter 7.

ciency standards for new automobiles, such as those adopted in the United States to raise new-car fuel efficiency from 14 miles per gallon in 1975 to 27.5 miles per gallon by 1985. With the longer term in mind, urban areas concentrate on developing efficient public transport systems to partially replace the less efficient automobile. Lastly, the focus turns to designing communities in such a way that automobiles are not needed. This obviously requires more time and a more sophisticated urban planning than has typically been the case in the past.

Commercially attractive homes can be built that are so energy-efficient they do not need furnaces.

The potential for boosting the energy efficiency of the world economy over the long term has scarcely been tapped. From a purely economic point of view, there are vast opportunities to invest in energy efficiency that would yield an annual return of 15 to 50 percent on capital. External or indirect benefits make the return on investment in energy efficiency difficult to calculate. For example, what costs should be assigned to the forests being destroyed by acid rain and to the economic modifications that will ultimately be required by CO_2-induced climate change? Although the economic costs of forest destruction are already evident in countries like Czechoslovakia, West Germany, and Poland, calculations on how much to invest in pollution control versus energy efficiency are still a matter of debate. There has been even less consideration of how much to invest in energy efficiency to minimize a global warming. Using exhaust controls to lower CO_2 discharge in the atmosphere has been rejected because costs are

prohibitive, leaving energy efficiency and a switch to renewable energy sources as the principal alternatives.

RENEWABLE ENERGY: SURGING FORWARD

Economic forces, environmental concerns, and technological advances have launched the transition from fossil fuels to renewable energy sources. The key question is whether the process is proceeding rapidly enough to minimize economic stresses and to avoid fossil-fuel-induced climate change and the wholesale destruction of forests by acid rain.

The transition can best be seen in the contrasting trends of various energy sources between 1979 and 1984. (See Table 10-7.) The production of oil, the world's leading source of energy, has declined by 3 percent annually over the last five years. The use of wood, ranked fourth in the world energy budget after the three fossil fuels, has been expanding by nearly 2 percent per year. Hydropower, second to wood among renewable energy sources, has expanded by some 3 percent per year. Together, wood and hydropower will be supplying more energy than natural gas by 1990. Fortunately, in terms of their connection to acid rain and CO_2 generation, neither coal nor natural gas is growing very rapidly.

The spectacular rates of growth have come from the newer sources of renewable energy. Wind electricity, for example, has been nearly doubling each year for the last several years, starting from a negligible base. And, from a somewhat larger base, geothermal has increased at 15 percent per year. Although these high rates of growth obviously cannot be sus-

Table 10-7. World Growth in Energy Production by Source, 1979–84

Energy Source	Annual Rate of Growth
	(percent)
Major Sources	
Oil	−3
Coal	+1
Natural Gas	+4
Wood	+2
Hydropower	+3
Minor Sources[1]	
Nuclear Electricity	+9
Geothermal Electricity	+15
Wind Electricity	+75
Alcohol Fuels	+30
Solar Panels	+20

[1]Sources supplying less than 3 percent of world energy output.
SOURCE: Worldwatch Institute estimates based on data from American Petroleum Institute, U.S. Department of Energy, California Energy Commission, and unofficial sources.

tained indefinitely, they do indicate the potential for renewables to become important energy sources well before the century is out.

The progress on developing several of these sources is detailed in Chapter 8. And, as indicated there, three other forms of renewable energy—wood fuel, geothermal, and wind power—that were covered in *State of the World-1984* continue to hold considerable potential. In contrast to hydropower, where the undeveloped potential is concentrated in the Third World, vast underused forests grow in the northern tier of industrial countries. In the United States, for example, the residential use of firewood has increased some 10 percent per year between 1973 and 1983. Impressive though this level of residential wood

burning is—the equivalent of over 100 million barrels of oil per year—it is overshadowed by the industrial use of fuelwood. Notwithstanding the recent growth in fuelwood use in the United States, Canada, and Scandinavia, there is a vast unrealized potential for further expansion in these countries and in the Soviet Union.[32]

The use of geothermal energy, a vast source that is continuously renewed by pressure and radioactivity within the earth, is expanding in both industrial and developing countries. It is used directly for hot baths, residential heating, and industrial process heat and indirectly to produce electricity. In Hungary, 70 hectares of greenhouses produce winter vegetables with heat drawn from underground sources. Corporations in the United States, the Philippines, and New Zealand have sited industrial plants astride geothermal fields in order to tap this subterranean source of heat directly. World geothermal electrical capacity, as noted in Chapter 8, is expected to surpass 10,000 megawatts before 1990. The exploration and engineering experience gained during the eighties is setting the stage for massive expansion during the nineties, mainly in the geothermal-rich countries that ring the Pacific plus several Mediterranean countries, such as Italy and Turkey.[33]

In wind energy, the lead has been taken by California, where there are now several thousand commercial-scale wind generators producing electricity on wind farms, as documented in Chapter 8. The key to this breakthrough is not a unique wind endowment, for there are many such sites around the world, but the availability of both state and federal tax credits for renewable energy development and a forward-looking state energy commission. With the technologies now being perfected in California, prime wind sites throughout the world will one day be converted into wind farms.

As the world moves beyond its heavy dependence on oil, shifting to a variety of renewable sources, the outlines of the new energy economy are beginning to emerge. Successful strategies will be tailored to each country's indigenous endowment of renewable resources. Some may rely heavily on one locally abundant form of renewable energy. Others may have highly diversified renewable energy economies. Nepal, Norway, and Paraguay, for example, all richly endowed with hydroelectric potential relative to population, could rely heavily on hydropower. Heavily forested countries, in contrast, could fashion an energy strategy centered on wood. For some countries, the United States among them, the wisest course is to develop the entire panoply of renewable energy sources—wood, windpower, hydropower, rooftop collectors, energy crops, geothermal energy, and photovoltaics.

In developing an economy sustained with renewable energy, Brazil is emerging as an early leader, focusing on the development of its vast hydroelectric potential, the use of wood as an industrial and residential energy source, and a fast-advancing agriculturally based alcohol-fuels program. With a pauper's endowment of fossil fuels and its once-ambitious nuclear program all but abandoned, the country is building an industrial economy that will be one of the first to be based on renewable energy. To maximize the chances of success, Brazil could rely less on the automobile and more on electrically powered intraurban and inner-city rail systems. This, combined with a program to boost automotive fuel efficiency, would reduce liquid fuel requirements and thus lessen the competition between the transport and food sectors for food-producing resources. Unfortunately, if Brazil does not act more effectively to curb its population growth, the favorable resource/population balance that currently gives it so many energy options will disappear.

Under the pressure of near total dependence on imported oil and mounting foreign debt, the Philippines Government designed an ambitious 10-year program aimed at reducing oil's contribution to the national energy budget from 91 percent to 56 percent by 1989. Although coal and nuclear power are expected to account for some 15 percent of its total commercial energy use by then, renewable sources—including hydroelectric, geothermal electric, wood, agricultural wastes, timber industry wastes, and fuel alcohol from sugarcane—could push the renewable energy share of total energy use to one third by the end of the decade.[34]

In the industrial world, to cite one leader in this field, Canada is investing heavily in development of its renewable energy resources, particularly wood and hydropower. Wood, long a principal fuel for Canada's export-oriented forest products industry, is now being used throughout the country. Canada's earlier investment in hydropower development is also now paying off as it exports surplus electricity to several New England states and New York.[35]

To speed the transition to renewable energy, there is a need for research support, information dissemination, tax incentives, grants, and other inducements that reflect the benefits not only of lessening dependence on imported oil but also of reducing acid rain. As of the mid-eighties only a few national governments are making a speedy transition from fossil fuels to renewable energy. Legislation and financial incentives will play an important role. For example, the U.S. Public Utility Regulatory Policies Act of 1978, which requires utilities to buy power generated by small systems at the avoided cost, has created a multitude of opportunities for renewable energy developers. The support of international development agencies, led by the World Bank, will also be a key factor. Development of hydropower, for example, has expanded at some 4 percent annually over the past five years partly because of World Bank efforts to help Third World countries reduce their dependence on imported oil.

In an ironic twist, Third World debt is spurring the global shift to renewable energy. Since such resources are largely indigenous, the outlays of foreign exchange are often nonexistent or negligible, limited to those for imported equipment or technical advice. In addition, many renewable energy sources are virtually inflation-proof. Once the initial investment is made, the cost of running a hydroelectric dam or a solar water heater is independent of rising fuel prices.

Third World debt is spurring the global shift to renewable energy.

The reinforcing role that renewables can play in the movement toward sustainability is an important one. As described earlier in this chapter, the reforestation that is badly needed in many areas—in part, to provide wood for cooking and heating in the Third World—will yield considerable ecological benefits in terms of stabilizing soil and water resources. In employment terms, too, renewables are attractive. Most require less capital and create more jobs than fossil fuels or nuclear power do. In this respect the timing of the transition could not be more fortuitous for Third World planners, coming as it does when record numbers of young people will be entering the job market.

If governments formulate a package of public policies that will speed the transi-

tion from fossil fuels to renewable energy sources, a potentially catastrophic warming of the earth can be avoided. The urgency of responding to this particular threat cannot be overestimated. The incentives need not be massive, but they need to be substantial enough to bring about the transition in time to avoid forest destruction and a wrenching climate change.

RECYCLING MATERIALS

The shift from a throwaway society to a recycling one can help restore a broad-based gain in living standards in several ways. The "virtue of necessity" of recycling was documented in *State of the World-1984:* On the environmental side, the reduction in energy use lowers carbon dioxide emissions, acid rain, and the environmental disruption associated with mining larger quantities of virgin ores. Where paper and cardboard are concerned, recycling takes some pressure off forests. Economically, recycling saves energy, reduces the area required for landfill, and also lowers the costs of garbage collection and disposal. From a social point of view, recycling can reduce litter. And because it saves energy and capital while creating jobs, it is well adapted to the global economic future— where capital and energy will be costly and labor relatively abundant.

In national security terms, a recycling society is less vulnerable to disruptions of raw materials flows. Perhaps more important, countries importing energy have an interest in recycling because it reduces energy use. Japan understands this: It increased the share of materials recycled from 16 percent in 1974 to 48 percent in 1978. This phenomenal increase, unmatched by any other country, was designed to lower oil imports.[36]

For the world as a whole, recycling rates in the mid-eighties are rather low, typically not much more than a quarter, although for aluminum the figure may now be close to one third. They vary widely among countries. Some Third World countries recycle extensively. Garbage disposal sites surrounding Third World cities are carefully gone over by hand to retrieve any useful material—paper goes to the paper mill, bones to the glue factory, and rags to a furniture factory for use in upholstery. In societies plagued with unemployment, this approach makes sense. Among the industrial countries, the highest recycling rates are usually found in densely populated countries that import energy and raw materials, such as the Netherlands and Japan.

The energy savings are greatest with aluminum, where recycling requires only 6 percent as much energy as aluminum produced from bauxite. Iron and steel recycling uses roughly 35 percent of the energy required to produce these materials from iron ore. With paper, the savings are 20–40 percent. For glass, the U.S. Environmental Protection Agency estimates that national returnable beverage container legislation would save 46 million barrels of oil per year—roughly 10 days of imports at 1984 levels. Some of this saving has of course been realized already, since nine states, home to roughly a fifth of all Americans, have passed returnable deposit legislation.[37]

No country has a materials recycling system nationwide. Several national governments have taken steps to facilitate recycling, but comprehensive programs are largely in the hands of local governments, either at the municipal or the state level. The impressive systems in a number of cities were described in last year's *State of the World.* Since then, Minneapolis, a city of close to 400,000 people, became the largest American community to start a source separation recycling program. Its voluntary program was launched on November 1, 1983. In the first month 476 tons of recyclable materials—paper, cans, glass, and oil—were collected; the second and third months netted 512 and 600 tons. At the start, one house out of six was participating, but within a year it is expected to reach one out of four. For now the city subsidizes the pickup at the rate of $10–17 per ton. Once the program is well established, however, the recycling firms will have to earn their income from sale of the materials they pick up.[38]

Machida, Japan, a city of 60,000 people, has a "Recycling Culture Center" that may be the world's most sophisticated recycling program. Its executive director, Muneo Matsumoto, explains the Center's name: "Merely collecting and processing garbage does not solve the problem. A lot of waste today comes from our modern culture, with its emphasis on mass produced plastic products and packaging. We have to change that culture from the very roots. We have to reconsider our entire way of life because that is the only way you reduce garbage. We wanted our citizens to think about this concept, so we decided to use the word culture in our official name." In addition to the usual separation of materials for recycling, the Center also renovates furniture, appliances, clothing, and bicycles, which are sold at bargain prices or given to the needy. If local regulations can be modified, the garbage residue, which is now incinerated, will eventually be used to cogenerate electricity and steam heat, with the latter piped to nearby homes, offices, and other facilities.[39]

Several forces are driving individual households, businesses, and communities toward comprehensive recycling, not least of which is the rising cost of energy. Another is the rising cost of landfill for municipal governments, which is what led Minneapolis to consider its source-separation recycling program. Between 1980 and 1990, city officials expected the cost of trash disposal to nearly quadruple. (See Table 10-8.) Both the greater distance to remaining landfill sites and the rising costs of ensuring environmental safety of disposal sites are boosting landfill costs.

Minimills are thriving in the United States at a time when the more conventional segment of the steel industry is in the doldrums.

A number of technological advances are facilitating materials recycling. One is the electric arc furnace, a steel-making technology that relies almost exclusively on scrap metal. Usually relatively small by steel industry standards, these minimills are thriving in the United States at a time when the more conventional segment of the steel industry is in the doldrums. With lower material costs and with far lower energy requirements, the steel minimills are steadily increasing their market share. (See Table 10-9.) In 1960 electric arc furnaces accounted for 2 percent of U.S. steel output. By 1985 this is expected to reach 32 percent and by 1990, 36 percent. This percentage thus indicates the minimal share of U.S.

scrap that will be recycled. As the other principal steel-making technology, the basic oxygen furnace, typically uses some 38 percent scrap, half or more of U.S. steel output in 1990 will be from recycled materials.

Another technology that is facilitating metal recycling is the reverse vending machine, which dispenses coins in return for empty aluminum cans. With scrap aluminum now worth some $500 per ton, the collection of aluminum cans has become economically attractive. Sweden, the world leader in this technology, plans to have 10,000 reverse venders in operation by 1990, recycling an estimated 97 percent of all aluminum cans. As of the end of 1984 there were some 2,200 of these machines in operation in the United States.[40]

As the environmental and economic

Table 10-8. Cost of Burying a Ton of Trash in Landfill for the City of Minneapolis, With Projections to 1990

Year	Cost Per Ton
	(dollars)
1980	11
1984	23
1990	40

SOURCE: Minneapolis City Government.

Table 10-9. U.S. Steel Produced in Electric Arc Furnaces, 1960–84, With Projections to 1990

Year	Annual Output	Share of Total Steel Production
	(million tons)	(percent)
1960	8.4	8.4
1965	13.8	10.5
1970	20.1	15.3
1975	22.7	19.4
1980	31.2	27.9
1981	34.1	28.3
1982	23.2	31.1
1983	25.1	31.5
1984	33.0	33.2
1990	43.4	36.0

SOURCES: American Iron and Steel Institute; data for 1990 from Jack R. Miller, "Steel Minimills," *Scientific American*, May 1984.

reasons for recycling become more compelling, national and local governments may require it. The city of Islip, New York, whose garbage dumps were polluting underground water with toxic chemicals, was ordered by the courts to adopt a mandatory resource recycling program. The Netherlands and Japan have both introduced some regulations, although neither government has come close to mandating a comprehensive materials recycling program. One problem faced by recyclers almost everywhere is price instability. The price swings in the market for recycled materials typically exceed those of the business cycle itself. To overcome this the Dutch government has established a price stabilization reserve for paper, under which the government buys paper when the price drops below the established price and then resells it when the market price rises again.[41]

Public interest groups often initiate the establishment of recycling programs. In some communities in the United States and Japan, citizens' groups are directly involved in educating people about the social advantages of recycling; in others they actually collect materials. In Boulder, Colorado, for example, volunteer groups involve themselves in the recycling program on weekends to raise funds. A similar approach is used in Japan where student associations take part in recycling programs to raise money.[42]

One benefit of source-separation recycling programs is the sense of participation they can provide people with. As Brian Hammond put it in the *New Scientist:* "In an increasingly impersonal world in which political and economic events seem as arbitrary and unalterable as the weather, many of us feel remote from the real levers of power. At the individual level recycling systems give us a chance to help to exercise control over at least one section of the whole complex

and bewildering macroeconomy."[43]

Apart from being an obvious integral part of any society that is sustainable over the long term, the rate at which countries move toward comprehensive recycling will affect both their living standards and their competitive position in the international marketplace. With energy becoming scarce, recycling can provide a higher standard of living at any given level of energy consumption. Those national economies that recycle will be more energy-efficient and hence more competitive in world markets than those that continue to throw away materials used just once.

COMPLEXITY, CHANGE, AND LEADERSHIP

Times of rapid change put a premium on leadership. During the long stretches of history when social change was so slow as to be scarcely perceptible there was little need for leadership. Maintaining the status quo does not impose the heavy demands on leaders that change does.

Change requires both intellectual and political innovation. Intellectual leadership identifies the need for change and determines in what direction society should move. Political leaders devise the policies and shape the priorities to move society in this direction.

More often than not insight comes from outside of government and usually from people rather than institutions—from people such as Rachel Carson or E.F. Schumacher. During the early sixties Rachel Carson awakened the world to the risks of chemical pollution associated with modern industrial society. A decade later E.F. Schumacher effectively challenged the "bigger is better" mode of technological thinking that was guiding the evolution of industrial societies.[44]

Times of rapid change put a premium on leadership.

More recently, a group of scientists led by astronomer Carl Sagan and biologist Paul Ehrlich have altered the way we think about nuclear war. Their research on the climatic and biological consequences of such a war led to a national conference, articles published in *Science* magazine, and a worldwide debate. Their findings, largely confirmed by Soviet scientists as well as the U.S. Defense Department, are revolutionizing thinking about the consequences of nuclear explosions. Recognition of the "nuclear winter" effect has made nuclear disarmament more urgent than ever.[45]

At the governmental level, the *Global 2000* study undertaken during the Carter administration contributed to worldwide understanding of complex environmental and resource trends. Other governments are now conducting national Year 2000 studies, many modeled on the *Global 2000* report. Among those completed or in progress are studies in Canada, China, Iceland, Japan, Mexico, the Philippines, South Africa, and South Korea. When completed, over one third of the world's people will live in countries that have taken this basic step toward understanding long-term resource trends.[46]

Perhaps the most challenging aspect of many problems facing humanity today is their gradual, insidious nature. Since the time horizon associated with issues such as population growth, soil erosion, CO_2 buildup, and deforestation does not mesh with the multiyear terms of elected political leaders, the temptation to ignore such topics is great.

Scientists, not politicians, are most likely to forge the institutions needed to confront these issues. The international scientific community has decades of experience investigating problems that are so large-scale and so long-term that only cooperative efforts yield useful information. In September 1984 the International Council of Scientific Unions proposed a new International Geosphere-Biosphere Program that will encompass the world's climate, biosphere, and the interactions of biological and geological cycles. The project was inspired as much by a sense of urgency about the scale of problems and the need for international cooperation in addressing them as by the quest for knowledge for its own sake.[47]

New international political institutions will be created for two reasons: to force countries to take remedial steps that no one nation would be willing to undertake alone, and to allow countries to gain from cooperation what they cannot gain from unilateral action. As mentioned in Chapter 5, 16 nations have joined a "30 percent club" pledging to reduce sulfur dioxide emissions by at least 30 percent over the next ten years. Although the two largest sulfur emitters, the United States and the United Kingdom, have refused to join, the trend toward cooperation is encouraging. No nation, acting alone, is capable of stopping airborne pollutants at its borders.

Countries are often slow to recognize the second reason for creating international institutions—that their self-interest is best served by cooperation. The insight that a resource formerly considered "national" is actually "global" can create a foundation for cooperative efforts. The Organization of Petroleum Exporting Countries would have foundered long ago if oil were not a global commodity. Intact tropical forests are beginning to be seen as a global resource as well. Writing in *Foreign Affairs,* tropical forest analyst Nicholas Guppy argues that an Organization of Timber Exporting Countries could slow deforestation while boosting the earnings of timber producers. Such an institution would require an unprecedented degree of cooperation from the 17 countries that export nine tenths of the world's tropical timber, but it could do more to save remaining forests than any other approach by making forest conservation a paying proposition.[48]

The advance of knowledge has accelerated its specialization. Unfortunately, the pendulum has swung too far in this direction, and much of today's knowledge is fragmentary as a result. This fragmentation has influenced not only the accumulation of knowledge at universities but also the way knowledge is used by governments and by the United Nations system, all of which seem crippled by an inability to act consistently and decisively. The knack for synthesis is lacking. In an Aspen Institute paper on governance, Joseph Slater, the Institute's president, notes "Many bright people can analyze situations with great skill, but many of them also tend to leave the pieces of the analytic mosaic scattered uselessly on the top of a table. It is truly great persons who show us how we can put these pieces together—indeed, that ability is the hallmark of greatness."[49]

Within the U.S. Congress, concern over the pace of technological change and the need for synthesis led to creation of the Office of Technology Assessment. Its purpose was to sketch the broad policy issues confronting Congress, issues that demanded interdisciplinary analysis and action. The Office of Technology Assessment has become a trusted, nonpartisan voice on many of the divisive issues of technology policy that confront Congress, the executive branch, and the public.[50]

Effective leadership in a time of rapid change demands not only a vision of the future, but the capacity to communicate that vision. The effort to put the world on a sustainable basis will take years of rapid, perhaps convulsive, economic and social change. Success in restoring a sustainable society will depend on the willingness and ability of political leaders to help their constituents understand change, why it is inevitable, and how to influence its direction. Psychologist Warren G. Bennis observes that great political leaders such as Jefferson, Lincoln, and Wilson were above all educators, "transforming murky problems into understandable issues . . . (filtering) the unwieldy flow of information into coherent patterns."[51] Without a proper understanding of the forces driving change, governments fail to respond to emerging problems, and problems become crises.

From time to time a person with a vision for the future, elected or appointed to a position of responsibility, nudges society toward a sustainable future. Jerry Brown, for example, as Governor of California, provided active leadership in adopting policies and programs to encourage the development of renewable energy resources. Today California not only leads the world in both wind-generated electricity and geothermal electricity, it has spawned new wind and geothermal industries that are moving to develop these resources in other parts of the world.

Ideology is not a substitute for intelligent, responsible policy. Pragmatism is the order of the day. Even countries with entrenched ideologies can embrace pragmatism. Recent years have seen a major shift in both the Hungarian and Chinese economies as leaders in these countries recognized that too much economic centralization was impeding progress. As a result, both have given a much freer rein to market forces. Chinese success in improving diets has flowed directly from the government's decision to reduce its involvement in agriculture while increasing its involvement in family planning.

While the Chinese Government has become more pragmatic in recent years, the U.S. Government seems to have become less so. Nowhere was this more evident than at the International Conference on Population in Mexico City in August 1984, where the United States argued that market forces alone could solve the population problem. This position, which ignored the vast body of demographic knowledge and belittled the perceptions of other governments, led to much criticism and even ridicule of the U.S. Government.

Much of the leadership required in the years ahead will come from grass-roots activists. Arresting and reversing the deterioration of living conditions is above all else a political process and it requires broad participation. Numerous activist groups have sprung up in many parts of the world to translate ideas into policy. None better exemplifies the interdependence of ecological, economic, and social systems than the Chipko Andolan or "Hug the Trees" movement in the Himalayan foothills of northern India.

The Chipko movement was born a decade ago of village women's concern about deforestation leading to excessive erosion and landslides, to increasingly destructive flooding on the plains below, and to a waste of local fuelwood resources. Since 1973, the Chipkos have challenged the government of Uttar Pradesh to enact a forest policy more sensitive to local needs. They have also set an example by mounting extensive voluntary reforestation efforts often superior to those designed by the government. And women have gained a new measure of authority in recognition of their leadership in the movement stemming from their previously unacknowledged role in collecting fuel and fodder for their communities.[52]

The threats to progress that the world faces today are of such immense proportions that people from all walks of life will have to participate in solving them. The years ahead are likely to be traumatic, and they could be catastrophic. The issues we have outlined already place great stress on the international political fabric.

The international community's capacity to deal with the new threats to progress may first be tested in Africa, where the dimensions of the unfolding food and water crises have not yet been fully grasped. Emergency food relief efforts—absolutely essential though they are—treat only the symptoms of the deteriorating situation. If Africa is drying out because of population-induced changes in land use, as postulated in Chapter 1, then the continuous, continent-wide decline in per capita food production can be reversed only by tree planting, family planning, soil conservation, and water resource development on a scale and with an urgency exceeding any international collaborative effort since the Allied Powers mobilized during World War II. It demands leaders who will shift the world's attention, and its resources, from maintaining East-West hostility to restoring the natural systems that ultimately sustain all societies.

Notes

Chapter 1. A False Sense of Security

1. Estimate of Africans fed with imported grain in 1984 based on import figures from U.S. Department of Agriculture (USDA), Foreign Agricultural Service, *Foreign Agriculture Circular* FG-8-84, Washington, D.C., May 1984, and on assumption that one ton of grain will feed roughly six people for a year.

2. Trend in grain production per capita from USDA, Economic Research Service (ERS), *World Indices of Agriculture and Food Production, 1950–83* (unpublished printout) (Washington, D.C.: 1984).

3. U.S. Agency for International Development, "Fiscal Year 1980 Budget Proposal for Ethiopia," Washington, D.C., 1978.

4. "Wound in the World," *Asiaweek*, July 13, 1984.

5. Peter Hendry, "Land Use and Living Space," *Ceres*, November/December 1983; "Chinese Reform Burial Customs," *Mazingira*, March 1984.

6. Alcohol fuels in Brazil are discussed at length in Chapter 8.

7. M. Mitchell Waldrop, "An Inquiry into the State of the Earth," *Science*, October 5, 1984; "Group Seeks Global Scientific Project," *New York Times*, September 29, 1984.

8. "Nyerere Urges African Debt Default," *Washington Post*, November 17, 1984.

9. Author's estimate based on U.S. data from USDA, Soil Conservation Service, "Preliminary 1982 National Resources Inventory" (unpublished printout), Washington, D.C., April 1984, and on Chinese data from Zheng Guanglin, "Preliminary Results From the *China 2000* Study: A Personal View," G.O. Barney & Associates, Inc., Arlington, Va., unpublished, July 1984. For a complete discussion of these calculations, see Lester R. Brown and Edward C. Wolf, *Soil Erosion: Quiet Crisis in the World Economy* (Washington, D.C.: Worldwatch Institute, September 1984).

10. Water table decline in Tamil Nadu from Carl Widstrand, ed., *Water Conflicts and Research Priorities* (Oxford, U.K.: Pergamon Press, 1980); information on northeast China from Vaclav Smil, *The Bad Earth: Environmental Degradation in China* (Armonk, N.Y.: M.E. Sharpe, Inc., 1984); shrinking Soviet seas from Dr. John Gribben, "Climatic Impact of Soviet River Diversions," *New Scientist*, December 6, 1979, and from Grigorii Voropaev and Aleksei Kosarev, "The Fall and Rise of the Caspian Sea," *New Scientist*, April 8, 1982; decline in U.S. irrigated area from USDA, *Agricultural Statistics 1983* (Washington, D.C.: U.S. Government Printing Office, 1983), and from unpublished data from Bureau of the Census, "1982 Census of Agriculture," U.S. Department of Commerce, Washington, D.C., 1984.

11. United Nations Food and Agriculture Organization (FAO), *Production Yearbook* (Rome: various years).

12. Davidson R. Gwatkin, *Signs of Change in Developing Country Mortality Trends: The End of an Era?*, Development Paper No. 30 (Wash-

ington, D.C.: Overseas Development Council, February 1981).

13. National Research Council, Board on Science and Technology for International Development, *Environmental Change in the West African Sahel* (Washington, D.C.: National Academy Press, 1983).

14. F. Kenneth Hare, "Recent Climatic Experience in the Arid and Semi-Arid Lands," *Desertification Control* (Nairobi), May 1984.

15. F. Kenneth Hare, cited in National Research Council, *Environmental Change.*

16. Eneas Salati and Peter B. Vose, "Amazon Basin: A System in Equilibrium," *Science,* July 13, 1984.

17. Ibid.

18. Philip M. Fearnside, "Brazil's Amazon Settlement Schemes," *Habitat International,* Vol. 8, No. 1, 1984.

19. Cited in Salati and Vose, "Amazon Basin."

20. All references in this paragraph discussed in ibid.

21. Hare, "Recent Climatic Experience."

22. Cited in ibid.

23. Ibid.

24. William W. Kellogg and Robert Schware, "Society, Science and Climate Change," *Foreign Affairs,* Summer 1982.

25. G.M. Woodwell et al., "Global Deforestation: Contribution to Atmospheric Carbon Dioxide," *Science,* December 9, 1983.

26. Estimates of carbon-emissions intensity of economic output based on data from United Nations, Department of International Economic and Social Affairs, "Fossil Fuels Production and Trade" (printout), New York, May 1984, from Gregg Marland and Ralph M. Rotty, *Carbon Dioxide Emissions from Fossil Fuels: A Procedure for Estimation and Results for 1950–81* (Washington, D.C.: U.S. De-

partment of Energy, June 1983), from Herbert R. Block, *The Planetary Product in 1980: A Creative Pause?* (Washington, D.C.: U.S. Department of State, 1981), and from International Monetary Fund, *World Economic Outlook* (Washington, D.C.: May 1984 and September 1984).

27. Kellogg and Schware, "Society, Science and Climate Change."

28. Ibid.

29. Ibid.

30. "Natural Disasters," Earthscan Press Briefing Document No. 39, Earthscan, Washington, D.C., May 1984.

31. V. Ramanathan et al., "Trace Gas Trends and Their Potential Role in Climate Change," National Center for Atmospheric Research, Boulder, Colo., unpublished, August 1984.

32. Stephen Seidel and Dale Keyes, *Can We Delay a Greenhouse Warming?* (Washington, D.C.: U.S. Environmental Protection Agency, 1983).

33. See Chapter 7 for a full discussion of the Department of Energy model and the Worldwatch Scenarios.

34. The concept of a "CO_2-benign" energy strategy was introduced by David J. Rose et al., *Global Energy Futures and CO_2-Induced Climate Change* (Cambridge, Mass.: Massachusetts Institute of Technology, 1983).

35. International Energy Agency, *World Energy Outlook* (Paris: Organisation for Economic Co-operation and Development, 1982).

36. Grain production data from USDA, ERS, *World Indices;* China's cropland prospects from Francis Urban and Thomas Vollrath, *Patterns and Trends in World Agricultural Land Use* (Washington, D.C.: U.S. Government Printing Office, 1984).

37. USDA, ERS, *World Indices.*

38. "Africa Faces 'Catastrophe'," *Mazingira*, May 1984; World Bank, *Toward Sustained Development in Sub-Saharan Africa* (Washington, D.C.: 1984).

39. Grain production data from USDA, ERS, *World Indices*.

40. Population data from Population Reference Bureau, *1984 World Population Data Sheet* (Washington, D.C.: 1984); grain production data from USDA, ERS, *World Indices*.

Chapter 2. Reducing Hunger

1. Decline in Africa's per capita grain output from U.S. Department of Agriculture (USDA), Economic Research Service (ERS), *World Indices of Agricultural and Food Production, 1950–83* (unpublished printout) (Washington, D.C.: 1984); share of Africa's population sustained by imported grain is author's estimate based on USDA data on grain production and imports.

2. Francis Urban and Thomas Vollrath, *Patterns and Trends in World Agricultural Land Use* (Washington, D.C.: U.S. Government Printing Office, 1984).

3. Ibid.

4. Drainage in Soviet Union from USDA, ERS, *USSR, Outlook and Situation Report* (Washington, D.C.: U.S. Government Printing Office, 1984); Great Plains states examples from Robert Gray, American Farmland Trust, Washington, D.C., private communication, November 9, 1984.

5. United Nations, Department of International Economic and Social Affairs, *Estimates and Projections of Urban, Rural, and City Populations, 1950–2025: The 1980 Assessment* (New York: 1982).

6. Linda Lee, "A Perspective on Cropland Availability," USDA, Washington, D.C., 1978; Organisation for Economic Co-operation and Development, *Land Use Policies and Agriculture* (Paris: 1976).

7. Akef Quazi, "Village Overspill," *Mazingira*, No. 6, 1978.

8. Author's discussions with Chinese officials in Beijing, April 1984; Peter Hendry, "Land Use and Living Space," *Ceres*, November/December 1983.

9. Dwight Perkins, "Constraints Influencing China's Agricultural Performance," in U.S. Congress, Joint Economic Committee, *China: A Reassessment of the Economy* (Washington, D.C.: U.S. Government Printing Office, 1975).

10. Motor Vehicle Manufacturers Association, *World Motor Vehicle Data Book, 1982 Edition* (Detroit, Mich.: 1982).

11. United Nations, Economic Commission for Latin America, *El Medio Ambiente en America Latina* (Santiago, Chile: May 1976).

12. "Should Agricultural Land Be Protected?," *OECD Observer*, September/October 1976.

13. Decline in harvested area of cereals from Urban and Vollrath, *Patterns and Trends in World Agricultural Land Use*.

14. "Chinese Reform Burial Customs," *Mazingira*, March 1984.

15. USDA, ERS, *World Indices*.

16. Science Council of Canada, "Population, Technology, and Resources," Ottawa, Ontario, July 1976.

17. Charles E. Hanrahan, Francis S. Urban, and J. Larry Deaton, *Longrun Changes in World Food Supply and Demand* (Washington, D.C.: USDA, ERS, 1984).

18. Based on unpublished data from Bruce Stone, International Food Policy Research Institute, Washington, D.C.

19. Centre for Monitoring Indian Economy, Economic Intelligence Service, *Basic Statistics Relating to the Indian Economy, Vol. 1: All India* (Bombay: 1984).

20. Data on irrigated area in 1978 from USDA, *Agricultural Statistics 1983* (Washing-

ton, D.C.: U.S. Government Printing Office, 1983); change in irrigated area since 1978 based on unpublished data from Bureau of the Census, "1982 Census of Agriculture," U.S. Department of Commerce, Washington, D.C., 1984.

21. USDA, ERS, *USSR Outlook and Situation Report.*

22. Hanrahan, Urban, and Deaton, *Long-run Changes in World Food Supply and Demand.*

23. USDA, ERS, *Inputs Outlook and Situation* (Washington, D.C.: February 1984).

24. Ibid.

25. Joseph Lastigzon, *World Fertilizer Progress Into the 1980's* (Muscle Shoals, Ala.: International Fertilizer Development Center, December 1981).

26. Ibid.

27. The Fertilizer Institute, *Fertilizer Reference Manual* (Washington, D.C.: 1982).

28. U.S. and Soviet fertilizer consumption from Fertilizer Institute, *Fertilizer Reference Manual;* U.S. and Soviet grain production from USDA, ERS, *World Indices.*

29. Response ratios based on fertilizer data from United Nations Food and Agriculture Organization (FAO), *FAO 1977 Fertilizer Yearbook* (Rome: 1978), and from Paul Andrilenas, USDA, ERS, private communication, September 28, 1983; grain production data from USDA, ERS, *World Indices.*

30. Brazil's import restrictions are discussed in USDA, ERS, *Latin America, World Agriculture Regional Supplement, Review of 1982 and Outlook for 1983* (Washington, D.C.: 1983).

31. USDA, ERS, *Inputs Outlook and Situation.*

32. Lastigzon, *World Fertilizer Progress.*

33. Calculated using the dollar price of urea at European ports, assuming a nitrogen content of 46.66 percent, and the dollar price of wheat for export at U.S. Gulf ports, based on data from International Monetary Fund, *International Financial Statistics* (Washington, D.C.: various annual issues).

34. FAO, *Agriculture: Toward 2000* (Rome: 1979).

35. FAO/UNIDO/World Bank projection cited in Lastigzon, *World Fertilizer Progress;* USDA forecast from USDA, ERS, *Inputs Outlook and Situation.*

36. Urban quoted in Robert C. Cowan, "Gene-Splicing Opens New World for Agriculture," *Christian Science Monitor,* July 7, 1981.

37. U.S. Office of Technology Assessment, *Impacts of Applied Genetics: Micro-organisms, Plants, and Animals* (Washington, D.C.: U.S. Government Printing Office, 1981).

38. Data on yields for corn, wheat, sorghum, and rice from USDA, ERS, *World Indices.*

39. Figure on artificial insemination from "The Livestock Industry's Genetic Revolution," *Business Week,* June 21, 1982; embryo transfer figure from Harrison Brotman, "Engineering the Birth of Cattle," *New York Times Magazine,* May 15, 1983.

40. In 1983, 142 million metric tons of grain were traded worldwide and 1,457 million metric tons harvested; the share of grain consumed in countries where harvested was 90.3 percent. Grain trade data from USDA, Foreign Agricultural Service, *Foreign Agriculture Circulars* FG-23-83 and FG-8-84, Washington, D.C., August 1983 and May 1984; harvest data from USDA, ERS, *World Indices,* with paddy rice converted to milled equivalent by Worldwatch Institute.

41. USDA, ERS, *World Indices.*

42. Urban and Vollrath, *Patterns and Trends in World Agricultural Land Use.*

43. Estimate of world topsoil loss due to erosion from Lester R. Brown and Edward C. Wolf, *Soil Erosion: Quiet Crisis in the World Economy* (Washington, D.C.: Worldwatch Institute, September 1984); southern Iowa study

from Paul Rosenberry, Russell Knutson, and Lacy Harmon, "Predicting the Effects of Soil Depletion from Erosion," *Journal of Soil and Water Conservation,* May/June 1980.

44. See, for example, Warren Hoge, "Brazil's Poor Raiding Food Stores in the Rio Area," *New York Times,* September 11, 1983; Margot Hornblower, "Price Riots Imperil Dominican Government," *Washington Post,* April 30, 1984; James Rupert, "Tunisians Riot Over Bread Price Rise," *Washington Post,* January 4, 1984; Jonathan C. Randal, "Morocco's Unrest Has Its Roots in Economic Woes," *Washington Post,* January 27, 1984; "Poland Prepares for Unrest Over Food Prices," *New York Times,* December 4, 1983. For an overview, see Paul Streeten, "Food Prices as a Reflection of Political Power," *Ceres,* March/April 1983.

Chapter 3. Managing Freshwater Supplies

1. Frits van der Leeden, *Water Resources of the World* (Port Washington, N.Y.: Water Information Center, Inc. 1975).

2. An annual supply of 1,000 cubic meters per person is typically given as necessary for a decent standard of living. See Carl Widstrand, ed., *Water Conflicts and Research Priorities* (Oxford, U.K.: Pergamon Press, 1980).

3. Vaclav Smil, *The Bad Earth: Environmental Degradation in China* (Armonk, N.Y.: M.E. Sharpe, Inc., 1984); Malin Falkenmark and Gunnar Lindh, *Water for a Starving World* (Boulder, Colo.: Westview Press, 1976); Gary S. Posz et al., "Water Resource Development in India," American Embassy, New Delhi, June 1980; food grain reduction from B.B. Sundaresan, "Water: A Vital Resource for the Developing World," in Peter G. Bourne, ed., *Water and Sanitation: Economic and Sociological Perspectives* (Orlando, Fla.: Academic Press, Inc., 1984); Zaire River flow from van der Leeden, *Water Resources of the World;* famine threat in Africa discussed in Chapters 1 and 2.

4. Inquiry on Federal Water Policy, "Water is a Mainstream Issue: Participation Paper," Canadian Minister of Supply and Services, Ottawa, 1984; Mardjono Notodihardjo, "Indonesia's Water Resources," in W. Hall C. Maxwell, ed., *Water for Human Consumption,* Proceedings of the Fourth World Congress of the International Water Resources Association (Dublin: Tycooly International Publishing Ltd., 1983); United Nations Economic Commission for Europe (UNECE), *Long-Term Perspectives for Water Use and Supply in the ECE Region* (New York: United Nations, 1981).

5. William W. Kellogg and Robert Schware, "Society, Science and Climate Change," *Foreign Affairs,* Summer 1982.

6. USSR Committee for the International Hydrological Decade, *World Water Balance and Water Resources of the Earth* (Paris: UNESCO, 1974).

7. Rice yields with different degrees of water control from Asit K. Biswas, "Major Water Problems Facing the World," *International Journal of Water Resources Development,* April 1983.

8. Estimate of global irrigated area and its contribution to production from W.R. Rangeley, "Irrigation—Current Trends and a Future Perspective," World Bank Seminar, Washington, D.C., February 1983. Irrigation demands based on FAO estimate for the 1974 World Food Conference that gross water demand for harvested crop irrigation averages 11,400 cubic meters per hectare. Estimate takes into account that rice requires twice as much water as wheat and other dry cereals. This figure, applied to an average expansion of irrigation of 4 million hectares annually, led to estimate of an additional 820 billion cubic meters annually for irrigation by 2000.

9. Wayne B. Solley et al., *Estimated Use of Water in the United States in 1980* (Alexandria, Va.: U.S. Geological Survey, 1983).

10. See John Harte and Mohamed El-Gesseir, "Water and Energy," *Science,* February

10, 1978, and Norman L. Dalsted and John W. Green, "Water Requirements for Coal-Fired Power Plants," *Natural Resources Journal*, January 1984; percent consumed from Solley et al., *Estimated Use in the United States.*

11. Major water-using industries from United Nations, *Resources and Needs: Assessment of the World Water Situation*, prepared for the U.N. Water Conference, Mar del Plata, Argentina, March 1977; trends in European countries from UNECE, *Long-Term Perspectives for Water Use and Supply;* Swedish Preparatory Committee for the U.N. Water Conference, *Water in Sweden* (Stockholm: Ministry of Agriculture, 1977).

12. Development decade goals cited in Biswas, "Major Water Problems."

13. United Nations, *Resources and Needs;* Solley et al., *Estimated Use in the United States.*

14. UNECE, *Long-Term Perspectives for Water Use and Supply;* World Health Organization, *Drinking Water and Sanitation, 1981–1990* (Geneva: 1981).

15. Widstrand, *Water Conflicts and Research Priorities.*

16. Water rendered unusable by pollution by year 2000 estimated at 3,000 cubic kilometers in Robert P. Ambroggi, "Water," *Scientific American*, September 1980.

17. Zheng Guanglin, "Research Program on China 2000," Institute of Scientific and Technical Information of China, Beijing, draft, February 1984; Smil, *The Bad Earth.*

18. U.N. Economic Commission on Latin America, *The Water Resources of Latin America: Regional Report* (Santiago de Chile: 1977); Bogota River cited in Peter Nares, "Colombian Towns Threatened by Polluted Bogota River," *World Environment Report*, May 30, 1984.

19. Thane Gustafson, "Transforming Soviet Agriculture: Brezhnev's Gamble on Land Improvement," *Public Policy*, Summer 1977.

20. Share of U.S. irrigated land from Resource Analysis Section, Colorado Depart-

ment of Agriculture, "Colorado High Plains Study: Summary Report," Denver, Colo., November 1983; for background on the Ogallala's development, see Kenneth D. Frederick and James C. Hanson, *Water for Western Agriculture* (Washington, D.C.: Resources for the Future, 1982), and Morton W. Bittinger and Elizabeth B. Green, *You Never Miss the Water Till . . .* (Littleton, Colo.: Water Resources Publications, 1980); data on water depletion from U.S. Geological Survey, *National Water Summary 1983—Hydrologic Events and Issues* (Washington, D.C.: U.S. Government Printing Office, 1984).

21. U.S. Department of Agriculture, *Agricultural Statistics 1983* (Washington, D.C.: U.S. Government Printing Office, 1983) and Bureau of the Census, "1982 Census of Agriculture," U.S. Department of Commerce, Washington, D.C., 1984; Nebraska corn production statistics from U.S. Department of Agriculture, Economic Research Service, *Economic Indicators of the Farm Sector: Costs of Production 1982* (Washington, D.C.: U.S. Government Printing Office, 1983).

22. See Dean Abrahamson and Peter Ciborowski, "North American Agriculture and the Greenhouse Problem," Report of the Humphrey Institute Symposium on the Response of the North American Granary to Greenhouse Climate Change, Minneapolis, Minn., April 1983, and Kellogg and Schware, "Society, Science and Climate Change."

23. Tucson information from Tony Davis, "Trouble in a Thirsty City," *Technology Review*, August/September 1984; Texas and Mexico references in Tommy Knowles and Frank Rayner, "Depletion Allowance for Groundwater Mining: Pros and Cons," *Journal of the American Water Works Association*, March 1978.

24. Reference to Tamil Nadu in Widstrand, *Water Conflicts and Research Priorities;* China references from Smil, *The Bad Earth.*

25. Thomas G. Sanders, "Population Growth and Resource Management: Planning

Mexico's Water Supply," *Common Ground,* October 1977; China references from "Sinking City Under Control," *Beijing Review,* February 23, 1981; Smil, *The Bad Earth;* Texas situation from Knowles and Rayner, "Depletion Allowance: Pros and Cons."

26. For U.S. citations, see U.S. Geological Survey, *National Water Summary 1983;* other countries cited in Tony Samstag, "Too Much of a Good Thing," *Development Forum,* April 1984.

27. Cropland figure from M.I. L'vovich and I.D. Tsigel'naya, "The Potential for Long-Term Regulation of Runoff in the Mountains of the Aral Sea Drainage Basin," *Soviet Geography,* October 1981; population and employment issues discussed in Thane Gustafson, "Technology Assessment, Soviet Style," *Science,* June 20, 1980; information on the Aral from Philip P. Micklin, Department of Geography, Western Michigan University, Kalamazoo, Mich., private communication, September 5, 1984; scientists' projections from G.V. Voropaev et al., "The Problem of Redistribution of Water Resources in the Midlands Region of the USSR," *Soviet Geography,* December 1983.

28. Estimate of water level decline from O.K. Leont'yev, "Why Did the Forecasts of Water-Level Changes in the Caspian Sea Turn Out to be Wrong?," *Soviet Geography,* May 1984; background information from Grigorii Voropaev and Aleksei Kosarev, "The Fall and Rise of the Caspian Sea," *New Scientist,* April 8, 1982; Micklin, private communication; Caspian fisheries discussed in Philip P. Micklin, "International Environmental Implications of Soviet Development of the Volga River," *Human Ecology,* Vol. 5, No. 2, 1977.

29. Philip C. Metzger and Jennifer A. Haverkamp, "Instream Flow Protection: Adaptation to Intensifying Demands," The Conservation Foundation, Washington, D.C., June 1984.

30. Inquiry on Federal Water Policy, "Water is a Mainstream Issue."

31. Anupam Mishra, "An Irrigation Project That Has Reduced Farm Production," Centre for Science and Environment, New Delhi, 1981.

32. Global estimate from V.A. Kovda, "Loss of Productive Land due to Salinization," *Ambio,* Vol. 12, No. 2, 1983; India and Pakistan estimates from Gilbert Levine et al., "Water," prepared for Conference on Agricultural Production: Research and Development Strategies for the 1980's, Bonn, West Germany, October 8–12, 1979; other areas from Biswas, "Major Water Problems," and various other sources.

33. Estimate of reservoir capacity based on M.I. L'vovich, *World Water Resources and Their Future,* translation ed. Raymond L. Nace (Washington, D.C.: American Geophysical Union, 1979); figures on large dam construction from van der Leeden, *Water Resources of the World,* and from Philip Williams, "Damming the World," Philip Williams & Associates, San Francisco, Calif., unpublished, April 1983.

34. U.S. Geological Survey, *National Water Summary 1983.*

35. UNECE, *Long-Term Perspectives for Water Use and Supply.*

36. Williams, "Damming the World."

37. Donor agency inspections from U.S. General Accounting Office, *Irrigation Assistance to Developing Countries Should Require Stronger Commitments to Operation and Maintenance* (Washington, D.C.: 1983); John Madeley, "Big Dam Schemes—Value for Money or Non-Sustainable Development?," *Mazingira,* Vol. 7, No. 4, 1983.

38. For an excellent discussion of these water and land interactions, see Malin Falkenmark, "New Ecological Approach to the Water Cycle: Ticket to the Future," *Ambio,* Vol. 13, No. 3, 1984; Malaysia example from Eneas Salati and Peter B. Vose, "Amazon Basin: A System in Equilibrium," *Science,* July 13, 1984; Dominica example from Robert S. Goodwin, "Water Resources Development

in Small Islands: Perspectives and Needs," *Natural Resources Forum*, January 1984.

39. For an assessment of selected large dam projects, see Environmental Policy Institute, "Fact Sheets on International Water Development Projects," Washington, D.C., 1984.

40. History and 1983 government support from Asit K. Biswas, "Water Where It's Wanted," *Development Forum*, August/September 1983; Yao Bangyi and Chen Qinglian, "South-North Water Transfer Project Plans," in Asit K. Biswas et al., eds., *Long-Distance Water Transfer* (Dublin: Tycooly International Publishing Ltd., 1983).

41. Bruce Stone, "The Chang Jiang Diversion Project: An Overview of Economic and Environmental Issues," in Biswas et al., *Long-Distance Water Transfer;* cost estimates also given in Asit K. Biswas, "US $12 Billion Plan to Redistribute China's Water Wealth," *South*, April 1982.

42. For discussion of Siberian diversion plans, see O.A. Kibal'chich and N.I. Koronkevich, "Some of the Results and Tasks of Geographic Investigations on the Water-Transfer Project," *Soviet Geography*, December 1983; quote is from Gustafson, "Technology Assessment, Soviet Style."

43. Philip P. Micklin, "Recent Developments in Large-Scale Water Transfers in the USSR," *Soviet Geography*, April 1984; cost estimates from Micklin, private communication, October 16, 1984; water-saving potentials and salinization risks from summary of remarks made by O.A. Kibal'chich at conference in Irkutsk, Soviet Union, August 1983, and published in *Soviet Geography*, December 1983.

44. U.S. Congressional Budget Office, *Efficient Investments in Water Resources: Issues and Options* (Washington, D.C.: U.S. Government Printing Office, 1983).

45. Thomas M. Power, "An Economic Analysis of the Central Arizona Project, U.S. Bureau of Reclamation," Economics Department, University of Montana, Missoula, Mont., 1978.

46. Costs to date from Steve Macauley, Supervisory Engineer for the State Water Project Analysis Office, California Department of Water Resources, private communication, October 23, 1984; pumping costs from California Department of Water Resources, *Management of the California State Water Project* (Sacramento: California Resources Agency, 1983).

47. Jack Foley, "Governor's Water Bill Dead for this Year," *San Jose Mercury News*, August 7, 1984; private communications with California Department of Water Resources personnel, June and August 1984.

48. Projects worldwide from Jay H. Lehr, "Artificial Ground-Water Recharge: A Solution to Many U.S. Water-Supply Problems," *Ground Water*, May/June 1982; Israel project cited in Robert P. Ambroggi, "Underground Reservoirs to Control the Water Cycle," *Scientific American*, May 1977; California Department of Water Resources, *The California State Water Project—Current Activities and Future Management Plans* (Sacramento: California Resources Agency, 1980); California Dept. of Water Resources, *Management of the Water Project;* Helen Peters, Groundwater Staff Specialist, California Department of Water Resources, private communication, October 1984; median cost estimate for new surface reservoirs from Ronald B. Robie, "Irrigation Development in California—Construction or Water Management?," in *Irrigation Challenges of the 80's* (St. Joseph, Mich.: American Society of Agricultural Engineers, 1981); Environmental and Energy Study Institute, *Weekly Bulletin*, March 26, 1984; Russell Brown, Subcommittee on Water and Power, Senate Committee on Energy and Natural Resources, private communication, October 1984.

49. Gangetic Plain estimates from Widstrand, *Water Conflicts and Research Priorities;* information on China from Smil, *The Bad Earth.*

50. Ambroggi, "Underground Reservoirs"; William R. Gasser, *Survey of Irrigation in Eight Asian Nations* (Washington, D.C.: U.S. Department of Agriculture, 1981); problems with the project cited in Ian Carruthers and Roy Stoner, *Economic Aspects and Policy Issues in Groundwater Development* (Washington, D.C.: The World Bank, 1981) and by Douglas Merrey, Agency for International Development, private communication, October 1984.

51. Wayne A. Pettyjohn, *Introduction to Artificial Ground Water Recharge* (Columbus, Ohio: National Water Well Association, 1981).

52. Lehr, "Artificial Ground-Water Recharge."

53. L'vovich, *World Water Resources and their Future.*

54. U.S. Office of Technology Assessment, *Water-Related Technologies for Sustainable Agriculture in U.S. Arid/Semiarid Lands* (Washington, D.C.: U.S. Government Printing Office, 1983); desalination cost estimates from U.S. Comptroller General, *Desalting Water Probably Will Not Solve the Nation's Water Problems, But Can Help* (Washington, D.C.: U.S. General Accounting Office, 1979); use in Arabian Peninsula from M. A. Khan et al., "Development of Supplies & Sanitation in Saudi Arabia," *African Technical Review,* June 1984.

55. A concise description of irrigation systems is contained in Office of Technology Assessment, *Water-Related Technologies for Sustainable Agriculture in U.S. Lands.*

56. Negev experiments from "Israel's Water Policy: A National Commitment," in U.S. Office of Technology Assessment, *Water-Related Technologies for Sustainable Agriculture in Arid/Semiarid Lands: Selected Foreign Experience* (Washington, D.C.: U.S. Government Printing Office, 1983); Office of Technology Assessment, *Water-Related Technologies for Sustainable Agriculture in U.S. Lands;* Jay H. Lehr, "Increased Irrigation Efficiency Will Ultimately Silence the Water-Short Blues of the Wasteful West," *Ground Water,* March/April 1983; Brazilian information from *IDB News,* Inter-American Development Bank, Washington, D.C., Vol. 10, No. 4.

57. Efficiency ranges from J. Keller et al., "Evaluation of Irrigation Systems," in *Irrigation Challenges of the 80's;* tailwater reuse discussed in Gordon Sloggett, *Energy and U.S. Agriculture: Irrigation Pumping 1974–1980* (Washington, D.C.: U.S. Government Printing Office, 1982); E.G. Kruse et al., "Advances in Surface Irrigation," in *Irrigation Challenges of the 80's.*

58. Nebraska program from Paul E. Fischbach, "Irrigation Management (Scheduling) Application," in *Irrigation Challenges of the 80's;* California system described by Edward Craddock, California Department of Water Resources, Office of Water Conservation, private communication, June 21, 1984; California Department of Water Resources, "The Mobile Agricultural Water Conservation Laboratory," information pamphlet prepared by the Office of Water Conservation, Sacramento, Calif.

59. "Israel's Water Policy: A National Commitment."

60. General Accounting Office, *Irrigation Assistance to Developing Countries;* D.B. Kraatz, *Irrigation Canal Lining* (Rome: U.N. Food and Agriculture Organization, 1977).

61. Worth Fitzgerald, U.S. Agency for International Development, private communication, April 25, 1984; Egyptian pilot project cited in Mark Svendsen et al., "Meeting the Challenge for Better Irrigation Management," *Horizons,* March 1983.

62. Harte and El-Gesseir, "Water and Energy"; "Thirsty Desert Plant Has Unique Water System," *The Phoenix Gazette,* June 27, 1984; ranges of water use for steel and paper from United Nations, *Resources and Needs;* reductions with aluminum recycling from R. C. Ziegler, "Environmental Impacts of Virgin and Recycled Steel and Aluminum," Calspan Corporation, Buffalo, N.Y., 1976.

63. Saul Arlosoroff, "Water Management Policies Under Scarce Conditions: A Case Study—Israel," presented at Conference on Water for the 21st Century: Will It Be There?, Dallas, Tex., April 1984.

64. Swedish Preparatory Committee, *Water in Sweden.*

65. Reductions by California pulp and paper industry from California Department of Water Resources, *Water Use By Manufacturing Industries in California, 1979* (Sacramento: California Resources Agency, 1982).

66. See 3M Company, "Low- or Non-Pollution Technology Through Pollution Prevention," prepared for United Nations Environment Programme, St. Paul, Minn., June 1982; Brazil study from Division for Industrial Studies, "Water Use and Treatment Practices and other Environmental Considerations in the Iron and Steel Industry," United Nations Industrial Development Organization, Vienna, Austria, December 1981.

67. John J. Boland, "Water/Wastewater Pricing and Financial Practices in the United States," Metametrics, Inc., Washington, D.C., August 1983.

68. For estimates of water and energy savings and costs of various water-conserving measures, see U.S. Environmental Protection Agency, Office of Water Program Operations, *Flow Reduction: Methods, Analysis Procedures, Examples* (Washington, D.C.: 1981); reference to West German toilets from *World Environment Report,* April 4, 1984.

69. Typical U.S. household savings from Environmental Protection Agency, *Flow Reduction;* Stefano Burchi, "Regulatory Approaches to the Use of Water for Domestic Purposes," *Natural Resources Forum,* July 1983; Barbara Yeaman, Consultant to Facilities Requirements Division, U.S. Environmental Protection Agency, private communication, August 10, 1984.

70. Adrian H. Griffin et al., "Changes in Water Rates and Water Consumption in Tuc-son, 1974 to 1978," *Hydrology and Water Resources in Arizona and the Southwest,* Vol. 10, 1979; Stephen E. Davis, "Tucson's Tools for Demand Management," *Hydrology and Water Resources in Arizona and the Southwest,* Vol. 8, 1979.

71. Lee Wilson and Associates, Inc., "Water Supply Alternatives for El Paso," prepared for El Paso Water Utilities Public Service Board, Santa Fe, N. Mex., November 1981.

72. Kahn et al., "Development of Supplies & Sanitation in Saudi Arabia"; Dennis J. Parker and Edmund C. Penning-Rowsell, *Water Planning in Britain* (London: George Allen & Unwin, 1980); Swedish Preparatory Committee, *Water in Sweden.*

73. Quote and estimates of advanced treatment costs from Axel F. Zunckel and Maria P. Oliveira, "South African Water Reuse Policy and its Practical Implications," in *Proceedings of the Water Reuse Symposium II,* Vol. 1 (Denver, Colo.: AWWA Research Foundation, 1981); reuse projections from Mike Nicol, "South Africa Will Require Wastewater Recycling Before Year 2000, Experts Say," *World Environment Report,* June 27, 1984; Hillel I. Shuval, "The Development of the Wastewater Reuse Program in Israel," in *Proceedings of the Water Reuse Symposium II.*

74. Value added figures cited in Ambroggi, "Water."

75. Great Britain practice from Burchi, "Regulatory Approaches to the Use of Water for Domestic Purposes"; subsidies in selected countries from J.A. Sagardoy et al., *Organization, Operation and Maintenance of Irrigation Schemes* (Rome: U.N. Food and Agriculture Organization, 1982); costs to U.S. farmers from Congressional Budget Office, *Efficient Investments in Water Resources.*

76. Knowles and Rayner, "Depletion Allowance: Pros and Cons"; Institute of Agriculture and Natural Resources, Cooperative Extension Service, "IRS Extends Ground

Water Depletion Deduction to Nebraska Irrigators," University of Nebraska, Lincoln, Nebr., March 18, 1983.

77. Importance of improved operation and maintenance discussed by Guy Le Moigne, Irrigation Advisor, World Bank, private communication, April 1984, and by Fitzgerald, private communication.

78. See Frances F. Korten, *Building National Capacity to Develop Water Users' Associations: Experience from the Philippines* (Washington, D.C.: The World Bank, 1982); quote from Ruangdej Srivardhanaat, "No Easy Management: Irrigation Development in the Chao Phya Basin, Thailand," *Natural Resources Forum,* April 1984.

79. See James A. Seagraves and K. William Easter, "Pricing Irrigation Water in Developing Countries," *Water Resources Bulletin,* August 1983; B. D. Dhawan, *Development of Tubewell Irrigation in India* (New Delhi: Agricole Publishing Academy, 1983).

80. Peter Rogers, "Fresh Water," prepared for The Global Possible Conference, World Resources Institute, Wye, Md., May 2–5, 1984.

81. James Huffman, "Instream Water Use: Public and Private Alternatives," in Terry L. Anderson, ed., *Water Rights: Scarce Resource Allocation, Bureaucracy, and the Environment* (Cambridge, Mass.: Ballinger Publishing Company, 1983).

82. Ibid.; Metzger and Haverkamp, "Instream Flow Protection."

83. For an excellent review of this decision, see Ellen Sullivan Casey, "Water Law—Public Trust Doctrine," *Natural Resources Journal,* July 1984; Harrison C. Dunning, "A New Front in the Water Wars: Introducing the 'Public Trust' Factor," *California Journal,* May 1983.

84. Dhawan, *Development of Tubewell Irrigation in India;* Tamil Nadu observation from Widstrand, *Water Conflicts and Research Priorities.*

85. Arizona Groundwater Management Study Commission Staff, "Summary: Arizona Groundwater Management Act," briefing presented to the Arizona Groundwater Management Study Commission and the Arizona State Legislature, June 5, 1980; Scott Hanson and Floyd Marsh, "Arizona Ground-Water Reform: Innovations in State Water Policy," *Ground Water,* January/February 1982; decline in irrigated area from U.S. Department of Agriculture, *Agricultural Statistics 1983,* and Bureau of the Census, "Census of Agriculture."

86. See Environmental Protection Agency, *Flow Reduction,* and Institute for Water Resources, *The Role of Water Conservation in Water Supply Planning* (Fort Belvoir, Va.: U.S. Army Corps of Engineers, 1979); policy changes under Reagan administration from "Water Resources," in The Conservation Foundation, *State of the Environment: An Assessment at Mid-Decade* (Washington, D.C.: 1984), and from Yeaman, private communication; California law from Reprint of Assembly Bill No. 797, *Legislative Council's Digest,* California Assembly, October 1983.

Chapter 4. Maintaining World Fisheries

1. 1983 fish production is author's estimate based on United Nations Food and Agriculture Organization (FAO), *1982 Yearbook of Fishery Statistics—Catches and Landings* (Rome: 1984) and various press reports on 1983 catch; share of world protein consumption calculated from FAO, *Fishery Statistics—Catches and Landings,* from FAO, *1981 Production Yearbook* (Rome: 1982), and from U.S. Department of Agriculture (USDA), Agricultural Research Service, *Composition of Foods,* (Washington, D.C.: U.S. Government Printing Office, reprinted 1975).

2. World Bank, *Fishery Sector Policy Paper* (Washington, D.C.: 1982).

3. FAO, *Yearbook of Fishery Statistics—Fishery Commodities* (Rome: various years).

4. Aquaculture Development and Coordination Programme, *Aid for Aquaculture Development in the Third World* (Rome: Norwegian Agency for International Development, United Nations Development Programme, and FAO, 1982); World Bank, *Fishery Sector Policy Paper*.

5. Per capita fish consumption in the Soviet Union and the United States based on data from FAO, *Fishery Statistics—Catches and Landings,* and from Population Reference Bureau, *1982 World Population Data Sheet* (Washington, D.C.: 1982); growth of the Soviet factory trawler fleet described in William W. Warner, *Distant Water* (Boston: Little, Brown & Co., 1983).

6. Japanese per capita fish consumption based on data from FAO, *Fishery Statistics—Catches and Landings,* and from Population Reference Bureau, *World Population Data Sheet.*

7. Michael K. Orbach, "Fishing in Troubled Waters," *Environment,* January/February 1980; Barry Lanier, "The Crisis in the World Tuna Market," *Infofish Marketing Digest* (FAO), November 1982; FAO, *Fishery Statistics—Catches and Landings;* FAO, Committee on Fisheries, "Fishery Commodity Situation and Outlook 1981/83," Rome, July 1983; Bob Johnstone, "Japan is Number One Squid-Eater of the World," *New Scientist,* November 3, 1983; M. Hotta, "The Japanese Market for Squid and Cuttlefish," *Infofish Marketing Digest* (FAO), July 1982.

8. FAO, *Fishery Statistics—Commodities.*

9. FAO, Fisheries Department, "Review of the State of World Fishery Resources," Rome, July 1983.

10. Ibid.

11. Ibid.

12. C.P. Idyll, "The Anchovy Crisis," *Scientific American,* June 1973.

13. David L. Fluharty, Institute for Marine Studies, University of Washington, Seattle,

Wash., private communication, November 3, 1984.

14. Earnings from Peru's anchovy catch in 1970 from Idyll, "Anchovy Crisis"; ratio of Peru's exports to debt from Lester R. Brown, "Overview," in Lester R. Brown et al., *State of the World-1984* (New York: W. W. Norton & Co., 1984).

15. Alaska king crab catch data from State of Alaska, Department of Fish and Game, "Westward Region Report to the Board of Fisheries," Anchorage, Alaska, March 1984; "King Crab Fishing Closed in Alaska," *New York Times,* October 3, 1983; 1982 survey of female crabs cited in Catherine C. Krueger, "Alaskan King Crab: A Decade of Boom and Bust," Institute for Marine Studies, University of Washington, Seattle, Wash., unpublished, March 1983.

16. FAO, Fisheries Department, "Review of World Fishery Resources."

17. Ibid; U.S. Environmental Protection Agency (EPA), *Chesapeake Bay Program: Findings and Recommendations* (Philadelphia: September 1983); decline in shad catch discussed in Robert H. Boyle, "A Rain of Death on the Striper?," *Sports Illustrated,* April 23, 1984.

18. FAO, Fisheries Department, "Review of World Fishery Resources."

19. Jay L. Maclean and Leticia B. Dizon, *ICLARM Report 1983* (Manila: International Center for Living Aquatic Resources Management, 1984).

20. John R. Beddington and Robert M. May, "The Harvesting of Interacting Species in a Natural Ecosystem," *Scientific American,* November 1982.

21. Quoted in ibid.

22. The biological dynamics of estuaries are thoroughly described in Bostwick H. Ketchum, ed., *Estuaries and Enclosed Seas* (New York: Elsevier Scientific Publishing Co., 1983).

23. EPA, *Chesapeake Bay Program.*

24. Robert J. Orth and Kenneth A. Moore, "Chesapeake Bay: An Unprecedented Decline in Submerged Aquatic Vegetation," *Science,* October 7, 1983.

25. EPA, *Chesapeake Bay Program.*

26. Boyle, "Rain of Death on the Striper?"; John W. Frece, "State Bans Harvest of Waning Rockfish," *Baltimore Sun,* September 12, 1984.

27. Peter McGrath and Mary Hagar, "An American Treasure at Risk," *Newsweek,* December 12, 1983.

28. Boyle, "Rain of Death on the Striper?"

29. "Turkey Struggles to Save its Seas," *New Scientist,* January 14, 1982.

30. Aquaculture Development and Coordination Programme, *Aid for Aquaculture Development.*

31. Ibid.; Federal Coordinating Council on Science, Engineering, and Technology, *National Aquaculture Development Plan* (Springfield, Va.: National Technical Information Service, September 1983).

32. Share of seafood consumption provided by aquaculture is author's estimate; Aquaculture Development and Coordination Programme, *Aid for Aquaculture Development;* Hans Ackefors and Carl-Gustaf Rosen, "Farming Aquatic Animals," *Ambio,* Vol. 8, No. 4, 1979.

33. International Center for Living Aquatic Resources Management, *The ICLARM-CLSU Integrated Animal-Fish Farming Project: Poultry-Fish and Pig-Fish Trials* (Manila, Philippines: ICLARM and Central Luzon State University, 1981); H. R. Rabanal, "Aquaculture in Asia and the Pacific," *Infofish Marketing Digest* (FAO), January 1983.

34. Richard T. Lovell, "Fish Culture in the United States," *Science,* December 21, 1979; Federal Coordinating Council, *National Aquaculture Development Plan.*

35. Federal Coordinating Council, *National Aquaculture Development Plan.*

36. R.T. Lovell, R.O. Smitherman, and E.W. Shell, "Progress and Prospects of Fish Farming," in Aaron Altschul and Harold Wilcke, eds., *New Protein Foods Vol. 3: Animal Protein Supplies, Part A* (New York: Academic Press, Inc., 1978).

37. China data from World Bank, *Fishery Sector Policy Paper;* Mississippi area in fish farms from Jeff Giachelli, Catfish Farmers of America, Jackson, Miss., private communication, April 1984.

38. World Bank, *Fishery Sector Policy Paper.*

39. "U.S. Aquaculture Lags But Could Be an Important Food Source," *News Report* (National Academy of Sciences), March 1978.

40. Lauren R. Donaldson and Timothy Joyner, "The Salmonid Fishes as Natural Livestock," *Scientific American,* July 1983.

41. "Free-Range Salmon," *The Economist,* October 1, 1983; Donaldson and Joyner, "Salmonid Fishes"; William J. McNeil, "Salmon Ranching: A Growing Industry in the North Pacific," *Oceanus,* Spring 1984; Fluharty, private communication.

42. Donaldson and Joyner, "Salmonid Fishes."

43. McNeil, "Salmon Ranching"; J. H. Ryther, "Mariculture, Ocean Ranching, and Other Culture-Based Fisheries," *BioScience,* March 1981.

44. Fluharty, private communication.

45. McNeil, "Salmon Ranching."

46. Donaldson and Joyner, "Salmonid Fishes."

47. "Free-Range Salmon."

48. Ibid.

49. McNeil, "Salmon Ranching."

50. FAO, "Review of World Fishery Resources."

51. Quoted in Gwen J. Struik, "Commercial Fishing in New Zealand: An Industry Bent on Extinction," *The Ecologist*, Vol. 13, No. 6, 1983.

52. Warner, *Distant Water.*

53. U.S. investment from Federal Coordinating Council, *National Aquaculture Development Plan;* for international lending, see World Bank, *Fishery Sector Policy Paper*, Aquaculture Development and Coordination Programme, *Aid for Aquaculture Development*, and Inter-American Development Bank, *Economic and Social Progress in Latin America—Natural Resources* (Washington, D.C.: 1983).

54. McNeil, "Salmon Ranching."

55. Data from "Indexes of Exvessel Prices for Fish and Shellfish, By Years," in National Marine Fisheries Service, *Fisheries of the United States* (Washington, D.C.: U.S. Department of Commerce, various annual issues).

56. The oil/krill ratio is mentioned by D. Norse, Organisation for Economic Co-operation and Development, in discussion comments appended to G.O. Barney, "The *Global 2000 Report* and its Implications for the United States," in Maurice Levy and John L. Robinson, eds., *Energy and Agriculture: Their Interacting Futures* (Chur, Switzerland: Harwood Academic Publishers, for The United Nations University, 1984).

57. Maclean and Dizon, *ICLARM Report 1983.*

58. FAO, *Agriculture: Toward 2000* (Rome: 1981).

Chapter 5. Protecting Forests from Air Pollution and Acid Rain

1. Edward C. Krug and Charles R. Frink, "Acid Rain on Acid Soil: A New Perspective," *Science*, August 5, 1983.

2. The survey was conducted by the Allensbach Institute and was referred to in James Buchan, "Germany's Dying Forests: 'It's Just Like Being at a Graveside'," *Financial Times*, November 19, 1983.

3. Anthony C. Tennissen, *Nature of Earth Materials* (Englewood Cliffs, N.J.: Prentice-Hall, Inc., 1974).

4. Sulfur emissions from Swedish Ministry of Agriculture, *Proceedings: The 1982 Stockholm Conference on Acidification of the Environment* (Stockholm, Sweden: 1982), and from Swedish Ministry of Agriculture, *Acidification Today and Tomorrow* (Stockholm, Sweden: 1982); International Nickel Company emissions from Subcommittee on Acid Rain, *Still Waters* (Ottawa, Canada: Ministry of Supply and Services, 1981); Mount Saint Helens emissions from U. S. Environmental Protection Agency, *The Acidic Deposition Phenomenon and its Effects: Atmospheric Sciences* (Vol. 1, draft) (Washington, D.C.: 1983); nitrogen oxide emissions from Fred Fehsenfeld, "Gas Phase and Precipitation Acidities in the Colorado Mountains," in *Acid Rain in the Rocky Mountain West*, Colorado Department of Health, Golden, Colo., Hearings, June 2–3, 1983.

5. For historical sketches of air pollution control, see Erik P. Eckholm, *Down to Earth* (New York: W. W. Norton & Co., 1982) and Edwin S. Mills, *The Economics of Environmental Quality* (New York: W. W. Norton & Co., 1978); emissions trends from Swedish Ministry of Agriculture, *Proceedings* and from Harald Dovland and Arne Semb, "Atmospheric Transport of Pollutants," in D. Drablos and A. Tollan, eds., *Ecological Impact of Acid Precipitation* (Oslo, Norway: SNSF Project, 1980).

6. Environment Canada, *United States-Canada Memorandum of Intent on Transboundary Air Pollution: Executive Summaries* (Ottawa, Canada: 1983); Swedish Ministry of Agriculture, *Proceedings.*

7. Estimates for Europe from Lars N. Overrein et al., *Acid Precipitation Effects on Forest and Fish: Final Report of the SNSF Project 1972–1980* (Oslo: Norwegian Interdisciplinary Research Programme, 1980); estimates for West Germany from Georg H. M. Krause,

private communication, January 1984; estimates for North America from Environment Canada, *United States-Canada Memorandum of Intent.*

8. INCO measurements from B. Freedman and T. C. Hutchinson, "Smelter Pollution Near Sudbury, Ontario, Canada, and Effects on Forest Litter Decomposition," in T. C. Hutchinson and M. Havas, eds., *Effects of Acid Precipitation on Terrestrial Ecosystems* (New York: Plenum Press, 1980).

9. Steven L. Rhodes and Paulette Middleton, "Acid Rain's Gang of Four: More than One Impact," *The Environmental Forum*, October 1983; Dovland and Semb, "Atmospheric Transport of Pollutants."

10. For a brief history of acid rain, see Eville Gorham, "What to Do About Acid Rain," *Technology Review*, October 1982; Gene E. Likens et al., "Acid Rain," *Scientific American*, October 1979.

11. Bryon W. Bache, "The Acidification of Soils" and B. Ulrich, "Production and Consumption of Hydrogen Ions in the Ecosphere," in Hutchinson and Havas, *Effects of Acid Precipitation;* William W. McFee, *Sensitivity of Soil Regions to Acid Precipitation* (Corvallis, Ore.: U. S. Environmental Protection Agency, Environmental Research Laboratory, January 1980); Swedish studies cited in Swedish Ministry of Agriculture, *Acidification Today and Tomorrow.*

12. Enhanced growth cited in Bernhard Ulrich, "Dangers for the Forest Ecosystem Due to Acid Precipitation," translated for U.S. Environmental Protection Agency by Literature Research Company, Annandale, Va., undated, and in Swedish Ministry of Agriculture, *Acidification Today and Tomorrow;* G. Abrahamsen, "Effects of Acid Precipitation on Soil and Forest: Leaching of Plant Nutrients," in Drablos and Tollan, *Ecological Impact of Acid Precipitation;* Dale W. Johnson, "Acid Rain and Forest Productivity," Oak Ridge National Laboratory, Environmental Sciences Division, Oak Ridge, Tenn., undated.

13. Ulrich, "Dangers for the Forest Ecosystem Due to Acid Precipitation."

14. Vermont research findings from "Testimony of Richard Klein," U.S. Senate, Committee on Environment and Public Works, Hearings, June 30, 1981; Oak Ridge findings from S. B. McLaughlin et al., "Interactive Effects of Acid Rain and Gaseous Air Pollutants on Natural Terrestrial Vegetation," Oak Ridge National Laboratory, Environmental Sciences Division, Oak Ridge, Tenn., undated.

15. Beech regeneration mentioned in Ulrich, "Production and Consumption of Hydrogen Ions"; Camels Hump seedlings data from Thomas G. Siccama, Margaret Bliss, and H.W. Vogelmann, "Decline of Red Spruce in the Green Mountains of Vermont," *Bulletin of the Torrey Botanical Club,* April/June 1982; Whiteface Mountain reference in Richard E. Rice, "The Effects of Acid Rain on Forest and Crop Resources in the Eastern United States," The Wilderness Society, Washington D. C., September 1983.

16. Swedish Ministry of Agriculture, *Proceedings.*

17. Von H. W. Zottl and E. Mies, "Die Fichtenerkrankung in Hochlagen des Sudschwarzwaldes," *Allgemeine Forst-und Jagdzeitung,* June/July 1983; Von C. Bosch et al., "Uber die Erkrankung der Fichte (Picea abies Karst.) in den Hochlagen des Bayerischen Waldes," *Forstwissenschaftliches Centralblatt,* June 1983.

18. Damage levels for ozone cited in Swedish Ministry of Agriculture, *Proceedings;* references to German scientists include Von H. Mohr, "Zur Faktorenanalyse des 'Baumsterbens'—Bemerkungen eines Pflanzenphysiologen," *Allgemeine Forst-und Jagdzeitung,* June/July 1983; Von Dr. Bernhard Prinz, "Gedanken zum Stand der Diskussion uber die Ursache der Waldschaden in der Bundes-

republik Deutschland," *Der Forst-und Holz-wirt*, September 1983.

19. L. J. Puckett, "Acid Rain, Air Pollution, and Tree Growth in Southeastern New York," U. S. Geological Survey, Reston, Va, 1981; Richard L. Phipps, "Ring Width Analysis," presented at Symposium on Air Pollution and the Productivity of the Forest, Washington, D.C., October 4–5, 1983.

20. Federal Minister of Food, Agriculture and Forestry, "Forest Damage Due to Air Pollution: The Situation in the Federal Republic of Germany," Bonn, November 1982; Federal Minister of the Interior, "The Federal Government's Reply to the Interpellation of the Deputies: Air Pollution, Acid Rain and Death of Forests," Bonn, August 25, 1982, translation from the German by U.S. Library of Congress, Congressional Research Service; Der Bundesminister Fur Ernahrung, Landwirtschaft and Forsten, "Neuartige Waldschaden in der Bundesrepublik Deutschland," Bonn, October 1983; summer 1984 survey mentioned in James M. Markham, "Angst on Autobahn: Would Slowdown Aid Trees?," *New York Times*, October 31, 1984.

21. Der Bundesminister Fur Ernahrung, Landwirtschaft und Forsten, "Neuartige Waldschaden"; Georg H. M. Krause, "Forest Effects in West Germany," presented at Symposium on Air Pollution.

22. Damage in Czechoslovakia from George H. Tomlinson and C. Ross Silversides, *Acid Deposition and Forest Damage - The European Linkage* (Montreal: Domtar, Inc., 1982); figure for the Erz Mountains from Bayerischen Staatsministeriums fur Ernahrung, Landwirtschaft und Fursten, "Waldsterben durch Luftverschmutzung," Munich, July 1983; damage in Poland from Eugeniusz Pudlis, "Poland's Plight: Environment Damaged from Air Pollution and Acid Rain," *Ambio*, Vol. 12, No. 2, 1983.

23. Austria referenced in Bette Hileman, "Acid Rain Meeting in Ottawa," *Environmen-tal Science & Technology*, Vol. 18, No. 5, 1984; the Netherlands, France, and Italy referenced in Environmental Resources Limited, *Acid Rain: A Review of the Phenomenon in the EEC and Europe* (London: Graham & Trotman Ltd., 1983); East Germany referenced in John J. Metzler, "Germany Battles Acid-Rain Pollution," *Journal of Commerce*, April 13, 1983; Romania referred to in "Romania Launches a Major Tree Planting & Conservation Plan," *World Environment Report*, June 2, 1980; Switzerland damage from Margaret Studer, "Swiss Tackle Air Pollution to Keep Forests Green," *Christian Science Monitor*, October 20, 1983; reference to various accounts of damage elsewhere include G. H. Tomlinson, "Die-back of Forests - Continuing Observations," Domtar, Inc., Montreal, June 1981 (including appendices) and Studer, "Swiss Tackle Air Pollution."

24. Damage in Scandinavia from Christer Agren, "Forest Death in Sweden" and "Norwegian Forest Owners Anxious About Damage to Woodlands," *Acid News*, January 1984; reference to damage in Soviet Union from "Volga Forests Dying from Toxic Pollution," *Washington Post*, January 6, 1984.

25. Federal Minister of Food, Agriculture and Forestry, "Forest Damage Due to Air Pollution"; Krause, private communication; Edgar Gaertner, "La Mort de la Foret," *Le Monde Diplomatique*, August 1983; J. M. Bradley, "What is Killing the Great Forests of West Germany?," *World Environment Report*, August 15, 1983.

26. Arthur H. Johnson and Thomas G. Siccama, "Acid Deposition and Forest Decline," *Environmental Science & Technology*, Vol. 17, No. 7, 1983; damage in North Carolina and expectations that tree deaths would be identified soon in other areas from Arthur H. Johnson, "Assessing the Effects of Acid Rain on Forests of the Eastern U.S.," Testimony before the U.S. Senate, Committee on Environment and Public Works, Hearings, February 7, 1984.

27. Camels Hump data documented in Siccama, Bliss, and Vogelmann, "Decline of Red Spruce"; broader spruce decline documented in Johnson and Siccama, "Acid Deposition and Forest Decline"; reference to commercially valuable spruce from Arthur H. Johnson, "Decline of High-Altitude Spruce-Fir Forests," presented at Symposium on Air Pollution; quote is from H. W. Vogelmann, "Catastrophe on Camels Hump," *Natural History*, November 1982.

28. A. H. Johnson et al., "Recent Changes in Patterns of Tree Growth Rate in the New Jersey Pinelands: A Possible Effect of Acid Rain," *Journal of Environmental Quality*, October/December 1981.

29. Paul R. Miller et al., "Photochemical Oxidant Air Pollutant Effects on a Mixed Conifer Forest Ecosystem," U.S. Environmental Protection Agency, Environmental Research Laboratory, Corvallis, Ore., 1977; Paul R. Miller, private communication, October 5, 1983.

30. Damage estimates from John Skelly, "Blue Ridge Mountains," presentation at Symposium on Air Pollution; studies of growth in pines include S. O. Phillips et al., "Eastern White Pine Exhibits Growth Retardation by Fluctuating Air Pollutant Levels: Interaction of Rainfall, Age, and Symptom Expression" and "Growth Fluctuation of Loblolly Pine Due to Periodic Air Pollution Levels: Interaction of Rainfall and Age," *Phytopathology*, June 1977.

31. Richard J. Meislin, "Mexico City's Flora Finds Life Too Foul to Bear," *New York Times*, September 12, 1983; "Malaysian Environment Not a Pretty Picture," *World Environment Report*, August 15, 1983; Maria L. Durando and Sergio R. Aragon, "Atmospheric Lead in Downtown Guatemala City," *Environmental Science & Technology*, Vol. 16, No. 1, 1982.

32. Reference to lower growth rates in commercially valuable species from Johnson, "Assessing the Effects of Acid Rain on Forests"; quote from Phillips et al., "Eastern White Pine Exhibits Growth Retardation."

33. United Nations Food and Agriculture Organization, *World Forest Products: Demand and Supply 1990 and 2000* (Rome: 1982).

34. Environmental Resources Ltd., *Acid Rain: A Review of the EEC and Europe.*

35. Von H. Steinlin, "Holzproduzierende Forstwirtschaft," presented at Conference on Forestry Management: Supplier of Raw Materials and the Environmental Factor, Gottingen, West Germany, November 14–15, 1983.

36. Richard Plochmann et al., "Pollution is Killing German Forests," *Journal of Forestry*, September 1983.

37. T. T. Kozlowski, "Impacts of Air Pollution on Forest Ecosystems," *Bioscience*, February 1980; United States Forest Service, *An Analysis of the Timber Situation in the United States 1952–2030* (Washington D. C.: U. S. Department of Agriculture, 1982); Thomas E. Ricks, "Timber Firms Moving to the South as Supplies in Northwest Diminish," *Wall Street Journal*, August 19, 1983.

38. Slowing of growth in valuable species from Johnson, "Assessing the Effects of Acid Rain on Forests"; sulfate deposition figures from Environment Canada, *United States-Canada Memorandum of Intent.*

39. Study on economic effects from Rice, "Effects of Acid Rain in the Eastern United States"; need to test species from Norman R. Glass et al., "Effects of Acid Precipitation," *Environmental Science & Technology*, Vol. 16, No. 3, 1982.

40. Forest industry perspective from John A. Thorner, American Paper Institute/National Forest Products Association Environmental & Health Program, private communications, December 1983–January 1984 and September 1984; Ely Gonick, "A Forest Industry Perspective on Acid Deposition," presented at Conference on Acid Rain & Forest

Resources, Quebec City, Canada, June 14, 1983.

41. Raymond J. P. Brouzes, "A Synopsis of Some Acid Rain-Related Forest Research and the Emerging Conclusions," Environment Canada, Hull, Quebec, Canada, unpublished, 1981.

42. F. H. Bormann, "The Effects of Air Pollution on the New England Landscape," *Ambio*, Vol. 11, No. 6, 1982.

43. H. H. Krause, "Acidic Atmospheric Deposition in Eastern North America: Forest Resources at Risk," presented at Conference on Acid Rain & Forest Resources; Douglas Martin, "Canada's Wasted Woodlands," *New York Times*, August 28, 1983.

44. Susceptible areas cited in Swedish Ministry of Agriculture, *Acidification Today and Tomorrow*; reference to soil acidity measurements from "Acid Rain Threatens Southern Hemisphere," *World Environment Report*, January 25, 1984.

45. Martin Alexander, "Effects of Acidity on Microorganisms and Microbial Processes in Soil," in Hutchinson and Havas, *Effects of Acid Precipitation*; Gary S. Hartshorn, "Ecological Implications of Tropical Plantation Forestry," in Roger A. Sedjo, *The Comparative Economics of Plantation Forestry: A Global Assessment* (Washington D. C.: Resources for the Future, 1983); for a discussion of the Third World fuelwood crisis and reforestation needs, see Sandra Postel, "Protecting Forests," in Lester R. Brown et al., *State of the World–1984* (New York: W. W. Norton & Co., 1984).

46. Hubbard Brook research from G. E. Likens et al., "Recovery of a Deforested Ecosystem," *Science*, February 3, 1978; added effects of whole-tree harvesting from Environmental Resources Ltd., *Acid Rain: A Review of the EEC and Europe.*

47. Swedish Ministry of Agriculture, *Proceedings.*

48. Benoit Barry, "Acid Rain and Forest Productivity," an interview with Dr. Gilles Robitaille, in *Milieu*, Autumn 1982.

49. Overrein et al., *Acid Precipitation Effects on Forest and Fish.*

50. See G. M. Woodwell, "Effects of Pollution on the Structure and Physiology of Ecosystems," in Lorne H. Russwurm and Edward Sommerville, eds., *Man's Natural Environment: A Systems Approach* (North Scituate, Mass.: Duxbury Press, 1974) and Bormann, "Effects of Air Pollution on the New England Landscape."

51. International Energy Agency, *World Energy Outlook* (Paris: Organisation for Economic Co-operation and Development, 1982).

52. Reference to three Eastern bloc countries from "Munich Conference Lays Groundwork for Sulfur Reduction Accord," *World Environment Report*, July 11, 1984.

53. Richard Schneider, "Acid Precipitation and Surface Water Vulnerability on the Western Slopes of the High Colorado Rockies," in *Acid Rain in the Rocky Mountain West*; Fehsenfeld, "Gas Phase and Precipitation Acidities."

54. Acidity measurements from "China Faces Environmental Challenge," *Science*, September 23, 1983, from "Chinese Data Indicates Serious Acid Rain Problem," *International Water Report*, July/August 1983, and from C. K. Varshney, "Acid Rain: The Unseen Threat," Press Institute of India, New Delhi, India, June 1983; China's energy plans from Wang Qingyi and Gu Jian, "How Will China Solve Energy Problem?," *Beijing Review*, August 29, 1983.

55. James Bruce, "Brazil Investing $300 Million To Increase Its Coal Production," *Journal of Commerce*, June 13, 1983; India's energy plans from K. Dharmarajan, "India—Energy Supply Policy and Management," *Natural Resources Forum*, July 1983; India's

emissions trends from C. K. Varshney and J. K. Garg, "A Quantitative Assessment of Sulfur Dioxide Emission from Fossil Fuels in India," *Journal of the Air Pollution Control Association*, November 1978; quote from Varshney, "Acid Rain: The Unseen Threat."

56. Environmental Resources Ltd., *Acid Rain: A Review of the EEC and Europe;* Rolf Zell and Michael Cross, "Germany's Acid Rain Laws Go Up in Smoke," *New Scientist*, September 29, 1983; Von Ludwig Muller, "Stand der Immissionsschutzrechtlichen Bestimmungen im Hinblick auf die Bekampfung des Waldsterbens," *Allgemeine Forst Zeitung*, Vol. 88, Nos. 51–52, 1983.

57. Larry B. Parker and Robert E. Trumbule, "Opportunities for Increased Control of Nitrogen Oxides Emissions from Stationary Sources: Implications for Mitigating Acid Rain," U.S. Library of Congress, Congressional Research Service, Washington D. C., December 1982.

58. Jumpei Ando, "Pollution Control in Japan," *Journal of Japanese Trade & Industry*, No. 5, 1983; see also Gregory S. Wetstone and Armin Rosencranz, *Acid Rain in Europe and North America: National Responses to an International Problem* (Washington D. C.: Environmental Law Institute, 1983).

59. For a good overview of pollution control technologies, see "Control Technologies" (Appendix B), in Wetstone and Rosencranz, *Acid Rain in Europe and North America.*

60. European experience with FBC from Working Group on the Evaluation of Pollution Control Technology for Coal Combustion, "Flue Gas Desulfurization Pilot Study Followup," Committee on the Challenges of Modern Society, North Atlantic Treaty Organization, Ottawa, Canada, June 1982, and from Environmental Resources Ltd., *Acid Rain: A Review of the EEC and Europe;* reference to Sweden project from "Fluidized Beds: In Power Stations At Last?," *New Scientist*, June 30, 1983; U.S. experience with FBC

described in Paul F. Fennelly, "Fluidized Bed Combustion," *American Scientist*, May/June 1984; conversion of Minnesota utility boiler from "Foster Wheeler Sells World's Largest Fluidized Bed Boiler," *Energy Daily*, August 13, 1984.

61. Larry B. Parker and Robert E. Trumbule, "Mitigating Acid Rain with Technology: Avoiding the Scrubbing-Switching Dilemma," U.S. Library of Congress, Congressional Research Service, Washington D. C., June 1983; "Ohio Edison Coal-Fired Plant to Test Simultaneous Removal of Sulfur, Nitrogen Oxides," *Energy Daily*, August 30, 1984.

62. Motor Vehicle Manufacturers Association, *Motor Vehicle Facts and Figures '83* (Detroit, Mich.: 1983); Ando, "Pollution Control in Japan"; "Swiss Air Pollution is Mostly Home-Made," *World Environment Report*, October 15, 1983; recent EEC developments from Charles E. Dole, "West Europe's Road to Emissions Control is Paved with Confusion," *Christian Science Monitor*, July 11, 1984.

63. Response of Japanese industries from Ando, "Pollution Control in Japan" and Paul Danish, "Japan Delays Building of Coal-Fired Plants," *Journal of Commerce*, October 10, 1983; energy consumption figures from *World Energy Industry* (San Diego, Calif.: Business Information Display, Inc., 1983).

64. See Christopher Flavin, *Nuclear Power: The Market Test* (Washington D. C.: Worldwatch Institute, December 1983).

65. The conflict inherent in private use of a common resource is described in the classic article by Garrett Hardin, "The Tragedy of the Commons," *Science*, December 13, 1968.

66. Wetstone and Rosencranz, *Acid Rain in Europe and North America.*

67. Gregory S. Wetstone and Armin Rosencranz, "Transboundary Air Pollution: The Search for an International Response,"

Harvard Environmental Law Review, Winter 1984.

68. EEC policy process and efforts to date are described in Wetstone and Rosencranz, *Acid Rain in Europe and North America;* Commission of the European Communities, "Proposal for a Council Directive on the Limitation of Emissions of Pollutants into the Air from Large Combustion Plants," Brussels, December 15, 1983; Gregory S. Wetstone, private communication, February 1984; Fred Pearce, "MPs Back Curbs on Acid Rain," *New Scientist,* September 6, 1984.

69. Ozone damage to crops documented in *Effects of Air Pollution on Farm Commodities,* Symposium Proceedings, Izaak Walton League, Washington D.C., February 18, 1982.

70. For effects of acid rain on crops, see Rice, "The Effects of Acid Rain in the Eastern United States"; acid rain's effect on materials described in Stephen R. Scholle, "Acid Deposition and the Materials Damage Question," *Environment,* October 1983; corrosion of plumbing, leaching of aluminum, and other effects described in Swedish Ministry of Agriculture, *Acidification Today and Tomorrow.*

71. Estimates of capital costs for scrubbers vary considerably. This calculation is based on a range of $150–300 per kilowatt. Administering a federal program of appliance efficiency standards is estimated to cost $3.5 million per year. Norris McDonald, Environmental Policy Institute, Washington, D.C., private communication, February 1984. Over 20 years, and assuming a 7 percent discount rate, the present value cost of the program is less than $40 million.

72. Canadian figures from Subcommittee on Acid Rain, *Still Waters;* recycling figures from William U. Chandler, *Materials Recycling: The Virtue of Necessity* (Washington, D.C.: Worldwatch Institute, October 1983); aluminum figures from R. C. Ziegler, "Environmental Impacts of Virgin and Recycled Steel and Aluminum," Calspan Corporation, Buffalo, N.Y., 1976.

73. Term used by David J. Rose et al., *Global Energy Futures and CO₂-Induced Climate Change* (Cambridge, Mass.: Massachusetts Institute of Technology, 1983).

Chapter 6. Conserving Biological Diversity

1. Lynn Margulis and Karlene V. Schwartz, *Five Kingdoms: An Illustrated Guide to the Phyla of Life on Earth* (San Francisco: W. H. Freeman and Co., 1982); Chris Peat and Will Diver, "First Signs of Life on Earth," *New Scientist,* September 16, 1982.

2. Elliott A. Norse and Roger E. McManus, "Ecology and Living Resources—Biological Diversity," in Council on Environmental Quality, *Environmental Quality 1980* (Washington, D.C.: U.S. Government Printing Office, 1980); Elliott A. Norse, "The Value of Species for Agriculture, Medicine, and Industry," presented at Extinctions, the First Annual National Zoological Park Symposium, Washington, D.C., September 11, 1982.

3. Robert and Christine Prescott-Allen, *Genes from the Wild: Using Wild Genetic Resources for Food and Raw Materials* (Washington, D.C.: International Institute for Environment and Development, 1983).

4. Paul and Anne Ehrlich, *Extinction* (New York: Random House, 1981).

5. James Lovelock, *Gaia: A New Look at Life on Earth* (New York: Oxford University Press, 1979).

6. David F. Salisbury, "Cloning Genes from Extinct Animals May Give Researchers Insights on Evolution," *Christian Science Monitor,* June 7, 1984; "Genes of Extinct Animal Are Cloned," *Washington Post,* June 6, 1984.

7. Daniel Simberloff, "The Next Mass Extinction?," *Garden,* March/April 1984; Roger

Lewin, "Extinctions and the History of Life," *Science,* September 2, 1983.

8. Richard A. Kerr, "Isotopes Add Support for Asteroid Impact," *Science,* November 11, 1983; Philip J. Hilts, "Comet-Extinction Link Gains Support," *Washington Post,* April 20, 1984; John Noble Wilford, "Study Hints Extinctions Strike in Set Intervals," *New York Times,* December 11, 1983; Lewin, "Extinctions and the History of Life."

9. Steven M. Stanley, "Mass Extinctions in the Ocean," *Scientific American,* June 1984.

10. George Gaylord Simpson, *Fossils and the History of Life* (New York: Scientific American Library, 1984).

11. Ehrlich and Ehrlich, *Extinction.*

12. Norman Myers, *The Primary Source* (New York: W. W. Norton & Co., 1984); Simberloff, "The Next Mass Extinction?"; Thomas E. Lovejoy, World Wildlife Fund-U.S., Washington, D.C., private communication, August 29, 1984.

13. Julie Ann Miller, "Entomologist's Paradise," *Science News,* June 2, 1984.

14. Ibid.

15. Council on Environmental Quality and U.S. Department of State, *The Global 2000 Report to the President, Volume 2, The Technical Report* (Washington, D.C.: U.S. Government Printing Office, 1980).

16. Thomas E. Lovejoy, "Refugia, Refuges and Minimum Critical Size: Problems in the Conservation of the Neotropical Herpetofauna," in William E. Duellman, ed., *The South American Herpetofauna: Its Origin, Evolution, and Dispersal* (Lawrence, Kans.: The Museum of Natural History, The University of Kansas, 1979).

17. Thomas E. Lovejoy and Eneas Salati, "Precipitating Change in Amazonia," in Emilio F. Moran, ed., *The Dilemma of Amazonian Development* (Boulder, Colo.: Westview Press, 1983).

18. Peter Raven, "Global Futures: The Third World," presented at the annual meeting of the American Association for the Advancement of Science, New York, May 25, 1984.

19. John Carey, "Mangroves . . . Swamps Nobody Likes," *International Wildlife,* September/October 1982; International Union for the Conservation of Nature and Natural Resources (IUCN), *Global Status of Mangrove Ecosystems,* Commission on Ecology Papers No. 3 (Gland, Switzerland: 1983).

20. "Wound in the World," *Asiaweek,* July 13, 1984; rate of deforestation in Southeast Asia from U.S. Office of Technology Assessment, *Technologies to Sustain Tropical Forest Resources* (Washington, D.C.: U.S. Government Printing Office, 1984).

21. "Wound in the World"; Bayard Webster, "Devastated Forest Offers A Rare View of Rebirth," *New York Times,* April 24, 1984.

22. "Wound in the World."

23. Eneas Salati and Peter B. Vose, "Amazon Basin: A System in Equilibrium," *Science,* July 13, 1984; E. Salati, T.E. Lovejoy, and P.B. Vose, "Precipitation and Water Recycling in Tropical Rain Forests (with Special Reference to the Amazon Basin)," *The Environmentalist,* Vol. 3, No. 1, 1983.

24. Simberloff, "The Next Mass Extinction?"

25. Margulis and Schwartz, *Five Kingdoms.*

26. Donald Duvick, "Genetic Diversity in Major Farm Crops on the Farm and In Reserve," presented at the 13th International Botanical Congress, Sydney, Australia, August 28, 1981.

27. National Academy of Sciences, *Genetic Vulnerability of Major Crops* (Washington, D.C.: 1972).

28. T.T. Chang, "Conservation of Rice Genetic Resources: Luxury or Necessity?," *Science,* April 20, 1984.

29. Ibid.

30. Garrison Wilkes, "Current Status of Crop Plant Germplasm," *CRC Critical Reviews in Plant Science*, Vol. 1, No. 2, 1983.

31. D.L. Plucknett et al., "Crop Germplasm Conservation and Developing Countries," *Science*, April 8, 1983.

32. Ibid.

33. Wilkes, "Current Status of Crop Plant Germplasm."

34. United Nations Food and Agriculture Organization, "Draft Report of Plenary - Part 8 (from Commission II)," Rome, November 22, 1983; John Walsh, "Seeds of Dissension Sprout at FAO," *Science*, January 13, 1984.

35. D.L. Plucknett, Consultative Group on International Agricultural Research, Washington, D.C., private communication, July 12, 1984.

36. Pioneer Hi-Bred International, Inc., *Executive Summary of the 1983 Plant Breeding Research Forum* (Des Moines, Iowa: 1984).

37. Donald N. Duvick, "Major United States Crops in 1976," *Annals of the New York Academy of Sciences*, February 25, 1977.

38. Charles Darwin, *The Origin of Species*, Mentor Edition (New York: New American Library, 1958).

39. National Academy of Sciences, *Little-Known Asian Animals with a Promising Economic Future* (Washington, D.C.: National Academy Press, 1983).

40. Noel Vietmeyer, "Unconventional Livestock," *Ceres*, November/December 1983; "'Extinct' Ox Breeding Hopes," *Mazingira*, March 1984; "Wildlife Watch," *Asiaweek*, June 15, 1984; National Academy of Sciences, *Little-Known Asian Animals;* Noel Vietmeyer, "Hog Wild," *International Wildlife*, May/June 1984.

41. Vietmeyer, "Hog Wild."

42. United Nations Environment Programme, "Animal Genetic Resources: Needs and Opportunities" (typescript), Nairobi, 1983.

43. Florencio Zambrana, "Seeds of Gold," *IDRC Reports*, August 1982; David F. Cusack, "Quinua: Grain of the Incas," *The Ecologist*, January 1984.

44. "Grains: Exploring New Harvests," *The Cornucopia Project Newsletter* (Emmaus, Pa.), Summer 1983; G. J. H. Grubben and D. H. van Sloten, *Genetic Resources of Amaranths: A Global Plan of Action* (Rome: International Board for Plant Genetic Resources, February 1981).

45. Ward Van Buren Lassoe, "Jojoba Oil: Another Price Drop," *Journal of Commerce*, May 22, 1984; "Responding to Jojoba's Lure," *Farmline*, April 1984; information on vernonia from "U.S. Plant Exploration Efforts Result in 'Very Promising' Potential New Crop for Third World Countries," *Diversity*, March/April 1984.

46. "Developing Guayule (Natural Rubber) as a Commercial Crop," in U.S. Office of Technology Assessment, *Water-Related Technologies for Sustainable Agriculture in Arid/Semiarid Lands: Selected Foreign Experience* (Washington, D.C.: U.S. Government Printing Office, 1983).

47. National Academy of Sciences, *Firewood Crops: Shrub and Tree Species for Energy Production Volume 2* (Washington, D.C.: National Academy Press, 1983); Christel Palmberg, "A Vital Fuelwood Gene Pool is in Danger," *Unasylva*, Number 133, 1981.

48. Winston J. Brill, "Agricultural Microbiology," *Scientific American*, September 1981.

49. R.S. Chaleff, "Isolation of Agronomically Useful Mutants from Plant Cell Cultures," *Science*, February 11, 1983.

50. U.S. Office of Technology Assessment, *Commercial Biotechnology: An International Analysis* (Washington, D.C.: U.S. Government Printing Office, 1984); U.S. Office of Technology Assessment, *Plants: The Potentials*

for *Extracting Protein, Medicines, and Other Useful Chemicals—Workshop Proceedings* (Washington, D.C.: U.S. Government Printing Office, September 1983).

51. Limitations on regeneration from tissue culture discussed in Office of Technology Assessment, *Commercial Biotechnology;* constraints on selecting useful traits discussed in Chaleff, "Isolation of Agronomically Useful Mutants."

52. James F. Shepard et al., "Genetic Transfer in Plants Through Interspecific Protoplast Fusion," *Science,* February 11, 1983; Brill, "Agricultural Microbiology."

53. Kenneth A. Barton and Winston J. Brill, "Prospects in Plant Genetic Engineering," *Science,* February 11, 1983.

54. A. Caplan et al., "Introduction of Genetic Material into Plant Cells," *Science,* November 18, 1983; a report of bacteria capable of introducing genes into some members of the grass family appears in "Trojan Bug," *The Economist,* October 13, 1984.

55. Barton and Brill, "Prospects."

56. Brill, "Agricultural Microbiology."

57. Harris Brotman, "Engineering the Birth of Cattle," *New York Times Magazine,* May 15, 1983.

58. Ibid.; estimate of market for biotechnology products from Office of Technology Assessment, *Commercial Biotechnology.*

59. David Dickson, "UNIDO Hopes for Biotechnology Center," *Science,* September 30, 1983; David Dickson, "India and Italy to Share Biotechnology Center," *Science,* April 27, 1984.

60. *MIRCEN News No. 5* (Paris), May 1983.

61. Allen T. Bull, Geoffrey Holt, and Malcolm D. Lilly, *Biotechnology International Trends and Prospects* (Paris: Organisation for Economic Co-operation and Development, 1982).

62. Eric Leber and Michael K. Bergman, "Biotechnology's Vast Implications for Energy and the Environment," *Public Power,* July/August 1983.

63. Barton and Brill, "Prospects"; Philip M. Boffey, "Plans to Release New Organisms into Nature Spur Concern," *New York Times,* June 12, 1984.

64. Robert C. Cowan, "US Officials Face Major Hurdles in Regulating Genetic Engineering," *Christian Science Monitor,* June 1, 1984; Philip M. Boffey, "Splitting Hairs Over Splitting Genes," *New York Times,* June 27, 1984.

65. Brill, "Agricultural Microbiology."

66. George M. Woodwell, "On the Limits of Nature," prepared for The Global Possible Conference, World Resources Institute, Wye, Md., May 2–5, 1984.

67. Michael E. Soulé and Bruce A. Wilcox, eds., *Conservation Biology* (Sunderland, Mass.: Sinauer Associates, Inc., 1980); conservation genetics is discussed in O.H. Frankel, "Genetic Diversity, Ecosystem Conservation, and Evolutionary Responsibility," in F. DiCastri, F. W. G. Baker, and M. Hadley, eds., *Ecology in Practice Part I: Ecosystem Management* (Dublin: Tycooly International Publishing Ltd., 1984)

68. Myers, *The Primary Source;* Mark J. Plotkin, Harvard Botanical Museum, Cambridge, Mass., private communication, May 30, 1984; Mark J. Plotkin, "Ethnobotany, Conservation, and the Future of the Tropical Forest," in Russell A. Mittermeier and Mark J. Plotkin, eds., *Primates and the Tropical Forest* (Washington, D.C.: World Wildlife Fund-U.S. and the L.S.B. Leakey Foundation, 1983); World Wildlife Fund-U.S., *Annual Report 1983* (Washington, D.C.: 1983).

69. Darwin, *Origin of Species.*

70. IUCN, *The IUCN Plant Red Data Book* (Gland, Switzerland: 1978, reprinted 1980); IUCN, *The IUCN Mammal Red Data Book Part 1: Threatened Mammalian Taxa of the Americas*

and the Australasian Zoographic Region (Excluding Cetacea) (Gland, Switzerland: 1982); IUCN, The IUCN Amphibia-Reptilia Red Data Book Part 1: Testudines, Crocodylia, Rhyncocephalia (Gland, Switzerland: 1982); IUCN, The IUCN Invertebrate Red Data Book (Gland, Switzerland: 1983); International Council for Bird Preservation, Endangered Birds of the World: The ICBP Bird Red Data Book (Washington, D.C.: Smithsonian Institution Press, 1981).

71. IUCN invertebrate categories from Mark Collins and Susan Wells, "Invertebrates—Who Needs Them?," New Scientist, May 19, 1983; status of national protection efforts from Thomas S. Elias, "Rare and Endangered Species of Plants—The Soviet Side," Science, January 7, 1983, and Catherine Fuller, World Wildlife Fund-U.S., Washington, D.C., private communication, September 18, 1984.

72. Laura Tangley, "Protecting the 'Insignificant'," Bioscience, July/August 1984; "Review of Invertebrate Wildlife for Listing as Endangered or Threatened Species," Federal Register, Vol. 49, No. 100, May 22, 1984.

73. Thomas E. Lovejoy et al., "Ecosystem Decay of Amazon Forest Remnants," in Matthew H. Nitecki, ed., Extinctions (Chicago: University of Chicago Press, 1984); Roger Lewin, "Parks: How Big is Big Enough?," Science, August 10, 1984.

74. Jeremy Harrison, Kenton Miller, and Jeffrey McNeely, "The World Coverage of Protected Areas: Development Goals and Environmental Needs," Ambio, Vol. 11, No. 5, 1982.

75. Margaret R. Biswas, "Biosphere Reserves—A World Network of Protection," Mazingira, Vol. 7, No. 4, 1983; information on Brazil and Africa from Lovejoy, private communication.

76. Norse and McManus, "Biological Diversity"; Norman Myers, "Genetic Resources in Jeopardy," Ambio, Vol. 13, No. 3, 1984.

77. Ira Rubinoff, "Tropical Forests: Can We Afford Not to Give Them a Future?," The Ecologist, November/December 1982.

78. Robert and Christine Prescott-Allen, "Park Your Genes: Protected Areas as In Situ Genebanks for the Maintenance of Wild Genetic Resources," presented at the World National Parks Congress, Bali, Indonesia, October 17, 1982.

79. "World Bank Issues First Official Statement on Environmental Policies," World Environment Report, June 13, 1984; Woodwell, "On the Limits of Nature"; Philip M. Fearnside, "Brazil's Amazon Settlement Schemes," Habitat International, Vol. 8, No. 1, 1984; Nicholas Guppy, "Tropical Deforestation: A Global View," Foreign Affairs, Spring 1984.

80. Rubinoff, "Tropical Forests"; Ira Rubinoff, "If We Lose the Tropical Forests, No Birds Will Sing," Washington Post, August 5, 1984.

81. Guppy, "Tropical Deforestation."

82. Frankel, "Genetic Diversity, Ecosystem Conservation, and Evolutionary Responsibility."

Chapter 7. Increasing Energy Efficiency

1. For a discussion of energy demand modeling, see John H. Gibbons and William U. Chandler, Energy: The Conservation Revolution (New York: Plenum Press, 1981).

2. See U.S. National Academy of Sciences, Changing Climate: Report of the Carbon Dioxide Assessment Committee (Washington, D.C.: National Academy Press, 1983), Stephen Seidel and Dale Keyes, Can We Delay A Greenhouse Warming? (Washington, D.C.: U.S. Environmental Protection Agency, 1983), and William W. Kellogg and Robert Schware, "Society, Science and Climate Change," Foreign Affairs, Summer 1982.

3. An international survey of 328 organizations that have published energy demand

projections was undertaken for the International Energy Workshop. The "median" projection for the year 2000 was 485 exajoules. See Alan S. Manne and Leo Schrattenholzer, "International Energy Workshop: A Summary of the 1983 Poll Responses," *The Energy Journal*, Vol. 5, No. 1, 1984. For projections beyond the year 2000 commonly used in analysis of the global carbon dioxide problem, see J. Edmonds et al., *An Analysis of Possible Future Atmospheric Retention of Fossil Fuel CO_2* (Washington, D.C.: U.S. Department of Energy, 1984).

4. Manne and Schrattenholzer, "International Energy Workshop: 1983 Poll Responses."

5. See Scenario B, Appendix, in Edmonds et al., *Possible Future Atmospheric Retention of CO_2*.

6. See, for example, William U. Chandler, *The Myth of TVA: Conservation and Development in the Tennessee Valley, 1933–1983* (Cambridge, Mass.: Ballinger Publishing Company, 1984); Edward Goldsmith and Nicholas Hildyard, *The Social and Environmental Effects of Large Dams, Volume 1* (Cornwall, U.K.: The Wadebridge Ecological Centre, 1984); Martin Weil, "Hydropower," *The China Business Review*, July/August 1982; Paul Aspelin and Silvio Coelho dos Santos, *Indian Areas Threatened by Hydroelectric Projects in Brazil* (Copenhagen, Denmark: International Work Group for Indigenous Affairs, 1981).

7. M. Desmond Fitzgerald and Gerald Pollio, "Financing Energy Developments 1983–2000," Chemical Bank, New York, undated.

8. Commercial energy uses by 15 countries from World Bank, *World Development Report 1984* (New York: Oxford University Press, 1984); United Nations Economic Commission for Europe (UNECE), *An Energy Efficient Future: Prospects for Europe and North America* (London: Butterworths, 1983); U.S. savings with most-efficient lights from Energy Information Administration (EIA), *International Energy Annual 1982* (Washington, D.C.: U.S. Department of Energy, 1983); Nadine Lihach and Stephen Pertusiello, "Evolution in Lighting," *EPRI Journal*, June 1984.

9. UNECE, *An Energy Efficient Future*; Andrea N. Ketoff (International Energy Studies, Lawrence Berkeley Laboratory, Berkeley, Calif.), "Facts and Prospects of the Italian End-Use Energy Structure," Rolf Bauerschmidt (Institute for Applied Systems Analysis and Prognosis, Hanover, West Germany), "An End-Use Oriented Energy Strategy for the Federal Republic of Germany," and Jean Marie Martin (Institute Economique et Juridique de l'Energie), "Alternative Energy Strategies for France," all presented at the Global Workshop on End-Use Energy Strategies, Sao Paulo, Brazil, June 4–15, 1984.

10. Marc Ross, "Industrial Energy Conservation," *Natural Resources Journal*, April 1984.

11. Haruki Tsuchiya (Research Institute for Systems Technology, Tokyo, Japan), "Case Study on Japan," presented at the Global Workshop on End-Use Energy Strategies, Sao Paulo, Brazil, June 4–15, 1984; World Bank, *Energy Efficiency in the Steel Industry with Emphasis on the Developing Countries* (Washington, D.C.: 1984).

12. Martin, "Alternative Energy Strategies for France."

13. Energy intensity of U.S. production from Ross, "Industrial Energy Conservation"; Ketoff, "Italian End-Use Energy Structure"; Bauerschmidt, "End-Use Strategy for Federal Republic of Germany."

14. Jose Goldemberg et al., "Brazil: A Study on End-Use Energy Strategy," presented at the Global Workshop on End-Use Energy Strategies, Sao Paulo, Brazil, June 4–15 1984; UNECE, *An Energy Efficient Future*; World Bank, *Energy Efficiency in the Steel Industry*.

15. Ketoff, "Italian End-Use Energy Structure"; Spain's efficiency in steel-making from

World Bank, *Energy Efficiency in the Steel Industry;* use of electric arc furnace from Jack R. Miller, "Steel Minimills," *Scientific American,* May 1984; steel recycling from imports, and world rate, from William U. Chandler, *Materials Recycling: The Virtue of Necessity* (Washington, D.C.: Worldwatch Institute, October 1983).

16. Various rates of return on investments from World Bank, *Energy Efficiency in the Steel Industry* and from U.S. Office of Technology Assessment (OTA), *Industrial Energy Use* (Washington, D.C.: U.S. Government Printing Office, June 1983); Ross, "Industrial Energy Conservation."

17. U.S. use of open hearth furnace from OTA, *Industrial Energy Use;* other countries from World Bank, *Energy Efficiency in the Steel Industry.*

18. World Bank, *Energy Efficiency in the Steel Industry.*

19. UNECE, *An Energy Efficient Future.*

20. Ed A. Hewett, *Energy, Economics, and Foreign Policy in the Soviet Union* (Washington, D.C.: Brookings Institution, 1984); Sumer C. Aggarwal, "Managing Material Shortages: The Russian Way," *Columbia Journal of World Business,* Fall 1980.

21. The uncertainty about introducing this technology is indicated in news stories such as "The Steelworkers Dig in Against a Cleveland Minimill," *Business Week,* January 23, 1984, and Steven Greenhouse, "Minimills: Steel's Bright Star," *New York Times,* February 24, 1984.

22. The implied rate of efficiency improvement in the mid-range projection of Edmonds et al., *Possible Future Atmospheric Retention of CO_2* (Scenario B) is 0.8 percent per year. If efficiency improvements in Soviet steel-making were consistent with this rate, it would require 68 years to reduce the current level of energy use per ton in the Soviet Union (31 gigajoules) to the current Japanese level (18 gigajoules). Brazilian plans

from Goldemberg et al., "Brazil: End-Use Strategy."

23. Miller, "Steel Minimills"; F.T. Sparrow, *Energy and Materials Flows in the Iron and Steel Industry* (Springfield, Va.: National Technical Information Service, April 1982); OTA, *Industrial Energy Use* ; World Bank, *Energy Efficiency in the Steel Industry;* Donald F. Barnett and Louis Schorsch, *Steel: Upheaval in a Basic Industry* (Cambridge, Mass.: Ballinger Publishing Co., 1983).

24. OTA, *Industrial Energy Use;* World Bank, *Energy Efficiency in the Steel Industry.* Note that capital costs are given in terms of tons of annual production capacity, and that total cost includes energy, labor, and amortized capital on a per-ton-produced basis.

25. Goldemberg et al., "Brazil: End-Use Strategy."

26. Chandler, *Materials Recycling: The Virtue of Necessity.*

27. Tsuchiya, "Case Study on Japan."

28. S.Y. Shen, *Energy and Materials Flows in the Production of Primary Aluminum* (Springfield, Va.: National Technical Information Service, October 1981); United Nations Environment Programme, "Industry and Environment," Nairobi, Kenya, July/September 1983; Organisation for Economic Co-operation and Development (OECD), *Aluminum Industry: Energy Aspects of Structural Change* (Paris: 1983); Goldemberg et al., "Brazil: End-Use Strategy"; UNECE, *An Energy Efficient Future;* Bauerschmidt, "End-Use Strategy for Federal Republic of Germany."

29. For an overview of industrial energy conservation, see Melvin H. Chiogioji, *Industrial Energy Conservation* (New York: Marcel Dekker, Inc., 1979).

30. Howard S. Geller, "The Potential for Electricity Conservation in Brazil," American Council for an Energy-Efficient Economy, Washington, D.C., February 1984, draft.

31. N. Mohan, "Techniques for Energy Conservation in AC Motor-Drive Systems,"

prepared for the Electric Power Research Institute, Palo Alto, Calif., September 1981.

32. OTA, *Industrial Energy Use.*

33. H.N. Hersh, *Energy and Materials Flows in the Production of Pulp and Paper* (Springfield, Va.: National Technical Information Service, May 1981).

34. Chandler, *Materials Recycling: The Virtue of Necessity.*

35. Bauerschmidt, "End-Use Strategy for Federal Republic of Germany." The energy intensity of German industry declined at an annual rate of 4.6 percent per year after 1979. Rates of return on chemical industry investments from OTA, *Industrial Energy Use.*

36. "PET Plastic Recovery," *Resource Recycling,* March/April 1983; L.L. Gaines and S.Y. Shen, *Energy and Materials Flows in the Production of Olefins and Their Derivatives* (Springfield, Va.: National Technical Information Service, August 1980).

37. J.E. Sapp, *Energy and Materials Flows in the Cement Industry* (Springfield, Va.: National Technical Information Service, June 1981); U.S. cement production and energy consumption from U.S. Department of Interior, Bureau of Mines, *Minerals Yearbook, 1982, Volume 1* (Washington, D.C.: U.S. Government Printing Office, 1983); Hewett, *Energy, Economics, and Foreign Policy in the Soviet Union;* Hugh Saddler, "Energy Supply and Demand in Australia: A Statistical Compendium," presented at the Global Workshop on End-Use Energy Strategies, Sao Paulo, Brazil, June 4–15, 1984; West European data from Bureau of Mines, *Minerals Yearbook, 1982, Vol. 1.*

38. Derived from Edmonds et al., *Possible Future Atmospheric Retention of CO_2* and from UNECE, *An Energy Efficient Future.*

39. These estimates assume that the average world car is driven 8,500 miles per year, obtains 21 miles per gallon of fuel, and that approximately 353 million cars exist. The assumptions for U.S. cars are 10,000 miles per year, 16 miles per gallon, and 125 million cars.

40. UNECE, *An Energy Efficient Future.*

41. Goldemberg et al., "Brazil: End-Use Strategy."

42. Ibid.

43. Jose Lutzenberger, Union for the Conservation of Nature, Rio Grande do Sul, Brazil, private communication, September 20, 1984.

44. Goldemberg et al., "Brazil: End-Use Strategy"; see also OTA, *Increased Automobile Fuel Efficiency and Synthetic Fuels* (Washington, D.C.: U.S. Government Printing Office, 1982), and Charles Gray, Jr. and Frank von Hippel, "The Fuel Economy of Light Vehicles," *Scientific American,* May 1981.

45. R. Feast, "Volvo Shows its Car of the Future," *Automotive News,* July 4, 1983; D. Scott and J. Yamaguchi, "High Performance with Economy Engine in Ultra-Light Body," *Automotive Engineering,* April 1983; J.P. Norbye, "Light-Weight Fuel-Sipper Gets 56 mpg," *Popular Science,* March 1982, as cited in Goldemberg et al., "Brazil: End-Use Strategy."

46. These calculations assume the average fuel economy of cars in Brazil is about 20 miles per gallon, that cars are driven about 9,300 miles per year, and that car ownership grows at 5 percent. This growth assumption represents a considerable decline from the 7 percent of the last five years, which was notable for continued high growth in auto ownership despite the severe recession. The actual growth rate has declined, however, from about 12 percent per year during the seventies. Goldemberg et al., "Brazil: End-Use Strategy."

47. See, "GM Says It Will Launch CVT In Europe Soon," *Ward's Engine Update,* July 1, 1983, as cited in Goldemberg et al., "Brazil: End-Use Strategy." But note also that problems with the mass production of CVTs has caused $30-million overruns at Van Doane

Transmissie in Holland. The company is being reorganized to increase efficiency; see *Ward's Automotive Reports,* August 27, 1984, as cited in the U.S. Department of Energy, *Monthly Data Report,* September 14, 1984. William U. Chandler, "The Fuel Efficiency of Tires by Manufacturer and Model," Environmental Policy Institute, Washington, D.C., September 1981.

48. Bauerschmidt, "End-Use Strategy for Federal Republic of Germany."

49. UNECE, *An Energy Efficient Future.*

50. Martin, "Alternative Energy Strategies for France"; UNECE, *An Energy Efficient Future.*

51. R.I. Salawu (University of Lagos, Nigeria), "End Use Energy Study, Nigeria," presented at the Global Workshop on End-Use Energy Strategies, Sao Paulo, Brazil, June 4–15, 1984.

52. See, for example, Gabriel Roth and George G. Wynne, *Learning from Abroad: Free Enterprize Urban Transportation* (London: Transaction Books, 1982), Herbert H. Werlin, "Urban Transportation Systems in the Developing World," *Ekistics,* May/June 1984, and J. Diandas, "Alternative Approaches to Transport in Third World Cities: Issues in Equity and Accessibility," *Ekistics,* May/June 1984.

53. V.M. Maslenikov, "Specific Features of the Development of the USSR Fuel-and-Energy Complex," presented at the Global Workshop on End-Use Energy Strategies, Sao Paulo, Brazil, June 4–15, 1984; UNECE, *An Energy Efficient Future;* Hewett, *Energy, Economics, and Foreign Policy in the Soviet Union.*

54. Goldemberg et al., "Brazil: End-Use Strategy."

55. Problems with U.S. railroads from Al Lewis, former Vice President, Louisville and Nashville Railroad, private communication, 1976; construction of waterways to compete with rail from Chandler, *The Myth of TVA.*

56. From Lee Schipper, *Internationell Jaemfoerelse av Bostaedernads Energifoerbrukning* (Stockholm: Swedish Council for Building Research, 1984). An English version and summary was submitted to *Energy Economics,* Journal of the International Association of Energy Economists. According to Schipper, figures are calculated in terms of useful energy/degree day/square meter of floor space. Floor space estimates include all dwellings and are somewhat uncertain. Useful energy is derived from actual energy consumed, figuring liquid and gaseous fuels at 66 percent conversion efficiency, electricity and district heating at 100 percent efficiency, wood and coal at 55 percent efficiency. The actual mix of fuels varies considerably from country to country and over time. See also, Bent Petersen, "The Danish Energy-Conservation Program in Buildings," in American Council for an Energy-Efficient Economy (ACEEE), *Doing Better: Setting An Agenda for the Second Decade, Vol. J* (Proceedings from the Panel on Programs Outside of the United States) (Washington, D.C.: 1984).

57. Lee Schipper, "Residential Energy Use in the OECD: 1970–1982—The Bottom-Up Approach," and "Energy Efficient Housing in Sweden," in ACEEE, *Doing Better, Vol. J.*

58. Charles A. Ficner, "The Evolution Towards R-2000: Past Experiences and Current Directions of the Canadian Energy Conservation Effort," in ACEEE, *Doing Better, Vol. J.*

59. Savings estimated by Worldwatch from Ficner, "The Evolution Towards R-2000," and from EIA, *International Energy Annual 1982.*

60. John P. Kesselring, Robert M. Kendall, and Richard J. Schreiber, "Radiant Fiber Burners for Gas-Fired Appliances and Equipment," and William H. Thrasher, Robert J. Kolodgy, and James J. Fuller, "Development of a Space Heater and a Residential Water Heater Based on the Pulse Combustion Principle," in ACEEE, *Doing Better, Vol. E* (Proceedings from the Panel on Appliances and Equipment).

61. Howard S. Geller, "Efficient Residential Appliances and Space Conditioning Equipment: Savings Potential and Cost Effectiveness as of 1984," in ACEEE, *Doing Better, Vol. E.*

62. Anthony Usibelli, "Monitored Energy Use of Residential Water Heaters," in ACEEE, *Doing Better, Vol. E;* Thrasher, Kolodgy, and Fuller, "The Pulse Combustion Principle."

63. David B. Goldstein, "Efficient Refrigerators in Japan: A Comparative Survey of American and Japanese Trends Towards Energy Conserving Refrigerators," in ACEEE, *Doing Better, Vol. E.*

64. Geller, "Efficient Residential Appliances and Space Conditioning Equipment."

65. Howard A. McLain and David Goldenberg, "Benefits of Replacing Residential Central Air Conditioning Systems," in ACEEE, *Doing Better, Vol. E.*

66. Rudy R. Verderber and Francis M. Rubinstein, "New Lighting Technologies, Their Status and Impacts on Power Densities," in ACEEE, *Doing Better, Vol. E;* hydroelectric output from EIA, *International Energy Annual 1982;* Lihach and Pertusiello, "Evolution in Lighting."

67. Betsy L. Gardiner, Mary Ann Piette, and Jeffrey P. Harris, "Measured Results of Energy Conservation Retrofits in Non-Residential Buildings: An Update of the BECA-CR Data Base," and Donald K. Schultz, "End Use Consumption Patterns and Energy Conservation Savings in Commercial Buildings," in ACEEE, *Doing Better, Vol. D* (Proceedings from the Panel on Existing Commercial Buildings).

68. Schipper, "Energy Efficient Housing in Sweden"; Lars Engebeck, "Are Building Codes Effective Tools for Reducing Energy Use in New Residential Buildings? Some Swedish Experiences," in ACEEE, *Doing Better, Vol. J.*

69. David Wilson, *The Demand for Energy in the Soviet Union* (London: Croom Helm, 1983); Hewett, *Energy, Economics, and Foreign Policy in the Soviet Union;* UNECE, *An Energy Efficient Future.*

70. Schipper, "Residential Energy Use in the OECD."

71. See Dennis C. Anderson, "Evaluation of Canada's Oil Substitution Program," and Ian Brown, "The Administration of Energy Conservation Programmes by Western European Governments," in ACEEE, *Doing Better, Vol. J.*

72. Bina Agarwal, "Why Stoves are Resisted," *Unasylva,* No. 140, 1983. For a description of recent trends in soil erosion, see Lester R. Brown and Edward C. Wolf, *Soil Erosion: Quiet Crisis in the World Economy* (Washington, D.C.: Worldwatch Institute, September 1984).

73. For a severe critique of wood-stove efficiency projects, see Gerald Foley and Patricia Moss, *Improved Cooking Stoves in Developing Countries* (Washington, D.C.: International Institute for Environment and Development, 1983).

74. See, for example, Gyan Sagar, "A Fuel-Efficient, Smokeless Stove for Rural India," *Appropriate Technology,* September 1980; "Stove Design" and "Stove Dissemination," *VITA News,* January 1984; George McBean, "Sushila Wants a New Stove," *UNICEF News,* Issue 3, 1983; John Worral, "Better Stoves Help Solve Firewood Crisis," *Christian Science Monitor,* March 14, 1984.

75. David J. Rose et al., *Global Energy Futures and CO_2-Induced Climate Change* (Cambridge, Mass.: Massachusetts Institute of Technology, 1983); the model has also been used in Seidel and Keyes, *Can We Delay a Greenhouse Warming?*

76. All assumptions and results for DOE Scenario B are described in detail in Edmonds et al., *Atmospheric Retention of CO_2.* Full details of the Available Technology and New

Technology Scenarios are available from Worldwatch upon request. The following key assumptions were the same in all projections: Population grows at about 1 percent per year from 1984 to 2025. Gross World Product grows annually at 3.15 percent until 2000, then slows to 2.6 percent. Price elasticity of demand for energy services is −0.9 in the buildings sector, −0.8 in the industrial sector, and −0.7 in the transportation sector in the OECD countries, and is −0.8 for all sectors in the rest of the world (for all years). Income elasticity of demand for energy is 0.8 for all regions (for all years). Primary energy prices are determined endogenously, and thus differ by scenario. Oil prices through 2000 increase annually in DOE's Scenario B, Worldwatch Available Technology, and Worldwatch New Technology at 1.7, 1.2, and 0.9 percent, and from 2000 to 2025 at 1.7, 1.7, and 1.6, respectively. Coal and biomass prices never increase above 0.8 percent annually in DOE's Scenario B or above 0.6 percent in either Worldwatch projection. The cost of nuclear-electric, hydroelectric, and solar-electric power changes at 1.6, 0, and −5.2 percent annually in all cases.

77. Estimated by Worldwatch from Herbert Block, *The Planetary Product in 1980: A Creative Pause?* (Washington, D.C.: U.S. Department of State, 1981); EIA, *International Energy Annual 1982;* World Bank, *World Development Report 1984.*

78. The incorporation of efficiency improvements was accomplished in the model by adjusting the rate of non-price-induced conservation as well as energy prices. The latter required an artificial shift in the supply curve, or the equivalent of an energy tax. For comparison, the energy demand projection for the United States grew from about 75 exajoules in the year 1983 (note that in the model all values are based on 1975) to 105, 85, and 83 exajoules in the DOE, Available Technology, and New Technology Scenarios, respectively. This compares with a range of 81 to 92 exajoules in *The Audubon Energy Plan 1984* (New York: National Audubon Society, July 1984).

79. Yves Albouy, World Bank, private communication, November 8, 1984.

80. Eric Hirst et al., "Recent Changes in U.S. Energy Consumption: What Happened and Why," in Annual Reviews, Inc., *Annual Review of Energy, Vol. 8* (Palo Alto, Calif.: 1983).

81. Jae Edmonds, Institute for Energy Analysis, private communication, Washington, D.C., October 24, 1984.

82. Energy Research Advisory Board, "Energy Conservation and the Federal Government: Research, Development, and Management," Report to the U.S. Department of Energy, Washington, D.C., January 1983.

83. Clark W. Bullard, "Energy Conservation in Buildings: Opportunities, Experience, and Options," in Annual Reviews, Inc., *Annual Review of Energy, Vol. 6* (Palo Alto, Calif.: 1981).

Chapter 8. Harnessing Renewable Energy

1. World Bank, Energy Department, *A Survey of the Future Role of Hydroelectric Power in 100 Developing Countries* (Washington, D.C.: 1984); J.L. Gordon, "Recent Developments in Hydropower," *Water Power & Dam Construction,* September 1983.

2. Philip B. Williams, "Damming the World," *Not Man Apart,* October 1983.

3. World Bank, *Energy in the Developing Countries* (Washington, D.C.: 1980).

4. Ministry of Mines and Energy, "Energy Self Sufficiency: A Scenario Developed as an Extension of the Brazilian Energy Model," Brasilia, July 1984; "Hydropower Bases Keys to China's Power Potential," *China Daily,* March 29, 1984; "The U.S. Demands a Fair Shot at Building a Huge Dam," *Business Week,* May 21, 1984.

5. Peter T. Kilborn, "Brazil's Hydroelectric Project," *New York Times,* November 14, 1983; Julival de Moraes and Victor F.

Salatko, "Coming: 12,600 Megawatts at Itaipu Island," *IEEE Spectrum*, August 1983.

6. Federal Ministry of Commerce, Trade and Industry, *Energy Supply in Austria* (Vienna: 1984); T.W. Mermel, "Major Dams of the World—1983," *Water Power & Dam Construction*, August 1983; U.S. Department of Energy, *Electric Power Annual, 1982 and 1983* (Washington, D.C.: 1983 and 1984); U.S. Department of Energy, *Inventory of Power Plants in the United States, 1982 Annual* (Washington, D.C.: 1983).

7. Pumped storage figure from Rita Barnett, U.S. Department of Energy, Washington, D.C., private communication, October 11, 1984.

8. Peter Hadekel, "Hydro-Quebec Looks to Energy Market for Surplus Power Exports," *Journal of Commerce*, September 24, 1984; "Boom Ahead for Canadian Kilowatts," *Energy Daily*, September 7, 1984; Walter D. Harris, "Canadian Power Surges South," *Public Power*, November/December 1982; Kevin Quinn, "Manitoba Agrees to Supply Western U.S. With Power for 35 Years, Beginning 1993," *Wall Street Journal*, June 4, 1984.

9. "Inga-Shaba Link Inaugurated," *Water Power & Dam Construction*, January 1984; World Bank, Energy Department, "1981 Power/Energy Data Sheets for 100 Developing Countries," Washington, D.C., March 1984.

10. Northern Quebec from Warren Perley, "Aluminum Industry Important to Economy," *Journal of Commerce*, September 24, 1984; Brazil from "Aluminum Port Nears Completion," *Journal of Commerce*, June 25, 1984; Siberia from Daniel Deudney and Christopher Flavin, *Renewable Energy: The Power to Choose* (New York: W.W. Norton & Co., 1983); Vincent W. Stove, "Aluminum Smelter Nears Full Capacity in Australia," *Journal of Commerce*, March 15, 1984; typical construction costs from World Bank, *Survey of Hydroelectric Power*.

11. United Nations Industrial Development Organization, "Small Hydro Power Development in the People's Republic of China," presented to the Third Workshop on Small Hydro Power, Kuala Lumpur, Malaysia, March 7-15, 1983; Wang Shoudao, "Small Hydro-Power Speeds Development in Hilly Regions," *China Daily*, March 27, 1984; data on 60 factories from Larry N. Stoiaken, "The Chinese Hydro Imports: Testing The North American Marketplace," *Alternative Sources of Energy*, July/August 1983; Hangzhou manufacturer quoted in "Chinese Manufacture Small Hydro Units," *Water Power & Dam Construction*, May 1984; "Guangdong Leads in Hydropower," *China Daily*, September 13, 1984.

12. Maria Elena Hurtado and Essam El-Hinnawi, "Hydro Power: China's Marriage of Convenience," *South*, January 1983; "Westinghouse Signs Agreement With China," *Alternative Sources of Energy*, March/April 1984; "China Barters Machines for Raw Materials," *Water Power & Dam Construction*, November 1983.

13. Allen R. Inversin, "Pakistan: Villager-Implemented Micro-Hydropower Schemes," National Rural Electric Cooperative Association, Washington, D.C., 1983; National Rural Electric Cooperative Association, "Status, Recommendations, and Future Directions for the Small Decentralized Hydropower Program," Washington, D.C., 1983.

14. William A. Loeb, "How Small Hydro Is Growing Big," *Technology Review*, August/September 1983.

15. "Statement of Keith L. Colbo," in U.S. Congress, Subcommittee on Energy Conservation and Power, *Northwest Power Planning Council & FERC*, Hearings, September 11, 1984; Response of Raymond J. O'Connor, Chairman of the Federal Energy Regulatory Commission, to an inquiry by the Subcommittee on Energy Conservation and Power, Committee on Energy and Commerce, U.S. House of Representatives, February 17, 1984.

16. "Var Developers Order 27 Standard Turbines," *Water Power & Dam Construction*, January 1984; F. Pazoul, "Developing Small-Scale Hydro in Czechoslovakia," *Water Power & Dam Construction*, March 1984.

17. Edward Goldsmith and Nicholas Hildyard, *The Social and Environmental Effects of Large Dams, Volume 1* (Cornwall, U.K.: Wadebridge Ecological Centre, 1984).

18. Elizabeth Kemf, "Rainforest Sacrificed To Build Amazon Dam," *World Wildlife Fund News*, July/August 1984.

19. World Energy Conference prediction from Asit K. Biswas, "World Status Report on Hydroelectric Energy," *Mazingira*, Vol. 7, No. 3, 1983; World Bank, *Survey of Hydroelectric Power*.

20. Ken Butti and John Perlin, *A Golden Thread: 2500 Years of Solar Architecture and Technology* (Palo Alto, Calif.: Cheshire Books, 1980).

21. D. Groues and I. Segal, *Solar Energy in Israel* (Jerusalem: Ministry of Energy & Infrastructure, 1984).

22. DeWayne Coxon, "Domestic Water Heating in Israel," *Sunworld*, Vol. 6, No. 4, 1982; Christopher Gadomski, "Amcor Profits from Close Dealer Ties," *Solar Age*, July 1984.

23. Costis Stambolis, "How Greece is Catching the Sun," *Financial Times*, November 23, 1983; "AFME Announces 1983 Programme," *World Solar Markets*, March 1983.

24. "Italy Slow to Use Solar Funds," *European Energy Reports* (London), March 9, 1984; British information from Michael Flood, *Solar Prospects* (London: Wildwood House, in association with Friends of the Earth, 1983); East European projections from "Elsewhere in the News," *Solar Energy Intelligence Report*, February 27, 1984.

25. Dick Munson, "Solar Energy in the Land of the Rising Sun," *Solar Engineering and Contracting*, May/June 1983.

26. "World Economics Curb ISES Euphoria," *World Solar Markets*, September 1983.

27. Y.B. Ng and C.T. Leung, "Solar Technology in China," *Sunworld*, Vol. 6, No. 4, 1982; "India," *World Environment Report*, July 25, 1984.

28. Peter Nares, "Solar Energy Seen Capable of Cutting Colombian Electricity Use 10%," *Solar Energy Intelligence Report*, October 24, 1983; "U.S. Solar Finds Lucrative Markets Outside the U.S.," *Solar Engineering & Contracting*, March/April 1984.

29. U.S. Energy Information Administration, *Solar Collector Manufacturing Activity 1983* (Washington, D.C.: 1984).

30. "Industry Analysts Surprised by EIA's Bearish Report," *Solar Age*, July 1984.

31. Energy Investment Research Inc., *The 1984 Solar Profitability Survey* (Greenwich, Conn.: 1984).

32. Molly Malloy, "The Solar Age 1984 State Tax Survey," *Solar Age*, June 1984; TVA information from TVA official, private communication, September 6, 1984; San Luis data from Amory Lovins, private communication, November 9, 1984.

33. "Selling Solar Like Encyclopedias," *Energy Daily*, October 20, 1983; Rebecca Voires, "Developing Profitable Distribution," *Solar Engineering & Contracting*, May/June 1984.

34. "Meatpacker Boasts Largest Solar Unit," *Journal of Commerce*, July 12, 1984.

35. "A Solar Success Story," *Solar*, May/June 1984; Wayne Johnson, "Third Party Financing Helps End-Users Save Without Fears About Performance," *Solar Engineering & Contracting*, May/June 1983.

36. "Passive Water Heaters Gaining Ground," *Solar Age*, August 1983.

37. William J. Putnam, "An Overview of Solar Thermal Domestic Hot Water Technology," in *Coming of Age*, Proceedings of the Renewable Energy Technologies Sympo-

sium, Anaheim, Calif., August 29–September 1, 1983.

38. David Godolphin, "Rising Hopes for Vacuum Tube Collectors," *Solar Age*, June 1982.

39. John W. Andrews and William G. Wilhelm, "Thin-Film Flat-Plate Solar Collectors for Low-Cost Manufacture and Installation," Brookhaven National Laboratory, Upton, N.Y., 1980; "Burton's Sundulator Collectors: $4.50/Square Ft.," *Solar Engineering & Contracting*, May/June 1983.

40. Carlo LaPorta, Solar Energy Industries Association, Washington, D.C., private communication, July 18, 1984.

41. Stephen W. Hinch, "Solar Power Goes on Line," *High Technology*, August 1984; "Roan Signs with PG&E to Sell Power from 15-MWE Parabolic Trough System," *Solar Energy Intelligence Report*, June 6, 1983.

42. "Israel, Japan Help to Finance Big Solar Project in California," *Energy Daily*, September 6, 1983.

43. Ira P. Krepchin, "Feast or Famine for Solar Dishes," *Solar Age*, September 1983.

44. Groues and Segal, *Solar Energy in Israel;* Jim Norris, McDonnell Douglas Corporation, private communication, November 12, 1984.

45. Timothy A. Fausch, "Solar Electric Plants: New Prosperity or Large-Scale Losers?," *Solar Engineering & Contracting*, May/June 1984; LaPorta, private communication.

46. David Halbert quoted in Nina Markov, "Solar Thermal: Exciting Developmments Reflect Promising Future," *Renewable Energy News*, May 1984.

47. John B. Woodard, "Solar Thermal Technology—Research and Development," in *Coming of Age.*

48. Alan Skinwood, "Recent Developments in Central Receiver Systems," *Sunworld*, Vol. 6, No. 4, 1982; Frank Kreith and Richard T. Meyer, "Large-Scale Use of Solar Energy with Central Receivers," *American Sci-*entist, November/December 1983; "USSR Details Gas/Solar Station Plans," *World Solar Markets*, August 1983.

49. J.J. Bartel, "Solar 10 MWe Pilot Plant Fact Sheet," Sandia National Laboratory, New Mexico, 1983.

50. Norman Down, "Solar One," *Solar*, January/February 1983.

51. Ibid.; Kreith and Meyer, "Large-Scale Use of Central Receivers."

52. Solar 100 description from Markov, "Solar Thermal: Exciting Developments"; ARCO Solar Industries, PG&E, and Rockwell International, "The Carrizo Plains Solar Central Receiver Plant," presented to the Solar Energy Industries Association Annual Meeting, November 10, 1982.

53. Down, "Solar One"; cost estimates from L.K. Ives and W.W. Wilcox, "Economic Requirements for Central Receiver Commercialization," in *Proceedings of STTF (Solar Thermal Test Facility) Testing for Long Term Systems-Performance Workshop*, Albuquerque, N.M., January 7-9, 1984, and from California Energy Commission, *Technical Assessments Manual* (Sacramento, Calif.: 1984).

54. Groues and Segal, *Solar Energy in Israel.*

55. Michael Edesess, "On Solar Ponds: Salty Fare for the World's Energy Appetite," *Technology Review*, December 1982.

56. Groues and Segal, *Solar Energy in Israel;* Richard Munson, "Israel's Shining Example," *Environmental Action*, June 1984.

57. "S. Calif. Edison Agrees to Build Solar Complex," *Journal of Commerce*, December 21, 1983.

58. W.W.S. Charters, "Solar Ponds in Australia," *Sunworld*, Vol. 7, No. 1, 1983.

59. "Solar Electric Market Put at 130 GWe in 2010," *Solar Energy Intelligence Report*, October 10, 1983.

60. Ibid.

61. For a good discussion of the history of alcohol fuels, see Hal Bernton, William Kovarik, and Scott Sklar, *The Forbidden Fuel: Power Alcohol in the Twentieth Century* (New York: Boyd Griffin Inc., 1982).

62. Howard S. Geller, "Ethanol From Sugarcane in Brazil," in Annual Reviews Inc., *Annual Review of Energy, Vol. 10* (Palo Alto, Calif.: forthcoming).

63. James Bruce, "Brazil's Alcohol Project Flourishing," *Journal of Commerce*, June 1, 1983; Jose Goldemberg et al., "Brazil: A Study on End-Use Energy Strategy," presented to the Global Workshop on End-Use Energy Strategies, Sao Paulo, Brazil, June 4-15, 1984; "The Sweet Smell of Brazil's Traffic," *World Bank News*, May 10, 1984.

64. Ministry of Industry and Commerce, "Assessment of Brazil's National Alcohol Program," Brasilia, 1981; Brian Murphy, "Brazil Ethanol Program Had Turbulent History," *Renewable Energy News*, September 1983; Genilson Cezar, "Brazil's Gasohol Success," *World Press Review*, June 1984; Geller, "Ethanol in Brazil."

65. Goldemberg et al., "Brazil: End-Use Strategy"; Ministry of Mines and Energy, "Energy Self-Sufficiency."

66. U.S. Department of Agriculture (USDA), Economic Research Service, *World Indices of Agricultural and Food Production, 1950-83* (unpublished printout) (Washington, D.C.: 1984); shifts in agricultural trends from Jose Lutzenberger, Union for the Conservation of Nature, Rio Grande do Sul, Brazil, private communication, September 20, 1984. For a further discussion of this issue, see Lester R. Brown, *Food or Fuel: New Competition for the World's Cropland* (Washington, D.C.: Worldwatch Institute, March 1980).

67. Geller, "Ethanol in Brazil."

68. World Bank, "The Energy Transition in Developing Countries," Washington, D.C., 1983; Bill Kovarik, "Third World Fuel Alcohol Push Shows Mixed Results," *Renewable Energy News*, September 1982.

69. Calestous Juma, "The Use of Power Alcohol in Kenya and Zimbabwe: An Overview," Science Policy Research Unit, University of Sussex, Brighton, England, February 1984; N.C. Krishnamurthy, World Bank, Washington, D.C., private communication, September 7, 1984.

70. Armand Pereira, "Employment Implications of Ethanol Production in Brazil," *International Labour Review*, January/February 1983; Vaclav Smil, "Can The Poor Countries Afford Biomass Energies?," presented to the Third International Conference on Energy Use Management, West Berlin, West Germany, October 26-30, 1981.

71. David Hallberg, President, Renewable Fuels Association, Washington, D.C., private communication, November 12, 1984.

72. Daniel C. Greer and Walter J. Kulakowski, "Current and Future Markets For Fuel Ethanol," presented to the Tenth Energy Technology Conference and Exposition, Washington, D.C., February 29–March 2, 1982; Solar Energy Research Institute, "Alcohol Fuels Program Technical Review," prepared for U.S. Department of Energy, Golden, Colo., Summer 1982; USDA, *A Biomass Energy Production and Use Plant for the United States, 1983-90* (Washington, D.C.: 1983); Tina Hobson, "Environmental Benefits Make Ethanol A 'Natural'," presented to the 1984 Washington Conference on Fuel Ethanol, Washington, D.C., September 12-13, 1984.

73. "Carter Lays Out Multi-Billion Dollar Plan for Gasohol," *Solar Energy Intelligence Report*, January 14, 1980; Andrew H. Malcolm, "Indiana Guzzles Gasohol, Unknowingly," *New York Times*, July 9, 1983; Richard House, "Brazil Turning Its Excess Cane Into Motor Fuel," *Washington Post*, February 19, 1984.

74. Phil Stevens, President, Ultrasystems, Inc., statement at the 1984 Washington Conference on Fuel Ethanol, Washington, D.C.,

September 12-13, 1984; Roger Pollak, "Alcohol Turns Cheese Wastes Into Profits," *Renewable Energy News*, April 1983; Michael E. C. Gery, "Alcohol Fuel Plant Runs on Wood Chips," *Renewable Energy News*, September 1983.

75. David E. Hallberg, Opening Remarks, 1984 Washington Conference on Fuel Ethanol, Washington, D.C., September 12-13, 1984; annual ethanol use projection from Marilyn J. Herman, President, Herman & Associates, statement at the 1984 Washington Conference on Fuel Ethanol, Washington, D.C., September 12-13, 1984.

76. USDA study cited by David E. Hallberg, "Commercialization of the Fuel Ethanol Industry: A Catalyst for Increased R&D Spending by the Private Sector," in *Coming of Age*.

77. Charles K. Ebinger et al., "Ethanol: National Security Implications," Center for Strategic and International Studies, Georgetown University, Washington, D.C., 1984.

78. Barry Commoner, "A Reporter at Large: Ethanol," *New Yorker*, October 10, 1983.

79. Bernton, Kovarik, and Sklar, *The Forbidden Fuel*.

80. Paul F. Bente, Jr., "Selected Examples of Emerging Bio-Energy Developments That May Lead to Substitutes for Conventional Liquid Fuels," presented to the Symposium on Biomass Substitutes for Liquid Fuels, Sao Paulo, Brazil, February 9-12, 1982; Joseph C. Roetheli, TVA Biomass Fuels Program, "Future of Alcohol Fuels," in *Coming of Age*; "Methanol Plant Opens Up New Prospects," *Latin American Markets*, July 30, 1984.

81. Hallberg, "Commercialization of the Fuel Ethanol Industry"; "Researchers Develop Formula To Make Ethanol From Algae," *Journal of Commerce*, January 5, 1982; Kristi Mauch, United Energy Corporation, Foster City, Calif., private communication, May 29, 1984.

82. Joseph G. Finegold et al., "Demonstration of Dissociated Methanol as an Automotive Fuel: System Performance," Solar Energy Research Institute, Golden, Colo., April 1981; Roger Staiger, statement at the Symposium on the Use of Methanol as a Fuel to Improve Air Quality in the South Coast Air Basin, El Monte, Calif., June 29, 1984.

83. U.S. Office of Technology Assessment, *Energy From Biological Processes, Vol. II* (Washington, D.C.: U.S. Government Printing Office, 1980); "France Markets Fuel Substitutes," *World Solar Markets*, January 1983; "Biomass Gasifier Developed at SERI Converts 60% Wood Feed to Methanol," *Solar Times*, October 1981; "Direct Wood Gasification Method Seen Leading to Methanol Production in Brazil," *Solar Energy Intelligence Report*, October 13, 1980.

84. Methanol use in U.S. automobiles from Pamela G. Hollie, "Du Pont, Citing Prices, To Halt Methanol Sales," *New York Times*, September 7, 1984; Burt Solomon, "Much to Arco's Delight, GM Changes Its View of Methanol," *Energy Daily*, August 6, 1984.

85. "Methanol Catches On In California," *Energy Daily*, September 6, 1983; Charles L. Gray, Jr., "Future Emission Control Technology for Methanol Vehicles," presented to the Symposium on the Use of Methanol as a Fuel to Improve Air Quality in the South Coast Air Basin, El Monte, Calif., June 29, 1984; Brazil and Norway testing, and Solar Energy Research Institute information, from Joseph G. Finegold, J. Thomas McKinnon, and Michael E. Karpuk, "Decomposing Methanol As Consumable Hydride for Automobiles and Gas Turbines," Solar Energy Research Institute, Golden, Colo., March 1982.

86. "Big Fuel Use Rise Eyed For Methanol, Ethanol," *Journal of Commerce*, January 17, 1984.

87. Ronald DiPippo, "Development of Geothermal Electric Power Production Overseas," presented to the Eleventh Energy

Technology Conference, Washington, D.C., March 1984.

88. James L. Easterly and Elizabeth C. Saris, "A Survey of the Use of Biomass as a Fuel to Produce Electric Energy in the United States," presented to the Eleventh Energy Technology Conference, Washington, D.C., March 1984; Government of Sweden, "Green Power: Biofuels Are a Growing Concern" (advertisement), *Scientific American*, August 1984; "Philippines Produces Wood Power," *World Solar Markets*, August 1983.

89. Project descriptions based on private communications with various developers and trade press reports.

90. Paul D. Maycock, "Current Status and Future Prospects of the U.S. PV Industry," Testimony presented to the Science Technology Committee, U.S. House of Representatives, September 11, 1984; "Kyocera Becomes First Foreign PV Manufacturer to Launch Full-Scale Marketing Effort in U.S.," *Photovoltaic Insider's Report* (Dallas, Tex.), June 1984; "Potential Impact of Hoxan Automated Plant on Thick Crystal Module Cost," *PV News* (Alexandria, Va.), September 1984.

91. Mike Batham, California Energy Commission, Sacramento, Calif., private communication, September 27, 1984.

92. Donald Marier, "Windfarm Update: A Banner Year Ends With a Flurry," *Alternative Sources of Energy*, March/April 1984; "Wind Power: A Question of Scale," *EPRI Journal*, May 1984.

93. California resource figure from Batham, private communication; San Gorgonio figures from Maurice Van Nostrand, "Unusual Farming for New Energy Source: The Wind," *Des Moines Register*, August 25, 1984.

94. Wind farm developments in various regions based on private communications and trade press reports.

95. Ten percent of U.S. energy use figure is derived from 1983 national energy use of 71 quadrillion BTUs of which hydropower was 3.9 quadrillion BTUs, from U.S. Department of Energy, *Monthly Energy Review*, August 1984; wood energy use estimated at 3.2 quadrillion BTUs by Dave Keenan, National Wood Energy Institute, Portsmouth, N.H. private communication, December 3, 1984.

96. *Cogeneration and Small Power Monthly* (Washington, D.C.), various issues.

Chapter 9. Stopping Population Growth

1. National population data throughout this chapter, unless otherwise specified, from Population Reference Bureau, *1984 World Population Data Sheet* (Washington, D.C.: 1984), and United Nations, *Monthly Bulletin of Statistics*, New York, various issues.

2. World Bank, *World Development Report 1984* (New York: Oxford University Press, 1984).

3. The evolution of China's family planning program is discussed in H. Yuan Tien, "China: Demographic Billionaire," *Population Bulletin* (Washington, D.C.: Population Reference Bureau, April 1983), and in Pi-Chao Chen, "11 M Chinese Opt for Only One Child Glory Certificate," *People* (London), Vol. 9, No. 4, 1982.

4. For a profile of the World Fertility Survey, see Robert Lightbourne Jr., Susheela Singh, and Cynthia P. Green, "The World Fertility Survey: Charting Global Childbearing," *Population Bulletin* (Washington, D.C.: Population Reference Bureau, March 1982).

5. For a discussion of the background of the U.S. policy position at the Mexico City meeting, see Erik Eckholm, "Population Growth: How U.S. Policy Evolved," *New York Times*, August 11, 1984; for an analytical review of the conference, see Dierdre Wulf and Peters D. Willson, "Mexico City: Consensus Amid Controversies," *International Family Planning Perspectives*, September 1984.

6. Rafael M. Salas, "Population: The Mexico Conference and the Future," statement to the International Conference on Population, Mexico City, August 6, 1984.

7. Population Reference Bureau, *1984 World Population Data Sheet.*

8. Stephen Rapawy and Godfrey Baldwin, "Demographic Trends in the Soviet Union: 1950–2000," and Murray Feshbach, "Trends in the Soviet Muslim Population—Demographic Aspects," in Joint Economic Committee, U.S. Congress, *Soviet Economy in the 1980's: Problems and Prospects* (Washington, D.C.: U.S. Government Printing Office, 1983).

9. Thomas W. Merrick, "Recent Fertility Declines in Brazil, Colombia, and Mexico," background paper prepared for World Bank, *World Development Report 1984;* population projection from World Bank, *World Development Report 1984.*

10. World Bank, *World Development Report 1984.*

11. "Age at Marriage and Fertility," *Population Reports* (Population Information Program, The Johns Hopkins University, Baltimore, Md.), November 1979; World Bank, *World Development Report 1984.*

12. World Bank, *World Development Report 1984;* see also, Kathleen Newland, *Infant Mortality and the Health of Societies* (Washington, D.C.: Worldwatch Institute, December 1981).

13. The suppression of fertility during breastfeeding is discussed in John Knodel, "Breast-Feeding and Population Growth," *Science,* December 16, 1977, and in R.V. Short, "Breast Feeding," *Scientific American,* April 1984.

14. International Labour Office, *World Labor Report* (Geneva: 1984).

15. Prevalence of Depo Provera from Joseph Speidel, Population Crisis Committee, Washington, D.C., private communication, November 7, 1984.

16. Ann Larson, "Patterns of Contraceptive Use Around the World," Population Reference Bureau, Washington, D.C., July 1981; Jeanette H. Johnson, "Vasectomy—An International Appraisal," *Family Planning Perspectives,* January/February 1983; "India Promotes the Pill," *People* (London), Vol. 10, No. 2, 1983; Tien, "China: Demographic Billionaire."

17. Larson, "Patterns of Contraceptive Use."

18. Contraceptive prevalence and cultural factors in Indonesia are discussed in Terence H. Hull, Valerie J. Hull, and Masri Singarimbun, "Indonesia's Family Planning Story: Success and Challenge," *Population Bulletin* (Washington, D.C.: Population Reference Bureau, November 1977).

19. Laurie Liskin et al., "Vasectomy—Safe and Simple," *Population Reports* (Population Information Program, The Johns Hopkins University, Baltimore, Md.), November/December 1983.

20. Johnson, "Vasectomy—An International Appraisal."

21. Ibid.

22. Ibid.

23. Laparoscopy and minilaparotomy are discussed in Cynthia P. Green, "Voluntary Sterilization: World's Leading Contraceptive Method," *Population Reports* (Population Information Program, The Johns Hopkins University, Baltimore, Md.), March 1978.

24. Speidel, private communication.

25. George Zeidenstein, "Contraception in the Population/Development Equation" (background paper prepared by Forrest C. Greenslade and George F. Brown, The Population Council, New York), presented at the First Conference of the Asian Forum of Parliamentarians on Population and Development, New Delhi, February 17–20, 1984.

26. Speidel, private communication.

27. Liskin et al., "Vasectomy—Safe and Simple"; U.S. Office of Technology Assessment, *World Population and Fertility Planning Technologies: The Next 20 Years* (Washington, D.C.: U.S. Government Printing Office, 1982).

28. Zeidenstein, "Contraception in the Population/Development Equation."

29. Bruce Stokes, *Filling the Family Planning Gap* (Washington, D.C.: Worldwatch Institute, May 1977).

30. World Bank, *World Development Report 1984*.

31. Geoff Tansey, "Turkey Looks Forward to Liberal Law," *People* (London), Vol. 10, No. 1, 1983; Nuray Fincancioglu, "Turkey's Liberal Law," *People* (London), Vol. 10, No. 3, 1983; Rami Chhabra, "India Promotes the Pill," *People* (London), Vol. 10, No. 2, 1983.

32. Quoted in Johnson, "Vasectomy—An International Appraisal."

33. Christopher Tietze, *Induced Abortion: A World Review, 1983* (New York: The Population Council, 1983).

34. Philip J. Hilts, "Legal Abortions Found Declining For First Time," *Washington Post*, July 7, 1984.

35. IPPF estimate cited in Tietze, *Induced Abortion*.

36. Barbara K. Herz, "Official Development Assistance for Population," World Bank, Washington, D.C., unpublished, September 1983.

37. Ibid.

38. World Bank, *World Development Report 1984*.

39. Ibid.

40. Gerald O. Barney, G. O. Barney & Associates, Inc., Arlington, Va., private communication, November 5, 1984.

41. Marshall Green, former U.S. Ambassador to Indonesia, speech presented at the Second Biennial Conference on the Fate of the Earth, Washington, D.C., September 20, 1984.

Chapter 10. Getting Back on Track

1. Latin American income figures from Inter-American Development Bank, *Economic and Social Progress in Latin America* (Washington, D.C.: 1983).

2. K. Dharmarajan, "India—Energy Supply Policy Management," *Natural Resources Forum*, July 1983; U.S. Department of Energy (DOE), *Estimates of U.S. Wood Energy Consumption from 1949 to 1981* (Washington, D.C.: U.S. Government Printing Office, 1982).

3. Indian soil loss estimates from K. G. Tejwani, Land Use Consultants International, New Delhi, private communication, July 3, 1983, and from Centre for Science and Environment, *The State of India's Environment 1982* (New Delhi: 1982).

4. Nigeria's oil output decline described in International Energy Agency, *World Energy Outlook* (Paris: Organisation for Economic Co-operation and Development, 1982).

5. World Bank, *World Development Report 1984* (New York: Oxford University Press, 1984).

6. David J. Walker and Douglas L. Young, "Technical Progress in Yields—No Substitute for Soil Conservation," Current Information Series No. 671, University of Idaho College of Agriculture, Moscow, Id., December 1982.

7. U.S. Department of Agriculture (USDA), Soil Conservation Service, "Preliminary 1982 National Resources Inventory" (unpublished printout), Washington, D.C., April 1984; calculation of distribution of excessive erosion by Worldwatch Institute using a maximum soil-loss tolerance level of 5 tons per acre.

8. Chinese data from Zheng Guanglin, "Preliminary Results From the *China 2000*

Study: A Personal View," G.O. Barney & Associates, Inc., Arlington, Va., unpublished, July 1984; Indian data from Tejwani, private communication, and from Centre for Science and Environment, *State of India's Environment;* India's national survey was recorded in National Commission on Agriculture, *Report of the National Commission on Agriculture, Part 5: Resource Development* (New Delhi: Government of India, 1976).

9. USDA, Foreign Agricultural Service, *Foreign Agriculture Circulars* SG-11-84 and SG-12-84, Washington, D.C., September 1984 and October 1984.

10. Frank R. Rijsberman and M. Gordon Wolman, eds., *Quantification of the Effect of Erosion on Soil Productivity in an International Context* (Delft, The Netherlands: Delft Hydraulics Laboratory, 1984).

11. American Farmland Trust, *Soil Conservation in America: What Do We Have to Lose?* (Washington, D.C.: 1984).

12. Estimate for conservation tillage in 1984 from Frank Lessiter, "Despite PIK, No-Till Turns In An Increase," *No-Till Farmer* (Brookfield, Wisc.), March 1984.

13. Research in Nigeria discussed in International Institute of Tropical Agriculture (IITA), *Tasks for the Eighties: A Long-Range Plan* (Ibadan, Nigeria: June 1981), and in IITA, *Tasks for the Eighties: An Appraisal of Progress* (Ibadan, Nigeria: April 1983).

14. "Soil Conservation in Kenya: An Interview with Carl-Gosta Wenner," *Ambio,* Vol. 12, No. 6, 1983.

15. Swedish International Development Authority, *Soil Conservation in Kenya 1980 Review* (Stockholm: December 1980).

16. United Nations Food and Agriculture Organization (FAO), Forest Resources Division, *Tropical Forest Resources,* FAO Forestry Paper 30 (Rome: 1982).

17. Analysis of FAO data for Asia is from U.S. Office of Technology Assessment

(OTA), *Technologies to Sustain Tropical Forest Resources* (Washington, D.C.: 1984).

18. OTA, *Technologies;* FAO, *Tropical Forest Resources.*

19. Industrial plantations in Brazil and tropics as a whole from OTA, *Technologies;* industrial plantations in India from Centre for Science and Environment, *The State of India's Environment.*

20. OTA, *Technologies;* FAO, *Tropical Forest Resources.*

21. Tree farming in Gujarat from OTA, *Technologies,* and from William Claiborne, "Indian Peasants Hope Tree Farming Will Make Them Rich," *Washington Post,* April 22, 1984. For a more thorough analysis of the Gujarat program, see Madhav Gadgil, S. Narenda Prasad, and Rauf Ali, *Forest Management in India: A Critical Review* (Bombay: Centre for Monitoring Indian Economy, 1982).

22. Erik Eckholm, "Seedlings Dot Nepal's Once-Barren Slopes as Country Battles Forest Crisis," *New York Times,* February 21, 1984.

23. OTA, *Technologies.*

24. Zheng, "Preliminary Results from *China 2000*"; Vaclav Smil, *The Bad Earth: Environmental Degradation in China* (Armonk, N.Y.: M. E. Sharpe, Inc., 1984).

25. Erik Eckholm, *Planting for the Future: Forestry for Human Needs* (Washington, D.C.: Worldwatch Institute, February 1979).

26. Francis Urban and Thomas Vollrath, *Patterns and Trends in World Agricultural Land Use* (Washington, D.C.: U.S. Government Printing Office, 1984).

27. G.M. Woodwell et al., "Global Deforestation: Contribution to Atmospheric Carbon Dioxide," *Science,* December 9, 1983.

28. Projection of tree planting in the tropics is authors' estimate based on an annual increase in the planting rate consistent with the increase of planting in 1980–85 over 1975–80, as reported in FAO, *Tropical Forest*

Resources. The annual share of carbon absorbed assumes that a total of six million hectares of new plantations are planted to leucaena, which can fix a maximum of 28 tons of carbon per hectare, and that the measured annual increase in atmospheric carbon (approximately 2.8 billion tons) does not increase or decrease before the turn of the century.

29. OTA, *Technologies;* Nicholas Guppy, "Tropical Deforestation: A Global View," *Foreign Affairs,* Spring 1984.

30. World Bank, *World Development Report 1984.*

31. Barbara Miller, "Super-Insulated Houses Slash Energy Use," *Appropriate Technology Times,* Spring 1980.

32. Growth in residential and industrial fuelwood use in the United States from DOE, *Estimates of U.S. Wood Energy Consumption.* Calculation of oil equivalent assumes 17.2 million BTUs per dry ton of wood, burned at 45 percent efficiency, and 5.8 million BTUs per barrel of fuel oil, burned at 65 percent efficiency.

33. For a more detailed discussion of geothermal energy development, see Christopher Flavin and Sandra Postel, "Developing Renewable Energy," in Lester R. Brown et al., *State of the World-1984* (New York: W.W. Norton & Co., 1984).

34. Philippine Ministry of Energy, *Ten Year Energy Program, 1980-1989* (Manila: 1980).

35. Patricia Adams, "Wood Energy: Rekindling an Old Flame," Energy Probe, Toronto, March 1981; Matthew L. Wald, "Canadian Power Will Lower Northeast's Bills," *New York Times,* September 14, 1984; Hydro-Quebec, *Annual Report 1983* (Montreal: 1983).

36. "Ring of Confidence for Japanese Recycling," *New Scientist,* January 24, 1980.

37. Energy savings from recycling from William U. Chandler, "Recycling Materials,"

in Brown et al., *State of the World-1984;* Environmental Protection Agency (EPA) estimate of energy savings from national container deposit legislation from EPA, *Fourth Resource Recovery and Waste Reduction Report to Congress* (Washington, D.C.: 1977); states with container deposit laws in effect from Chandler, "Recycling Materials."

38. Andrew H. Malcolm, "For Minneapolis, Trash Means Cash," *New York Times,* March 7, 1984; for one community's efforts, see Craig W. Dawson and Clint Pires, "Risking Success: Recycling in St. Louis Park, Minnesota," *Resource Recovery,* March/April 1984.

39. Geoffrey Murray, "Putting 220 Tons of Garbage A Day Where It Belongs," *Christian Science Monitor,* March 10, 1983.

40. "Aluminum Recovery? Can Do!," *Sweden Now,* February 1982; 1984 estimate from telephone survey of U.S. reverse vending machine manufacturers conducted by Worldwatch Institute, October 1984.

41. These examples are discussed in Chandler, "Recycling Materials."

42. Boulder, Colo., example from Clara Germani, "Sweet Smell of Success: Creative Recycling Firm Draws in Volunteers—And a Profit," *Christian Science Monitor,* May 11, 1984; Japan student associations described in *Saikuru No Chishiki* (Tokyo: The Clean Japan Center, 1983).

43. Brian Hammond, "Recycling Begins At Home," *New Scientist,* July 17, 1975.

44. Rachel Carson, *Silent Spring* (Boston: Houghton Mifflin, 1962); E.F. Schumacher, *Small is Beautiful: Economics as if People Mattered* (New York: Harper and Row, 1973).

45. R.P. Turco et al., "Nuclear Winter: Global Consequences of Multiple Nuclear Explosions," *Science,* December 23, 1983; Paul R. Ehrlich et al., "Long-Term Biological Consequences of Nuclear War," *Science,* December 23, 1983; Paul R. Ehrlich et al., *The*

Cold and the Dark: The World After Nuclear War (New York: W.W. Norton & Co., 1984).

46. Gerald O. Barney, G.O. Barney and Associates, Inc., Arlington, Va., private communication, November 5, 1984.

47. M. Mitchell Waldrop, "An Inquiry into the State of the Earth," *Science,* October 5, 1984.

48. Guppy, "Tropical Deforestation."

49. Joseph E. Slater, *Governance* (New York: Aspen Institute for Humanistic Studies, 1976).

50. Role of the U.S. Office of Technology Assessment discussed in John H. Gibbons, "Technology Assessment for the Congress," *The Bridge* (Journal of the National Academy of Engineering), Summer 1984.

51. Warren G. Bennis, "Where Have All the Leaders Gone?," *Technology Review,* March/April 1977.

52. Emergence of the Chipko Andolan movement discussed in Centre for Science and Environment, *State of India's Environment.*

Index